Metaphorical Stories in Discourse

When Hillary Clinton conceded in 2008 that she did not quite "shatter the glass ceiling," and when Rick Perry in 2012 called Mitt Romney a "vulture capitalist," they used abbreviated *metaphorical stories*, in which stories about one topic are presented as stories about something entirely different. This book examines a wide range of metaphorical stories, beginning with literary genres such as allegories and fables and then focusing on metaphorical stories in ordinary conversations, political speeches, editorial cartoons, and other communication. Sometimes metaphorical stories are developed in rich detail; in other examples, like "vulture capitalist," they may merely be referenced or implied. This book argues that close attention to metaphorical stories and story metaphors enriches our understanding and is essential to any theory of communication. The book introduces a theoretical structure, which is developed into a theory of metaphorical stories, and then illustrates the theory by applying it to actual discourse.

L. DAVID RITCHIE is Professor of Communication at Portland State University, where he has taught since 1990. He is the author of three books, including *Metaphor* (Cambridge University Press, 2014).

Metaphorical Stories in Discourse

L. David Ritchie
Portland State University

CAMBRIDGE
UNIVERSITY PRESS

CAMBRIDGE
UNIVERSITY PRESS

University Printing House, Cambridge CB2 8BS, United Kingdom

Cambridge University Press is part of the University of Cambridge.

It furthers the University's mission by disseminating knowledge in the pursuit of education, learning, and research at the highest international levels of excellence.

www.cambridge.org
Information on this title: www.cambridge.org/9781107168305
DOI: 10.1017/9781316717172

© L. David Ritchie 2017

This publication is in copyright. Subject to statutory exception and to the provisions of relevant collective licensing agreements, no reproduction of any part may take place without the written permission of Cambridge University Press.

First published 2017

Printed in the United Kingdom by Clays, St Ives plc

A catalogue record for this publication is available from the British Library.

Library of Congress Cataloging-in-Publication Data
Names: Ritchie, L. David author.
Title: Metaphorical Stories in Discourse / L. David Ritchie, Portland State University.
Description: Cambridge : Cambridge University Press, 2017. | Includes bibliographical references and index.
Identifiers: LCCN 2017011386 | ISBN 9781107168305 (hard back : alk. paper)
Subjects: LCSH: Metaphor. | Narration (Rhetoric)
Classification: LCC P301.5.M48 R57778 2017 | DDC 808/.03–dc23
LC record available at https://lccn.loc.gov/2017011386

ISBN 978-1-107-16830-5 Hardback

Cambridge University Press has no responsibility for the persistence or accuracy of URLs for external or third-party internet websites referred to in this publication and does not guarantee that any content on such websites is, or will remain, accurate or appropriate.

Contents

Preface		*page* vii
1	*"Shattering the Glass Ceiling"*: A Metaphor Becomes a Metaphorical Story	1
2	Stories and Narratives	20
3	Language and Metaphor	47
4	Allegory	79
5	Parables and Fables	105
6	Metaphorical Stories	120
7	Story Metaphors and Aphorisms	133
8	Story-Metaphors in Journalism and Public Affairs	150
9	Barack Obama Talks about Race	170
10	Metaphorical Stories about Climate Change	188
11	Metaphorical Stories in Visual Communication	215
12	Metaphorical Stories and Their Place in Discourse	234
Notes		254
References		256
Index		267

Preface

The cover image, from a 16th-century painting by Pieter Bruegel the Elder titled "The Blind Leading the Blind," depicts a line of blind men connected by their staffs or by a hand on the shoulder of the man in front. All are in poses suggesting forward motion. The title phrase is a familiar aphorism, often used as a metaphorical description of a situation in which a person who is giving advice knows no more than those who are receiving the advice, or in which a leader of a group is no better informed than any other member of the group. "*Blind*" implies "*unable to see.*" "*To see*" is more generally used as a metaphor for "to know," and "*leading*" is generally used as a metaphor for both "governing" and "advising," so as used in this aphorism, "*blind*" implies something like "the ignorant giving advice to the ignorant." TO SEE IS TO KNOW is an example of what is often called a *conceptual metaphor*, in which a general class of abstract ideas (KNOWING or UNDERSTANDING) is understood and experienced in terms of objects or activities in the here-and-now physical world (EYESIGHT). The aphorism "*blind leading the blind*" expresses this common conceptual metaphor in a blend with another common conceptual metaphor, LIFE IS A JOURNEY and with the *irony* implied by describing a seemingly contradictory idea (how can a blind person lead anyone else? How can a person who has no knowledge of a topic provide advice to anyone else?) The painting itself is an example of a particular kind of visual metaphor, inasmuch as it illustrates a common metaphorical aphorism (the title of the painting). The topic of the aphorism is not included in this image; it is left to the viewer to apply the metaphor.

The painting does not stop at depicting the metaphorical situation, a row of blind men following other blind men. It also illustrates a *metaphorical story*: The blind man at the front of the procession has fallen, apparently because he stumbled on a rock shown in the path next to him. The man behind is stumbling, off balance, and evidently about to fall over the fallen man, leading to the expectation that the four men following the second will also stumble and fall. The story: A group of blind men is led by another blind man who cannot see where he is going and consequently stumbles over an obstacle in the path, as a result of which all of the men will end up falling.

Understanding this painting involves some mental activities that are likely to be totally automatic; a typical viewer is unlikely to be aware of them at all. The underlying conceptual metaphor must become activated – or rather, the aspects of the conceptual metaphor that are relevant to the painting must be *partially* activated and connected with the images. The title of the painting helps by cuing the familiar aphorism. The title may also cue one or more situations in which the viewer has read or heard this aphorism in connection with a particular topic; if so, those situations are also likely to be recalled, and connected with the painting.

I first became interested in metaphorical stories when, as part of a workshop on metaphor analysis organized by Lynne Cameron at the University of Leeds, I participated in a line-by-line analysis of a speech by Tony Blair, then British prime minister and leader of the Labour Party. In this speech, Blair developed a story about a marital dispute that involves the wife throwing dishes ("crockery"), a commonplace in TV situation comedies and newspaper comic strips, as a metaphor for his own dispute with a discontented segment of the Labour Party. As I studied that speech, I also noticed a number of phrases that implied metaphorical stories but did not spell them out (e.g. the Conservative Party as a burglar, trying to enter government "*through the back door*"). As I analyzed other texts, including several conversations about relations between police and community, I encountered other metaphorical stories and other short phrases that allude to or imply metaphorical stories. Some, like Blair's "*throwing crockery*" story, drew on popular culture. Others drew on or developed conceptual metaphors in quite original and creative ways.

These early experiences led to this book, and many of the examples used in this book are drawn from those early studies. Initially I attended primarily to casual, nonliterary metaphorical stories; only as I began to prepare this book did I broaden the scope to include the literary genres such as allegories and parables that have been the focus of most previous research on this topic. Even then, I have retained a primary focus on metaphorical stories that are related or alluded to in "ordinary" (nonliterary) discourse. I quickly discovered that political discourse, including news coverage and editorial cartoons as well as ordinary conversations about political topics, is a rich source of entertaining and often witty metaphorical stories. As a consequence, many of the examples in this book are drawn from political discourse including speeches, editorials, and editorial cartoons.

An inevitable consequence of drawing examples from contemporary history is that the context of the examples continually changes as history continues to move and develop. As the context of a metaphorical story changes, the understanding of it must also change – and the context of political discourse can change quite rapidly. One example of this interaction between history and language / language analysis appears in Chapter 1, much of which is devoted to analysis of a passage from Hillary Clinton's concession speech during the 2008 U.S. Democratic Presidential Primary. Even as I wrote the analysis of the "*glass ceiling*" passage, I was fully aware that she intended to campaign for president again, and that she would likely succeed at least in becoming the Democratic candidate. As I write this preface, and complete the final revisions on the manuscript, she was nominated and campaigned for the highest office in the United States, won the popular vote, but lost the Electoral College vote. The meaning of that iconic metaphorical story from her 2008 speech has, unavoidably, changed to accommodate the new reality that was established on November 8, 2016.

Other examples that appear in various parts of the book involve news coverage of the European Union. Between the time I wrote these passages and the present time, when I am completing my revisions and polishing of the manuscript, the British people voted to leave the EU; by the time the book appears, negotiations for "Brexit" will be well under way. Again, the meaning of the MARRIAGE and FAMILY metaphors long used in news analysis of European politics will unavoidably change as the historic and cultural context changes.

In these and other instances in which history will have the opportunity to make some of my analysis seem obsolete or naive, I have noted the potential effects of historical changes on how the metaphors may be understood, but to attempt to keep fully abreast of a rapidly changing context would be futile. Accordingly, I can only hope that readers will approach the examples discussed throughout the book by considering the context in which the initial analyses were written.

The final version of this volume benefited greatly from the advice and suggestions of an anonymous final reviewer, as well as from the advice and suggestions of three initial reviewers. My thinking about the various topics represented in this book has been influenced and shaped by conversations with a large number of colleagues, especially Lynne Cameron, Cynthia-Lou Coleman, Alice Deignan, Elizabeth El Refaie, Ray Gibbs, Jr., Beate Hampe, Mike Hanne, Eric Jensen, Elena Negrea-Busuioc, Elena Semino, Gerard Steen, Min Zhu, and many others. I am deeply indebted to my editor, Andrew Winnard, and the production staff at Cambridge University Press for their assistance and advice throughout the writing and production process. As always, I owe more than I can express to the support, encouragement, and advice of my wife LaJean Humphries.

1 *"Shattering the Glass Ceiling"*
A Metaphor Becomes a Metaphorical Story

> Although we weren't able to *shatter* that *highest, hardest glass ceiling* this time,
> thanks to you, it's got about *eighteen million cracks in it...*
> And the *light is shining through* like never before,
> *filling us all with* the hope
> and the sure knowledge that *the path will be a little easier* next time.
> – Hillary Clinton concession speech, Washington, DC, June 7, 2008.

This brief segment from Hillary Clinton's concession speech during the 2008 U.S. Democratic presidential primary campaign blends several apparently distinct metaphors into a coherent whole that expressed something very important to her and to millions of her supporters. The segment can be understood in several ways, most obviously as a story about her first (2008) campaign for the Democratic Party nomination for president, and about the disappointing end to that campaign. It also illustrates several points about metaphor use and comprehension that I will expand on throughout this book. The metaphors, which I have marked in italics (see inset for an explanation of terminology and typographical conventions[1]), are all quite conventional – indeed, many who heard and read about her speech may not have recognized all of them as metaphors.

> **Notation**: I mark metaphorical phrases by placing metaphorical elements in italics and the entire phrase within quotation marks (or in a block quote, as above). I use single quotes for invented examples ('my lawyer is a *shark*') and double quotes for attested examples from actual discourse ("*filling us all with* the hope"). I refer to the metaphorical word or phrase (e.g., "*filling us with*") as the "*vehicle*" and the entity, object, or concept described (in this case, Clinton's strong showing in the campaign) as the "*topic*." The idea that is described or expressed (in this case, "causing people to experience something intensely") is the *apparent meaning*. The relationship between vehicle, topic, and apparent meaning is described as "the vehicle *mapping onto* the topic."

The passage as a whole also tells a story; it is an example of something quite different, which has not received much attention among metaphor researchers and scholars: a *metaphorical story*. I will begin this chapter by discussing the passage as a story. Then I will show how the individual metaphors might be explained by several conventional approaches to metaphor, and finally I will show how understanding it as a *metaphorical story* adds to the meaning of the passage. In the last half of the chapter, I will introduce several other blends of story and metaphor that will be discussed in detail in later chapters, including metaphors transformed into stories, stories implied by metaphors, and visual images that portray, evoke, or imply metaphorical stories. By the end of this book I hope to have convinced you that many metaphors, including very familiar metaphors, imply and bring to mind stories, that these stories contribute in fundamental ways to understanding metaphors, and that metaphors can often be fully understood *only* through the implied stories.

Stories from Hillary Clinton's Concession Speech

"We make narratives many times a day, every day of our lives" (Abbott, 2008, p. 1). Clinton's concession speech is no exception. She began with an ironic comment about the social context, "this isn't exactly the party I'd planned, but I sure like the company," which implies a contrast with an alternate story in which she would have given a victory speech, not a concession speech. She proceeded to tell the story of her campaign, opening with a brief generic story about her campaign volunteers, in which she expressed her gratitude toward "everyone who *poured* your *hearts* and your hopes *into* this campaign, who drove for miles and lined the streets waving homemade signs, who scrimped and saved to *raise* money, who knocked on doors and made calls, who talked, sometimes argued with your friends and neighbors." This was followed immediately by two specific stories, each expressing a different facet of the campaign. The first story exemplifies dedication and sacrifice, and anchored the campaign in very young women like "thirteen-year-old Anne Riddell from Mayfield, Ohio, who had been saving for two years to go to Disney World and decided to use her savings instead to travel to Pennsylvania with her mom and volunteer there."

> **Terminology**: For the present I will refer to any sequence of causally or thematically related events as a *story*. When the story is presented in a more highly structured way, with a goal, opposition or setback, and resolution, I will refer to it as a *narrative*. Stories and narratives will be defined and discussed in greater detail in Chapter 2.

The second story referred to the story of women's suffrage, and anchored the campaign in the very old, women who were "born before women could vote," exemplified by Florence Stein of South Dakota, who was eighty-eight years old and insisted that her daughter bring an absentee ballot to her hospice bedside. Her daughter and a friend put an American flag behind her bed and helped her fill out the ballot. She *passed away* soon after and, *under* state law, her ballot didn't count, but her daughter later told a reporter, "My dad's an ornery, old cowboy, and he didn't like it when he heard Mom's vote wouldn't be counted. I don't think he had voted in twenty years, but he voted *in place of* my mom."

Each of these stories provides a context in time and place; both satisfy some of the elements usually associated with a complete narrative. The story about Florence Stein is the more complete of the two: It includes a setback (Stein's death) and a resolution (her husband cast a vote for Clinton in his wife's memory). It also represents a minor victory that implicitly contrasts with the major primary election defeat Clinton had just experienced. Finally, it embeds Clinton's story in the broader, more universal story of women's struggle for political rights, a story to which Clinton referred repeatedly throughout the speech.

After several more brief stories about her own campaign, Clinton congratulated Obama on his victory and briefly recounted the story of her relationship with Obama, followed by a summary of Obama's own story. Then she merged the two stories, as a basis for urging her followers to work for Obama's election: "We may have *started on* separate *journeys*, but today our *paths have merged*. And we're all *heading toward* the same *destination*, united and more ready than ever to win in November and to *turn our country around*, because so *much is at stake*."

According to Schank and Berman (2002, p. 288) a story is "a structured, coherent retelling of an experience or a fictional account of an experience. A satisfying story will include ... themes, goals, plans, expectations, expectation failures (or obstacles), and perhaps, explanations or solutions." According to Bruner (2002, p. 18), "narrative in all its forms is a dialectic between what was expected and what came to pass. For there to be a story, something unforeseen must happen."

These and many other passages from Clinton's concession speech satisfy both of these definitions. The speech as a whole is a retelling of Clinton's experience, shared with her supporters. This particular passage has the form of a story about a *"journey"* that she and Obama have been taking separately but now are taking together. That is the *vehicle* of the metaphorical story: The *topic* is the campaign for the presidency, which they were undertaking separately and in competition but are now taking together. The topic story is motivated by her goal of being nominated and her defeat by Obama, and thus it also satisfies Bruner's criterion that "something unforeseen must happen." It provides a partial resolution by transferring her and her supporters' hopes and aspirations to her victorious rival, Barack Obama, and extending the story of the campaign into a *future* story of Obama's victory – and beyond, to an eventual successful campaign by a woman, who might just possibly be Hillary Clinton.

After another series of future-oriented stories focused on the coming campaign, Clinton returned to the theme that was implicit in her opening stories: "But I am a woman and, like millions of women, I know there are still *barriers* and biases out there, often unconscious, and I want to *build* an America that respects and *embraces* the potential of every last one of us." She then exhorted her supporters to "*aim high*," and drew the following comparison:

As we gather here today in this historic, magnificent building, the fiftieth woman to leave this Earth is orbiting overhead. If we can blast fifty women into space, we will someday *launch* a woman into the White House.

This passage was followed immediately by the "*glass ceiling*" passage, which reprises and summarizes the entire story of the campaign. In parallel to the overall story of her campaign, the "*glass ceiling*" story describes a reversal of expectations, the "*glass ceiling*" that led to the failure of her expectations, along with an explanation and a potential solution. Although this story does not culminate in the protagonist overcoming the obstacle, it does include her receiving help along the way, and it does culminate in her promise that the story is not "*over*," that the canonical ending, overcoming obstacles and succeeding, will happen "next time."

A more extensive and detailed account of narrative and storytelling will be provided in Chapter 2.

"Glass Ceiling" and Other Metaphors in the Clinton Speech

Even relatively brief stories often include metaphors. In the brief story about Clinton's defeat and her subsequent support of Obama's campaign, several metaphors related to "*journey*" appear. The "*glass ceiling*" story also includes several metaphors in addition to "*glass ceiling*." In fact, it is saturated with metaphors: about a third of the 53 words in the passage are metaphors or part of a metaphorical phrase. The speech as a whole is only slightly less densely populated with metaphors.

Traditionally, metaphors have been defined as substituting one word for another, or comparing one word with another. Traditional metaphor theory focused primarily on noun-for-noun metaphors, often invented ('a lawyer is a *shark*') or taken out of context ("Juliet is *the sun*"). Clinton's speech includes only a few metaphors that consist of a single noun (e.g., "*hearts*," "*journey*," and "*destination*") and none that take the traditional form of "x is a y." The speech also contains some other parts of speech used as single word metaphors ("*poured* your *hearts* and hopes," "*under* state law," "*barriers* and biases," "*launch* a woman into the White House"). However, most of the metaphors in

Clinton's speech, including "*aim high*" and "*glass ceiling*," have to be analyzed as phrases of two or more words.

Conventional approaches to metaphor comprehension. Linguists and other metaphor researchers have proposed a variety of approaches to explain how people understand metaphors. One approach is to look at attributes or qualities of the metaphor vehicle that might be '*transferred*' to the topic. "*Ceiling*" transfers the attributes of being a '*higher*' part of a '*space-enclosing structure*' to the topic, which in this sentence is not explicitly mentioned. From the context we can infer that the topic has something to do with conditions that prevented Clinton, a woman, from achieving career advancement. "*Glass*" transfers the attributes of "*hard*" and '*transparent*' to the topic, which is most directly the word it modifies, "*ceiling.*" Since the topic of "*ceiling*" is '*obstacles* preventing career *advancement*,' by extension "*glass*" transfers attributes of "*hard*" and '*transparent*' to '*obstacles* preventing career *advancement*.' The apparently simple two-word metaphor requires a complex, two-stage interpretation beginning with the nominative metaphor (the noun, "*ceiling*") and proceeding with the noun "*glass*," grammatically transformed into a metaphorical adjective. This apparently simple interpretation also requires that we make inferences based on the immediate context (a political concession speech by a woman who sought the Democratic nomination for president) as well as on the larger cultural context, including the history of women's participation in U.S. politics and the origin of the "*glass ceiling*" metaphor and its previous uses in other contexts.

A related approach is to show how the metaphor vehicle establishes an *ad hoc* category of things (or actions) that have similar attributes (Glucksberg, 2008; Wilson & Sperber, 2004). *Glass* is hard and transparent, and *ceiling* is a part of a structure that is above the speaker or other reference point. "*Glass ceiling*" establishes a category of things that are hard, transparent, and overhead. To *shatter* is to break or destroy violently; *a crack* is a line along which a brittle substance is weakened or partially but incompletely broken. To "*shatter a glass ceiling*" establishes a category of actions that break or destroy something hard, transparent, and overhead.

Clinton was clearly *not* talking about a physical structure. Her political advancement was not blocked by a hard, flat surface above her head. Her political advancement *may* have been blocked by subtle and unacknowledged ('*unseen*') biases against women serving as political leaders, biases that are unacknowledged ('*transparent*'), difficult to counteract, and even more difficult to change ("*hard*"). In order to make sense in the context of Clinton's speech, since she is clearly *not* talking about a physical structure, the qualities transferred from vehicle to topic, the qualities that form the basis for an *ad hoc* category, require further metaphorical interpretation (Ritchie, 2003b). It is conventional to refer to an organizational hierarchy in terms of vertical location in space (e.g., to '*move up in* the organization' means to *get a series of promotions*). By extension, "*ceiling*" is a '*barrier to upward motion,*' a "*hard*" ceiling is a '*difficult barrier to upward motion,*' and a "*glass ceiling*" is a '*barrier that is unseen until one encounters it,*' also a '*barrier through which one can see the levels one is unable to reach.*' As the italics indicate, all of these explanations are themselves metaphorical, so they do not really explain how people make sense of the phrase, but they at least express the idea in terms of more conventional and familiar metaphors (Ritchie, 2003a).

Broadening and narrowing. Wilson and Sperber (2004) argue that all language is ambiguous, so that understanding *any* language, including metaphorical language, requires a process of broadening the meaning of words and phrases to encompass the topic, and narrowing the meanings to exclude irrelevant or inapplicable meanings. According to Wilson and Sperber, then, "*ceiling*" and '*barrier*' are broadened to include "any aspect of a situation that impedes one from accomplishing something" and narrowed to exclude "part of a building or other physical object." '*Upward motion*' is broadened to include "achieving a position of greater power and prestige" and narrowed to exclude "physical movement in a vertical direction." These ideas help move us a little closer to understanding how a metaphor like "*glass ceiling*" can come to make sense in the context of Clinton's speech. However, like the attribute transfer and categorization account, Sperber and Wilson's account still does not specify how this process of broadening and narrowing happens, and how it leads to a particular interpretation of a metaphorical phrase (Ritchie, 2003b; 2009).

Conceptual Metaphor Theory (CMT). In 1980, George Lakoff and Mark Johnson introduced a radically new way of looking at metaphors – Conceptual Metaphor Theory (CMT). According to CMT, the linguistic form of most metaphors is but an overt expression of an underlying *conceptual* metaphor, a cognitive relation in which one concept (usually more abstract) is experienced as or understood in terms of another concept (usually less abstract) from a different kind of experience. These *conceptual* metaphors are expressed in a number of *linguistic* metaphors; for example, KNOWLEDGE IS LIGHT and UNDERSTANDING IS SEEING are the basis for common metaphorical expressions like '*I see what you mean,*' '*keep someone in the dark,*' 'the *Age of Enlightenment,*' '*an illuminating conversation*,' and the ironic aphorism "*blind leading the blind*" (cover image; Preface; Chapter 11). The metaphors in the brief passage in which Clinton joins her campaign to Obama's, discussed in a previous section, express a common conceptual metaphor POLITICS IS A JOURNEY: "We ... *started on* separate *journeys* ... our *paths have merged*. And we're all *heading toward* the same *destination*, ... turn our country around."

Notation: Following the convention introduced by Lakoff and Johnson, I designate conceptual metaphors by placing them in small capital letters, e.g., KNOWLEDGE IS LIGHT and UNDERSTANDING IS SEEING.

According to Lakoff and Johnson (1980; 1999), conceptual metaphors are based on correlations in experience. For example, because young children tend to feel loved at the same time that they feel the physical proximity and warmth of a caregiver, this repeated association leads to the conceptual metaphors LOVE IS PHYSICAL WARMTH (or EMOTION IS TEMPERATURE) and LOVE IS PHYSICAL PROXIMITY. These conceptual metaphors are expressed in common expressions like 'a *warm* reception,' 'an *icy* stare,' and 'a *close* friend.' Looking closely at an object or pattern is often associated with understanding it better, and it is easier to see an object in sufficient detail to understand it when it is well illuminated; these associations provide the basis for KNOWLEDGE IS LIGHT and UNDERSTANDING IS SEEING. Taller people tend to be more powerful, stronger, and more persuasive, and high places are militarily easier to defend, thus POWERFUL IS UP, a conceptual metaphor reinforced by location of temples and palaces on high hills, location of the executive suite on the top floor of corporate headquarters, and the nearly universal custom (among many species of animal as well as humans) of showing respect and submission by bowing or otherwise lowering one's head and upper body (Schubert, Waldzus, & Seibt, 2008).

In "*shatter* that *highest, hardest glass ceiling*," "*shatter*" and "*cracks in it*" are expressions of TO OVERCOME IS TO BREAK and "*hardest*" is an expression of DIFFICULT IS PHYSICALLY HARD. "*Highest*" and "*ceiling*" are expressions of POWERFUL IS UP. "*Glass*," "*light*," and "*shining through*" are expressions of KNOWING IS SEEING, KNOWLEDGE IS LIGHT, and HOPE IS LIGHT. The latter interpretation is strengthened by the next line, "*filling us all with the hope*." Here, "*filling us all with*" seems to be a linguistic manifestation of HOPE IS A SUBSTANCE and A PERSON IS A CONTAINER. The final line of this passage, "knowledge that *the path will be a little easier* next time," expresses A CAREER / ELECTION IS A JOURNEY.

Metaphor and metonym. Metonym is an expression in which the vehicle and topic belong to the same domain; in metaphor, vehicle and topic come from different domains. However, as the discussion of CMT makes clear, these categories are not always distinct. If common conceptual metaphors originate in correlations in our experience of the world, then many of them started as metonyms: in a "*close*" or "*warm*" relationship, the actual physical proximity (and resultant body warmth) of the caregiver stands as a metonym for the entire experience of being loved and cared for. In an example much discussed by Lakoff and Johnson, ARGUMENT IS WAR, the conceptual relationship is probably based on early experiences in which arguments are associated with physical violence or threats of violence. In a corporate office building, senior executives usually occupy offices that are literally *higher* in the building; '*higher* authorities' is thus both a metonym and a metaphor for organizational power.

Ruiz de Mendoza and Galera-Masegosa (2011) identify two types of metonym: part-whole metonyms ('*all hands* on deck,' in which the hand stands for the entire person) and whole-part metonyms ('*the court* ordered his immediate release,' in which the institution stands for the person or persons who belong to it). As will be discussed in greater detail in Chapter 3, these are not discrete categories: metaphors and metonyms are often blended, and it is sometimes difficult to classify a word or phrase as either metaphorical or metonymic. For many, '*passed away*' is a metaphorical euphemism for death, but for others it is a metonymic expression of the actual passage of a spiritual essence out of the body to some other location in time and space. In Robert Frost's (1969) poem, "The Road Not Taken," the entire story can be read as a literal account of a ride through the woods, a metonymic account of a ride through the woods as part of an independent-minded life, or a purely metaphorical account of the poet's choices of vocation and topic. The relationship of metonym to metaphor will figure in several sections of this book.

Perceptual simulations. In the past decade or so, scientists who study mind and brain have begun to turn away from the classic idea that mind is separate from the body, including the physical brain. Barsalou (1999; 2007) demonstrated that in principle all thought, including abstract logic as well as language use and comprehension, can be accomplished through *perceptual simulations*. In perceptual simulations, the perceptual neural systems (hearing, sight, awareness of our own inner physical state, etc.) and the motor control neural systems, used to contract (and relax) muscles for various kinds of movements, become partially activated, just as if the brain had actually perceived a sight or sound, or had actually begun to clench a fist or tense a leg muscle.

Gibbs (2006; 2008) has conducted a series of experiments supporting his contention that language activates perceptual simulations. In particular, a metaphor activates simulations associated with the vehicle. When people hear '*grasp* the concept,' the neural systems that would be used to grasp a physical object become weakly activated. Similarly, Zhong and Leonardelli (2008) have shown that people experience social exclusion as being physically cold (this will be discussed in greater detail in Chapter 3; for a comprehensive review, see Bergen, 2012).

According to Perceptual Simulation Theory, we would expect that people who hear "*shatter* that *highest, hardest glass ceiling*" would experience a partial simulation of a transparent pane that was blocking someone's upward motion then being violently shattered. "It's got about *eighteen million cracks in it*" would be experienced as a partial simulation of a glass pane with a network of cracks, like a windshield that has been struck by a heavy object but not broken. "The *light is shining through*" would be experienced as a partial simulation of bright light coming through the cracked glass pane. "*Filling us all with the hope*" would be experienced as simulations of fullness, hope, and optimism. "*The path will be a little easier*" would probably be experienced as simulations of motion along a smooth, level path.

These and other theories about the identification, use, and comprehension of metaphors will be discussed in greater detail in Chapter 3.

Understanding the *"Glass Ceiling"* Passage as a Metaphorical Story

Taken together, these approaches help us to understand how the various words and phrases in this passage from Clinton's speech might be understood, but they leave out something important. Like the "*different paths*" story discussed before, the "*glass ceiling*" passage tells a story about someone trying to break a hard transparent overhead structure but only putting cracks in it. The speech in which the passage appears, taken as a whole, tells an overtly different story, about a woman trying to achieve a high-status position and failing to achieve her objective, possibly because of unacknowledged ('*invisible*') gender biases. In this section I will show how our understanding of the passage is enriched by treating the entire passage as part of a *metaphorical story*, specifically as the *vehicle* in a metaphor. The immediate *topic* of the story metaphor is the story, or part of the story, about Clinton's campaign, but it also maps onto a more general topic story about women's struggle for equal opportunity and equal access to positions of power and influence.

> Although we weren't able to *shatter* that *highest, hardest glass ceiling*
>   this time,
> thanks to you, it's got about *18 million cracks in it*...
> And the *light is shining through* like never before,
> *filling us all with the hope*
> and the sure knowledge that *the path will be a little easier* next time.

Each metaphor in the passage seems to express a distinct idea, but taken as a sequence, they blend into a single complex story that maps metaphorically onto the story of Clinton's campaign to become the first female president of the United States, within the larger context of women's long struggle for political, economic, and social equality.

"*Glass ceiling*," a now-familiar metaphor, was initially coined by Gay Bryant (1984), former editor of *Working Woman* magazine; Bryant was also quoted in an *Adweek* article by Nora Frenkiel (1984): "Women have *reached* a certain *point* – I call it the *glass ceiling*. They're in the *top* of *middle* management and they're *stopping* and *getting stuck*." This quote blends two common conceptual metaphors, A CAREER IS A JOURNEY and SOCIAL POWER IS UP. It also implies another familiar metaphor in which these two conceptual metaphors are merged, '*climbing the corporate ladder.*' The metaphor, "*glass ceiling*," only makes sense in the context of an implied story about a person climbing a ladder and being blocked from making further progress by an overhead barrier. "*Glass*" implies that the person is able to *see* farther up, above her position on the ladder, but "*ceiling*" implies she is stopped from '*making further progress.*'

The "*glass ceiling*" metaphor has appeared in many articles and as a visual metaphor in political cartoons over the past 30 years, almost always in reference to members of some group who manage to earn promotions to a certain level, then are prevented by various '*structural obstacles*' and '*invisible*' biases from "*reaching*" the '*higher levels,*' which they can '*see*' but never "*reach.*" It was incorporated into the name of a unit of U.S. government, the Federal Glass Ceiling Commission (1991–1995), formed to investigate barriers affecting the careers of not only women but other demographic groups as well, including ethnic minorities and persons with disabilities. In the context of Clinton's speech, then, "*glass ceiling*" refers to the story of past attempts of women politicians, including Clinton, to achieve high political office ('*climb the political ladder*') and their failure to '*break through*' to the "*highest*" office in the nation: the presidency.

Most elements of a narrative are either explicitly present or strongly implied by the passage. Although the element of resolution is still only implied, the '*unseen obstacle*' has been weakened ("about *eighteen million cracks in it*") and further '*progress*' is implicitly promised. Clinton's narrative is more complex than Bryant's initial story, and blends elements from several conceptual metaphors. It begins with a metaphorical story about attempting to destroy a ceiling made of glass, but only damaging it. Then it shifts to a story about light shining through the damaged "*glass ceiling,*" and ends with a story about the "*path*" that Clinton and her supporters are "*traveling.*" As a series of story fragments this narration is hardly coherent, but it maps smoothly onto the story of Clinton's political career, in which the presidency is the "*highest*" (POWERFUL IS UP) and the '*barriers*' to attaining the presidency are the "*hardest*" (DIFFICULT IS HARD).

With "we *weren't able to shatter* ... thanks to you, it's *got about eighteen million cracks in it,*" Clinton transformed the canonical career story into a story of a collective ("we") attempt not merely to '*break through*' the '*unseen barrier*' but to "*shatter*" it – to destroy it completely. The attempt failed, but the barrier is weakened – not "*shattered*" or even '*broken*' but at least "*cracked.*" Not only is it "*cracked,*" it has "*about eighteen million cracks.*" In the canonical story, the '*transparency*' of the "*glass*" implies that the ambitious woman can '*see*' the "*higher* office," with all of its privileges and power; it also implies that the biases preventing her from *"reaching the top"* are not *'visible.'* But *"the light is shining through like never before"* exploits another aspect of the *'transparent glass'* metaphor: *"Light"* is a common metaphor for both *knowledge* and *hope*, and that *"light"* of knowledge and hope is now *"shining through"* the *"glass ceiling."*

The second metaphor in the passage, "it's got about *eighteen million cracks in it*," transforms the original metaphor in a way that changes the implications about the present state of affairs from one of frustrated talent to one of potential future *'progress.'* The next series of metaphors, culminating in a JOURNEY metaphor, *"the path* will be *a little easier* next time," extends the story into the future and changes its valence from one of past defeat and present resignation to one of potential future victory. The vehicle story as a whole is the story of a woman who attempts to *'climb the ladder,'* encounters a *'transparent,'* hence *'invisible' 'barrier,'* through which she can *'see the top'* but not *'reach the top.'* She tries, and fails, to *"smash through"* the invisible barrier, but she does manage to *"put a million cracks in it,"* with the result that it will be easier for her, or some other woman in the future, to *"break through the glass ceiling"* and *'reach the top.'*

The canonical *'career ladder'* story underlying the *"glass ceiling"* metaphor is part of the CHANGE IS MOTION and POWER IS UP metaphor fields, in which career promotion is expressed sometimes as *'climbing higher'* and sometimes as *'moving forward'* or *'progressing.'* Just as *'climbing higher'* implies a *'career ladder,' 'moving forward'* implies a *'career path,'* a metaphor invoked by Clinton's final phrase, "the *path* will be *a little easier* next time." These separate (but interrelated) metaphors are blended together in a single story metaphor about trying to *'break'* or even *"shatter"* a *"glass ceiling,"* but only *"cracking it."* However, it now has so many *"cracks"* that *"light"* (knowledge and hope) is *"shining through."* This invites or leads into another story, located in the future, in which "the *path will be a little easier*" – and by implication, the *"glass ceiling"* will then be *'broken.'* All of this is mapped onto the story of Clinton's attempt to secure the Democratic nomination – and win election to the presidency, in which she achieved much more than previous women, with the result that a future candidate (perhaps Clinton herself) will have a greater chance to succeed.

The base metaphor vehicles, *'ladder,' "level,"* and *"ceiling"* / *'obstacle,'* all imply a small space, a ladder in a room. At first glance the time (in the vehicle story) seems to be a minute or so, all that it takes to climb a ladder. The person on the ladder might conceivably wait for some time – at most, perhaps, a few hours – at the level on the ladder where further progress is blocked. The corresponding topics, *career, position, unwritten rules, and unspoken biases* exist in the much larger space of a corporate headquarters (for Bryant) or national politics (for Clinton). The topic story also occurs over a much larger extent of time – advancement to middle management ('*climbing the ladder*') may take a decade or longer, and several years may pass before the woman in the topic story realizes that further promotion is '*blocked*' by unwritten rules and unspoken biases ('*unseen obstacles*'). Thus, "*glass ceiling*" maps a vehicle story located in a few square feet and taking place within a few minutes or maybe an hour onto a topic story that may be located over a space of thousands of miles and take place over several decades. In Clinton's telling of the story, by implication the topic story is the pursuit of political rights – and power – by American women that has continued for two centuries and will extend for an indefinite time into the future.

The first part of the story maps readily onto the topic story, Clinton's unsuccessful attempt to obtain the Democratic nomination, with the unspoken implication that her defeat resulted from a '*barrier*' to further '*upward motion*' (a "*ceiling*"), a gender bias that is unacknowledged hence '*unseen*' ('*glass*'; thus, the "*glass ceiling*"). Thus far, the metaphor is consistent with, and draws on, the standard use and interpretation of "*glass ceiling.*" However, the second part of the passage transforms the metaphor vehicle into a story about a hopeful and potentially successful *future* campaign, and by extension suggests a similar transformation of the topic story, with the further implication that she (or some other female candidate) will win the next time.

"*The light is shining through*" does not imply any defined time or space: It does permit expanding time and space somewhat beyond that of the "*ladder*"/ "*glass ceiling*" story. "*The path will be a little easier* next time" potentially extends the vehicle story in both space and time, but not to nearly the same extent as a political campaign, which crosses back and forth across an entire nation, and in the United States extends over a full year or longer. A *path* is not clearly bounded in space, nor is a journey along a path clearly bounded in time, although one ordinarily does not think of a literal path as extending more than a few miles, or taking more than a few hours, perhaps a few days, to traverse. Thus, the entire story metaphor still maps a relatively restricted extent of time and space onto a much larger time and space.

The metaphorical story about putting "*about eighteen million cracks*" in a "*glass ceiling*" maps directly onto the story of Clinton's successes in several of the primary elections and the fact that she *did* succeed in being taken seriously as a viable candidate for president. The extension into a metaphorical story about the future, when "*the path will be a little easier,*" maps onto the implied story of a future woman candidate who will be "*launched into the White House.*" This metaphor itself is foreshadowed by the thematically connected advice to young women in the audience to "*aim high*" and the exultant story about the 50th woman astronaut who was orbiting the Earth as Clinton spoke.

Two ideas become apparent from this discussion. First, note the separate entailments of the metaphor "*glass,*" which "allows us to *see* the unattainable *higher levels"* and also 'presents a *barrier that cannot be seen.*' These two interpretations are compatible, and both have appeared in other discussions of *"glass ceiling,"* so it is reasonable to combine them. Second, note that Clinton doesn't actually provide the mapping – she just tells the vehicle story and leaves it to the audience to map it onto the topic, the story of her unsuccessful bid for the nomination. Also note that the metaphorical phrase, *"glass ceiling,"* implies a metaphorical story, and lends itself to elaboration and application to many different topic stories. These ideas will be covered in more detail throughout this book.

As a side note, Clinton's use of this metaphor, and the blend of metaphor with her actual political history, has had an interesting effect on vernacular understanding of the metaphor. In fall 2014 (when Clinton had not yet announced her candidacy for 2016) during a classroom discussion of this metaphor, several women in the class put *can be broken* above *hard* as a relevant quality of *glass*. Thus it seems that the *"glass ceiling"* does indeed have "about *eighteen million cracks* in it"; some of these cracks were *'visible'* in that classroom discussion. At least in part as a result of Clinton's campaign *"glass ceiling"* has been transformed from a metaphor of frustrated ambition to a metaphor of hope.

Interpreting metaphors. How do we know that particular persons interpret *career advancement* as *'moving up,'* and *biases that prevent career advancement* as a *"ceiling"*? How do we know that particular persons interpret the metaphor *"glass"* in terms of both *'unseen'* and *'transparent'*? The short answer is that we don't and we can't. Even literal language is ambiguous (Wilson & Sperber, 2004), and figurative language is even more ambiguous. Both in our everyday interactions and as researchers, we rely on what we know about past uses of language – but with full awareness that different people may be thinking of different meanings associated with a metaphor vehicle. We also rely on clues from the surrounding context, which in this case includes the nature of workplace biases, which are rarely acknowledged and in many cases may not even be conscious. As researchers we can also garner clues from previous researchers and commentators. For example, according to the Federal Glass Ceiling Commission (1995, p. 4), *"glass ceiling"* describes "the *unseen*, yet *unbreachable barrier* that keeps minorities and women from *rising* to the *upper rungs* of the corporate *ladder*, regardless of their qualifications or achievements" (italics added to mark metaphors). In 1986, the same year Gay Bryant's book was published, Hymowitz and Schellhardt included the phrase in the title of an article in the *Wall Street Journal*: "The glass ceiling: Why women can't seem to break the invisible barrier that blocks them from the top jobs." Similarly, Hesse-Biber and Carter (2005) explain that *"glass ceiling"* is used to describe *"invisible barriers"* ("glass") through which women can see elite positions they cannot reach ("ceiling"). And of course

14   *"Shattering the Glass Ceiling"*

we sometimes have direct evidence from members of the audience itself, as when women in my classroom provided the "can be broken" entailment of "*glass*."

The '*transparent barrier*' interpretation of "*glass ceiling*" is sufficiently obvious that Nicholson (2008) could use it in a cartoon based on a wordplay where he transformed "*glass ceiling*" into "*class ceiling*." The cartoon shows two women, dressed in business suits and one man dressed in what appears to be carpenter's overalls standing on a glass surface (a "*glass floor*"). The man and one woman are looking up through a "*glass ceiling*"; the other woman is looking down through the "*glass floor*" at three other women, one of whom is cooking, one doing janitorial work, and one working on an assembly line. The cartoon makes sense only if "*glass*" is understood to entail '*transparent*' as well as "*barrier to vertical motion*."

All of these clues tell us that many people do interpret "*glass ceiling*" in ways consistent with the foregoing discussion, but they do not tell us how specific persons in Senator Clinton's audience may have understood the metaphor, or even how Senator Clinton may have intended the metaphor. Indeed, the metaphor is sometimes used in a lexicalized way to which both the '*transparent*' and the "*barrier*" entailments are irrelevant: In a recent book about the role of language in human evolution, Dunbar (2014) refers to the "*glass ceiling*" that has prevented other primates from evolving anything like language. Since members of a species lacking language would presumably not be able to '*perceive*' the capabilities they are unable to attain, '*transparent*' is irrelevant. It seems most likely that Dunbar was just using the metaphor in a generic sense of '*barrier*,' with no intention of activating other entailments. (Regarding intentionality in metaphor use, see Steen [2015], discussed in Chapter 3.) Even the '*upward motion*' entailment of "*ceiling*" is inconsistent with the doctrine, in evolution theory, that evolution has no objective or '*direction*.' Dunbar's use of the metaphor in a much broader sense reminds us that metaphors often become partially or wholly lexicalized, and applied in contexts very different from the context in which they originated. Indeterminacy in the face of ambiguous language is a weakness of interpretive research that can be alleviated but never completely overcome. In Chapters 3, 4, 11, and 12, I will discuss methodological issues involved in metaphor research, including the problem of ambiguity, in more detail.

Metaphorical stories in visual communication. Nicholson's "*class ceiling*" cartoon is a good example of another phenomenon, which will be covered in greater detail in Chapter 11: visual images, especially in advertising, editorial cartoons, and other forms of cartoon art, often illustrate, draw on, or imply conceptual metaphors, which are sometimes but not always familiar from idiomatic metaphorical expressions. Nicholson's cartoon is particularly interesting because it extends the '*upward mobility*' and '*ambition frustrated* *by unacknowledged biases*' stories implicit in Gay Bryant's initial use of the metaphor '*downward*' as well as '*upward*' in the corporate hierarchy. The more customary topic story about a woman's ambition to '*rise beyond middle management*' is represented by images of two people in business suits gazing upward through a glass ceiling. A different topic story about working-class men and women who are unable even to reach '*middle*' management (and the '*middle* class') is represented by a third figure, looking downward through a glass floor at three figures below doing manual labor (janitorial and assembly-line work), for whom the "*glass* floor" of those in the middle is a "*glass ceiling*." The combination of these images blends these two versions of the implicit metaphorical story into a single metaphorical story about the rigidity of socioeconomic class structure in contemporary U.S. society, reinforced by the wordplay title "*class ceiling*."

Metaphorical Stories and Story Metaphors

Extended metaphorical stories. When first encountering the idea of *metaphorical stories*, it is likely that most people, including social scientists and scholars who study language, will not think of examples like Hillary Clinton's concession speech. For most people, *metaphorical stories* are more likely to call to mind the allegories, fables, and parables that have been told and retold over many centuries; these have also received the most attention from scholars in the literary disciplines. Probably the most commonly encountered form of metaphorical story encountered in literature is the *allegory*, which is sometimes explained as a metaphor that has been so extended that it becomes something more than a metaphor (Crisp, 2001). More specifically, allegory refers to examples like *Pilgrim's Progress*, in which the topic is often not explicitly mentioned, but the metaphorical mapping is guided by the use of overtly metaphorical names such as "Sinner," "Everyman," "Idleness," and "Christian," and place names like "Slough of Despond." In the typical allegory, the vehicle story is created as a self-contained world with its own rules. Characters are given allegorical names, but are rarely developed beyond the stereotypes suggested by these names. According to Crisp, the topic of the allegory is not directly mentioned, although the allegorical language provides abundant clues to guide interpretation – and it is assumed that the process of interpretation will illuminate and add meaning to the topic.

Perhaps more familiar to lay persons are fables like Aesop's story of the Fox and the Grapes, from which the commonplace metaphor '*sour grapes*' derives, and parables like Jesus's parable of the Prodigal Son. Some of these, like Aesop's animal fables and some of Jesus's parables, resemble allegory in that the topic is not mentioned within the story, although both the topic and the intended interpretation is often made explicit in a coda or "moral" at the end of the story. In others, like Jesus's parable of the wise man who built his house on solid rock, contrasted with the foolish man who built his house on sand, the mapping onto the topic is incorporated into the story. Parables often take a form closer to metonym than to metaphor, and many of Jesus's parables are overtly metonymic. The Prodigal Son in the well-known vehicle story leads a sinful life, repents, and is forgiven, mapping onto and at the same time providing an example of the more general topic story of sin, repentance, and forgiveness; the Good Samaritan in the vehicle story displays kindness and charity, mapping onto and providing an example of the topic story about kindness and charity. Both of these parables afford both a metonymic and a metaphorical interpretation. In contrast, the story about building one's house on the sand is clearly *not* intended as a lesson in safe home construction: it is purely metaphorical, with no elements of metonym.

Until quite recently, the study of stories and storytelling has been largely concentrated in disciplines associated with literary criticism and literary studies generally, although there has also been some attention to stories elicited during therapeutic interviews as a diagnostic and treatment method within clinical disciplines. Within literary disciplines, research on metaphorical stories has focused primarily on allegory. Chapter 5 will discuss these familiar and formal types of metaphorical stories, many of which illustrate religious or philosophical ideas, but some of which simply illustrate ideas about the "human condition." Chapter 6 will examine metaphorical stories that appear in non-literary discourse, including speeches like Senator Clinton's concession speech as well as casual conversations.

Metaphorical story scenarios. Based on an analysis in which he applied Conceptual Metaphor Theory to partisan political discourse, Lakoff (1996) argued that political thought and rhetoric in the United States is organized around two linked conceptual metaphors, A NATION IS A FAMILY and LEADERS ARE PARENTS. According to Lakoff's analysis, conservatives generally prefer metaphors based around a STRICT PARENT metaphor and liberals prefer NURTURANT PARENT as a metaphorical base. Musolff (2006) generalizes and extends this idea, arguing that conceptual metaphors are often developed into *scenarios*, such as the LOVE-MARRIAGE-FAMILY scenario discussed by Lakoff. According to Musolff, political discourse within (and about) the European Union is often characterized by FAMILY-based scenarios such as COOPERATION BETWEEN STATES IN MARRIAGE. Metaphorical story scenarios will be discussed in greater detail in Chapter 7.

Abbreviated and Implied Story Metaphors

Often in discourse, stories are just mentioned or alluded to, with the apparent expectation that listeners will understand the reference; this is true of metaphorical stories as well. Well-known fables or parables may be invoked by simple reference to a character ('he's kind of a *Prodigal Son*,' 'he's being a *Good Samaritan*') or phrase ('that sounds like *sour grapes*,' 'he *cried wolf* once too often'). Hearers may not always activate the full underlying story, but it is likely that they often do – and the speaker's intended meaning may not be fully understood without activating the story and applying it to the subject of the remark. Brief metaphors often require activation of a metaphorical story to be fully understood. 'It's time to *fall back and punt*' makes no sense without activating the story of a team in American football, facing a third down with several yards to go, and mapping it onto a topic story about whatever situation provoked the remark.

Aphorisms (usually metaphorical) distill a bit of commonsense wisdom in a way that requires activation of at least a vehicle story and usually require mapping it onto a topic story. A *'bull in a china shop'* is merely something or someone in the wrong place until a story about a bull clumsily destroying the entire contents of the shop is activated, and mapped onto an already-salient story about some behavior of the subject of the remark, usually metaphorically *'clumsy'* behavior that *'destroys'* social harmony, interpersonal trust, or some other valued social state of being. *'Let sleeping dogs lie'* merely seems like advice to *be kind to exhausted pets* until a vehicle story about someone awakening a sleeping dog and getting bitten is contrasted with a vehicle story about the same person tiptoeing around the dog and not getting bitten, and both vehicle stories are mapped onto the topic, some potentially troublesome social situation.

Sometimes a nonmetaphorical story is mentioned in a way that invites mapping it as a metaphor vehicle onto a topic story. The refrain, "where will you *meet* your *Waterloo*?" from the popular song "Waterloo"[2] (Wilkin & Loudermilk, 1959) means little without activating the story of Napoleon's disastrous defeat (which is mentioned in the song) and mapping it onto a story of potential personal disaster. Glucksberg and McGlone (1999) provide the example 'Cambodia is Vietnam's *Vietnam*,' which appeared in several media commentaries on Cambodia's 1978 invasion of Cambodia. This metaphor requires activating the story of the long and costly U.S. engagement in Vietnam and mapping it onto the story of Vietnam's subsequent intervention in Cambodia. Brief stories, metaphors that imply stories, and allusions to stories that invite or demand a metaphorical interpretation will be discussed in detail in Chapters 6 and 7.

Metaphorical Stories and Story Metaphors in Language Play, Irony, and Humor

Metaphorical stories and story metaphors often have an element of irony. The ironic use of *'Vietnam'* as vehicle in a metaphorical comment on Vietnam's own actions makes 'Cambodia is Vietnam's *Vietnam*' particularly interesting. The song "Waterloo," mentioned in the last section, uses a playful reference to the story of Napoleon's defeat to make a serious comment about life. The overall playful tone of the song is underscored by playful transformation of the conventional metaphor *'every dog has its day'* into a diminutive form in "Every *puppy* has its day." Popular music is replete with playful use and distortion of metaphors. One of Johnny Cash's satirical songs, "Flushed from the Bathroom of Your Heart" (Clement, 1968), consists entirely of a string of humorously vulgar and ridiculous metaphorical stories about love, all in the same vein as the title. Gamson (1992, p. 23) reports an exchange between two participants in a focus group after the conclusion of the formal conversation that includes an exchange in which one participant uses a conventional metaphor to claim that his participation in the conversation had been forceful and forthright: "I didn't *pull any punches* anyways …" and another participant transformed the metaphor into a playfully deflating tease: "You didn't *throw any* either." Playful transformation of metaphors into stories, and the use of metaphorical stories and story-metaphors in irony and jokes will be discussed in greater detail in Chapter 7. Chapters 8 through 10 will examine metaphorical stories and story metaphors in three specific discourse contexts: journalism, a campaign speech by Barack Obama, and several speeches on the topic of climate change.

Yet another form of figurative language, *hyperbole* (extreme exaggeration) is apparent in Clinton's phrase "it's got *a million cracks in it*." Hyperbole is often, as here, combined with metaphor and metonym, sometimes as a means of emphasizing the speaker's point but also often in a spirit of playfulness (referring to ordinary life setbacks as "your *Waterloo*" is an example).

Metaphorical Stories in Visual Communication

Language-based metaphors are often depicted in political cartoons (and other cartoons), as well as in advertising and other visual media. Nicholson's (2008) cartoon in which he visually transformed *"glass ceiling"* into *"class ceiling"* has already been discussed. Almost every year at New Year's, cartoons appear showing the Earth with an ice pack on its head, suggestive of a headache, possibly a hangover. Bruegel's painting *The Blind Leading the Blind*, reproduced on the cover of this book and discussed in the Preface and Chapter 11, is another example.

Visual metaphors, including metaphorical stories, are also a staple of commercial advertising. The Schick razor company recently ran a series of ads for the Schick Quattro, a razor designed for trimming women's pubic hair (colloquially referred to as *"bush"*). One ad in the series shows a formal garden featuring three potted topiary plants (bushes), one in the shape of a perfect cube, the second a perfect sphere. The third, a small inverted cone, is strategically placed in front of a nude statue in the neoclassical style, so it looks like a triangle of neatly trimmed pubic hair on the statue. This visual metaphor is quite complex; part of what it accomplishes is to activate a story about topiary gardening and map it onto an implicit story about intimate personal grooming. Metaphorical stories that are implied by visual images, and visual images that draw on metaphorical stories to comment about a topic will be discussed in Chapter 11.

Summary

The importance of metaphor in storytelling has long been recognized, although until recently most analysts followed Aristotle's lead in treating metaphor as primarily a matter of embellishment or decoration. Until recently scholarly attention has focused almost entirely on instructive story metaphors, especially allegories, as well as fables and parables. Story-based jokes have been extensively analyzed in the humor literature, but remarkably little attention has been given to the metaphorical aspects of many story jokes. Similarly, although story metaphors appear with some frequency in formal discourse such as political speeches as well as in informal conversations, their metaphorical aspects have received almost no attention.

Even less attention has been given to the playful transformation of metaphors into stories, or to the stories that are often implied by metaphors. In this book I argue that analysis of story metaphors is crucial to discourse analysis. I also argue that even metaphors that take the form of a single word or short phrase often imply a story, and that the implied story must be activated in order to fully understand the metaphor.

2 Stories and Narratives

> And the Lord God called unto Adam, and said unto him, "Where art thou?" And he said, "I heard thy voice in the garden, and I was afraid, because I was naked; and I hid myself." And he said, "Who told thee that thou was naked?"
> – Genesis 3:9–11

Anthropologist Robin Dunbar (2014) singles out religion and storytelling as two crucial characteristics that distinguish humans from other species. Creation stories, like the one from which this passage was taken, answer questions like: Who are we? How did we get here? Why is life so difficult? Along with stories about the group itself, both recent and in the remote past, these stories anchor individuals' identities as members of a social order in a particular relationship with ancestors and gods.

> **Examples from actual discourse**
> I will draw examples, throughout the book, from a variety of texts that are in the public domain, including speeches such as Hillary Clinton's concession speech discussed in Chapter 1. I will also draw examples from conversations organized and facilitated, as part of class assignments, in several advanced seminars I have taught during the past 10 years. In each case, participants were invited to spend 60–90 minutes in an open-ended conversation about a topic of general interest; the student facilitators audio-recorded and transcribed the conversations.
>
> All of the conversations were held in or near Portland, Oregon (a midsize city in the Pacific Northwest), between 2005 and 2012. I will provide additional contextual information wherever it is relevant to the discussion. Topics included police-community relations and public safety; the problem of homelessness; and the formation of artists' identities as artists.
>
> All of these projects had IRB approval and were conducted in accordance with normal procedures for the protection of human participants in research, including informed consent, assignment of fictional names, and deletion of information that might identify participants.

A very different example of storytelling comes from a conversation among a group of African American men who met, at the request of two graduate students in Communication (as part of an assignment in an advanced seminar), to discuss relations between the community and the police force.

Stories and Narratives

The background was a series of incidents, both in Portland and in other U.S. cities, in which unarmed African Americans had been killed by police officers during routine stops for minor traffic violations and other routine interactions, and which had resulted in allegations of racial bias in police practices. About halfway through a 90-minute conversation, one of the participants told the following story about an incident that had happened in Portland a few years earlier:

Tony Stevens was ex-Marine, Vietnam era. He had a guy came in. Robbed a gas station. Tony grabbed the guy and held him down. The police came in. In spite of what everybody in the surrounding area was telling them, the police jumped on Tony, and choked him to death. Why? The perpetrator was White and Tony was Black. And this was a detective that did it. This was when Potter was chief of police. There are certain *patterns* that happen. (Ritchie, 2010).

Portland has a relatively small and cohesive African American population for a city its size, and it is very likely that the other participants in the conversation already knew the Tony Stevens story. Since the story had received extensive media coverage, it is also likely that the two students who organized and facilitated the discussion knew something about the story, although they may not have known the details. In the context of the conversation it appears that the story was offered, not to inform anyone of new facts, but rather to illustrate a point about the "*patterns* that happen" in the community. As with the Garden of Eden story, many of the details are left to be filled in by the audience based on background contextual knowledge. The details provided by the narrator (Stevens was an ex-marine, the skin color of the participants, the officer involved was a detective, and the identity of the police chief) all serve to foster, reinforce, or refute possible inferences about the story.

Compared with Hillary Clinton's extended story about her unsuccessful campaign for the Democratic presidential nomination, both of these passages are relatively short, but they also have a fairly complex structure. Both passages relate a sequence of thematically and causally related events. Both passages would satisfy most people's ideas about what constitutes a "story." But compare these to another brief passage from the same conversation about police-community relations. A few minutes after the Tony Stevens story, the same speaker related a story about the shooting of an unarmed African American citizen in a different state. A second participant, Bob, remarked, "Well it has happened here too. Kendra who got shot over there on … on the bridge by a police officer."

A few years earlier an unarmed young African American woman named Kendra James had been shot and killed by police officers during a routine traffic stop. The incident was in the news for several months, and led to a public meeting between police and city officials and members of the community (see Ritchie & Cameron, 2014). The mere mention of the name "Kendra" would be likely to bring the entire sequence of events to mind for any person of color who lived in the city at that time. The participants in the conversation, including the student facilitators, could be reasonably assumed to know about the incident and the ensuing public controversy as part of their background cultural knowledge. Would this single sentence, spoken in a context of shared background knowledge and beliefs, qualify as a story? Would the mere name "Kendra" or "Tony Stevens" qualify as a story in the context of this conversation?

Even shorter, but arguably more completely developed, is a "six-word novel" attributed to Ernest Hemingway: "For sale: Baby shoes. Never worn."

What Is a Story?

Although we all have an intuitive sense of what a story is, based on a lifetime of hearing, reading, and telling stories, we do not necessarily agree about what counts as a story. To complicate matters, some scholars and researchers distinguish between a *story* and a *narrative* (e.g., Labov, 2013; Snaevarr, 2010) but others do not (Bruner, 2002; Schank & Berman, 2002). Moreover, some researchers and scholars give quite broad definitions and some give very restrictive definitions.

Abbott (2008) defines *narrative* very broadly as "the representation of an event or a series of events," a "*fuzzy* set," without clear boundaries between what is and what is not a narrative. Labov (2013) defines a "minimal narrative" quite simply as "a sequence of two independent clauses" (p. 15), which would include the brief reference to Kendra James, but he also provides a much more restrictive definition for a "fully developed narrative," which "begins with an abstract, an orientation with information on persons, places, times and behavior involved; the complicating action; an evaluation section, which identifies the point of the narrative; the resolution; and a coda" (p. 5). Schank and Berman (2002) define *narrative* in similar terms as a "structured telling," which will ordinarily include "themes, goals, plans, expectations, expectation failures (or obstacles), and perhaps, explanations or solutions" (p. 287). Bruner (2002, p. 15) asserts more succinctly that "narrative in all its forms is a dialectic between what was expected and what came to pass. For there to be a story, something unforeseen must happen." "Something unforeseen" is similar to Labov's concept of a "complicating action" and Schank and Berman's "expectation failures," although "something unforeseen" is arguably more inclusive, since it is not necessarily "complicating" and may not represent a failure of expectations. What all of these concepts have in common is that something about the sequence of events in a narrative sets it apart and

What Is a Story?

makes it unusual. It differs from the ordinary and offers the prospect of learning something new, hence it is interesting in and for itself.

Snaevarr (2010) draws a different line between *narrative* and *story*: "Story is *what* is being recounted, independent of the medium used. Narrative is the *way* the story is told ... narrative (or discourse) is the signifier, the story is the signified" (p. 168). In this sense, the full sequence of events surrounding the death of Kendra James would be the *story*, and Bob's brief mention of it the *narrative*. Labov (2013), however, proposes a definition under which narrative is a sub-category within a more general concept of story: "Since we have constrained narrative to mean a very particular kind of speech event, *story* may be allowed to float freely for any talk about a sequence of events" (p. 18).

Following Labov, I identify *any* recounting of a series of causally or thematically related events as a *story*, and classify it as a *narrative* only if it includes at least a minimal structure: actions toward a goal; something unexpected such as a reversal, obstacle, opposition, setback, or failure of expectation; an attempt to overcome the reversal; and a final resolution of the conflict or contradiction that led to the reversal. However, as with Hemingway's six-word novel, much of this may be only implied. I will use the phrase *actual event sequence* to express Snaevarr's distinction between what is being recounted and how it is expressed. What is being recounted, the *actual* event sequence, can never be known: even participants and direct witnesses can know only the stories they construct for themselves, based on what is salient to them about their perceptions – shaped by their prejudices and expectations, supplemented and modified by the stories they hear from other participants and witnesses.

Often, stories are merely mentioned: when the cultural and historical context is known and salient, a name ("Kendra James," "Adam and Eve"), location ("Garden of Eden," "Waterloo," "Appomattox Courthouse[1]"), or theme ("forbidden fruit," "first kiss," "police shooting") may serve as a *story index* (Schank & Berman, 2002) with the potential to activate in the minds of listeners an entire story, or certain parts of it. As "first kiss" and "police shooting" illustrate, different listeners may experience very different stories in response to a story index; even a more specific index like "Kendra James" often activates different stories for listeners who bring different contextual knowledge and presuppositions to the discourse (Ritchie & Cameron, 2014). In the United States, "Appomattox Courthouse" still, after 150 years, activates very different stories for different audiences, based mainly on where they live and whether they identify more with the northern region of the United States or with the "Old South," the states of the former Confederacy. Even when the story indexed by "Appomattox Courthouse" is narrated in detail it may be understood quite differently by descendant of a

Confederate soldier and a descendant of a Union soldier, regardless of the point of view expressed by the narrator.

Structure of stories and narratives. To sum up and reprise, an *event sequence* is an actual sequence of events that can be arbitrarily bounded in time, space, and/or theme. As such, it has no structure until a person with a point of view perceives, selects, and organizes events in some way. A *story* is two or more events taken from a teller's perception of an event sequence and reported in a way that implies at least some causal and thematic relationship among these events. "I went to the store and bought some fruit" is a minimal story – it recounts two events that are implicitly related both by causality (one can infer that buying the fruit was the purpose, and the desire to buy the fruit the cause, of going to the store) and by theme (a store is one place where fruit is found for purchase). It lacks any of the other elements of a narrative – there is no opposition, no reversal, no conflict, hence no resolution. "Kendra who got shot over there on … on the bridge by a police officer" is a more fully developed story. It almost qualifies as a narrative, although to understand it as a narrative the listener must fill in details about motives, the conflict that led to the shooting, the ensuing political controversy, and the resolution; these details may be drawn from background knowledge or generated from the listener's intuitive imagination.

A *narrative* is a set of events taken from a teller's perception of an event sequence and organized in a structure that includes a setting (time and place), at least one person (a protagonist) who attempts to accomplish something, opposition or conflict leading to a reversal or setback, followed by a resolution. The resolution may lead to accomplishment of the protagonist's goals, but may be achieved in some other way such as acceptance of a new state of affairs. A narrative sometimes includes assistance from a third party (or other external force) that contributes to resolution of the conflict. A narrative often ends with a *coda*, which comments on the story and its relevance to the conversation in which the story appears or to other concerns common to teller and audience. The perception and selection of events, as well as other features of the narration, almost inevitably expresses or implies a particular perspective or point of view.

The short dialogue between Adam and God, quoted at the beginning of this chapter, comes about halfway through a story about the origins of humanity and the loss of innocence that is embedded in a larger story about the creation of the world, and begins another, much longer, story about a particular tribe and its relationship with a deity. The Garden of Eden story is usually understood from the perspective of the "first man" (or in more gender-inclusive terms, the "first couple"). From this perspective the story is bounded by the first couple's initial innocent awareness ("they were both naked, the man and his wife, and were not ashamed") and their ultimate loss of innocence and bitter exile: "therefore the Lord God sent him forth from the garden of Eden, to till the ground from whence he was taken." The coda to the story also includes language that suggests the perspective of God the Creator: "And the Lord God said, 'Behold, the man is become as one of us, to know good and evil: and now, lest he put forth his hand, and take also of the tree of life, and eat, and live forever'; therefore the Lord God sent him forth from the garden of Eden."

The story about Adam and Eve and their eviction from the Garden of Eden illustrates several features common to theories about narrative and storytelling. It has a *setting*, *persons* who *attempt to accomplish something*, *opposition* or conflict leading to *a reversal*, followed by a *resolution*. The *setting* is an idyllic garden, which includes "every tree that is pleasant to the sight, and good for food," as well as the tree of life and the tree of knowledge of good and evil. The story begins with the creation of Adam. God puts Adam in charge of the garden, and commands him not to eat from the tree of knowledge of good and evil, warning him that if he does so he will die. This initial command and warning set up a potential conflict which will reappear, in Eve's conversation with the serpent, to move the story forward.

Following this introductory passage, in something of a digression, the narrator describes how God created the animals and Adam named them. Finally the narrator returns to the main story by relating how God created Eve as a companion for Adam. This orienting section ends with the evaluative statement that Adam and Eve "were both naked, the man and his wife, and were not ashamed." This section fits Labov's (2013) concept of an "an orientation with information on persons, places, times and behavior." Consistent with Schank and Berman (2002), it sets forth the crucial themes (an idyllic life in a lush garden; innocence and lack of shame) and expectations with implicit goals: Adam and Eve are expected to obey God's commands and in turn they expect to continue living blissfully and happily in the garden.

A *complicating action* (Schank & Berman, 2002) is introduced immediately in the first sentence of the next chapter, in the guise of a serpent who "was more subtil than any beast of the field." There follows a dialogue in which the serpent convinces Eve to eat the fruit of the forbidden tree, Eve convinces Adam to do likewise, and this leads to what Schank and Berman call an *expectation failure*. The state of blissful ignorance/innocence is broken and, when the two people see that they are naked they experience shame, followed by fear of being found out. This complicating action is immediately followed by the climax of the story, as quoted at the beginning of this chapter: "And the Lord God called unto Adam, and said unto him, 'Where art thou?' And he said, 'I heard thy voice in the garden, and I was afraid, because I was naked; and I hid myself.' And he said, 'Who told thee that thou was naked?'" This challenge is followed by a blame sequence, and then the *evaluation* and *resolution*, in which God passes judgment on the three miscreants. In the final passage, God realizes the possibility that Adam and Eve might discover the tree of life and become immortal, and so banishes them from the garden and guards the tree of life with a flaming sword. This constitutes a brief story about a potential future, and could be construed as part of the resolution, but it can also be construed as a *coda* (Labov, 2013), an independent passage that comments on the narrative and on its relevance to the present. As this example illustrates, the boundaries between elements of a narrative are not always clearly marked, even in artfully constructed (literary) stories, and that is even truer of conversational storytelling.

As it is presented in the second and third chapter of Genesis, the story of Adam and Eve is relatively sparse, with only the most crucial details reported. There is no mention of how long the couple enjoyed the garden before the temptation. Only the bare bones of the serpent's dialogue with Eve are reported, and no details at all are given as to how Eve was able to convince Adam to eat the fruit; these and many other details are left to the imagination of the audience. This sparseness might seem to be explained by the location of the story within the opening section of an ancient religious text, by its prehistory as part of a long oral tradition, or by its mythic quality. But as Cameron (2007) points out, simple, austere, literal language is often more powerful than more elaborated telling, and simple direct language figures in most ordinary conversation as well as in mythic and religious stories like the story of Adam and Eve.

Short as it is, the Tony Stevens story is also recounted in simple, direct language, and also has all the elements of a narrative: characters, location, and a plot. The Tony Stevens story begins with a problem or challenge ("a guy ... robbed a gas station"), proceeds to an attempted resolution ("Tony grabbed the guy and held him down. The police came in"), followed by a reversal ("the police jumped on Tony"), final resolution ("choked him to death"), and a coda explaining the significance of the story and connecting it to a broader *generic* story ("There are certain *patterns* that happen"). "*Patterns*," which appears in the coda, is the only metaphor in the entire story.

The story of Adam and Eve and the Tony Stevens story are both fully developed narratives: They include purposes, conflict, setbacks, and resolution – although in both stories, the resolution is presumably quite unsatisfactory to the protagonists. Each story ends in a coda, although the coda in the story of Adam and Eve can also be understood as part of the resolution – if the story is understood from the perspective of God, then the concern that Adam and Eve might gain immortality is a residual contradiction that can only be resolved by expelling them from the garden and posting a guard with a flaming sword in front of the tree of life.

In ordinary conversations, stories may be told by a single person, often spread over several speaking turns, sometimes with supportive comments and questions, occasionally interrupted by other comments or even other stories. Personal stories are often co-narrated, sometimes by several people who either participated in a particular event or have experienced similar events (Bulow, 2004; Norrick, 2010). The narrator may provide detailed information about setting and context, but often – particularly when the context is familiar to most members of the audience – most of the details may be left for the audience to fill in. As the "baby shoes" story illustrates, leaving crucial details to be filled in by the audience can greatly enhance the power and persuasive effects of a story.

Lakoff (2008) observes that complex narratives are composed of smaller, simpler narratives based on *"frames"* or *"scripts."* Lakoff claims that much of our thinking is accomplished with these frames or scripts, consistent with Schank and Abelson's claim that our memory consists of stories. Narratives are often woven together from several constituent stories, which may themselves be fully developed, or may merely be mentioned or indexed. Sometimes stories overlap, so that a series of events that could itself be developed as a complete narrative is merely mentioned as an incidental part of another narrative. Brief as it is, the Tony Stevens story incorporates elements of several other stories. "Ex-marine, Vietnam era" indexes the story of Stevens's military service and overlaps with the entire story of the Vietnam War, including the prominent role of African American soldiers in that war. "Robbed a gas station" is the crucial part of a story that stands on its own, and figures in this story only as the motivation for Stevens's actions. "What everybody in the surrounding area was telling them" implies the individual stories of several spectators – it also sets up and implies an alternative story in which Stevens would have been greeted as a hero and thanked by the police. The contrast with that alternative story, the story that might be expected to happen but did not happen, sets up the bitter irony of the actual story, as well as a secondary, thematic contradiction, the "patterns that happen." In the context of the conversation, the Tony Stevens story is itself embedded within an ongoing story about the troubled relationship between the police department and the African American community.

The coda of the Tony Stevens story can be divided into four parts. The first part is a simple explanation of why the police officers attacked Stevens instead of the robber. The second part of the coda, "this was a detective that did it," implies a story about the training and experience required for promotion to police detective and the actions that would be expected to result from that training and experience. The third part, "this was when Potter was chief of police," implies a story about Potter's leadership and his attempts to improve police relations with the African American community. These two story indexes set up the final part of the coda, "There are certain *patterns that happen.*" They also provide a basis for generalizing the concept of "*patterns* that happen" to include not just tragic deaths like that of Tony Stevens but also patterns of police training, institutional racism, and political leadership.

Labov and Waletsky (1967) consider a story to be a narrative *only* if the events are related in the order in which they occur. Labov (2013) acknowledges that many passages that have been classified and analyzed by narrative researchers in the intervening years would not qualify as narrative under this restrictive definition. In the Tony Stevens passage, for example, the speaker relates the prior event, "robbed a gas station" after the scene setting event, "a guy came in." Even the Garden of Eden story includes a flashback, when Eve explains to the serpent that she and Adam have not eaten any of the fruit from the tree of knowledge because God had forbidden them to do so. Flashbacks are a common feature of storytelling in ordinary conversations as well as formal literature. Sometimes the event sequence is inverted for various aesthetic reasons such as maintaining dramatic tension or, as in Conrad's (1958) novel *Lord Jim*, as a framing device. Often in conversational storytelling events are told out of order when the narrator (or another participant in the conversation) realizes that explanatory background information is needed. Stories are often embedded as flashbacks within larger stories, to provide background information, comment on the main story, or for any of a number of other purposes.

NASA scientist Jim Hansen opened his TED talk about climate change (see Chapter 10) with a story embedded in a question, "What do I know that would cause me, a reticent, Midwestern scientist, to get myself arrested in front of the White House protesting?" Before answering the question and thereby completing the story about the protest and his arrest, he flashed back to a story of his childhood: "I was lucky to grow up at a time when it was not difficult for the child of a tenant farmer to *make his way* to the state university. And I was really lucky to go to the University of Iowa where I could study *under* Professor James Van Allen who built instruments for the first U.S. satellites." This brief story of his youth was followed by a more elaborate story of his research on the "*greenhouse* effect," interlaced with several other stories, including an abbreviated hypothetical story set in a future in which his grandchildren criticize him: "Opa understood what was happening, but he didn't *make it clear*."

Hansen could easily enough have told this complex, multipart story in strict chronological order, but it would have been much less interesting. By shifting back and forth, from recent past (his arrest) to distant past (his childhood), future (his grandchildren's potential dismay about his failure to act) and back to the present, Hansen invited his audience to fill in the causal gaps and generalize the implications from Hansen's life and activities to their own. The power of this sort of narrative "time-travel" is even more apparent with

Hemingway's "six word novel." By placing the resolution, "For sale," first, the author activates a familiar script and provides motivation for the reader to fill in all the rest. In both literary and conversational storytelling, events are frequently narrated out of sequence.

Abbott (2008) points to a similar phenomenon, "narrative gaps," information about characters' life history, motivations, etc., that is not supplied; these gaps can add considerably to a story's power. As Abbott points out, in the novel *Wuthering Heights*, Brontë provides no answers to crucial questions such as, where did the child Heathcliff come from? Why did the adult Heathcliff hang Isabella's dog? Abbott also claims that the presence of these narrative gaps distinguishes fiction from true stories – but even true stories have gaps. Jim Hansen's story about studying under James Van Allen, then going on to design the first Venus flyby mission has many gaps. How did he manage to get a job at NASA? Why were scientists at NASA studying climate patterns on Earth? What leads his grandchildren to reflect on Hansen's career? The Tony Stevens story also has many gaps. Who called the police? What happened between the time the police arrived and the time they "jumped on" Stevens? Who were the bystanders and what exactly did they say to the police officers? Why was Stevens present at the scene of the attempted robbery?

Neither violations of chronological order nor explanatory gaps seem to pose difficulties for audiences; to the contrary, both are regular features of storytelling, often used for deliberate effect. Accordingly, I will use a broader definition of narrative, that includes stories with flashbacks as well as stories in which the narrator omits material the audience can be reasonably expected to fill in.

Master-plots and character types. Abbott (2008) argues that we organize our thinking as well as discourse about actual life around *master-plots* such as betrayal, revenge, rags-to-riches, a quest, and so on; these are represented by folktales, novels, and plays like *Cinderella, Don Quixote, Othello, The Odyssey*. At an abstract level these master-plots appear to be universal, but culture-specific master-plots and versions of master-plots have more practical force in ordinary life. Politicians, marketers, and other persuasion professionals shape narratives to activate these master-plots; debates are often conducted by activating competing master-plots. Bruner (2002) relates in detail how the defense and prosecution in the Lizzie Borden trial sought both to establish their own narrative to account for the known and uncontested facts and to undermine the other side's narrative. Hogan (2003; see also Mar & Oatley, 2008) narrows the field even further: based on analysis of narrative themes in a variety of literary works, Hogan found that the most common themes are relationships, specifically love and conflict; this finding is consistent with Dunbar's (1996) research on the predominance of social themes in ordinary conversations.

Master-plots usually involve stereotypical character types, which come to be associated with familiar characters like Iago, Judas, Lear, Oedipus, Cinderella, Willy Loman. Tragic characters like Othello tend to be complex and multidimensional – Abbott (2008) refers to these as *"round"* characters, in contrast to the *"flat,"* uncomplicated characters of satire and comedy. However, Abbott's distinction seems rather too simple: it seems fair to ask whether Don Quixote, Bottom (in *Midsummer Night's Dream*), or Arthur Dent in the *Hitchhiker's Guide* series (Adams, 1979) are truly *"flat."* In any event, named or not, certain types are encountered in many narrative modes – the flirt, the scoundrel, the hypocrite, the well-meaning fool, etc. These types are readily recognized in literature, and they provide a ready resource for conversational storytelling as well.

Setting. Abbott claims that narrative is *"the principal way in which our species organizes its understanding of time"* (2008, p. 3; italics in original). Events in a story happen in a time and a place – two ingredients of setting. Sometimes the time and place are specified; sometimes they are left to be inferred by the audience. In Jim Hansen's story about growing up, he explicitly stated the places, a tenant farm and the University of Iowa, and gave the time as his own youth, so that the audience could estimate the approximate years based on his current age. In the Tony Stevens story, the place is just "a gas station"; the time is unstated, but, from the statement that Stevens was a Vietnam-era marine, an approximate time can be inferred. The story of Hillary Clinton's campaign happens in several states, a few of which are named, and in the year preceding the speech in which she told it; the story of her support of Obama's campaign, like Jim Hansen's story of his grandchildren criticizing him, takes place in the future.

Even when a story is not "located" in an exact time and place, the narrated details, events, and entities create an implicit sense of place and time, what Abbott calls a "story world" (see also Gerrig, 1993). In addition to the story world in which the action is set, stories also frequently activate *possible worlds* in which things might be different. The Garden of Eden story implies a possible world in which Eve would have been more resolute in resisting the serpent and continued to live in blissful innocence (and ignorance) with her mate, Adam. In the Tony Stevens story, the phrase "in spite of what everybody ... was telling them" creates a possible world in which the police officers would have understood that Tony was the hero not the culprit, leading to a very different outcome. By the officers' actions it can also be inferred that they entertained and acted according to yet another possible world, one in which Stevens was the criminal and the actual robber was an innocent bystander. These *alternate worlds* often motivate and give meaning to the stories. Sometimes, as in the Tony Stevens, Garden of Eden, and *Baby Shoes* examples, the story can only be fully understood in terms of the alternate worlds.

Stories contain – and exist within – the time and place of their story world. They also exist within the world of the narrator. A story invokes both the time it takes for the narrated events to occur, within the story, and the time it takes to read or hear the story. There may be long gaps in time within the story ("a few years later . . .") but there may also be gaps in the telling or reading, because of interruptions of one sort or another. In some complex narrations, like *Tales of 1,001 Nights* and the novel *Lord Jim*, the world in which the story is narrated is itself a story world. Clark (1996) refers to this phenomenon as *layering*. Even true stories may be several layers deep, as when a witness's testimony is described in a news account, complete with the witness's report of a conversation with the defendant. Clark observes that layering is transparent in only one direction: When I read *The Hitchhiker's Guide* (Adams, 1979), I am aware of Arthur Dent but Arthur Dent is not aware of me. However, as Abbott points out, this directionality is often violated for artistic effect. Abbott gives the example of an old Daffy Duck cartoon in which Daffy struggles with the cartoonist over how the story is to progress. A visual example is Escher's etching in which two hands draw each other. Yet a third example comes in Tolkien's (1955) *Return of the King*, in a scene in which Frodo and Sam joke about whether their story might appear in a saga and, if it does, how people who read it might react to the passage describing their current predicament. "Any well-written narrative holds us because there is a plurality of possible worlds lying ahead of us" and these worlds jostle with each other for our attention (Abbott, 2008, p. 192).

Storytelling in Conversations

Until recently, research on nonliterary storytelling relied heavily on stories from structured contexts like interviews (Norrick, 2000), reflecting in part researchers' interest in diagnostic and therapeutic potential of stories, but also reflecting the ease of obtaining interview data relative to informal conversation data. There has also been recurring concern about the validity of recorded conversations, based on the necessity of obtaining informed consent. However, if the recording equipment is not too obtrusive and the facilitator acts in a natural way, and if the topic of the conversation is sufficiently engaging, participants often seem to forget that the discussion is being recorded. In my own research, I have found low-structure focus group conversations to be a rich source of storytelling. Compared to interviews, conversational storytelling is more interactive, less formal in structure, and more spontaneous, as demonstrated by frequent digressions and disfluencies, uncompleted thoughts, and extraneous comments. Conversational stories are also frequently interrupted, may be dispersed over several speaking turns, and are often at least partially co-narrated (Ritchie, 2010; 2011a; 2011b; 2011c).

According to Norrick, storytellers clearly mark both the opening and closing of a story, frequently summarizing the action or formulating the point of the story. Storytellers respect norms of "storytelling rights" (e.g., one person does not have a right to tell a story if the primary protagonist is present) and "tellability" – relevant, of general interest, and suitable to the present social context. However, Norrick acknowledges the "dark side of tellability" – stories may be tellable from the perspective of interest and relevance, but violate group norms regarding topic matter, disgust, etc.

In my own data, the "rules" described by Norrick and other researchers are frequently violated without comment, which may reflect the fact that my data have usually been collected in the context of casual socializing, with the conversation opened by reference to a particular topic and with limited subsequent intervention by the facilitators. The relative freedom with respect to "rules" such as "storytelling rights" and "tellability" in my data may also be a characteristic of the population from which most of the data were gathered: men and women in their late 20s and early 30s, most of them working at least part time and many of them attending college at least part time, very few of them in established careers or established relationships. Among this demographic group, there may be relatively less concern about content that might seem irrelevant, disgusting, or immoral by members of an older group, and less competition for the floor than might be the case with a younger group. Most researchers also include "newsworthiness" as a feature of "tellability," but in my data conversation participants seem to enjoy telling and listening to stories even when they are already well known to most or all participants. (This is particularly true of shared stories about a family, social group, or relationship.)

As Norrick (2000) and Labov (2013) both note, audience participation is important in eliciting, and sometimes in telling stories. Stories sometimes occur in thematic chains, in which a story follows up a theme or topic introduced by a previous speaker, but in my own data the contextual relevance is not always obvious. Labov (2013) notes that extended narratives of 15 minutes or more are often found in natural conversations, but in my own data, stories longer than two or three minutes are rare.

Types of Story

People tell many kinds of stories, to serve a variety of purposes. Researchers and scholars (e.g., Labov, 2013; Schank & Berman, 2002) have classified stories in a number of ways, according to features such as whether they report events that actually happened (*experiential* stories) or were invented (*fictional* stories), whether they are reported as having happened to the narrator (*first-person*) or someone else (*third-person*). Experiential stories in ordinary conversations include self-aggrandizement, embarrassing stories, humorous retelling of an actual incident, and retelling of dreams or fantasies

(Norrick, 2000). Fictional stories range from stories that could have happened (and are sometimes told as if they actually happened) to complete fantasies that could not possibly have happened. A special type of fictional story is the *myth* or *mythic story*, which is often but not necessarily told as having actually happened. People also frequently tell *generic* stories about events that typically happen to themselves, or that anyone might experience (Norrick, 2000); Labov (2013) calls these *pseudo-narratives*. These generic stories may be signaled by conditionals such as *would* (Labov, 2013) or by phrases like "Every time I..." or "Sometimes..."

These story types are not absolute, and the boundaries often shade into one another. Both first-person and third-person experiential stories are often based on actual events but embellished with fictional or mythic elements. The Garden of Eden story occupies an ambiguous status: for many people it is an example of an experiential third-person story, but for most people it is an example of a *mythic story*, a story told *as if* it happened to a real person even though the protagonists may or may not have actually existed. By comparison, the Tony Stevens story and the story indexed by *Kendra* in the same conversation are *experiential third-person stories*: they report events that actually happened to someone else. However, even these two examples slightly blur the lines, since they are introduced as specific *experiential examples* of *generic* stories, something that "happens all the time," as signaled by the coda to *Tony Stevens*, "There are certain *patterns* that happen."

Third-person experiential stories may be repeated from previous conversations; they are also often repeated or adapted, from mass media. It is unclear from the transcript of the conversation whether the Tony Stevens story was initially learned from newspaper accounts – given the relatively small size of the African American community in Portland, the city where the events happened and the conversation was recorded, the speaker may have heard it from others who were present. Hillary Clinton almost certainly heard the stories about 13-year-old Anne Riddell and 88-year-old Florence Stein from members of her campaign staff who, we can assume, had been instructed to record and report stories of this nature.

An example from a conversation among a group of Latino college students in the public safety series was reported as having come from mass media. The subject of ethnic profiling had arisen, and one of the participants repeated the following story as an example:

ADAM: For instance, I was reading, I read about it both ah, the *Mercury* and also in the, in the *Tribune*, how, ah there was a, she was a, PCC[2] instructor, thirty-four years old, she was standing on the corner of 82nd, and I forgot which intersection on 82nd, well waiting for the bus, well they took her in and arrested her for prostitution. She ah, she wanted to, she decided to sue the city, but they settled for like a thousand dollars, like, it was like no big deal. But I mean ...

34   Stories and Narratives

MARY: A thousand?
ADAM: A thousand dollars.
MARY: Are you sure about that?
ERICH: She must have been really provocatively dressed or something. That's really uncommon to have happen.
EDGAR: This was on 82nd?
ADAM: Yeah, they held her for,
EDGAR: Geez
ADAM: ... uh, in the back of the car ... They took her down to the station ...
MARY: When was this?
ADAM: Back in April.
MARY: This year?
EDGAR: PCC instructor? Wow.
ADAM: Yeah, a PCC instructor, 34 years old, arrested for prostitution. I mean the profiling ... is pretty blatant.

Like the Tony Stevens story, this story was told in a sparse way with minimal detail, but it still satisfies the criteria of a good story. The narrator described both the protagonist and the setting as well as the protagonist's objective (catch a bus, probably on the way either to or from work). A reversal arose in the form of an unexpected arrest, then the protagonist turned the tables and threatened action against the city, resulting in a resolution. The challenge ("Are you sure about that?") is not unusual in a conversation when a story includes an unusual element – although it is unclear whether Mary questioned the assertion that the settlement was for $1,000 because she thought it unusually high or unusually low. Erich's offer of a possible explanation, that the protagonist "must have been really provocatively dressed or something," is also common. Both challenges threatened the contextual relevance of the story as an example of police profiling; Erich's challenge in particular activated a "blame the victim" script that is a common response to stories involving sexual harassment. However, Adam's coda reinstated the "moral" of the story, and it did not elicit further challenge.

In conversations, listeners frequently offer back-channel supportive vocalizations, questions, and evaluative comments, as in the preceding example. Sometimes these comments challenge certain aspects of the story; often they either serve to elicit further information or add to the entertainment value of the story. The following story comes from a conversation about community-police relations in a wealthy suburb of Portland (part of the same series as the preceding example). The participants were all college students who graduated from local high schools, and much of the conversation centered around the ineffectual response of authorities, including teachers and parents as well as police, in dealing with the drug and alcohol-fueled culture of the local high school, in the wealthiest part of the suburb. This story illustrates the

Types of Story

participants' cynical attitude toward these authority figures, but it appears to have been offered primarily for its entertainment value:

ALEX: Uh, yeah, I know, like, one weekend, when my parents were ah, out of town, my brother decided to throw a party and when my parents got back, ah, they didn't question him, they were just glad because he cleaned the house. [Laughter.]
FRED: They didn't question why he cleaned the house?
BETH: Yeah ...
FRED: "Why did the teenager clean the house?" [Laughter.]
ALEX: They also didn't ask why the foosball table was on the back deck.
FRED: Um, the moment my dad came home and saw that the house was clean, he would have asked what I have been ...

In this example, Fred's question and its repetition as an imagined quote underscored Alex's point, rather than challenging it. His final coda, comparing Alex's parents with his own, also seems to have had a similar motivation. It also expresses a culturally shared cynicism about teenagers (doing chores like cleaning the house is so unusual that it is in itself a cause for suspicion), reinforcing the implications of the fictionalized quotation (phrased in the form of a familiar joke riddle setup), "Why did the teenager clean the house?" (This kind of adaptation of familiar scripts as a rhetorical resource is common in casual conversations.) Third-person stories are often, like both the Tony Stevens story and the "82nd Avenue" story, introduced to illustrate or support a point, but they are also often, as in this example, repeated for their entertainment value.

In conversations it is also common for stories to be interrupted or interwoven with other stories, and to spread over several speaking turns. Although the "canonical" approach is for a single narrator to tell a story, as in the Tony Stevens example, people also frequently collaborate in telling stories that they all know about or, in many cases, jointly experienced. In the following example, from the same conversation in the wealthy Portland suburb, Fred and Beth collaborate in retelling a story that had recently figured prominently in news media coverage. A third participant, Ellie, had just related a story about the failure of the police to investigate a classmate accused of collecting child pornography from the Internet "not that he enjoys it, but he has it just to have it."

ALEX: Yeah, that reminds me of, like, that case they had a little while ago about the kids ...
BETH: Oh, the sex thing?
ALEX: Yeah, the setting up ...
BETH: That was in Pennsylvania, sending naked pictures of themselves. Not even naked pictures, scantily clad pictures of themselves.
ALEX: Yeah, teenage girls sending ...

BETH: [Interrupting.] Several teenagers.
ALEX: ... Naked or partially naked pictures of themselves ...
BETH: None of them are full nudity
ALEX: To ... um, I'm not sure, to their friends, uh both male and female. And ...
BETH: And some of them were never sent.
ALEX: And, so, they got caught on child pornography.
BETH: Yeah.
ALEX: For both the girls who took the pictures and the guys who received them.
FRED: Not all the girls got charged ...
BETH: I heard a couple people got caught, even though, they actually never, it was just picture of themselves and they didn't have any other pictures, just pictures of themselves. And at least one picture was only of a girl in a bikini. Nothing scantier than that
ALEX: And yeah, the fact, that, you know, that gets brought up in this debate and that ...
BETH: And then something like THAT
ALEX: Doesn't get ...
ELLI: Where it was actual real life eww kiddie porn ...

Although the topic introduced by the facilitator at the beginning of this conversation was "public safety and police-community relations" the participants were far more interested in discussing the inability of police, school officials, and parents to control the behavior of young people in the community. The apparent violation of community norms regarding drugs and sexual behavior can be seen here as consistent with a *group* norm, probably reflecting norms of their peer group in this wealthy suburb. Since the participants all expressed disgust about "kiddie porn" one can infer that it lies well outside their moral standards – but *talking about it* was not counter-normative, and they clearly found the story interesting and entertaining.

This passage also illustrates an interesting aspect of group narration – clearly they were all aware of the story, so there was no "news value," but different speakers were able to offer tidbits of information that may *not* have been known to the others. It seems evident that both the "teenager who cleaned the house" and the "kiddie porn" stories were interesting, and the group seemed to be participating in collaboratively constructing a detailed reliving of the stories. This is consistent with Gerrig's (1993) concept of *"transportation into the story-world,"* a condition that apparently involves a dynamic and sustained simulation of key perceptual features of the story world. Green (2004) claims that stories are much more persuasive when listeners are thus *"transported."* It is likely that they are also more entertaining when listeners are transported.

Although we tend to think of a story as something that happened in the past, they are sometimes set in the future; this applies not merely to science fiction stories but also to stories that serve purposes such as instructing, coordinating, planning, inspiring, or fantasizing. Often participants begin with a story from the past and extend it into the future, as a prediction or warning of what *might* happen. This kind of projection into the future is apparent in Jim Hansen's brief account of a conversation his grandchildren *might*, in future years, have about himself (and by implication, about his entire generation): "Opa understood what was happening, but he didn't *make it clear*." It is also apparent in Hillary Clinton's concession speech: "*the path will be a little easier* next time."

In a conversation among a group of American Muslims from the "public safety" series, two participants, Sarah and Samira, collaborated in developing a frightening future scenario based on the experience of Japanese Americans during World War II:

SARAH: Well you were talking about, like, the Japanese and how they were detained like after World War II, and what happ – well not after World War II, what happened after the Pearl Harbor bombing, and then, even like, during that time, like, all Ger – almost all German Americans were *put in* detainment, even though, like, after the fact, like, only 10 percent of the German Americans that were detained were even *part of* the Nazi party, and then they found out that *none* of the Japanese Americans were *part of* espionage. And two-thirds of them were like American. American, they had like already [had been here for generations]

SAMIRA: Right, but they were in camps.] They put them [in camps.]
SARAH: [But, they] put them in camps.
SAMIRA: Yes they did.
SARAH: And then, it's *past*. and now they *feel* safe in their commu – like, you know what I mean, that's past. So I think, *Insha'Allah*, Maybe, as *awareness grows*, this will pass too.
SAMIRA: 'Cause I was just waitin' for the time when they was gonna *try* and *round up* all African Americans and put 'em in a camp, which would've been a *mess*. [laughter]
SARAH: And my – my own mother said to me, like
SAMIRA: You know?
SARAH: Don – did you know that they're going to try to do the same kind of thing to Muslims? Like, aren't you scared? Aren't you, aren't you scared that being Muslim now that, umm, if ... if, you know, they have some new thing in the war, that they're going to *round up* all, all *Muslims*? In the United States, and put you in some camp? And I was like ...
AISHA: Did you ... did you hear that recently?
SARAH: No my *mother* said this to me.

Like the "kiddie porn" story, this story is co-constructed by two participants, each of whom supplies relevant information, which was probably known to all participants – but may have been news to some of them. In both of these examples, it appears that the primary reason for offering the information was to "get it on record," establish it as part of the story world under construction.

It also appears that both Sarah and Samira have entertained this horrifying fantasy before – it is likely that the scenario was actively circulating among American Muslims in the van of the post 9/11 panic that swept over the United States. Aisha's question, "Did you hear that recently?" may indicate that she had *not* heard the scenario, or it may indicate that she thought it was "old news." In any event, this story is also an example of a story that seems to reaffirm group membership and identification – "We are all members of this vulnerable group; we are all at risk." Simulating the perceptual features associated with being put into concentration camps is undoubtedly unpleasant, but it would have the effect of enhancing the feeling of identification and solidarity with other members of the (potentially) persecuted group.[3]

First-person experiential stories. An example of a first-person experiential story occurred early in yet another conversation in this series, among four Latino college students:

MANUELA: When I was living in the uh Northwest near umm Emanuel hospital umm, like it was like two summers ago actually umm .. one time I was going to school in the morning and taking the streetcar and I was walking minding my own business and there was this umm ... this woman who was just.. crossed the street to where I was walking and she pepper-sprayed me and tried to steal my wallet.
EDUARDO: "What!?"
PENA: "Wow!"
MANUELA: Yeah and of course I *freaked out*. Um thankfully I got some help and the woman didn't take my purse. The hospital was just like the next block away, there was this man who helped me, who took me to the emergency room. I remember a cop came and later and asked me, how tall is she? What was her race? What she looked liked? And I gave him the details and um and I never *heard* anything, if they caught her, or if this had happened before in that area. Cuz I never really think because it was a *nice* neighborhood. Umm and heard never anything bad or people get assaulted or cars being broken in.

This story satisfies the normal canons of "telling rights" (it happened to the narrator) and "tellability" (it has surprise value and is inherently interesting; it is also relevant to the overall topic of public safety and police-community relations). The narrator established the setting, including place and time as well as her motives and frame of mind. The "complicating action" was introduced abruptly and unexpectedly – just as she experienced it. The supportive backchannel comments are typical of this kind of story – they simultaneously reinforced the surprise value and offered support for the teller-as-victim. In the coda, Manuela affirmed the relevance of the story to the police-community relations topic, and also countered any potential inferences about the quality of the neighborhood in which she lived.

Types of Story

The "kiddie porn" example illustrates a common characteristic of conversational storytelling, in which one story activates another story on a related topic – sometimes these "story chains" can continue through several thematically or topically related stories. Another kind of story-chaining happens when another participant refers back to an earlier story in a different context, and often to a different purpose. A few minutes after Manuela told the story about the pepper spray attack, the group turned to the topic of the kinds of difficulties faced by police officers, and some of the strategies they use to negotiate their social roles. Eduardo compared the experience of police officers to our own everyday experiences, then compared this to a story that a third participant had just recounted about her house being burglarized, and finally returned to the pepper spray incident:

EDUARDO: Just like us.. we have good days and bad days, right. Like good days, good things happens some days, sometimes you are not getting your house *broken into* (Laughs)
MANUELA: Or assaulted (Laughs)
EDUARDO: Or assaulted (Both Eduardo and Manuela are laughing) with the hand Mace and stuff,
MANUELA: Yeah
EDUARDO: But like you know. But I bet you are pretty pissed for the rest of your day (Everyone Laughs)
MANUELA: Yeah I was pissed (Laughs) of course who wouldn't be?

Here, Eduardo extended the previous stories into a possible world in which being victimized by crimes is so routine that *not* being victimized constitutes "a good day." The irony elicits a humorous response from Manuela, who extends the possible world to include her own bad experience. By thus "normalizing" the pepper spray incident in this way, it appears that Manuela was able to activate the comic and ironic elements of the attack and downplay the traumatic aspects. Eduardo's comment, "I bet you are pretty pissed for the rest of your day," simultaneously expressed sympathy for her initial trauma and reinforced her present appreciation for the irony and humor of the story.

Much of the literature on conversational storytelling (and on conversation in general) implicitly treats conversation as a *competitive* activity, in which participants engage in an apparently relentless struggle for dominance and hierarchical status (e.g., Billig, 2005; Edwards, 1997; Labov & Waletsky, 1967). This may in part reflect their sources of data; it also seems to reflect a Hobbesian, Social Darwinist view of society as a kind of unceasing "struggle of one against all." In my own data, drawn from casual social conversations among groups of middle-class friends with ages ranging from late 20s through early 60s, a more collaborative and cooperative spirit is apparent. Participants tolerate disfluencies, deviations from norms of "tellability" and "relevance," and participants support each other emotionally, as illustrated by Eduardo's support of Manuela's ironic conversion of her traumatic pepper spray experience into humor.

Another expression of the collaborative, *non*competitive nature of much casual conversation is the frequent use of self-deprecation (see also Terrion & Ashforth, 2002). In a conversation about homelessness among a group of college students, all in their late 20s, one of the participants told, with obvious relish, a story about a homeless person (a "bum") who turned the tables and got the better of her:

SUZY: I have had the funniest ... funniest bums though ... one of them asked me for a cigarette.. one and a half or two years ago. He pulled out a rosary!, He was like ... you're lying to the LORD! [general laughter] and I was totally ... and I was like shit he called me on it.
He held up the rosary. You're lying to the LORD! He did a jig and ran down the street.

(Ritchie, 2011c, p. 493)

This story keys into the experience, common to virtually all cities of any size, of encountering apparently homeless people who beg for money or sometimes cigarettes, and the "white lies" people tell to avoid a face-threatening direct refusal. Several stories about being hit up for money or cigarettes by homeless people had previously been told by other participants in the conversation. The setup, "I have had the funniest ... funniest bums," conditioned the narrator's audience to expect a humorous story and the self-quotation "shit he called me on it" acknowledged the narrator's own loss of face, while expressing approval of the "bum's" success in overturning the social status hierarchy, if only briefly.

Urban legends. People often tell stories about mythic, impossible, or highly unlikely stories – ever-popular themes include UFO sightings and apparent instances of mental telepathy, ghostly "presences," or other "supernatural" happenings. A related type of story is what Brunvand (1981) calls "urban legends." These differ from "tales of the supernatural" in that the story is objectively possible (although unlikely enough to be interesting), is told as having actually happened, and occasionally even reported in a news article, even though when it does appear in a newspaper it can rarely be traced to any real person or event. Typically these stories are introduced as "something heard from a neighbor's cousin," or "something I read in the newspaper." In one of Brunvand's examples, an ad is placed in the paper offering a brand-new Cadillac for $50. Everybody thinks it is a typo except a high school kid, who calls the listed number and buys the new car for almost nothing. It turns out that a wealthy man's will directed that his Cadillac be sold and the money given to his mistress – so his widow sold the car for $50. (Not long after I came across Brunvand's book I heard this story from my father, who claimed to have read about it in the Boise *Statesman*, Idaho's lead newspaper. He did not have either the article or the original classified ad, however.)

A story that probably fits the *urban legend* category appeared early in the conversation about homelessness:

JACK: On the east coast I think, Boston or somewhere my friend was telling me about this.. it was all over the news ... like ... homeless people were taking shits in peoples cars ... inside their cars ... because they didn't ... have a place to go the bathroom ... they, they would like get arrested or ... whatever because they yah know
PETE: That's the number one public nuisance in Amsterdam
JACK: So they started shittin in people's cars ... like inside their cars ... they'd get in, take a shit, get out and you come back to your car [general laughter] ... and there's shit
ROB: that's brilliant! That's subversive ... people who own cars wait!
PETE: get a bike!
ROB: shit! I drove (laughter)
BRANDY: you can't shit inside somebody's bike.

(Ritchie, 2011c, p. 492)

The introduction to this story marks it as a probable urban legend: "On the east coast I think, Boston or somewhere my friend was telling me about this ... it was all over the news." Like the "You're lying to Jesus" story, it has a satisfying quality of Carnival-like moral inversion in which the "meek shall be exalted," which is reinforced by a sense of "poetic justice" – society does not provide sanitary facilities for homeless people, and this is the unintended consequence. Rob's coda, "people who own cars wait!" and Pete's supportive "get a bike!" both relate to Portland's "bicycle culture," in which commuting by automobile is devalued. Rob's admission that he had driven a car to the event, like Suzy's story about "lying to Jesus," ironically turns the tables on himself.

Social Functions of Storytelling

A traditional view of language holds that it originated in the need to transmit information about threats and opportunities in the environment, such as predators and food sources, and to coordinate action with respect to these threats and opportunities (e.g., Bickerton, 2009). These models are consistent with the *'computer'* metaphor for cognition, which became popular during the early days of the computer era and is closely associated with the code model of language, and contemporary discussions of language often seem to assume that this is still the primary function of language. As a result, figurative language such as metaphor and irony, as well as all forms of language play (punning, nonsense, etc.) are treated as problematic and corrupt – or disregarded altogether.

In refutation of the information-first view of language evolution and function, Dunbar (1996; 2003; 2014) cites evidence that the size of the cerebral cortex (essential for language use) relative to body mass is correlated with the size and social complexity of the species' or sub-species' typical primary group but *not* with ecological factors such as food source, predation threat, or forging strategies. Dunbar (1996) reports that about two-thirds of all talk in ordinary conversations is focused on relationships. From this and other evidence, he proposes that language initially originated as an extension of the social grooming observed among other primates as well as many other mammals, as a way of coping with the stresses associated with complex social hierarchy, including building and maintaining networks of social support.

Mar and Oatley (2008) claim that literary narratives in particular provide models of the social world that serve both instruction in the complexities of social interaction and socialization to societal expectations. Literary narratives are carefully constructed to promote deep immersion in the story world, through which readers experience simulations of thoughts and emotions associated with depicted events. Readers thus come to understand underlying social processes and learn to predict outcomes of social interactions. Simulations also contribute to theory of mind by cultivating the ability to know what other persons might experience and think in situations similar to those depicted. At the more "macro" level of a culture, "works of imaginative literature – stories – are one means by which we make sense of our history and our current life and by which we make predictions and decisions regarding our future world" (Mar & Oatley, 2008, p. 176).

Dunbar (2014) observes that moving, singing, and laughing in unison all generate oxytocin, which contributes to social bonding. On this basis, he proposes that the bonding effects of unison singing and laughing may have provided a primary impetus for the adaptation of early language to information exchange – i.e., planning for the next gathering of the extended social group. *Play* also releases oxytocin, and animal researchers have found that, at least among mammals, opportunities for play serves as well as food as a reward in conditioning experiments.

All of this suggests that storytelling, both when the stories are told in a way that listeners are transported into the story world and when stories elicit humor, will serve as a means to create and reinforce social bonds. Collaborative storytelling and various forms of language play should also contribute to maintaining social bonds and group solidarity. Virtually all of the casual conversations in my own data include examples of language play and collaborative storytelling. The stories in both Hillary Clinton's concession speech and Barack Obama's *More Perfect Union* speech (discussed in detail in Chapter 11) appear likely to serve a similar purpose, at a broader scale.

Obama's speech also contains many passages that have an overtly informative purpose, but very little of Clinton's speech offers information that is likely to be newsworthy to her intended audience. In sum, the entertaining and collaborative elements in discourse, especially storytelling, are at least as important as and probably more important than informative functions.

Cognitive Aspects of Storytelling and Comprehension

Schank and Abelson (1995) claim that memory consists primarily of stories: "Virtually all human knowledge is based on stories constructed around past experiences, and ... new experiences are interpreted in terms of old stories" (pp. 1–2). They acknowledge the independent existence of factual knowledge ("whales are mammals"), what many theorists call "encyclopedic knowledge," but dismiss it as relatively unimportant, observing that many facts are themselves based in stories. For example, the fact "I was born in Kellogg, Idaho," is anchored in the story of my parents' sojourn there while my father worked in one of the mines before entering the army during the Second World War – a personal story embedded in a larger story of my family, itself embedded in two separate societal-level stories, about the mining industry and about the world war.

"Such very short versions are not the results of 'table look-up in memory,' that is, finding the birthplace slot and reading its value. This may work for computers, but it doesn't make any sense psychologically. Search in human memory is a search for stories" (Schank & Abelson, 1995, p. 3). Because our memory and our understanding are so dependent on stories, it can be very difficult to absorb new information if it does not fit our known stories. Since the social context influences the way we tell a story, retelling a story in the same context multiple times can reshape the memory; we tend to believe our own stories. This also helps to explain social influences: The stories favored by the people we associate with are the stories we are most likely to tell, consequently the stories we come to believe.

Schank and Abelson claim that most of our opinions are based on stories in our memory. Most of our stories can be accessed by means of a large number of "indexes" – names like *Kendra James* or *Tony Stevens*, phrases like *police shooting* or *blind justice*. As these examples illustrate, even when people know the same stories they may be indexed by different words and phrases; conversely, the same phrase can index quite different stories for different people (or for the same person in different circumstances. Schank and Abelson also dispute the "logician model" of memory: "every problem can be reduced to first principles and decided on the basis of some logic. Knowledge, in this view, is about rules of inference and principles, not stories ... humans are not really set up to hear logic. People, however, like to hear stories ... People need a context to help them relate what they have heard to what they already know" (p. 8).

Kahneman and Tversky (1982, p. 201) suggest that in many situations, "questions about events are answered by an operation that resembles the running of a simulation model." Different circumstances will lead people to run the simulation in different ways, with different results. They presented subjects with a story about a traveler who misses a flight because of a delay getting to the airport. Subjects predicted that the traveler who barely missed the flight will be more upset than the traveler who missed it by 30 minutes or more. They concluded that people expect the traveler to run a simulation model along the lines of *how I could have made the flight*: it is easier to imagine how one might have arrived 5 minutes earlier than to imagine arriving 30 minutes earlier.

There is a tendency "to underestimate the likelihood of events that are produced by slow and incremental changes" (Kahneman & Tversky, 1982, p. 207). Since a plan (or other scenario) consists of a chain of plausible links, any one of which can fail, leading to the failure of the entire plan or scenario, this bias can lead to underestimating the risk of failure and overestimating the risk of success for a complex plan or scenario. It seems plausible, for example, that this could help to explain the widespread disbelief in climate change: the causal chain connecting increasing atmospheric CO_2 with climate change is long and complex, hence difficult to experience as a coherent story, and easy to discredit even when each link is supported by overwhelming evidence (see Chapter 10).

Mar and Oatley (2008) cite evidence that readers develop a mental representation of a text as they process it, and that this representation takes the form of detailed perceptual simulations of the persons, places, and events depicted in the text (see also Barsalou, 2007; Gibbs, 2011). Thagard (2011; Thagard & Aubie, 2008; Thagard & Stewart, 2011) has developed a neurologically plausible account of how these simulations might actually be processed. Thagard and Aubie (2008) argue that conscious emotional experience involves the continual coordination and integration of neural representation of internal states as well as evaluations of external events. Thagard and Stewart (2011) show that creativity involves combining mental representations – patterns of neural activity, representing previously unconnected concepts or events, in working memory. The "aha!" experience that results when a combination seems particularly surprising, relevant, and valuable stimulates pleasurable emotional state that enhances storage of the creative combination in long-term memory.

How stories change over time. Schank and Abelson (1995) point out that stories change in predictable ways through retelling, either by the same person or by different persons. In the process of *"distillation"* the events are reduced to simple propositions that fit with known story schemas. In the process of *"suppression,"* inconsistent elements are suppressed and consistent elements highlighted. Larger stories that are shared by many members of a culture may become *"captioned,"* summarized in an indexing phrase that can serve to call to mind the entire story, or relevant elements of a story.

Integrating cognitive and social levels. According to Mar and Oatley (2008). a primary function of literary narrative is to represent the cultural and social world in a simplified and abstracted way that can be directly experienced and comprehended by individual members of society. This includes works of fiction that serve as a kind of "thought experiment" through which a reader can explore possible situations, responses, and consequences. It also includes works of biography and history that allow readers to immerse themselves in past events and in the situations experienced by other persons.

In their discussion of creativity, Thagard and Stewart (2011) explicitly reject an individualist account of creative thought. Citing the collaboration of Crick and Watson on the discovery of the structure of the DNA molecule, they point out that the social interactions between the two scientists enabled them to bring together their separate knowledge and representations, which in turn led to dramatic changes in each person's individual representations. Carrying the thought further, Crick and Watson, both together and individually, interacted with several other scientists (Watson, 1968), often in a rather playful spirit; all of these *social* interactions contributed to their individual and joint combination of neural representations leading to the "aha! moment" of creative discovery (Ritchie, 2009).

Conclusion

Stories are an important, perhaps the major, component of memory (Schank & Abelson, 1995) as well as reasoning (Kahneman & Tversky, 1982). Storytelling is an important component of language use, plays a significant role in social bonding and group identity maintenance, and may have played a primary motive role in the evolution of language (Dunbar, 2014); most ordinary conversations are replete with stories of various lengths and various types. Although storytelling may be competitive and rule-bound in social contexts such as groups of adolescent males in which competition for social status is a dominant theme (Billig, 2005; Edwards, 1997), in more collaborative social settings it is often much more relaxed and characterized by tolerance and mutual supportiveness (Ritchie, 2010; 2011b; 2011c).

Although stories are sometimes told in order to relay new information, a primary motivation in casual conversation seems to be shared enjoyment and, often, reliving well-known incidents and situations. Both fictional and actual stories are sometimes told to illustrate a point or characterize sequences considered typical; these often take on a metaphorical quality, in which a story about one kind of event is related as a way of commenting on an event of an entirely different sort – Hillary Clinton's story about *"almost shattering the glass ceiling,"* discussed in Chapter 1, is an example. Other examples will be discussed throughout this book.

3 Language and Metaphor

> The document they *produced* was eventually signed but ultimately *unfinished*. It was *stained* by this nation's *original sin* of slavery, a question that *divided* the colonies and *brought* the convention to a *stalemate* until the founders chose to allow the slave trade to *continue* for at least twenty more years, and to *leave* any final resolution to future generations. . . .
>
> This is *where we are* right now. It's a racial *stalemate* we've been *stuck in* for years. Contrary to the claims of some of my critics, Black and White, I have never been so naïve as to believe that we can *get beyond* our racial *divisions* in a single election *cycle*, or with a single candidacy – particularly a candidacy as imperfect as my own.
>
> But I have asserted a *firm* conviction – a conviction *rooted in* my faith in God and my faith in the American people – that working together we can *move beyond* some of our old racial *wounds*, and that in fact we have no choice is we are to *continue on the path* of a more perfect *union*.
>
> – Then Senator Barack Obama, *A More Perfect Union*, Philadelphia, PA, March 18, 2008

A few days ago I spilled a few drops of coffee on a printed copy of one of the transcripts I am consulting for this chapter: as a consequence of my carelessness, the transcript is *stained* by coffee. If a leaky display case allowed a few drops of rusty water to fall on a copy of the U.S. Constitution, that document might be *stained* by rust. The meaning of these statements is evident, but what does it mean to say that a document is stained by an *original sin*? And when Obama said, "This is *where we are* right now," was he referring to a historic building in Philadelphia? If not, what did he mean?

Most members of contemporary society would agree that slavery was (and is) a great wrong, and most people who believe in a just God (and many people who do not believe in God at all) would agree that slavery is a *sin*. According to the beliefs of most Christian denominations, the disobedience or rebellion described in the story of Adam and Eve (discussed in Chapter 2) that led to their expulsion from Paradise was the *original* sin, the sin that happened at the *origin* of humankind. The guilt for that sin and the punishment of suffering and mortality (exclusion from paradise) was passed along to their offspring and all future generations. But what does it mean to refer to *slavery* as original sin?

It is also a sin that happened at the origin – this time, the origin of the United States. But how can that concept apply to a *document*? How can it *stain* a document?

These phrases, along with the other italicized phrases in the above-quoted passage, are of course *metaphors*. Some of these metaphors are quite complex, and I will return to them several times in this and later chapters. In Chapter 1, I briefly summarized several approaches to the analysis of metaphors. In this chapter, I will expand and extend that discussion. I will begin by reviewing traditional ideas about language that are particularly relevant to metaphor, then proceed to some recent developments in theories about metaphor use and comprehension, as a foundation for exploring the convergence of metaphor with storytelling in later chapters.

Language and Metaphor

According to most definitions, a true language includes both a *vocabulary* and a *syntax*. A vocabulary consists of some set of symbols such as words or gestures, most of which have an abstract and arbitrary relationship to associated meanings. These meanings can sometimes be identified as particular places (Gettysburg), persons (General George Pickett), or actions (Pickett's charge),[1] but words often refer to *concepts* or *categories*, which may be partially or entirely abstract. For example, "document" here refers to a class of objects, sheets of paper (or parchment) with words and phrases written on them to represent thoughts about some topic; the word is often narrowly applied to writing that has some official or legal status. But "document" as it is used here *also* refers to the words and phrases and the thoughts they represent, in particular to the U.S. Constitution. It is those thoughts and ideas that are *"stained"* by slavery, not the piece of parchment or paper on which they are written or printed or even the words and phrases in which they are expressed.

Syntax (or grammar) includes changes to word sound (or shape), word order, or both sound and order that connects meanings of individual words into a coherent idea, alters the meanings of individual words, or adds meaning independent of word meanings. "The document they *produced*" means something quite different from 'they produced the document,' and "the document they *produced* was eventually signed" means something quite different from 'the document they signed was eventually *produced*.' McNeill (2005) claims that gestures should also be considered part of language; it seems reasonable to include other signals such as intonation and facial expression as part of both syntax (since they also qualify or alter meaning) and vocabulary (since they often have culture-specific meanings and can be used in place of words). In written communication, a similar perspective applies: use of italics, underlining, bold print, visual characteristics of the font, spacing and punctuation, and of course diagrams and pictures can all qualify or alter the meaning of the language represented.

Language as coded information. As discussed in Chapter 2, a common view holds that language is primarily a vehicle for transferring information from one person to another, and originated in the need to transmit information about threats and opportunities in the environment, such as predators and food sources, and to coordinate action with respect to these threats and opportunities (e.g., Bickerton, 2009). In this view, often associated with the *'computer'* metaphor for cognition, thinking is done in a kind of "language of the brain" or *mentalese* (Bergen, 2012). Ideas are encoded from mentalese into the words and syntax of a natural language such as English, then further encoded into symbols such as the sounds of a spoken language, gestures of a sign language, pictograms, or sequences of letters from an alphabet. These symbols are then *'sent'* to a *'receiver'* who decodes them. If the ideas are correctly encoded into symbols by the *'source,'* the *'receiver'* can decode the symbols into exactly the same ideas by drawing on the shared code. Implicit in code models is the assumption that *'sender'* and *'receiver'* use the exact same code for encoding and decoding messages, i.e., that words and phrases have precise, unambiguous, and universal relationships to meanings. These assumptions are reflected in traditional analysis of metaphor as a process of *'transferring'* meanings from vehicle to topic and in the practice of discussing metaphors without regard for the particular context in which they are encountered. (I will return to the metaphorical quality of the words in italics within quotation marks in a later section.)

Metaphor as attribute transfer or category formation. As discussed in Chapter 1, traditional discussions of metaphor almost invariably focused on simple nominal metaphors in the form 'x is y,' e.g., 'Achilles is *a lion*,' "Juliet is *the sun*," and 'my lawyer is *a shark*.' These are usually either invented to illustrate a theoretical point (e.g., 'my lawyer is *a shark*'), or, like "Juliet is *the sun*," taken out of context. In actual discourse, metaphors in the form 'x is y' are relatively rare, and nouns generally account for well under half of all metaphors: Cameron (2003) reports 63 percent of all metaphors in one sample as verbs and verb phrases, and only 22 percent nouns or noun phrases (nominal metaphors). Even when nouns are used metaphorically, they rarely appear in the 'x is y' form. In the passage from Obama quoted at the beginning of this chapter, only eight metaphors, about a third of the total, are based on nouns (e.g., "*stalemate*"); the others consist primarily of verbs ("*brought*," "*move beyond*") and adjectives ("*firm* conviction").

As noted in the preceding section, traditional views of language hold that the primary purpose of communication is to transmit ideas from the speaker or writer ('a *source*' – Obama in this case) to the hearer or reader ('a *receiver*' – Obama's audience) by *encoding* the ideas into propositions that can be judged to be either true or false. If the ideas are correctly encoded by the '*source*,' the '*receiver*' can decode them into exactly the same ideas. However, metaphors state propositions that are either patently false (sharks do not attend law school; the nearest star is not named *Juliet*) or cannot be judged as true or false: Is a more perfect union located somewhere, and if so is there a path leading to it? Does the original signed copy of the U.S. Constitution have stains on it?

Until relatively recently metaphorical language was regarded as decorative at best and misleading at worst – and consequently viewed with suspicion by many philosophers. According to this view a metaphor may add interest to a passage, but it does not add anything to the meaning and may, to the contrary, obscure or hide the meaning. According to this view, in the extract from Obama's speech, the metaphor vehicle "*stalemate*" was simply substituted for the literal phrase *unresolved disagreement*, and adds no meaning to the literal phrase. However, in recent decades scholars and researchers have begun to take metaphors more seriously, and to ask what meaning they might add to an utterance, and how people make sense of them.

Attribute transfer. One explanation for how readers or listeners make sense of metaphorical language holds that a metaphor somehow '*transfers*' attributes that are part of the meaning encoded by the vehicle to the topic. 'Achilles is *a lion*' transfers a quality, such as *bravery* or *ferocity*, that is encoded as part of the meaning of *lion*, to *Achilles*. "Racial *division*" transfers a quality such as *being set apart from one another* from *a physical object* to *a society*. "*Firm* conviction" transfers qualities such as *solid* and *difficult to move* from *an object or substance* to *convictions*.

Analogical mapping: Structure-Mapping Theory. Gentner and Bowdle (2001) argue that metaphor is a kind of analogy, in which one or more aspects of the topic are compared to certain aspects of the vehicle. Thus, "*stained by* the *original sin* of slavery" might reasonably be converted to "slavery is like *original sin* and the contradiction between provisions for continued slave-owning and the ideals underlying the Constitution is like a *stain* on the document." Gentner and Bowdle developed an elaborated model around this insight. Simple metaphors like the timeworn example 'Achilles is a *lion*' may not require full elaboration, but interpreting a more complex metaphor begins with a one-to-one mapping in which elements of the vehicle are mapped onto elements of the topic. Mapping is never complete: only relevant elements are mapped, and a single element of one domain is mapped onto only one element of the other. However, the process of mapping vehicle onto topic can lead to additional insights. Figure 3.1 illustrates how this might work for "*stained by* the *original sin* of slavery."

"*Original sin* of slavery" maps *slavery* onto "*original sin*." "*Stained by*" maps *slavery* onto "*a defiling substance*." "*Stained by* the *original sin* of

```
┌─────────────────────────────────────┐          ┌──────────────┐
│ Allowing institutionalized slavery  │─────────▶│ original sin │
└─────────────────────────────────────┘          └──────────────┘

┌─────────┐                                      ┌───────────────────┐
│ Slavery │─────────────────────────────────────▶│ Defiling substance│
└─────────┘                                      └───────────────────┘

┌─────────────────────────────────┐              ┌──────────────────────────┐
│ Contradiction with democratic   │─────────────▶│ stain by defiling substance│
│ ideals                          │              └──────────────────────────┘
└─────────────────────────────────┘

┌─────────────────────────────┐               ┌──────────────────────────────┐
│ Responsibility for slavery- │◀──────────────│ responsibility for sin       │
│ related social ills         │               │ inherited from Adam and Eve  │
└─────────────────────────────┘               └──────────────────────────────┘

┌─────────────────────────────┐               ┌──────────────────┐
│ Correcting slavery-related  │◀──────────────│ atonement for sins│
│ ills                        │               └──────────────────┘
└─────────────────────────────┘

┌─────────────────────────────┐               ┌────────────────────────────────┐
│ Sacrifice to correct ills   │◀──────────────│ Christ's sacrifice to atone for│
└─────────────────────────────┘               │ sins of world                  │
                                              └────────────────────────────────┘
```

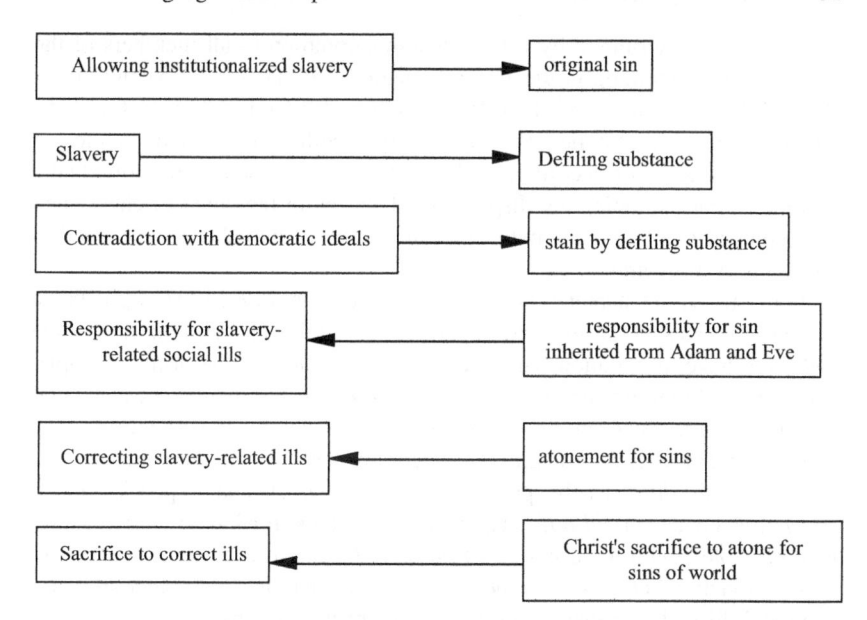

Figure 3.1 Structure map for "Stained by the original sin of slavery"

slavery" maps *contradiction with democratic ideals* onto "*stain by a defiling substance.*" For members of the audience familiar with the Christian doctrine of *original sin*, these mappings suggest mapping the shared responsibility for the sin of Adam and Eve onto a shared responsibility for the sustained consequences of slavery; the need to atone for sins onto the need to remedy the continued problems that can be traced to slavery, and Christ's sacrifice of atonement on the cross onto a need to sacrifice to correct these lingering social ills.

Although structure-mapping theory does not explain how metaphors are actually processed, for reasons that will be explained later in this section, it provides a useful analytic tool for understanding the relationships among entailments of a metaphor.

Category formation. Most contemporary cognitive scientists agree that knowledge is organized in memory in *categories*, sets of experiences that hold certain defining qualities or traits in common. These categories are themselves arranged in hierarchies, e.g., the category *mammal*, defined by features such as *warm blooded* and *supplying nutrition to infants through mammary glands*, includes *dog*, which includes *German shepherd*, which includes a particular dog named *Rex*. Applying this idea to the code theory of language, each word refers to a specific category: nouns refer to categories of entities, verbs to categories of action (or state of being), and so on. Categories were initially thought to be determined by lists of features common to all members of the category, but beginning in the 1970s Eleanor Rosch (1973; 1975) and others showed that categories are often defined and understood, not by feature lists, but according to prototypes. People identify specific objects, actions, etc., to conceptual categories according to how closely they match the individual's prototype. For example, any disposition of pieces in the game of chess such that a player is not in check but cannot move except into check is assigned to the category *stalemate*.

As discussed in Chapter 1, Glucksberg and Keysar (1990; 1993) argue that a metaphor creates an *ad hoc* category, based on a relevant trait that the vehicle and topic have in common, with the metaphor vehicle as the prime example. To use two of their examples, 'Achilles is *a lion*' creates an *ad hoc* category of 'entities that are brave and fierce,' of which *lion* is the prime example and 'My lawyer is *a shark*' creates an *ad hoc* category of 'entities that are predatory and vicious,' with *shark* as the prime example. From Obama's speech, "racial *stalemate*" creates an *ad hoc* category of "situations in which effective action is impossible," with the chess situation of *stalemate* as a prime example, and "*firm* conviction" creates an *ad hoc* category of 'qualities that render an entity solid and difficult to move,' with *firm* as the prime example.

Limitations to both transfer and categorization theories. There are several reasons why scholars and researchers have relied so much on artificial and invented examples such as 'Achilles is *a lion*' and 'my lawyer is *a shark*.' It is often difficult to find a natural example that fits one and only one theoretical idea, as "*original sin* of slavery" illustrates. For experimental research, the unlimited variability of natural language makes it very difficult to conduct rigorous experiments using actual discourse because the validity of an experiment depends on the ability of the researcher to hold everything constant except the variable that is of interest. It is much easier to accomplish this level of control by inventing metaphors that fit the desired criteria.

To be sure, for some metaphors that appear in natural discourse, the transfer and categorization approaches seem straightforward. The *U.S. Constitution* is an abstraction, a set of ideas expressed in natural language – but the italicized phrase also refers to an *object*, a written document, ink on parchment or some other material. As an *object*, the Constitution was *literally* "produced." It is the product of the physical labor of writing, putting ink onto parchment. The mental processes, including the often rather difficult social interactions required to secure agreement about the exact words and phrases to be written, are by extension part of this *production*. According to this line of reasoning it is probably more accurate to describe the word "*produced*" as it is used here as a *metonym* (see Chapter 1, p. 12), in which the physical action of producing a document – an object – is applied to the entire process, including the individual thoughts about the topic and the debates among participants, that led to formulating the text as well as writing it down. As this example illustrates, the distinction between metonyms and metaphors is often ambiguous, and the two terms may more accurately be considered to anchor two ends of a continuum rather than to define discrete categories.

Whether it is analyzed as a metaphor or metonym, according to the theories discussed in this section the vehicle *"produced"* transfers the idea of *make or manufacture* from *physical document* to *ideas expressed in writing on a physical document.* "Produce," then can be seen as establishing an *ad hoc* category of *processes involving physical or mental effort that result in a new idea or object.* The object – the original signed copy of the Constitution – *could* be stained by a spill or leak. The abstract ideas represented by what is written on the object cannot be stained by coffee or dirty water – but if *"stained"* is given a metaphorical interpretation, it *can* be *"stained"* by actions or situations that contradict the ideals on which it was based and the principles it sets forth.

Some other applications of the transfer idea to the discourse samples discussed thus far also seem relatively straightforward, although they often present more complexity than is at first apparent. Continuing with the passages from Obama, the vehicle *"stain"* transfers the idea of *'defilement'* (itself a common metaphor) from physical objects (such as the paper on which the Constitution is written) onto associated concepts (the ideas expressed by the Constitution). In *"firm* conviction" the vehicle, *"firm"* transfers the qualities of *'solid'* and *'unyielding'* from *an object* to *a conviction.* In the passage from Gay Bryant, discussed in Chapter 1, "the *top* of *middle* management," the vehicle *"top"* transfers the idea of *'as high as one can get'* from *vertical motion* to *organizational hierarchy* and the vehicle *"middle"* transfers the idea of *'between two extremes'* from *vertical position* to *organizational hierarchy.* From Hillary Clinton's concession speech, discussed in Chapter 1, the passage, "now it's time to *restore* the *ties that bind* us together and to *come together around* the ideals we *share,"* offers several serviceable examples. The vehicle *"restore"* transfers the idea of *'return to a prior condition'* from objects to relationships. *"Ties that bind"* transfers the quality of *'connection'* from *physical objects* to *social relationships.* *"Come together around"* transfers qualities of *'association'* from *physical proximity* to *mental agreement,* and "the ideals we *share"* transfers qualities of *'possession'* from *physical objects* to *ideas.* In each case, it is a simple matter to transform the statement about transference into a statement about establishing an *ad hoc* category, with the vehicle as a prime exemplar, around the idea or quality transferred (Chiappe & Kennedy, 2001).

A difficulty with both of these approaches is what I have elsewhere called the *"circularity"* issue (Ritchie, 2003b). The qualities of *bravery* and *ferocity* associated with a *lion* are intended to apply literally to Achilles, and the status of *resulting from an effortful process* associated with *producing* writing on a piece of parchment is intended to apply literally to the ideas expressed in the writing. By contrast, none of the qualities associated with a *shark* are intended to apply literally to *my lawyer* (who may be a vegetarian and a poor swimmer with a lifelong fear of water but still be a '*shark*' in relation to clients and/or opponents). In Obama's speech, the idea of physical location associated with "*get beyond*" and "*divisions*" makes no sense with respect to ideas and attitudes about race (except perhaps in a discussion of housing discrimination).

The customary interpretation is that the metaphor transfers the quality of *predatory* from '*shark*' to *lawyer*, or establishes a category of *predatory entities*, with '*shark*' as the primary exemplar. However, the quality of '*predatory*' is itself metaphorical. *My lawyer* may be an avid hunter and fisher who enjoys dining on venison and salmon – but that is *not* what is intended by the phrase, 'my lawyer is *predatory*,' much less the phrase, 'my lawyer is *a shark*.' The same objections apply to the qualities supposedly '*transferred*' by the other metaphors discussed in the last paragraph, such as '*defilement*' (associated with "*stain*") and '*solid*' and '*unyielding*' (associated with "*firm*"). In brief, relevant qualities associated with some metaphor vehicles, like *brave* and *fierce*, associated with '*lion*,' are straightforwardly transferred to the topic, but in most examples the qualities transferred are themselves metaphorical, hence require further interpretation. "This is *where we are* right now" provides an interesting – and not uncommon – case. Standing alone, it is a literally true statement, a truism. (Where else could we be?) But in context it was clearly intended to express a meaning that had nothing to do with the physical location of Obama and his audience.

Metaphors like "*firm* conviction" and "*launch* a woman into the White House" pose yet another difficulty for traditional approaches. "*Firm*" must obviously be interpreted metaphorically – but the qualities, *solid* and *unyielding*, do not apply to abstract concepts like *convictions*. Similarly, aside from circus and carnival acts (or the U.S. astronaut program), a *woman* is ordinarily not the sort of object one *launches* – certainly not into the White House! In effect, metaphors of this sort transform not just the vehicle word, but an entire phrase. In order to have a "*firm* conviction," "*firm*" must be transformed into a quality that can apply to *convictions* or *conviction* must be transformed into something that can be described as *firm*, i.e., into an '*object*,' or both, so that the entire phrase becomes something different, distinct from either of the constituent words or the concepts they represent. I will return to this issue later in this chapter.

Code model of language as metaphor. As suggested by the typography, language such as '*sender*' and '*receiver*' is metaphorical. Aside from written communication ('*snail*' mail' in computer jargon), nothing is actually *sent*. A speaker generates, and a hearer detects a pattern of compression waves;

the molecules of air between them do not move from speaker to hearer, but merely move back and forth as the compression waves propagate. Thagard and Stewart (2011, p. 19) express a similar idea: "We avoid the term 'content' because it misleadingly suggests that the meaning of a representation is some kind of thing rather than a multifaceted relational process."

In an influential essay originally published in 1979 and republished in 1993, Michael Reddy generalized and extended this observation, showing that most of the words and phrases we use to discuss language (our common *metalanguage*) are fundamentally metaphorical, based on an implicit CONDUIT (or TRANSMISSION) metaphor in which words are represented as *'containers'* and ideas as *'objects.'* According to the CONDUIT metaphor, creating a message is *'putting* ideas *into* words' that will *'carry'* the ideas to a *'receiver'* who can *'get* the meaning *out of* the words.' (The use of *'sender'* and *'receiver'* in electronic communication is also metaphorical, since nothing is actually sent from one to the other; the signal is propagated as an electromagnet wave, just as the signal in ordinary speech is propagated as a pattern of compression waves.)

Building on his analysis of metaphorical metalanguage about communication, Reddy challenged the fundamental assumptions of code models, arguing that we have no way to know how others connect meanings with symbols. In place of the *'conduit'* metaphor, Reddy proposed a "*toolmaker's* paradigm." Reddy argues that messages are constructed and presented as clues from which others can infer what the originator must have intended and *reconstruct* a message based on those inferences. In a model like Reddy's, contrary to the assumptions of the code model, meanings are always indeterminate and usually ambiguous.

Implications for metaphor terminology. Over the years theorists and researchers have used a number of different terms in discussing and analyzing metaphors. Many of these terms are themselves metaphorical, and each of them implies something different about the nature of metaphors and how they are used and understood. Reddy's analysis of the *'conduit'* metaphor suggests that it might be worthwhile to consider the metaphorical implications of the language we use to discuss metaphors. In the following, I will use the example of a metaphorical nickname given to U.S. Civil War General Thomas Jackson, "Stonewall," because he was said by another general to have "stood his ground like a *stone wall*" at the Battle of Bull Run. The word was later used as a verb by President Nixon, who directed his aides to "*stonewall*" the investigators, i.e., avoid responding to their questions.

The word or phrase used metaphorically ("*stonewall*"): *'Vehicle'* and *'source'* or *'domain'* are the most common terms used to identify the metaphorical word or phrase itself. If "*Stonewall*" is labeled as the *'vehicle,'* it metaphorically *'carries'* the meaning. If it is labeled as the *'source'* or '*domain*,' it is a '*location*' from which the meaning is taken. '*Source*' can also be interpreted as a '*container*,' consistent with Reddy's "*conduit*" metaphor. Following Ortony (1993), I prefer '*vehicle*' because '*source*' can also refer either to the speaker/writer who originates a metaphorical passage or to the general set of concepts from which a metaphorical word or phrase is drawn. '*Vehicle*' avoids this ambiguity.

The word, phrase, concept, or entity to which the metaphor is applied (General Jackson; Nixon's directive to his aides): *Topic* and '*target*' are the most common terms used to identify the concept to which the metaphor is applied – General Jackson in the Civil War example, the expected response of Nixon's aides to questioning by investigators in the Watergate example. '*Target*' metaphorically implies that meaning is a '*missile*' that is '*aimed at*' the concept – General Jackson or the behavior Nixon demanded of his aides (cf. '*mudslinging*,' in which an insult or accusation is a '*missile*'). *Topic* does not seem metaphorical at all; it is simply a term for what discourse is about. I generally prefer *topic* because it is consistent with ordinary usage, and because '*target*' has implications of aggressive violence that are sometimes but by no means always appropriate.

What the metaphor is about, the idea that it expresses (for "*stonewall*," stubborn refusal to yield or cooperate). *Tenor* (British *tenour*) and *meaning* are often used to designate the general drift of what the metaphor expresses; neither term is metaphorical. Authors sometimes use '*target*' or '*topic*' (metaphorical in this usage) to designate what the metaphor expresses. Metaphorically, as noted in the last paragraph, '*target*' implies that what the metaphor expresses is the target and the metaphor itself a missile aimed at that target; '*topic*' implies that what the metaphor expresses is what the discourse is about. In my own past writing I have used '*topic*' in this way, but I have come to the conclusion that this usage is confusing. Instead, I will henceforth use *meaning* of *interpretation*, consistent with ordinary usage. I will usually qualify the term as *apparent*, *potential*, or *inferred* meaning, as acknowledgment that most metaphors can support a variety of interpretations, and the analyst can never be certain how a speaker intended or an audience interpreted a metaphor. (I will return to the topic of intention later in this chapter.)

The overarching concept or set of concepts from which a metaphor is drawn (objects that are difficult to remove or to get past). '*Domain*,' '*source*,' and '*source domain*' have all been used to designate the general concept or set of concepts from which a metaphorical word or phrase is drawn. I will use '*source domain*' to distinguish this concept from the common use of '*source*' to indicate a speaker or writer who originates an utterance.

Relevance. In the past few decades, the traditional view of language has been challenged and refined in several ways. As noted in earlier sections, traditional models of metaphor use and comprehension give little or no attention to context – indeed, even metaphors like "Juliet is *the sun*" and "life is *a stage*," which in Shakespeare are richly embedded in the social and interactive contexts of the story worlds established by the respective plays, are frequently analyzed independently, with no reference to the surrounding language or the scenes in which they appear. This context-free approach is justified by the assumption that language is a code based on fixed relationships linking meanings to words, from which it follows that meanings – and comprehension – should be largely independent of context.

Sperber and Wilson (1986/1995) proposed an account of language use and comprehension in which context plays a central role – although they did not provide a satisfactory explanation of the concept of *context* itself. Sperber and Wilson propose that all communication is motivated by a drive for *relevance*, and this drive for relevance is fundamental to communication for both originator and perceiver/interpreter of a signal. Communication depends on a "mutual cognitive environment," those ideas that interacting persons believe they hold in common about the state of the world, including the current state of the interaction between them. Mutual cognitive environment includes various mutually accessible *cognitive contexts*, by which they seem to mean something like the traditional concept of a *schema* – a set of interrelated ideas about some concept.

From Sperber and Wilson's discussion of *cognitive contexts*, it is reasonable to infer that the more conventional meaning of *context*, which includes what has gone before in a conversation, the social and physical setting, cultural knowledge, and so on, is partially represented as part of the mutual cognitive environment. *Partially*, because only the aspects of context that are salient to all participants are available in the mutual cognitive environment: the aspects of *context* in this more conventional sense that are salient and accessible to all participants in an interaction are included as *cognitive contexts* (i.e., representations) within the mutual cognitive environment. Elements of *context*, more broadly understood – such as surrounding discourse, the nature of relationships among participants, what is going on in the environment, and recent current events are all, in principle, represented in *cognitive contexts* and hence part of the *mutual cognitive environment*, although Sperber and Wilson do not discuss this in detail.

Sperber and Wilson define the *relevance* of a communicative action (language, gesture, etc.) as increasing in proportion to the change to one or more mutual cognitive contexts that results (or might result) from processing it, and decreasing in proportion to the mental effort required to achieve those effects. (Thagard's convolution model of conceptual integration, discussed in Chapter 2 and later in this chapter, provides a neurologically plausible explanation of how changes to cognitive context might actually come about.) Indirect language, including unfamiliar metaphors, if it requires more processing effort must achieve greater contextual effects in order to justify the additional effort.

Wilson and Sperber (2004) argue that language is inherently ambiguous, and all language use requires broadening and/or narrowing the basic or customary meanings of words. They argue that metaphor is not, at least in this sense, distinct from literal language, in that exactly the same process of broadening and narrowing is required for comprehending all language, including metaphorical language. For example, in 'be sure to put your empty bottles out for recycling,' *empty* does not exclude the possibility that one of the bottles may have a few drops of liquid (or a dead fly) in the bottom, and the bottles certainly have air in them, so they are never strictly speaking *empty*. The meaning of the word *empty* is broadened to include bottles that contain air, and may also have a little liquid or a dead fly in them. Similarly, in 'her husband *drinks* too much,' the word *drink* is narrowed to refer only to alcohol. In the passage from Obama's speech, *document* refers both to the written artifact (ink on paper or parchment) and to the words and phrases that are written on it – and, arguably, to the ideas expressed by these words and phrases.

Wilson and Sperber's approach to metaphor is similar to Glucksberg's approach, inasmuch as a metaphor vehicle creates an *ad hoc* category to which the topic is assigned, but Wilson and Sperber specify a more complete explanation of how this actually occurs. Applying Wilson and Sperber's approach, 'My lawyer is *a shark*' broadens the meaning of *shark* to create a category that includes all entities that display predatory behavior. The meaning of *'predatory'* must also be broadened to create a category that includes all forms of behavior that entail profiting at the expense of others, and narrowed to exclude actual killing and eating. In "a conviction *rooted in* my faith in God," from Obama's speech, "*rooted in*" is broadened to create a category of relationship that includes something like *logically entailed by* and narrowed to exclude subterranean parts of a plant. In "our old racial *wounds*," also from Obama's speech, "*wounds*" is broadened to create a category that includes the emotional, social, and economic effects of prejudice and discrimination. (Given the history of physical violence in race relations in the United States, "*wounds*" is not necessarily narrowed to exclude *physical harm*.) In "*launch* a woman into the White House," from Clinton's concession speech, "*White House*" is broadened to create a category that includes *the office of president* and narrowed to exclude *any residential structure painted white*; "*launch*" is broadened to create a category that includes *elect as president* and narrowed to exclude *set abruptly into motion*. "*Stain*" is broadened to include *dishonor* or *discredit* and narrowed to exclude *discolor with a differently colored substance*. How all this happens, Sperber and Wilson never quite explain: like attribute transfer and categorization theories, their theory is fundamentally circular, in that it relies on metaphorical mappings that are not themselves explained by the theory (Ritchie, 2009a).

Semantic association models. Children acquire their first few words through association – they hear words like 'mama,' 'daddy,' and 'puppy' when these entities are present. However, this is soon supplemented, then largely replaced, by contextual learning. Landauer and Dumais (1997) point out that children must acquire 10 to 12 new words every day from early childhood until well into adolescence, and they provide convincing evidence that most of these words are at least initially understood through their relationships with the contexts in which the words are encountered. This includes the social and physical context of oral communication, but as children gain reading skill, an increasing number of new words are encountered and understood entirely in the context established by other words. Landauer and Dumais and their colleagues developed a sophisticated program called Latent Semantic Analysis (LSA) that measures the relationships of each word in a typical person's vocabulary with other words, then represents these relationships in a way that permits the analyst to compare any two words on about 200 "*dimensions*." Several other similar programs have been developed in the last few decades; these include programs for translating between languages and the computer routines used by Google and other search engines to select the most appropriate responses to search terms (and to select the paid ads most likely to appeal to a person who enters a particular search). The details of these programs need not concern us; what is of interest here is that they seem to capture, in an abstract way, something about the way humans might use statistical relations among words and phrases to understand language. (These relationships are probably represented in strength, number, and pattern of synaptic connections, but this aspect of cognitive processing is still poorly understood – and, interesting as it is, need not concern us here.)

Psychologists have known for decades that, when a particular word is presented to a person, it will activate ('*bring to mind*') a series of related words, and the words brought to mind by a stimulus word can be strongly affected by the context, including previous words as well as the external environment. This supports the claim that knowledge is represented in *schemas*, sets of interrelated ideas about a topic. When a person encounters a word or other stimulus related to a schema, the entire schema becomes partially activated, so that other related words and phrases come more readily to mind (the "*priming*" effect). For metaphor theory, an implication of this idea is that a vehicle term, such as "*launch*" or "*glass ceiling*," will activate ("*prime*") a set of related words, phrases, and ideas. Some of these may be totally irrelevant to the topic of the metaphor, but others may either seem directly relevant (as *brave* and *fierce* seems directly relevant to *Achilles*) or may activate *other* words and phrases that seem relevant. '*Shark*' activates words like *attack, kill,* and *predator* that do not seem relevant to *lawyer*. However, *attack* and *kill* may in turn activate emotions and emotion-related words like *fear* and *merciless* that *do* seem relevant to *lawyer*; these secondary activated concepts then activate related parts of the hearer's *lawyer* schema.

Kintsch (2008) has shown that it is possible to use LSA to identify the words that are common to the schemas associated with vehicle and topic in a simple, direct metaphor (including the secondary associations), and thereby derive interpretations that are quite similar to those provided by humans for the same metaphors. This suggests that the neural connections in the human brain among words and phrases themselves may be implicated in language comprehension generally, including metaphor comprehension. In "*stained* by the *original sin* of slavery," "*stain*" may activate schemas associated with blood and other bodily fluids, which are themselves associated with emotion-related words related to shame, guilt, and humiliation, so that these other, more abstract ideas are attached both to *slavery* and to *the Constitution* and thereby serve to explain how the one concept is related to the other.

Conceptual Metaphor Theory (CMT). As discussed in Chapter 1, Lakoff and Johnson (1980) argued that commonplace idioms like '*close* relationship' and '*rising* inflation,' often referred to as '*dead*' metaphors, reflect underlying conceptual relationships between abstract concepts and more basic embodied experiences. Thus, '*warm* feelings,' '*icy* glare,' and 'a *hot* love affair' all express an underlying relationship between emotion and physical warmth that can be summarized as AFFECTION IS WARMTH. '*Rising* prices,' '*high* temperature,' and '*low* rate of return' express MORE IS UP. Lakoff and Johnson claim that both our conceptual thought and our communication are organized by means of hundreds of these conceptual metaphors, which are themselves based on correlations in experience. It is important to note that Lakoff and Johnson offer CMT *not* as a theory of language, but as a theory of how the mind works. In expressions shown in small capital letters, like LOVE IS A JOURNEY and MORE IS UP, the designated phrases are not intended to be understood as verbal metaphors, but as relationships between the underlying general concepts identified with LOVE and JOURNEY, MORE and UP.

Lakoff and Johnson point out that common abstract concepts like affection, argument, and marriage are expressed through multiple conceptual metaphors, each based on different correlations between abstract concepts and ordinary physical and social experience, and each addressing a different aspect of the underlying abstract concept. ARGUMENT, for example, may be experienced and understood as WAR ('*attack*' an opponent's claim), LOCATION ('*take* a *position* on the topic'), or JOURNEY ('*reach* a conclusion'). As Lakoff and Johnson concede, the conceptual metaphor ARGUMENT IS WAR, which they discuss at length, can as readily be understood as a metonym, since arguments often entail threatened or actual physical violence, and occasionally result in actual warfare. Similarly, in Obama's *More Perfect Union* speech, when he says that he chose to *"continue the long march* of those who *came before,"* he can be understood as speaking metonymically (the civil rights movement was organized around many literal marches, notably the march depicted in the recent movie *Selma*) as well as metaphorically (POLITICAL CHANGE IS A JOURNEY).

Conversely, the same vehicle can also express a number of different abstract concepts. Like politics, a CAREER and a MARRIAGE can be A JOURNEY. A career or marriage can also be *"stuck in"* a *"stalemate"* or *'reach a fork in the road'* or a *'dead-end.'* Several other phrases in Obama's speech also reflect JOURNEY metaphors: "This is *where we are* right now," "we can *move beyond . . . ,"* and *"continue on the path* of a more perfect union."

CMT provides a better explanation than any of the other theories discussed so far for *"stained* by this nation's *original sin* of slavery": WICKED IS DIRTY and GUILT IS A STAIN are common conceptual metaphors, each giving rise to many verbal metaphors (*'dirty* deeds,' *'a real stinker,' 'rotten to the core,' 'blood on his hands'*) and, of course, the hand-washing scene from *Macbeth*. For "a *firm* conviction" we have CHANGE IS MOTION and A CONVICTION IS AN OBJECT. "A conviction *rooted in* my faith in God" implies a complex set of conceptual metaphors in addition to CHANGE IS MOTION, including CONVICTION IS A PLANT and FAITH IS FERTILE SOIL. I will return to this topic in a later section.

Lakoff and Johnson (1980; 1999) and others have identified hundreds of conceptual metaphors that seem to be based on experienced correlations between abstract concepts (like *love*) and perception or experience-based concepts (like *warmth, physical proximity,* and *motion through space*). These are also reinforced culturally, e.g., through related metaphorical phrases encountered in conversation and news broadcasts. Lakoff and Johnson assert that these conceptual metaphors are both culturally and cognitively stable, and form the basis of general human cognition. Lakoff and Johnson (1999) further explain that more complex conceptual metaphors are formed through a process of conceptual blending (Fauconnier & Turner, 2002), which would (at least partially) explain how a complex concept like *"glass ceiling"* might arise. I will discuss conceptual blending in more detail later in this chapter and in Chapter 4. These conceptual metaphors also provide fertile resources for visual communication: I will discuss several examples in Chapter 11.

CMT has been criticized on several grounds. Some critics claim that it is circular, because Lakoff and Johnson (1980) cite verbal expressions as evidence for underlying conceptual metaphors – which are then offered as explanations for the same verbal expressions. To some extent this criticism misses the point that CMT is primarily a theory of cognition, specifically how conceptual knowledge is acquired and organized, and only secondarily a theory about language – but it is related to a more valid criticism, that the theory fails to make it clear what it means to experience one concept as another, for example, to experience *a career* as a *ladder* or *promotion* as *upward motion*. Along with the other theories discussed in the preceding sections of this chapter, Lakoff and Johnson's presentation of CMT has also been criticized because it was based entirely on intuitive interpretations of metaphor expressions, with little or no objective evidence of the assumed underlying conceptual relationships. These criticisms have been addressed (if not entirely resolved) by recent developments in cognitive science, in particular by evidence that language use and comprehension at least sometimes involves partial neural simulation of the experiences and actions described by the language (Bergen, 2012; Gibbs, 2009), which I will discuss in a later section of this chapter.

Grammatical Metaphor. Lakoff and Johnson describe conceptual metaphors as experiencing a topic in terms of a metaphor vehicle, but another way of expressing this relationship is *transcategorization*, in which a concept from one conceptual category is expressed – and experienced – as a concept from a different category (Halliday, 1998). Halliday argues that conceptual metaphors are but one kind of transcategorization, and that transformation of a word or phrase from one grammatical category to another should also be analyzed as a form of metaphor, which he calls Grammatical Metaphor (GM). In an example from Mao (2010), 'these ideas have been subject to widespread criticism,'[2] the action designated by the verb *to criticize* is transformed into an entity designated by the noun criticism, which is capable of being spread widely. In CMT, this example would be classified as an *objectification* metaphor, in which an abstract concept is presented as an object (Ritchie & Zhu, 2015). However, the concept of GMs extends well beyond objectification; nouns can be transcategorized into verbs or adjectives, adjectives transcategorized into nouns or verbs, and so on. As Halliday shows, analysis of these transcategorizations in a text can sometimes contribute significantly to understanding the author's underlying assumptions.

GM is defined as any expression that replaces one kind of grammatical structure with a different kind of grammatical structure to express a concept from a totally different domain (Ritchie & Zhu, 2015). In "a *firm* . . . conviction *rooted in* my faith," the verb *to convince* is transformed into an object, the noun conviction, which can then be described as *firm* – and is also capable of entering into causal relations. The noun *root* is transformed into a verb, *to root*, and then into a quality, the adjective *rooted*, which can be applied as a descriptor to conviction. Two similar examples come from the current political debate about the effects of CO_2 on the atmosphere (Chapter 12). In "climate change" the noun *climate* is transformed into an adjective, representing a quality that can applied as a descriptor to the verb *change*, transformed into and objectified as a noun. In "environmental warming," the noun *environment* is transformed into an adjective representing a quality and the adjective *warm* is transformed into a verb, then into a noun. In both examples transforming the verb into a noun creates an entity that can enter into causal relations.

Mao (2010) points out that transcategorization also occurs when one speech act is re-presented as another. For example in a rhetorical question, an imperative ('Ask permission!') may be transformed into an interrogative ('Don't you think you should ask first?') Ritchie and Zhu discuss an example from Norrick and Spitz (2010), in which an apparent statement of personal taste is presented as a transcategorization of a satirical comment. In a discussion of what to serve for a planned meal, DV's mother proposes quiche and DV responds that he does not like quiche, because "real men don't eat it," an apparent reference to the pop-culture book *Real men don't eat quiche* (Feirstein & Trippett, 1982). Irony generally can be analyzed as grammatical metaphor, since it always represents a transformation of an *intended* speech act into an *apparent* speech act. In an example from the story about a teenager holding a wild party in his parents' absence (discussed in Chapter 2), the speaker presents an ironic comment on the counter-stereotypical behavior of the storyteller's brother in the transcategorized form of a question/riddle setup, "Why did the teenager clean the house?" This is an especially complex example, because the riddle, especially in jokes such as "knock-knock" and "elephant" jokes, is itself a transcategorization from question to joke; in this example it is further transcategorized to a comment on the other participant's story about his brother.

Halliday's discussion of grammatical metaphors leaves some important questions unanswered. He claims that metaphorical transformation (transcategorization) always moves from relationship to process to quality to entity, so verbs can be metaphorically transformed into qualifiers or nouns and qualifiers into nouns but not the reverse. However, his own concept, transcategorization, contradicts this claim since it is formed by transforming the noun *category* into the verb *categorize* and then back into a different noun *categorization* (Ritchie & Zhu, 2015). Ritchie and Zhu propose that the direction of transformation (and consequently whether a particular example should be analyzed as a grammatical metaphor) can in some cases be decided on the basis of etymology (which form is linguistically primary). However, two problems with this approach immediately arise: it is not always apparent which form is primary, and in any case it is unlikely that etymological primacy is salient (or even known) to ordinary language users.

A more pragmatic approach is to consider whether it makes any difference to the understanding of a passage whether or not a particular expression can be classified as a grammatical metaphor. In the passage from Obama quoted at the beginning of this chapter, "*divided*" appears first as a past tense of a verb, metaphorically referring to disputes about the status of slavery during the

Constitutional Convention. In the following paragraph it appears again as a noun, "racial *divisions*." Analyzing this transformation as a grammatical metaphor can add to our understanding of the passage and its effects since, as (reified) *things*, "*divisions*" can exist independently of any action and can enter into causal relations. Similarly, "a conviction *rooted in* my faith in God" can usefully be analyzed as a transformation of the noun *root* that potentially intensifies the perceptual simulations activated by the phrase; as a verb, "*root*" can be understood as active and dynamic. Admittedly this does not adequately answer the procedural questions associated with classifying particular expressions as grammatical metaphors – but it does provide some guidance for how to allocate the scarce resource of analytic attention in particular situations.

Mental spaces and conceptual blending. Researchers who use programs related to LSA often use metaphors based on physical space to describe the relationships among concepts and clusters of concepts. They talk about clusters of concepts as '*mental spaces*' organized in two or more '*dimensions*.' They estimate the differences between concepts or clusters of concepts by various methods, including word association and word sorts, and describe these estimated differences as '*distances*' along the various '*dimensions*' that constitute subjects' '*conceptual space*.'

In developing Conceptual Integration Theory, Fauconnier and Turner (2002) took the "*mental space*" metaphor in a different direction. They define "mental *spaces*" as "small conceptual *packets*" connected to "long-term schematic knowledge called '*frames*,'" as well as to "long-term specific knowledge." Conceptual Integration Theory specifies a minimum of four mental spaces, two "*input spaces*," a "generic *space*" defined by whatever the two inputs have in common, which provide the basis for linking the input spaces, and a "*blended space*" that contains elements drawn from each input space. The blended space may also contain additional elements from long-term memory. Comparison of elements drawn from the separate input spaces and elaboration of all these elements in the blended space ("*running* the *blend*") can produce a wholly new set of concepts as "*emergent structure*" in the blended space.[3] Figure 3.2 shows how the "*blended space*" approach might be applied to the "*ivory tower*" metaphor (Ritchie & Schell, 2009). In this example, the two input spaces are *academic science* and *ivory tower*, both of which can be connected to a generic space based on the ideal of separation from the ordinary cares and worries of everyday life.

In this example, most of the elements imported into the blended space from input space 2, ivory tower, must be metaphorically interpreted, as must the emergent element, "*unstable foundation*." In principle, each of these primary metaphorical interpretations could themselves be modeled by similar, although simpler diagrams.

Language and Metaphor

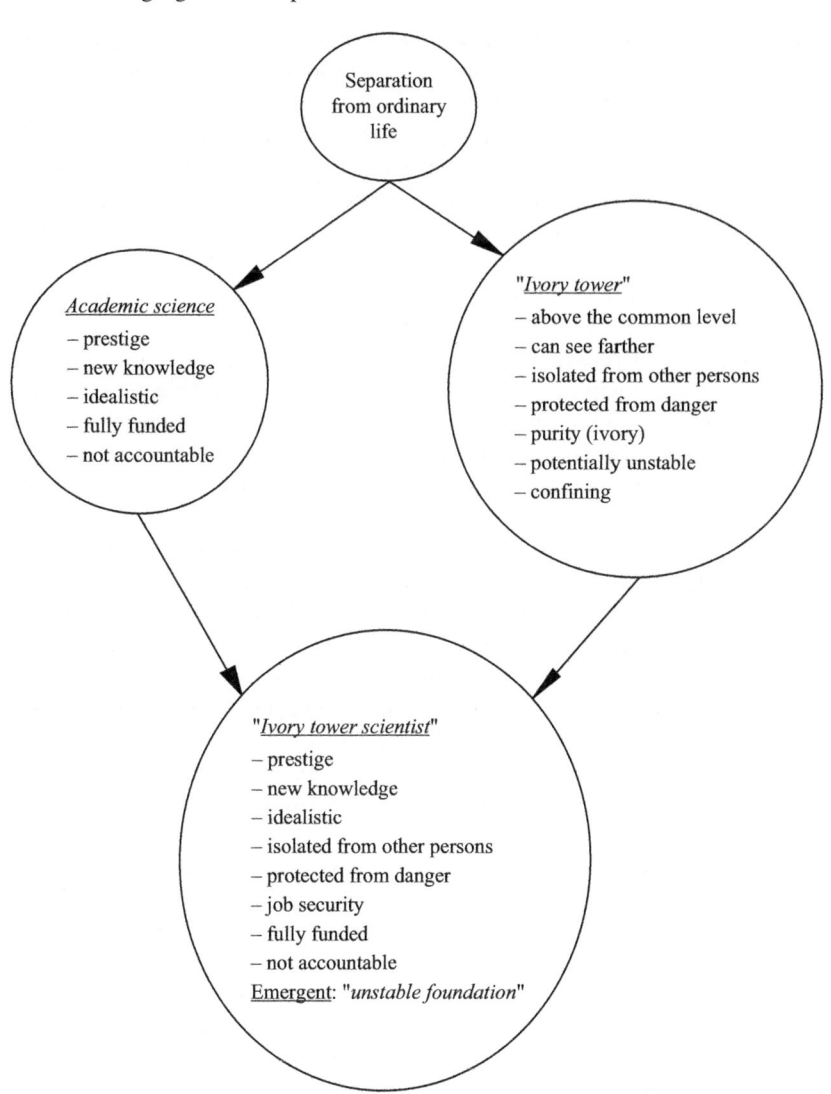

```
                    ┌─────────────┐
                    │ Separation  │
                    │from ordinary│
                    │    life     │
                    └─────────────┘
                    ↙             ↘
    ┌──────────────────┐      ┌────────────────────────────┐
    │ *Academic science*│      │ "*Ivory tower*"            │
    │ – prestige       │      │ – above the common level   │
    │ – new knowledge  │      │ – can see farther          │
    │ – idealistic     │      │ – isolated from other persons│
    │ – fully funded   │      │ – protected from danger    │
    │ – not accountable│      │ – purity (ivory)           │
    └──────────────────┘      │ – potentially unstable     │
                              │ – confining                │
                              └────────────────────────────┘
                    ↘             ↙
                ┌────────────────────────────┐
                │ "*Ivory tower scientist*"  │
                │ – prestige                 │
                │ – new knowledge            │
                │ – idealistic               │
                │ – isolated from other persons│
                │ – protected from danger    │
                │ – job security             │
                │ – fully funded             │
                │ – not accountable          │
                │ Emergent: "*unstable foundation*"│
                └────────────────────────────┘
```

Figure 3.2 *"Ivory tower" as a "blended space."*

Gibbs (2000) has pointed out that Conceptual Integration Theory does not provide a coherent unified theory, and has not been specified in a way that allows it to be tested empirically – a criterion for good scientific theory.

A related criticism of Fauconnier and Turner's approach is that they have not really explained what they mean by a "*mental space*" or how the hypothesized "*blending*" might occur. They describe the "*mental spaces*" as "neural assemblages," and conceptual integration or "*blending*" as a process of altering existing synaptic connections or developing entirely new ones, but they do not explain how any of this might actually work in the brain. It is also questionable whether the "generic *space*" specified in the theory is applicable to all metaphors (Ritchie, 2004; 2006; 2013). It seems useful for understanding "*ivory tower*," as shown in Figure 3.2, but it is difficult to conceive of a "generic *space*" for a metaphor like "*glass ceiling*." What "generic *space*" could possibly provide a source for both *gender biases* and *barrier to upward movement* without encountering the circularity problem? The connection is clear only after PRESTIGE IS UP has been explained.

Nevertheless, Conceptual Integration Theory provides a useful tool for analyzing some complex metaphors, either alone or in combination with the structure mapping approach described in a previous section of this chapter. As Gibbs (2000, p. 349) notes, analysis using CIT can lead to interesting insights and suggest some "localized hypotheses ... which may be experimentally examined."

Perceptual simulations. As discussed in Chapter 1, Barsalou (1999; 2007) proposed that cognition, including language processing, relies on perceptual symbols abstracted from neural activity associated with perception and physical action. Perceptual information is abstracted and combined in a series of stages, leading to a "convergence zone" where perceptions of the same object or situation in various modes (vision, sound, tactile, etc.) are consolidated into a single mental representation. At the most abstract level, perceptual experience is consolidated into complex concepts, such as "*shatter*," "*glass*," and "*ceiling*" from the Clinton example or "*divide*," "*wound*," and "*path*" from the Obama example.

Barsalou proposed that a *conceptual* nervous system parallels the *perceptual* nervous system. *Simulators* associated with each concept are capable of generating partial simulations of neural patterns that would be activated by an actual encounter with the object or situation. Simulations are always partial and ordinarily include only those perceptual features that are relevant to the present cognitive task, such as processing a particular utterance. "*Wound*" might under some circumstances activate simulations of blood and bandages, but in the context of "racial *wounds*" these perceptual features are less likely to be activated. For an avid chess player, "*stalemate*" will activate much more detailed simulations of chess pieces on a board than it will for a novice or for someone who has never played the game.

Barsalou acknowledged that abstract symbols and semantic associations play a role in language processing, particularly when deep processing is not required, but he argues that more elaborate language processing and conceptual thought are accomplished by activating and manipulating *perceptual symbols* based on simulators at a high level of abstraction. Abstract concepts like *equality* and *fairness* can be understood by simulators of *interoception* (perception of our body's inner state) and *introspection* (perception of our own thoughts). *Equality* can be represented by a simulation of the cognitive awareness that two perceptions match, *fairness* by a simulation of the emotion of satisfaction associated with receiving fair treatment. Barsalou (1999) argues that abstract perceptual symbols based on these and other interoceptions and introspections are sufficient for all abstract thought, even logic and philosophy. There is no need for a separate "language of the mind."

Extensive research using a variety of methods has supported the claim that literal language is accompanied by perceptual simulations, although it has yet to be established how central these simulations are to language comprehension. Behavioral evidence comes from a variety of experiments in which participants read a sentence, then are shown a picture of an object and asked to indicate whether the object was mentioned in the sentence. The sentences typically imply that the object will be in one of two positions (e.g., high or low), orientations (horizontal or vertical), etc., and subjects are asked to respond, for example by determining whether the sentence matches an image. Typically subjects respond more quickly when the image matches the position, orientation, etc. implied by the sentence (for a detailed review, see Bergen, 2012).

Behavioral research using similar experimental designs has also provided substantial evidence in support of the claim that perceptual simulations are activated during metaphor processing (Gibbs, 2006; Gibbs & Matlock, 2008). Other researchers have also shown that metaphors can influence behavioral responses. Ijzerman and Semin (2009) found that people who experience physical warmth express stronger affection for friends. Zhong and Liljenquist (2006) found that subjects who were induced to recall a past *unethical* action more frequently chose a gift of a cleansing wipe; those who had been induced to recall a past *ethical* action more frequently chose a gift of a pencil.

Research using neuroimaging techniques has consistently shown that perceptual areas of the brain are activated when literal language is processed (Casasanto & Gijssels, 2015). Results of similar studies with metaphorical language have been more equivocal; Casasanto and Gijssels (2015) conclude that evidence from neuroimaging studies is *not* consistent with detailed activation of modality-specific brain areas during metaphor processing. Given the strength and extent of behavioral evidence for the activation of perceptual simulations during metaphor processing, it seems more likely that metaphorical language activates simulations at the more abstract levels where information from multiple perceptual modes are consolidated into unified concepts. As Bergen (2012, p. 208) suggests, while processing metaphors it is likely that we "construct embodied simulations that are slightly less detailed than ones we construct for literal language but that are no less motor or perceptual."

The social and cultural context of the communicative interaction may also influence both whether we construct simulations and how detailed the simulations are.

Context and elaboration. Zwaan (2014) argues that both *symbolic* cognition (abstract symbols) and *grounded* cognition (perceptual simulations) are active during language use and comprehension. According to the symbolic cognition perspective a few logical or computational rules are applied to a large set of arbitrary amodal symbols (*mentalese*). Even well-known and familiar words are understood through definitions in the form of propositions stored in a mental lexicon. Language processing assembles these propositions into a mental representation in the form of interrelated propositions. On the other hand, *grounded cognition* manipulates nonarbitrary and multimodal symbols grounded in neural systems of perception, action, and emotion. Zwaan argues that both processes are required for a complete account of language use and understanding. Grounded cognition supplies the connection to actual perception and action; symbolic cognition is necessary for abstract concepts such as property and ownership, economic payment systems, and so on. Zwaan's proposal is consistent with Barsalou's (2007) theory of Language and Situated Simulation (LASS), although Barsalou claims that symbolic cognition is engaged primarily for simple cognitive tasks and insists that deeper conceptual processing requires activation of perceptual simulations.

Zwaan (2014; 2015) also insists on the importance of the broader context of language use. Language refers to ideas and actions that exist within a rich setting of agents, objects, events, etc., and utterances occur in a context that includes other language, along with knowledge and beliefs about the broader context. This broader context is necessary for comprehension. The broader context also mediates the balance between symbolic and grounded representations. Zwaan argues that both symbolic and grounded symbol systems are active in most language processing. The more a communicative interaction concerns objects, persons, and actions that are particular and present, the more the interaction will rely on grounded symbols and the less important abstract symbols will be. Conversely, the more the communicative interaction concerns remote, physically absent, or general objects, persons, and actions, the more abstract symbols will be used and the less important grounded symbols will be.

As noted in the preceding, Barsalou (2007) argues that perceptual symbols, grounded in the brain's perceptual, motor, and emotional systems, are employed for deeper and more elaborate processing and abstract symbols for shallower and more cursory processing. A third perspective on the balance between modes of language processing comes from Petty and Cacioppo's (1981) Elaboration Likelihood Model. Petty and Cacioppo propose that depth of processing, the degree to which a hearer/reader processes and elaborates on a message, is a factor of both *motivation* and *ability to process*. *Motivation* includes personal relevance as well as "need for cognition," the enjoyment of thinking about new concepts and ideas. *Ability* includes the knowledge of cultural and situational factors that Zwaan (2015) summarizes as *context*, as well as situational factors such as distraction or tiredness.

Hurley, Dennett, and Adams (2011) propose an account of humor that applies generally to "need for cognition." They argue that a joke or other humorous situation poses a conceptual puzzle, and the pleasure of laughter evolved as a reward for solving the puzzle. Many of the metaphors discussed in this book have a similar quality of posing a puzzle, and it seems likely that the pleasure people get from thinking about the implications of a metaphorical story may arise from a puzzle/reward process similar to what Hurley, Dennett, and Adams describe. Conversely, motivation to process may be *undermined* by factors in a message that activate negative emotions such as extreme fear, disgust, or reactance.

Zwaan (2015) points out that much of psycholinguistic research – including most of the studies reviewed by Casasanto and Gijssels (2015) – relies on simple and more or less conventional metaphors with very little context. In brief, this is consistent with the claim that more novel and complex metaphors presented in a richer context and processed by people with both motivation and requisite background knowledge are more likely to activate mode-specific neural systems.

Deliberate metaphor use. If hearers are motivated to cooperate in the communicative interaction, they are more likely to expend cognitive effort on aspects of the message that the speaker emphasizes, rather than on peripheral features that are not emphasized. Steen (2015) argues that hearers are more likely to process a metaphor deeply if the metaphor is perceived as *deliberate*, that is, if it is perceived to have been intentionally used as a metaphor, if the communicator has deliberated over the message and explicitly chosen to use a particular metaphor rather than some other expression. Although Steen's definition emphasizes the intentions of the *source*, he operationalizes the concept in terms of the *message*. A metaphor is *deliberate* when its structure signals the need to shift attention from the topic to the metaphor vehicle.

Evidence of deliberate metaphor includes novelty, the use of extended metaphors (repeated phrases based on the same conceptual metaphor), and surrounding language that calls attention to the metaphoricity, as in the following passage from a *TIME* magazine article about Alzheimer's disease: "Imagine your brain as *a house filled with lights*. Now imagine someone *turning off the lights* one by one. That's what Alzheimer's disease does" (Nash, 2000, quoted in Steen, 2015, p. 182. See Chapter 6 for a more detailed discussion). The opening phrase, "imagine your brain," signals the reader to shift attention from the topic, Alzheimer's disease, to the vehicle, a "*house filled with lights*" and "*turning off the lights* ..." (Cameron and Deignan

[2003] refer to this kind of phrase as a "*tuning device*.") Steen further explains that novel and extended metaphors tend to be deliberate, and these features consequently are likely to "*trigger*" a deeper level of processing. The passage from *TIME* is novel, and it is *extended* in that it develops a single metaphor vehicle across an extended passage.

Steen (2015, p. 2) acknowledges that "addressees do not always verbally pick up on such intentions of deliberate metaphor use," but he does not discuss what might influence whether or not addressees attend to the evidence of deliberate metaphor use, but focusses only on features of the message that might provide evidence of the intentions of the source. As a consequence he has something important to say about metaphor *use*, but not enough to say about metaphor *comprehension*.

When is a metaphor likely to induce simulation? To sum up, attributes of the communicative context, the message, and the receiver influence whether the receiver engages in message elaboration, including simulation of the metaphor vehicle. Important attributes of the context include embeddedness (the degree to which the interaction is concerned with immediate and specific objects, actions, and persons), background cultural and social knowledge, what has already been said, and the nature of the social interaction. In an informal or playful interchange, messages may be elaborated simply because they are interesting and intrinsically rewarding; in a more serious interchange, elaboration will be restricted to what is needed to make sense of and respond appropriately to a message. Attributes of the receiver include *need for cognition*, enjoying language for its own sake, along with other knowledge factors, knowledge of relevant social and cultural information and other ability factors. A person who has never lived in a home with electricity would be unlikely to understand the Alzheimer's disease metaphor well enough to elaborate on it. By the same token a person with limited knowledge of the long struggle for civil rights would understand "*continue the long march*" from Obama's speech, if at all, on only the most cursory level.

Aspects of a metaphor that may induce cognitive elaboration and perceptual simulations include novelty and creativity, the use of unusual or particularly dynamic language in the message, specifically calling attention to the metaphor, and extended development of the metaphor. As I will discuss in later chapters, if a metaphor is either presented as a story or implies a story, that may also induce a listener to extend and complete the story. Conversely, if a metaphor is upsetting or contradicts deeply held beliefs, a reader or hearer may reject it and avoid further processing.

Contextual influences on individual interpretations. The examples from the Obama speech raise another issue that has not been addressed by Lakoff and Johnson. CMT seems to assume a more or less universal mapping of topic onto vehicle, but many metaphors are understood quite differently, even by members of the same language community. To use a commonplace example, I have asked a number of different English-speaking audiences to spell and explain the metaphor 't - - the line.' I consistently get an equal number who spell it *'toe'* and *'tow.'* Even within these groups there are many interpretations. 'Toe the line' may imply the imaginary line that soldiers 'toe' in a military formation, or the starting line in a footrace. 'Tow the line' has been interpreted as a tugboat, the rope in a game of tug-of-war, and an advertising banner behind an airplane. Each of these is based on different background knowledge and word associations. In this case, at least, the overall interpretations are similar enough for most purposes: "conform to social expectations." The implications differ slightly: in general, *'toe'* implies passive, and *'tow'* implies active compliance. I have tested several other metaphors, often with similar results. For example, I always interpreted *'the grass is always greener on the other side of the fence,'* consistent with my farm background, in terms of the futility of trying to keep cows in a fenced pasture. Students from suburban backgrounds interpret it in terms of suburban lawns, and the need to work harder to keep one's own lawn looking as nice as the neighbor's lawn.

"Racial *wounds*," from Obama's speech, is likely to activate a wide range of simulations, as is "a racial *stalemate* we've been *stuck in* for years." "*Stuck in*" might imply glue or mud, a narrow, tight passageway, or a rush-hour traffic jam. "*Original sin*" is an even better example, since the associated doctrine varies widely among Christian denominations, and may not be well understood by many Christians, much less by non-Christians. For people who process the concept of "*original sin*" as a guilt that is passed down to future generations, whether or not they had anything to do with the sinful act, the "*stain*" will have much greater immediacy and relevance than for people who more or less ignore the word *original* and merely process the idea that slavery is "*a sin*": for these people, the "*stain*" applies to the time before the Civil War and the Emancipation Proclamation, but may not have any bearing on present circumstances. Even hearers who attend to the word "*original*" may, if they are unaware of the Christian doctrine, hear it as a reference to those who were alive at the time and owned slaves, and hence not understand how it might apply to contemporary Americans.

Convolution and the cognitive-affective model. Thagard (2011, p. 132) defines analogies as "systematic comparisons in which a source situation provides information about a target situation." He argues that comprehending analogies is cognitively difficult because of the many ways in which two complex ideas can be compared. He identifies three constraints that make this process easier: similarity, structure, and purpose. Two concepts can be mapped onto each other if one or more elements of the source and target are similar in meaning or appearance (similarity); if some elements of the source are related to each other in a way that corresponds with the relationship among elements of the target (structure); and/or if the source and target concepts serve similar cognitive functions (purpose).

Thagard (2011) has developed a *convolution* account of how concepts are combined, which he suggests is parallel to Fauconnier and Turner's approach. Thagard and Aubie (2008) have applied the convolution model to emotional experience, Thagard and Stewart (2011) have applied it to creativity, and Thagard (2011) applies it to analogy in general and allegory in particular. I will discuss Thagard's analysis of allegory in greater detail in Chapter 4.

Thagard claims that, when processing a text, readers develop simulations, which allow us to understand and predict the behavior of complex systems in which many processes interact. Thagard and Stewart (2011) show that creativity involves combining mental representations – patterns of neural activity, representing previously unconnected concepts or events, in working memory. Here, 'working memory' is defined as the currently active parts of long-term memory – roughly what Sperber and Wilson (1995) mean by 'cognitive environment.' Mental representations consist of patterns of neural activity, including all sensory modalities and motor control. 'The generation of new representations involves binding together previously unconnected representations in ways that also generate new emotional bindings' (Thagard & Stewart, 2011, p. 2). This combination or (in Fauconnier & Turner's [2002] term) conceptual blend is accomplished through a process of *convolution*, "an operation that binds together wave functions or vectors" or patterns of activation within a neural population. Thagard and Stewart (2011) show how patterns of neural activity including both appraisal and affective evaluation portions of emotions can be bound together, in such a way that the constituent concepts (represented as patterns of neural activation) remain separable and distinct. Thus, aspects of *slavery* and *original sin*, including information about these concepts and our emotional (appraisal plus affect) response to them can be bound together into a new concept while the original concepts remain distinct. Thagard (2011) has developed an analytic tool, Cognitive-Affective Diagramming, for applying these concepts to particular analogies and allegories, which I will discuss in greater detail in Chapter 4.

Analogy vs Conceptual Metaphor. *Comparing to or experiencing as.* Gentner and Bowdle (2001) assume that metaphor is fundamentally an extension of analogy, in which the topic is compared to the vehicle in such a way that attributes of the vehicle, including relations among sub-concepts, affords a basis for drawing conclusions and making predictions about the topic. Lakoff and Johnson (1980) claim that metaphor is fundamentally cognitive and distinct from analogy, and that a metaphor induces us to experience the topic *as* the vehicle. Thagard (2011) also seems to regard metaphor as a kind of analogy – but his explanation of convolution is generally compatible with the conceptual metaphor view: the topic is not merely compared to the vehicle; it is *combined with* the vehicle in a way that creates an entirely new and distinct concept.

The view of metaphor as a kind of analogy is consistent with a more traditional lexical approach, in which the vehicle to topic mapping is accomplished linguistically, by selecting words and phrases related to the vehicle and connecting them with the topic. The conceptual metaphor view is consistent with Perceptual Simulation Theory, in which neural systems associated with the vehicle are partially activated and blended (or *convoluted*) with neural systems associated with the topic. Barsalou (2007) suggests that lexical processing may be used for low-effort shallow processing, what Petty and Cacioppo (1981) call the 'peripheral route' but perceptual simulations are activated during deeper, more elaborate processing, what Petty and Cacioppo call the 'central route,' which leads to greater retention and more cognitive change. Petty and Cacioppo argue, at least in the context of persuasive communication, that the central route processing is used when the individual has both the motivation (interest and relevance) and the ability (mental capacity, language skills, and background knowledge) to process and elaborate on a message.

These considerations would lead to the expectation that "*stained by* the *original sin* of slavery" would be more likely to be processed by activation and blending of multi-modal perceptual simulations if the hearer or reader has a sufficient knowledge of both the history of slavery in the United States and the doctrine of *original sin*, and is sufficiently concerned about slavery, sin, or both to be motivated to think more deeply about Obama's metaphor. Ideas and emotions associated with sin and culturally shared guilt, possibly accompanied by emotional responses to the idea of a wrathful God, would be activated. Along with simulations of the suffering and deprivation of slavery, they would be blended into a highly charged composite emotion in which the actions and compromises of the framers of the Constitution may be charged with a new or at least intensified emotional and religious experience, possibly leading to extensive cognitive change. For those lacking the motivation, the most salient ideas associated with *sin* (it's wrong and people don't approve of it) might be activated in a shallow way and associated with the most salient ideas associated with *slavery* (owning other people and forcing them to work for nothing) leading to a composite proposition such as 'forcing people to work for nothing is wrong,' which to most people would seem like a truism, and so would not lead to much if any cognitive change. Because the cognitive effects are much greater for the more in-depth processing, the *relevance* as defined by Sperber and Wilson (1986/1995) is also greater; this increment to relevance justifies the extra effort required of Obama to use the metaphor and expected of his audience to process it.

In general, traditional approaches that treat metaphors as lexical (*lexical metaphors*) map relevant attributes of the vehicle onto the topic. The nature of the topic is not changed by lexical interpretation of a metaphor; the topic merely takes on slightly different attributes in the context established by the utterance or text, or existing attributes are enhanced or otherwise elaborated. This is in effect a *'linear,' 'one-way'* mapping. CMT goes beyond this, with the claim that the topic is experienced as the vehicle. For simpler metaphors, like 'sin is *dirt*,' this still has a linear aspect to it: the desire of research participants who have talked or even thought about doing something unethical to cleanse themselves by literally washing their hands supports this idea, that unethical behavior *is experienced as* dirt or becoming dirty.

The process of convolution (Thagard, 2011) creates a new concept distinct from both vehicle and topic. When Rick Perry called Mitt Romney a "*vulture* capitalist," the metaphor created a new sort of entity, an entity that combines the features and behaviors culturally imputed to both vultures and capitalists. It does not seem quite accurate to express this in terms of CMT, as 'experiencing a capitalist as a vulture,' because the blend changes and is distinct from *both* input concepts. In contrast to the one-dimensionality of lexical metaphors, or even of simpler conceptual metaphors, a blended metaphor is multidimensional or perhaps omni-dimensional: it creates a new concept that amalgamates but also potentially goes beyond the input concepts.

If this claim is true, it must require considerably more mental effort than merely transferring a couple of obvious qualities, or even than merely experiencing a partial simulation of the vehicle in conjunction with the topic. This extra effort and additional processing is unlikely to occur if the individual is distracted, lacks relevant background knowledge, or is otherwise inhibited from in-depth processing; nor will it occur if the individual lacks motivation or interest to undertake the extra processing. As Petty and Cacioppo (1981) point out, personal relevance is one source of motivation; intrinsic interest, with the expected payoff of enjoying an amusing idea may also provide sufficient motivation for extensive processing. That would seem to apply to "*vulture capitalist.*" For "*original sin of slavery*," the payoff is not amusement or enjoyment, but a deeper understanding of the current state of race relations in the United States. (It is also possible that some members of Obama's audience had a *negative* motivation – they were motivated to *avoid* thinking about the entailments of the metaphor.)

Synthesis: Context-Limited Simulation Theory (CLST)

Cameron (2007) observes that it is impossible to determine whether a conceptual metaphor is activated in the mind of either a speaker or a listener on any particular occasion, and accordingly recommends discussing metaphors in terms of *thematic* metaphors rather than *conceptual* metaphors. While I agree with her assessment of the situation, I find the evidence quite convincing that abstract concepts are shaped by, if not based on, conceptual metaphors, and that many metaphorical expressions derive from these underlying conceptual metaphors. However, I am not convinced by the claim that conceptual metaphors take a form implied by expressions such as LOVE IS A JOURNEY, or that they are necessarily always activated when a metaphor is encountered. I draw a rather different conclusion from the evidence: repeated experiences such as movement through space, upward and downward motion, changes in temperature, etc., lead to the development of *generic* conceptual metaphors such as UP/HIGH, DOWN/LOW, WARM/COLD, JOURNEY, PHYSICAL CONFLICT (WAR), DIRT, etc. These generic conceptual metaphors are available as relatively abstract multimodal simulators to help us understand (and express) a variety of abstract concepts. Thus we have MORE IS UP, POWERFUL IS UP, HEALTHY IS UP, etc., all drawing on the same underlying conceptual field, VERTICAL DIRECTION AND MOTION. Since most abstract concepts are complex, we comfortably "mix metaphors," drawing on *several* conceptual fields to express an experience. LOVE IS A JOURNEY; it is also A CONSTRUCTION PROJECT, A DANCE, A GAME, and even WAR. However, when motivation or ability to process is low, metaphors may receive only a very cursory, shallow lexical processing, with at most a brief and weak activation of perceptual simulations associated with the vehicle.

Various aspects of context and perceived relations of relevance strongly influence how a speaker draws on these conceptual fields to formulate, and how a hearer draws on them to understand, an utterance. This is the essence of Context-Limited Simulation Theory (CLST), proposed in Ritchie (2006). A central task of this book is to update and extend CLST by addressing the role of metaphorical stories (primary subject of this book) and story-metaphors in metaphor use and understanding. I will revisit CLST in Chapter 12, after reviewing and analyzing evidence regarding the role of stories in metaphor, and the interaction of narrative and metaphorical processes in both cognition and social interaction.

Methodological Addendum to Chapter 3: Identifying and Classifying Metaphors

Consistent with Lakoff and Johnson, I understand metaphor as experiencing or representing events, entities, etc., from one domain as or in terms of a completely different domain. In practice, metaphor is a somewhat fuzzy category. In particular, metaphor overlaps with metonym, in which the vehicle and topic domains are not entirely distinct. A frequently discussed example is the conceptual metaphor ARGUMENT IS WAR, since argument can sometimes escalate into physical conflict, and war does not necessarily entail active physical conflict. Many metaphors appear to have originated in metonymic relationships: 'a *warm* relationship' and 'a *close* relationship' both implicate metonymic as well as metaphorical mappings. In the song, "I've got my love to *keep me warm*," is it the *thought* of my love that keeps me "*warm*" (a metaphorical relationship) or is it snuggling up to my lover's literally warm body (a metonymic relationship)? For the purposes of this book the distinction is not particularly important.

Identifying metaphors. In order to maintain consistency both within and between studies, I recommend (and follow) procedures outlined by Cameron (2006; 2007), modified according to suggestions by Dorst and Kaal (2012). It is always a good idea to begin by reading through the text to be coded, in order to understand the context. Then identify candidates for metaphor status and check each word or phrase by consulting a reputable dictionary that includes historical and etymological information. I use the Merriam-Webster online dictionary. I generally rely on the first definition, supplemented by the derivation. The history and derivation is particularly important for phrases that have become so familiar that a metaphorical meaning is listed as a secondary meaning. I follow Dorst and Kaal in recommending that this initial test be supplemented by attention to apparent topical incongruity: Is the apparent meaning in context incongruous with the topic? This is important because sometimes each word in a passage seems literally appropriate, but the overall intention is clearly metaphorical (Obama's "This is *where we are right now*").

To identify grammatical metaphors, I have simplified Halliday's approach as follows: identify the basic grammatical form of the word and compare it to the grammatical form as it is used in the passage. For example, the verb form *to fail* is more basic than the noun form *failure* consequently, failure is marked as a GM (grammatical metaphor). Then compare the two forms, taking account of the overall meaning of the passage, to determine the transformations that lead from the basic grammatical form to the observed form. (Ordinary English is full of grammatical transformations, and not all of them are of sufficient importance to be worth extended analysis – but that is true of conceptual metaphors as well.)

As noted earlier in this chapter, this procedure is far from conclusive: There are many words for which, regardless of original etymology, multiple grammatical forms are understood as equally basic in everyday usage – in which case classification on the basis of original etymology is of little interest to the researcher who is analyzing actual discourse. (Arguably, even the example of *fail/failure* might fit this caveat.) Since this book is directed primarily toward an audience interested in actual discourse, including written texts and oral conversation, it is probably more important to consider examples in their discourse context. If a speaker uses both *fail* and *failure* in the same passage (or *divide* and *division* as in the Obama example) it may be less interesting and useful to determine which version is original and which is transcategorized than to analyze how the two forms interact with one another in the discourse context.

Interpretation. As noted in previous sections, people do not necessarily have the same background knowledge, and even when they do, the same ideas or knowledge may not be salient to everyone. Even in a fairly homogeneous group, interpretations of a common metaphor like "*toe the line*" are consistently varied. Metaphors like "*original sin*" are even more likely to evoke different interpretations that draw on different theological teachings and different concepts of *sin*. In the same speech, Obama refers to "my wife, who *carries the blood of slaves and slave-owners in her veins.*" Some members of his audience have extensive knowledge of the prolonged period of sexual exploitation and rape of Black women by White men. Some members may have been completely ignorant of this history. Some members may be aware that "*blood*" is a common metaphor for *genetic heritage* and some not. Some may realize that this metaphor is based on an old theory that genetic inheritance is carried by a tiny bit of the father's blood carried in the sperm. In short, for almost any metaphor there is a wide range of possible interpretations. This is true even if the claims of CMT and Perceptual Simulation Theory are fundamentally correct: the conceptual metaphors and perceptual simulations that activate metaphors in the mind of a speaker, and those that are activated by metaphors in the mind of a hearer, are necessarily dependent on the knowledge and schemas, the *cognitive contexts*, that are activated and salient at the time.

A consequence of this is that hearers cannot know with any certainty what a speaker intended, and a speaker cannot know with any certainty how a hearer will understand a metaphor. Interpretations – conceptual metaphors and simulations – may vary among listeners on the same occasion, and within the same listener on different occasions. Moreover, the same restriction applies to the researcher and theorist. Accordingly, the best a researcher can do is to acknowledge this diversity, identify a range of *possible* or *potential* interpretations, and infer the *most likely* interpretation based on factors such as customary usage of this metaphor and related metaphors, other evidence in the text or conversation in which the metaphor appears, and evidence from other research. Where possible, it is also useful to confirm an interpretation by consulting participants in the discourse event itself or other members of the same speech community. This is not to say that a participant (listener *or* speaker) should have the final word – there are many reasons to doubt that a speaker's retrospective recall is in any way definitive evidence of the thought processes that produced an utterance, and speakers may be unaware, even in the moment, of subtle influences on their choice of language. However, I am also wary of the interpretations of even the best-informed researchers when these are based on *a priori* theorizing, especially when these interpretations contradict the understanding of participants. As Sigmund Freud is reputed to have said once, "Sometimes a good cigar is just a good cigar."

4 Allegory

> Now, who, if endowed with intelligence, will believe that a first, a second, and a third day, and an evening and a dawn, took place without sun, moon, and stars? And that the day that should have been the first took place even without sky? Who is so stupid as to believe that God, like a human farmer, has planted a garden in Eden toward the East and put a visible and sense-perceptible tree of life therein, so that one, by eating its fruit with one's bodily teeth, could acquire life, and also could participate in good and evil after munching what is taken from that tree? If, then, God is said to stroll in the garden/ Paradise in the evening, and Adam to hide under the tree, I do not think that anybody will doubt that these things indicate symbolical truths in an allegorical way, by means of what looks like a historical account, and yet has never happened corporeally.
> – Origen, *Commentaries on the Book of Genesis*,
> quoted in Ramelli (2011, p. 368)

The word *allegory* has been used to describe many kinds of metaphorical texts, and defined in many different ways. The noun, which derives from ancient Greek *allegoria*, "other speaking" (Crisp, 2005a), has sometimes been used broadly to include all metaphor, but it is more commonly restricted to some combination of metaphor and story. The related noun, *allegoresis*, refers both to the practice of giving an allegorical interpretation to existing texts and to the practice of creating allegorical texts. Crisp (2008) defines allegory as an extended or "super-extended" metaphor, a fiction that is subject to a continuous and consistent metaphorical interpretation (Crisp, 2001), any metaphorical passage in which overt reference to the "*target*" (topic) domain is omitted (Crisp, 2005b). Gibbs (2011, p. 121) gives an equally broad definition of allegory as "a cognitive action in which people apply a metaphoric mode of understanding to situations and discourse that typically does not contain metaphorical language per se." Gibbs (2011) implicitly anchors the concept to storytelling: "Allegory involves an extended metaphor in which the entire narrative introduces and elaborates upon a metaphoric source domain ... to evoke larger life themes."

In this chapter, I will briefly review several examples of literature that are clearly allegorical, along with some of the recent discussion of allegory by metaphor theorists and researchers. The aim is not to provide a comprehensive discussion of allegory – that would require a very large book in itself (Whitman, 2003). The aim of this chapter is twofold. First, because allegory is a familiar form of metaphorical story, it is useful to begin with an examination of a few texts that are often cited as examples of allegory. Second, based on a discussion of literary allegories, this chapter will distinguish allegory as a literary form from other kinds of metaphorical story as a basis for discussing the allegorical elements that may be found in other forms of metaphorical story.

Allegory in Antiquity

By the sixth and fifth century BCE, Greek philosophers were attempting to come to terms with stories about the all too human behavior of the Gods, as portrayed by Homer, Hesiod, and others, while honoring the genius of these early authors. One strategy was to give these texts an *allegorical* interpretation, in which each of the gods, and their various interactions with each other and with humans, stands for some abstract idea or principle. According to Whitman (2003), allegorical interpretation of this sort allows thinkers to come to terms with texts produced in very different cultural situations. The Stoic philosophers initially assigned scientific and ethical meanings to mythological stories (for example Zeus represents the ether, Hera represents the air), then extended the strategy by creating their own allegorical expressions of core philosophical ideas. Indeed, Ramelli (2011) argues that, for the Stoics, allegory was inseparable from philosophy. "Allegoresis had been used since the very beginning of Stoicism, from Zeno's commentaries on Homer and Hesiod onwards" (Ramelli, 2011, p. 336). Chrysippus, in *On Divinities*, argued that poetry, myth, and cultic traditions require an allegorical interpretation in order to detect the truth hidden in them (Ramelli, 2011).

By the first century, Jewish philosophers and scholars were adapting the Greek allegorical methods to the exegesis of Judaic scripture. For example, Philo of Alexandria claimed that "the biblical injunction not to eat the fruit of trees for three years (Leviticus 19:23) suggests that the fruit of instruction remains intact throughout the threefold division of time into past, present, and future" (as quoted in Whitman, 2003, p. 7). Christian philosophers and exegetes, especially the "esoteric" commentators Clement and Origen (second and third centuries CE) in turn used allegorical interpretations of Plato, Aristotle, and other pre-Christian Greek writers to establish the truth of Christian faith, and adapted the same methods of allegorical exegesis to the Christian Bible itself (Ramelli, 2011).

As the passage from Origen quoted at the beginning of this chapter illustrates, allegorical interpretation was sometimes used to come to terms with apparently contradictory or otherwise intellectually embarrassing passages. However, the preferred approach was to treat biblical passages as simultaneously literal and allegorical. According to this approach, the events described (such as the Great Flood) really happened, but they also express allegorical meanings. An example of this approach is a passage from Paul's letter to the Galatians:

> Tell me, ye that desire to be under the law, do ye not hear the law? For it is written, that Abraham had two sons, the one by a bondmaid, the other by a freewoman. But he who was of the bondwoman was born after the flesh; but he of the freewoman was by promise. Which things are an allegory: for these are the two covenants; the one from the mount Sinai, which gendereth to bondage, which is Agar. For this Agar is Mount Sinai in Arabia, and answereth to Jerusalem which now is, and is in bondage with her children. ... what saith the scripture? "Cast out the bondwoman and her son: for the son of the bondwoman shall not be heir with the son of the freewoman." (Galatians 4:21–30)

Paul's interpretation here is a complex expression of several themes, including the replacement of the "old" covenant of enslavement and Jewish Law by the "new" covenant of emancipation and spiritual law, which is spelled out in explicit detail in other epistles (Whitman, 1991). Paul also replaces the idea of generational succession, birth "after the flesh" with succession by "divine covenant," thus associating the Jews of his time with Ishmael, not Isaac – who is thus cast as the *spiritual* progenitor of the Christians, gentile as well as Jew: "So then, brethren, we are not children of the bondwoman, but of the free" (Galatians 4:31).

In this explicit bit of allegorical exegesis Paul extends the idea of allegory to include a temporal dimension, in which historical events both prefigure future events and signify spiritual ideas and principles. "'Allegory' of this kind suggests not just the turning of a story, but a transformation in history" (Whitman, 1991, p. 163). Commenting on the passage from Galatians in his fifth-century treatise *On the Trinity*, Augustine explicitly codified the distinction between allegories that express abstract ideas in a fictional story, expressed only in words (*in verbis*) and allegories in which these ideas are present *in facto*, in actual historical events (Whitman, 1991). Much of the Christian use of allegory follows the same model as Paul's interpretation of the story of Sarah and Hagar, giving an allegorical reading to events while asserting their historical facticity.

Well before the Christian era, Stoics and other philosophers were concerned about the related problems of how to present philosophical, ethical, and spiritual ideas to unsophisticated audiences, and how to conceal sacred mysteries from the uninitiated, who are not prepared to receive and understand them. Allegory was presented as a solution to both problems. On the one hand, when esoteric mysteries are expressed in complex allegories, they can be clearly revealed to those who have been initiated into the esoteric knowledge needed to interpret the allegory. On the other hand, if religious and ethical ideas are wrapped in suitable allegorical stories, unsophisticated audiences can only catch some glimmer of the underlying ideas while more sophisticated audiences can appreciate the full richness of the message. Early in the Christian era Latin poet Prudentius wrote an allegorical account of a battle, the *Psychomachia*, written in the epic style of Virgil, in which Christian faith is attacked by pagan idolatry. The battle includes seven personified vices who attack and are defeated by seven personified virtues: Chastity is attacked by Lust; Anger attacks Patience, and so on. I will discuss this allegory, which is often regarded as the first medieval allegory, in the next section along with other classical examples.

Initial definition: *Allegory* refers to a style of displaced writing about abstract ideas, including scientific and philosophical as well as religious and ethical ideas in which persons, places, and actions stand for abstract ideas and relations among abstract ideas. *Allegoresis* refers to a practice of inventing or finding an allegorical interpretation of existing texts, a practice of creating texts that express abstract allegorically, or both. The texts may be overtly allegorical or they may be written in such a way that a simple, nonallegorical reading is readily accessible. According to many of the Stoic philosophers, texts may be legitimately subject to allegorical interpretation regardless of the author's intentions. Allegory may displace ideas across domains (as when Zeus stands for ether) or across temporal eras (as when Sarah and Hagar stand for Jews and Gentiles or, in Paul's reinterpretation, for Christians and contemporary unbaptized Jews). The allegorical story may be historically true (Sarah and Hagar) or entirely fictional (Odysseus's visit to the Underworld).

Allegory in the Late Medieval and Early Modern Ages

> ... I was writing of the Way
> And Race of Saints, in this our Gospel-day,
> Fell suddenly into an Allegory
> About their Journey, and the way to Glory.
> ...
> Sound words I know Timothy is to use,
> And old Wives' Fables he is to refuse;
> But yet grave Paul him nowhere doth forbit
> The use of Parables; in which lay hid
> That Gold, those Pearls, and precious stones that were
> Worth digging for, and that with greatest care.
>
> From *Pilgrim's Progress: The author's apology*

Throughout the Middle Ages, scholars developed '*multilevel*' methods of scriptural exegesis. A fourfold approach was commonly followed, in which an event like the Great Flood or the Exodus out of Egypt was simultaneously understood as (1) historical fact; (2) allegory, with particular focus on typological fulfillment of Old Testament figures in Christ or the Church; (3) morally, as a representation of conversion and salvation of the soul through grace; and (4) analogically, representing the passage of the soul to Heaven (Whitman, 2003). Concerns about the difficulty of presenting sacred mysteries to those unready to receive and understand them, and allegory as a partial solution to this problem, also persisted through the Middle Ages and up to the Reformation era, and the allegorical interpretation of ancient mythology continued throughout the Renaissance.

However, Luther and other reformers rejected both the idea that common folk are incapable of understanding religious truths and the use of allegorical interpretations, and advocated a simple, literal reading of Christian scripture (Whitman, 1991; 2003). By the 18th century, theologians increasingly approached the Christian Bible from a "rationalist" and historical/critical perspective based on investigation of the text's origins and development. At the same time the Romantics objected to allegorical interpretations of all ancient texts because they feared losing the original meanings.

It is particularly interesting that, during this time in which philosophers and theologians came to devalue and reject allegory as an approach to biblical exegesis, several extended allegories were produced, not for the purpose of biblical exegesis or reinterpreting pre-Christian classical texts, but as a way of representing abstract and often complex political, religious, and social ideas. Beginning with Prudentius in the fifth century, authors discovered the power of allegory as a means, not only of expressing abstract ideas but also of expressing potentially dangerous political criticism against both religious and secular leaders. In this section I will discuss four examples that represent different approaches to the genre. *Psychomachia*, *The Divine Comedy*, *The Faerie Queene*, and *Pilgrim's Progress* differ from one another in many ways, but a common thread runs through them that will help extend and refine the definition of allegory given above.

Psychomachia (fifth century CE): Written by the Latin poet Prudentius in the style of Virgil's *Aeneid*, *Psychomachia* relates a war between Christian faith and paganism, in which paganism is defeated. The poem opens with a prayer to Christ that parallels the prayer to the Muse that open classical epic poems like the *Odyssey*:

> Say, with what *arms* the human *soul* expels
> Each *vice*, that harbours in her inmost cells;
> What *troops* she sends the *rebels* to defeat ...
> ... And *Christian minds* are made the *seat of war*.
> (Italics in original. All quoted passages are from Prudentius, 1723 edition.)

The poem is divided into a series of cantos, each devoted to the single combat between a vice and a matching virtue, all depicted as female warriors, beginning with the combat of *"Faith"* and *"Idolatry."* *"Faith"* enters the battle unarmed, "wholly trusting to a dauntless heart, / No shield she carried, nor envenom'd dart." *"Idolatry"* attacks; *"Faith"* throws *"Idolatry"* to the ground and steps on her neck, choking the life out of her.

The metaphor is sustained in many of the cantos in the description of the combat and the weapons used. In the battle between the maid *"Chastity"* and the harlot *"Lust,"* *"Lust"* throws flaming torches (SEXUAL PASSION IS FIRE) and tries to choke *"Chastity"* with sulfur and smoke. Then *"Chastity"* throws a rock that breaks *"Lust's"* arm, and cuts off her head with a sword. The poet compares this battle to the victory of the biblical Judith. In the battle between *"Pride"* and *"Humility,"* *"Humility"* also, like *"Faith,"* enters the field of battle unarmed. *"Pride"* sees *"Humility's"* lack of sword and shield, and scoffs at the opposing forces, gloats at how she subdues men everywhere, beginning with Adam, who "friendly *Pride* taught him with leaves that nakedness to hide." Disdaining to stain her sword "With the ignoble blood of such a crew" *"Pride"* decides to crush them under the feet of her courser. But the steed falls into a hidden ditch, dug and covered over by *"Fraud,"* which *"Humility"* avoided. The steed falls on top of *"Pride"* and crushes her to death. *"Humility's"* *"Guardian"* gives her a sword with which she severs the head of the fallen *"Pride."* Then *"Hope"* declaims over the fallen *"Pride,"* and compares this battle to similar previous fights, including David's fight against Goliath.

Crisp (2008) claims that in classical allegory, in contrast to extended metaphor, the metaphorical mapping is sustained but never made explicit. However, this claim is contradicted by several passages in which Prudentius explicitly refers to the allegorical connection between the battles he depicts and the topic of his poem. For example, after *"Patience"* mildly proclaims her triumph over *"Wrath,"* the poet comments,

> *thus* our wars we wage,
> Without th' *inhuman* marks of *bloody* rage;
> From discipline, like this, we never part,
> For *hardy suff'rance* is our *martial art*.

Here Job is introduced; then the poet comments:

> without *her* no *virtue* keeps the field;
> Without *her* presence ev'ry *virtue's* faint.

The poem closes with a coda in which the poet explicitly maps the entire story onto his own personal spiritual *"struggles"* (FAITH IS WAR):

> Oft have I felt the influence of the God,
> When in my foul he fix'd his fair abode,
> Did strength to ev'ry faculty impart,
> And drive the crowd of rebels from my heart,
> But soon these glitt'ring scenes of joy were o'er,
> And vice, and darkness triumph as before;
> Wars, horrid ward within my bosom rage,
> And man's two natures furiously engage.

Crisp's intention was to argue that allegory and extended metaphor are distinct and separate, and argue against the claim that these two types fade into one another along a continuum, with many texts exhibiting some but not all features of allegory. However, the presence of explicit mapping in *Psychomachia*, otherwise a nearly perfect example of allegory, undermines this claim, and it is easy to find examples of literary text that fall between the extremes of pure allegory and non-allegorical extended metaphor. One such example is provided by Dante's *Divine Comedy*.

The Divine Comedy (Dante, 1320): *The Divine Comedy* combines several genres. Overall it takes the form of a blend of epic and allegory, recounting the author's journeys through the regions of Hell, Purgatory, and Heaven. A metaphorical mapping of this journey is stated in the opening triplet:

> Midway through life's journey, I went astray
> From the straight road and woke to find myself
> Alone in a dark wood[1]

A guide appears at once – the pre-Christian Roman poet Virgil, representing the scholarly tradition of wisdom and intellect, who is himself unable to enter Heaven because he lived too early to have the opportunity to profess faith in Jesus, be baptized, and thereby be redeemed from the "*stain*" of original sin. Virgil accompanies Dante through *Inferno* and *Purgatorio*, then hands him off to another guide, Beatrice, representing pure spiritual Love, who guides him through *Paradiso*. Consistent with the epic format, the author/traveler faces many dangers. During his journey through Hell, these take the form of encounters with the demons and various features of the landscape, which are metaphorically mapped onto the torments of the damned souls, and which Virgil helps Dante to avoid. During his journey through Paradise, the dangers are of a different sort: Dante's mortal senses are inadequate to cope with the glorious splendor of the Heavenly state of bliss, which is metaphorically expressed as fire and intense light. Here, Beatrice advises him on how to perceive the glories of Paradise without being blinded by them.

Throughout, the focus is on what Dante learns about the spiritual life from what he experiences and sees, and particularly from conversations with the persons he encounters. Most of these are actual historical figures, many of them contemporaries of Dante. The physical *"journey"* maps explicitly onto Dante's JOURNEY OF LIFE in the opening lines; then it implicitly maps onto his JOURNEY OF UNDERSTANDING; this mapping is reinforced by passages throughout in which Virgil and others provide theological explanations and instruction.

Especially in the *Inferno*, the poem also has the character of political commentary, even polemic, as Dante describes the crimes and sins committed by figures from recent history, including popes and rulers as well as merchants and other notables, and assigns torments (in *Il Inferno*) and cleansing punishments (in *Purgatorio*) to these figures, each punishment reflecting the nature of the sins Dante ascribes to them. The action is also interspersed with moral homilies and instruction in Catholic doctrine, illustrated by the punishments meted out in *Il Inferno* and *Purgatorio*. In *Il Paradiso*, the poem is interlaced with theological argumentation that follows the form in some places of a catechism, as when Dante is asked to recite his faith and his reasons for believing, and in many places it follows the form of a philosophical dialogue, in which Dante's questions about apparent paradoxes are answered with philosophical arguments, sometimes by these saints, sometimes by Beatrice. Sometimes Beatrice encourages him to give voice to these questions and doubts; sometimes she reads his mind and voices them for him, then answers them.

The *"journey"* described by the poem is doubly metaphorical, representing both Dante's own life and the JOURNEY OF FAITH AND UNDERSTANDING that all Christians must undertake. It is significant that explanations of Divine Justice in *Il Inferno* and *Purgatorio* are provided by the poet Virgil, representing Intellect and Inspiration; explanations of Faith and Grace are provided by Beatrice, representing Love. These elements clearly fit the definition of allegory as stated by Harris and Tolmie (2011): a genre in which abstract personification of moral concepts like Gluttony and Lust (Faerie Queene) act within a conceptually laden locale like the Celestial City (Pilgrim's Progress) or the Cave of Error (Faerie Queene). On the other hand, Harris and Tolmie's definition is apparently contradicted by the amount of attention given to historical figures and events, especially in the first two books, and the literal explanations of both recent history and Catholic doctrine throughout, as well as the philosophical argumentation in *Il Paradiso*.

The Faerie Queene (Spenser, 1590): *The Faerie Queene* is presented in the form of an Arthurian romance, complete with magicians, witches, and fantastical beasts and demons. Spenser wrote in his introductory letter that his purpose was to "fashion a gentleman or noble person in virtuous and gentle discipline." Elements of the poem also map onto the topical struggle between Catholicism and Protestantism, as well as onto recent English history, including a justification and critique of Tudor rule. Six books represent six virtues, *Holiness, Temparance, Chastity, Friendship, Justice,* and *Courtesy.* Spenser's letter to Sir Walter Raleigh, presented as a preface to the work, suggests that the figure of King Arthur, who appears throughout, represents *Magnificence,* "the perfection of all the rest," and the Faerie Queene, *Gloriana,* represents *Glory.*

In addition to representing specific virtues, characters in the poem also map onto contemporary and historical figures, real and mythic. Queen Elizabeth I is represented by *Gloriana,* the Faerie Queene, and several other figures; some of these representations are laudatory, some critical of her and her court. Her half sister Mary, Queen of Scots, is represented by the evil and deformed witch *Duessa.* King Arthur appears repeatedly, performing heroic exploits under his own name. The protagonist of Book I, *The Redcrosse Knight,* according to a passage in Book I, will come to be revered as Saint George, patron saint of England.

The poem follows the exploits of several knights, each representing different virtues, as they battle dragons, sorcerers, and other mythical figures. Book I begins with an elf warrior, the *Redcrosse Knight,* with his lady *Una,* the daughter of a king and queen who are being held captive by an evil dragon; the elf warrior has been charged by the Faerie Queene with the quest of killing the dragon and liberating the captives. (Later in the book it is revealed that *Redcrosse* is not an elf but the son of a royal human couple stolen from his parents and given to the faeries to rear.) After the *Redcrosse Knight* fights and defeats the dragon *Errour,* he is tricked by a dream sent by the wizard *Archimago* into believing that *Una* is unfaithful to him, and flees in the night, abandoning her. He meets and defeats another knight, *Sans Foy,* the eldest of three brothers. *Sans Foy* is accompanied by the sorceress *Duessa,* who presents herself as *Sans Foy*'s captive as a means of trapping *the Redcrosse Knight.*

Duessa leads *the Redcrosse Knight* to a castle, the *House of Pride,* which is built "on so weake foundation ... on a sandie hill," and "all the hinder parts, that few could spie, / were ruinous and old, but painted cunningly" (p. 56). There they are ushered by *Vanitie* into the presence of the queen *Lucifera,* who is characterized as a usurper "that made her selfe a Queene, and crond to be, / Yet rightfull kingdome she had none at all, / Ne heritage of native sovereaintie, / But did usurpe with wrong and tyranie" (p. 58). *Lucifera* rules with the advice of "six wisards old," named *Idlenesse, Gluttony, Lechery, Avarice, Envie,* and *Wrath. Sans Foy*'s brother, *Sans Joy,* shows up, and challenges *Redcrosse,* who defeats him also. However, *Duessa* conceals the defeated *Sans Joy* within a dense fog, then spirits him away to save his life. Fearing treachery, *Redcrosse* leaves the *House of Pride. Duessa* catches up with him, tricks him into bathing in a spring that weakens him, then betrays him to the giant *Orgoglio*, who imprisons him in the dungeon of *Despair*. *Una* escapes from the sorcerer and overcomes various perils and meets Arthur, who defeats the giant *Orgoglio* and frees the *Redcrosse Knight* from *Duessa* and the Dungeon of *Despair*. However, the *Redcrosse Knight* has been weakened by his long imprisonment, so Una leads him to the *House of Holiness*, where he is healed. There he is also introduced to the ideal of a spiritual life, which he vows to follow. He then accompanies *Una* to her parents' land, where he defeats the dragon who has held them captive, frees them, and is betrothed to *Una*. However, the marriage cannot take place until he returns to the Faerie Queene to complete one final quest.

The Faerie Queene is a complex weaving of allegories. The political, moral, and religious allegory is reflected in much of the naming, with places like the House of *Pride*, dungeon of *Despair* and the House of *Holiness* and person names like named *Idlenesse, Gluttony, Lechery, Avarice, Envie,* and *Wrath*. Each place is associated with activities and events matched to its allegorical name, and each person with name-appropriate behavior, all of which serves to keep the metaphorical mapping active in the reader's working memory.

Pilgrim's Progress (Bunyan, 1678/1969): *Pilgrim's Progress* opens with a brief framing narrative: "As I *walk'd* through the *wilderness* of this world, I lighted on a certain place where was a den, and I laid me down in that place to sleep; and as I slept, I dreamed a dream." This frame is continued in a series of dreams, which allows the narrator to insert himself and his authorial commentary from time to time, and at the same time in effect provides a cover story for the more fanciful parts of the narrative. "*Wilderness*" appears as a metaphor for Earthly existence in many texts (*The Faerie Queene* and *The Divine Comedy* also open in a "*wilderness*" setting) – and it still shows up in contemporary idioms, both secular and religious, for example, '*It's a jungle out there.*' "*I walk'd*" also activates a standard conceptual metaphor that forms the basis for the entire book, LIFE IS A JOURNEY, although it is rapidly narrowed and focused into a more specific application of the JOURNEY conceptual metaphor, SALVATION IS A JOURNEY. The book as a whole takes the form of a novel in two parts – a narrative and a sequel. Both part one and part two of *Pilgrim's Progress* have all the defining features of a complete narrative, with a protagonist who sets out on a quest, strives to achieve an objective, experiences and overcomes a sequence of setbacks. It is presented in two parts, a narrative about *Christian*, followed by a parallel, but inter-connected novel about *Christian*'s wife, *Christiana*.

The plot is motivated by the book *Christian* is reading (by implication, the Bible, although that is never made explicit), from which he learns that the city in which he was born and lives, the *City of Destruction*, is to be destroyed along with all who live there. The quest he sets out on is to escape the fate of being destroyed along with his city. Early in the first part, *Christian* pleads with his wife and children to accompany him on his quest and so escape destruction along with him, but they refuse to come with him, so he sets out alone, in spite of his professed love for them. The plot of the second part is motivated when *Christiana* learns that her husband was successful in his quest, and determines to join him after all.

The characters and places in *Pilgrim's Progress* all bear names that identify them with moral, psychological, or spiritual qualities. *Christian* lives in the city of *Destruction* and journeys toward the *Celestial City*. His neighbors are *Obstinate* and *Pliable*. He meets *Evangelist*, who sets him on his way, and whom he encounters again from time to time. His misadventures include sinking into *the Slough of Dispond* and passing in *darkness* through the *Valley of the Shadow of Death*. He *turns aside* onto an *easier path* and is caught by the giant, *Despair*, and thrown into the dungeon of *Doubting Castle*.

Prefiguring the modern psychological novel, each part of the book presents *two* parallel stories, an external saga of heroic adventure and an internal story of spiritual struggle and growth. These two stories are intertwined in a way that contradicts Crisp's (2005b, p. 116) claim that "allegories ... never refer directly to their metaphorical target." In the first part, the immediately apparent story is about *Christian*, who learns from a book he is reading (the Bible) that the city where he lives is going to be destroyed. After worrying for some time about how to escape destruction, he encounters *Evangelist*, who sets him on a road to safety. At this level the story reads like *The Odyssey* (with *Evangelist* in the role of Athena) or any of dozens of "road novels": *Christian* encounters a series of setbacks and misadventures, including swamps, giants, ogres, and so on. Each of these has a metaphorical name that guides the mapping onto the topic story about *'the road to salvation.'* However, the story is *also* a psychological novel, about the hero's struggles with his neuroses, or *'internal demons.'* These are often, though not always, matched with the metaphorically named external demons.

Christian carries a *burden* on his back that, like the book he reads, is not explained – it is left to the reader to arrive at an interpretation based on background knowledge of Christian theology. On the other hand, the very first obstacle encountered in the *physical journey* narrative is the *Slough of Dispond*, into which he and his companion *Pliable* stumble, so that they become mired and are unable to go farther. Here, both men become literally despondent (in the psychological novel); *Pliable* responds by becoming angry with *Christian* and giving up the quest, but *Christian* recovers his determination and his will enough to struggle to the other side of the bog, where he encounters the metaphorically named *Help*, who (literally) helps him out of the bog and sets him back on the road. Later in the book, when he is caught by the giant, *Despair*, and thrown into the dungeon of *Doubting Castle*, he is (in the parallel psychological novel) beset by literal despair and doubt, which he must overcome before he recalls that he was given a *key* that will *unlock the doors* to the *dungeon* and let him *escape the castle* of *doubt and despair*.

Even Christian's interactions with the helpers he meets along the way, such as *Evangelist*, have this dual quality, in which the topic as well as the vehicle is often explicit, sometimes within the flow of the psychological novel, sometimes as commentary. For example, in the passage (pp. 21–29) in which Christian follows the advice of *Worldly Wiseman* and turns aside in hopes of freeing himself of his *burden*, *Evangelist* reassures him that "all manner of sin and blasphemies shall be forgiven unto men; be not faithless, but believing." The *Evangelist* concludes by instructing *Christian* about the three reasons why he must "utterly abhor" the counsel of *Worldly Wiseman* with his "carnal ways." The novel – throughout both Parts One and Two – is interrupted with these homilies (which may well have come straight from the sermons Bunyan preached to his congregation); they take up a large part of the novel.

In sum, *Pilgrim's Progress* is presented as a story with a well-developed narrative structure, and abstract qualities are represented by naming both places and characters. The characters have personalities that fit their names, and they behave in each place in a way that fits the metaphorical place-name. However, even over and above the character and place-names, there are *many* ways in which the author indicates how the vehicle story is to be mapped onto the topic story. This includes a surprisingly modern "psychological novel" element that runs throughout the first part (but is less overt in the second part) as well as the frequent literal religious homilies. In spite of his generic abstract name, *Christian* is well developed as a character, although the other persons in *Pilgrim's Progress* are rather one-dimensional.

Allegory as a literary genre. Although they differ in several ways, these examples share some important common themes that point toward a specification of allegory as a genre. All four represent religious ideas and concepts in allegorical form; in the first and last, *Psychomachia* and *Pilgrim's Progress*, the ideas are almost exclusively religious. However, both *Divine Comedy* and *Faerie Queene* freely intermix political ideas with the religious ideas. In *Divine Comedy* the political ideas are overt; Dante places popes, cardinals, and princes in situations in Hell that clearly represent his views of their political as well as spiritual sins. In the *Faerie Queene*, most of the political concepts are presented in allegorical form, often intermixed with religious and moral ideas. *The Divine Comedy* and *The Faerie Queene* also differ from *Pilgrim's Progress* in their heavy admixture of classical mythology and pagan ideas such as the elves/ faeries and sorcerers who inhabit *The Faerie Queene*. Finally, *The Divine Comedy* intermixes literal discussion of recent Italian history as well as Church history into the allegorical action, especially in the first two books. English history is also present in *The Faerie Queene*, although in a more mythic, symbolic, and in many places metaphorical form. *Pilgrim's Progress* is totally separated from secular history.

All four texts are presented as some form of narrative. *Divine Comedy* presents a coherent story, with many shorter narratives woven in throughout, but it lacks the element of surprise and reversal that characterizes a true narrative. *Pilgrim's Progress* is a fully developed and coherent narrative; each book presents a journey with a goal, and a series of adventures based on setbacks that are overcome. Book I and Book II of *Pilgrim's Progress* together constitute an overarching narrative of domestic relationship, in which *Christian*'s wife, *Christiana*, along with their children initially refuse to accompany him on his quest, but later embark on their own journey, culminating in reuniting the family – in the *Celestial City*, i.e., after death of the corporeal body. Each book of *Faerie Queene* presents a coherent narrative based on a knightly quest, based on the traditional design of the Arthurian romance. These are woven together in a grand narrative in which the knights errant are pitted against the wiles of *Archimago* and *Duessa*, and against the various giants, monsters, and evil knights with whom *Archimago* and *Duessa* are allied.

The narrative plot itself is clearly allegorical in *Divine Comedy*, *Faerie Queene*, and *Pilgrim's Progress*. Dante's journey through Hell, Purgatory, and Paradise allegorically represents the intellect's JOURNEY OF UNDERSTANDING and the soul's JOURNEY OF SALVATION. In the first two stages of his journey he is guided by *Virgil*, who represents the classical ideals of poetic and philosophical understanding. In the final stage he is guided by *Beatrice*, who represents the courtly ideal of spiritual love (prefiguring later Romantic ideas). The struggles of the Faerie Queene's knights against Archimago and his allies represent both Queen Elizabeth's political struggles and the struggles of Good against Evil, Christianity against Paganism. *Christian*'s flight from the city of *Destruction* and his journey toward the *Celestial City* allegorically represents the ordinary Christian's JOURNEY OF SALVATION, bearing the '*burden of sin.*' In *Faerie Queene*, the religious allegory might be characterized as the QUEST FOR SALVATION, although it is also reasonable to interpret the knights' journeys in terms of LIFE IS A JOURNEY.

All of these texts use allegorical names. *Pilgrim* uses almost exclusively allegorical names, both for characters and for places. *Divine Comedy* uses only a smattering of allegorical names – most names are historical or mythological, but the named persons are given allegorical relations to the particular moral sins / virtues they are represented as having committed during life. *Faerie Queene* mixes the two devices. In both *The Divine Comedy* and *The Faerie Queene*, the characters represent abstract ideas even when, like *Arthur* in *Queene*, they are not given allegorical names. In all of these examples, the allegorical meanings are supported and reinforced by actions and events. *Sans Loy*, in *Queene*, acts in a lawless manner. When *Christian*, in *Pilgrim*, falls into the *Slough of Dispond*, he becomes despondent, and when *Redcrosse*, in *Faerie Queene*, is thrown into the Dungeon of *Despair*, he experiences debilitating despair. Sometimes the allegorical meanings are merely stated and briefly illustrated, but as in the example of the dungeon of *Despair*, they often serve to advance the plot and develop the character.

Revised definition. *Allegory* is a literary text based on a metaphorical story in which the narrative plot as well as persons, places, and events are constructed with a consistent metaphorical relation to abstract ideas, and sometimes also to actual (historical or contemporary) persons, places, and events. An allegory is usually organized around a single unifying conceptual metaphor or a set of metaphors, e.g., FAITH IS COMBAT in *Psychomachia* and *Faerie Queene*, SALVATION IS A QUEST in *Faerie Queene*, and SALVATION IS A JOURNEY in *The Divine Comedy* and *Pilgrim's Progress*. Allegories often have didactic, instructional, or illustrative functions, as all of these examples have; they may also serve as social commentary and critique. Often, as in *The Faerie Queene*, these functions are all present. Allegories are also sometimes constructed around real events or around narratives that were not necessarily originally written with allegorical intent, as in Paul's allegorizing of the story of Abraham's two sons.

This definition is largely but not completely consistent with Harris and Tolmie (2011), who further note that "the genre is characterized by abstract personifications, concepts that walk and talk, like Reason and Conscience (*Piers*), Gluttony and Lust (*Queene*) ... by topifications, conceptually laden landscapes like the Celestial City (*Pilgrim's*) the Cave of Error (*Queene*) ... within the frame of a journey or quest" (p. 112). It is also somewhat consistent with Crisp's (2008) general discussion of allegory, although his claim that all language in allegory is source related and literal is contradicted by all of these examples. It is true that the characters and places in *The Faerie Queene* and *Pilgrim's Progress* are presented as real people and places, and events are presented as events that actually happened; in brief these works are presented as ordinary narrative accounts. However, the "story-frame" of the presentation is repeatedly broken by the "concepts that walk and talk," persons and places that bear allegorical names and demonstrate the characteristics of abstract moral and spiritual qualities (e.g., the dragon "*Errour*," "*Christian*," "*Evangelist*," the dungeon in the castle "*Despaire*," "*Slough of Dispond*"). Crisp dismisses these as equivalent to mere nicknames, but in many examples, especially *Pilgrim's Progress*, they play crucial roles in advancing the plot, and in general are too obtrusive to be dismissed so easily. Moreover, in each of these examples, the characters as well as the poet enact and comment on the psychological and spiritual qualities implied by the names. Bunyan, Prudentius, and Spenser explicitly address the allegorical nature of the writing in a preface, and all four authors insert Christian homilies that explicitly connect source with target. All four examples include passages of explicit, literal theological argumentation and moral instruction; these passages constitute nearly half of *Il Paradiso*.

The relatively narrow definition of allegory proposed above is particularly important for distinguishing between allegorical elements and other metaphorical stories that are embedded in the text, not as part of the allegory but to serve explanatory or expository purposes. An example comes in *Faerie Queene* near the end of Book I (p. 209) when Spenser uses a nautical metaphorical story to describe the storytelling process:

> *Now strike your sailes you jolly Mariners,*
> *For we be come unto a quiet rode,*
> *Where we must land some of our passengers,*
> *And light this wearie vessel of her lode.*

Early in Book II, explaining why *Duessa* and the *Archimage* relented in their attacks on *Redcrosse* and turned their attention to another knight, *Guyon*, Spenser tells us that

> His *credit now in doubtfull ballaunce hong*;
> For *hardly could be hurt, who was already stong.*

And a few lines later, "The *fish that once was caught, new bait will hardly bite.*" Like the language used in the narrative itself, this language is apparently literal but clearly metaphorical, and it is recognizably distinct from the overall allegorical design of both the poem generally and the adventure to which these lines are a preface. Limiting the definition of allegory as I propose provides a ready means both for distinguishing the stories implied by these metaphors from the allegory they serve and for understanding how they contribute to the transition between Book I with its focus on *Redcrosse* and Book II with its focus on the knight *Guyon*. Otherwise we would be left with only a paraphrase of a line from *Animal Farm*: all allegories are equal, but some allegories are more equal than others.

To summarize the argument thus far, as a literary genre *allegory* is identified with a handful of typical characteristics. Allegory is a metaphorical story organized around one or more unifying conceptual metaphors. The narrative plot of the vehicle story as well as persons, places, and events in the story map in a way that is consistent with the unifying conceptual metaphors onto corresponding elements of the topic story, and this relationship is often reflected in names. Allegory may serve didactic functions or provide philosophical or political commentary on the topic. In the next section of this chapter, I will discuss some recent research on how people understand allegorical elements of metaphorical stories and some examples of discourse in which allegorical elements are (apparently intentionally) introduced into metaphorical stories.

Allegoresis: Creating, Finding, and Interpreting Allegorical Elements in Literary Texts

Gibbs (2011, p. 121) claims that the "allegorical impulse" (*allegoresis*), the tendency to give allegorical interpretations to ordinary events as well as to literary creations, is fundamental to cognition. He also reports experimental evidence that people readily detect and interpret allegory in poetry and satirical writing.

In one study (Gibbs & Boers, 2005), college student participants read a poem, Robert Frost's (1969) "The Road Not Taken," and describe their thoughts about its meaning. Participants were asked to read the poem in three line segments, one per page, and write interpretations of each segment. Then they read the complete poem one more time and wrote down what they now thought it meant. Participants provided very few personal associations, suggesting that they focused on the poet's message, not their own concerns, and more than 70 percent of the interpretations were metaphorical.

In another series of studies, students read a satirical story in which Garner (1994) rewrote a series of folktales, including "The Three Little Pigs," using language associated with "politically correct" ideas, e.g., "along came a big, bad wolf with expansionist ideas ..." When students were asked to interpret the stories and explain the point of them, 65 percent gave an allegorical interpretation, but only 23 percent explicitly mentioned satire. Of the responses that gave an allegorical interpretation, 67 percent interpreted the author's intention as supporting political correctness. However, when the author was described as politically conservative, liberal, or neutral in a follow-up study, students attributed intentions to the author that were consistent with the author's reported political views.

Gibbs and Boers conclude that, at least among college students, a sizable majority readily and easily provide allegorical interpretations, although they do not necessarily arrive at the *same* allegorical interpretations. Even among college students, people are less able to perceive satire and, when they do, they are if anything even more likely to interpret it according to preconceptions based on their own beliefs or on what they think the author believes. Citing Jerzy Kosinski's (1970) story *Being There*, Gibbs also points out that people sometimes interpret statements that were intended literally as metaphorical.

These results generally support the claim that most people readily understand metaphor and allegory, but it would be interesting to know more about the 35 percent of participants who did *not* give an allegorical or metaphorical interpretation to a poem like "The Road Not Taken," and the 77 percent in the *Politically Correct* study who did not explicitly mention satire. Did these participants see the metaphorical and satirical implications but not mention them? Are they capable of understanding allegory and satire in some but not all texts? How would participants respond to a selection from *Psychomachia* or *Pilgrim's Progress*, where the allegory is more clearly marked? Further research is obviously needed.

Cognitive processing. Drawing on his previous research with metaphorical phrases like *'tear apart the argument'* (Gibbs, Gould, & Andric, 2005–2006) and *'grasp the concept'* (Wilson & Gibbs, 2007), Gibbs argues that people understand allegory through embodied simulations of the source (vehicle) actions. When people read "The Road Not Taken," they experience a partial activation of the actions described by the author – the visual perception of a "yellow wood" (suggesting autumn) where "two roads diverged," and so on, up to starting to go forward on "the one less traveled by." This is consistent with Gerrig's (1993) claim that people experience a story by being *"transported into"* the *"story-world,"* and Green's (2004) claim that *"transportation"* leads to greater persuasiveness. However, the account is not complete; activation of partial simulations of the source (vehicle) is only half the story. Somehow, to complete the allegorical understanding, a simulation of the topic must also be activated, and related in some way to the source. One account of how this might take place is suggested by Conceptual Integration Theory (Fauconnier & Turner, 2002), briefly described in Chapter 3. Another, more fully specified account is provided by Thagard's (2011) convolution and cognitive-affective model, also discussed in Chapter 3. Crisp (2008) applies Conceptual Blending Theory in developing an allegorical reading of a poem from William Blake, and Thagard applies convolution theory to George Orwell's *Animal Farm*. I will review both of these analyses in the next section, followed by Oakley and Crisp's (2011) analysis of allegory in a popular music video.

Conceptual Integration Theory (Fauconnier & Turner, 2002), also known as blending theory, briefly described in Chapter 3, provides a useful tool for analyzing metaphors, including allegories. Crisp (2008, p. 291) acknowledges that blending theory is "almost vacuous in its most general versions," and that there is "no evidence from experimental psychology for the occurrence of blending." However, he argues that it does have content as a theory of figurative thought, and develops a detailed analysis of Blake's poem "A Poison Tree" in support of this claim. Toward this end, he distinguishes between "extended metaphor" and allegory: "While extended metaphor involves both source-related and target-related language, allegory involves only source-related language" (2008, p. 291). As noted in the preceding, this definition is immediately problematic, since it would exclude three of the most commonly cited examples of allegory, all three of which involve extensive source-related language. This objection could be circumvented by separating out the passages of religious homily and theological argumentation from the story line, which would entail distinguishing between allegories and works of literature that contain allegorical passages. It is far from clear why this is a useful step to take. It is also important to distinguish passages of extended metaphor that have no narrative structure from allegories, in which the narrative structure itself is metaphorical.

Crisp (2008) supports the distinction by noting that, in extended metaphor, the topic is explicitly mentioned alongside the vehicle, so that the reader is consciously aware of the blended space, using an example from Charles Causley's (1975) "A Ballad for Katherine of Aragon":

> O war is a *casual mistress*
> And the world is *her double bed*
> *She has* a few *charms in her* mechanized *arms*
> But *you wake up* and *find* yourself dead.

Because both war and mistress are mentioned together, "the reader consciously experiences a strange, seemingly impossible, fusion of war and mistress, a metaphorical blend ... Allegory may, as a part of the unconscious cognition underlying it, involve blended spaces, but the reader is not directly aware of these" (Crisp, 2008, p. 292). Crisp's intention is to argue against the idea of a continuum connecting extended metaphor to allegory. Crisp uses a detailed analysis of William Blake's "A Poison Tree" to develop the distinction between allegory and extended metaphor. According to Crisp, allegory develops a fictional world in overtly literal language as if it were a real world, and extended metaphor provides an explicit metaphor mapping.

"A Poison Tree." Crisp (2008) argues that "A Poison Tree" begins as a literal narrative then, about halfway through, is transformed into allegory. Crisp's argument is supported by the assumption that reference is absolute: either an utterance refers to something else or it does not. Based on this definitional assumption, Crisp concludes that the vehicle story must either refer to the topic or not refer to the topic, and since extended metaphor does refer to the topic and, according to Crisp's definition, allegory does not, "there must be an exact point in a text where a reader shifts from extended metaphor to allegory" (p. 294). Given these assumptions, the transformation from literal story to allegory must happen at some specific point, which, Crisp acknowledges, might be located anywhere between line 4 and 10. In the following, I have separated the section of the poem, the last half of line 4 through all of line 8, in which the transition might be found according to Crisp's reasoning.

> A Poison Tree
> 1 I was angry with my friend:
> 2 I told my wrath, my wrath did end.
> 3 I was angry with my foe:
> 4 I told it not,
>   my wrath did grow.

Allegoresis

> 5 And I water'd it in fears,
> 6 Night and morning with my tears;
> 7 And I sunn'd it with smiles,
> 8 And with soft deceitful wiles.
> 9 And it grew both day and night,
> 10 Till it // bore an apple bright;
> 11 And my foe beheld it shine,
> 12 And he knew that it was mine,
> 13 And into my garden stole
> 14 When the night had veil'd the pole:
> 15 In the morning glad I see
> 16 My foe outstretch'd beneath the tree.
>
> (Blake, 1966, p. 218[2])

The poem begins with a simple literal statement, "I was angry with my friend," followed by a second line that ends with a simple lexical metaphor: "I told my wrath, my wrath did *end*." This is followed by a parallel couplet: "I was angry with my foe: / I told it not, my wrath did *grow*." The second phrase in line 4 is ambiguous: "my wrath did *grow*" can be read as a simple lexical metaphor for "I became angrier," but it also introduces the extended botanical metaphor developed in lines 5–8 (a metaphorical story), beginning with "I *water'd it in fears*," leading to line 10, where Crisp claims the poem makes the transition to allegory: "Till it bore an apple bright."

Crisp's (2008) claim that there must be a precise location for the shift from extended metaphor to allegory follows from his assumption that reference is an "either/or" phenomenon and his definition of allegory as an extended account that includes no reference to the topic. But these claims are both purely a matter of definition, and overlook allusion, which can be understood as a form of *indirect* reference. If the concept of reference is allowed to expand to include indirect reference, and if it is recognized, as I have shown earlier in this chapter, that allegory frequently includes reference to the topic, then the middle section of Blake's poem can be seen as a gradual, rather than abrupt, transition from literal to allegorical. In each line of this middle section, the pronoun "it" clearly refers simultaneously to *my wrath* and the metaphorical "*tree*," tying the literal story, beginning with "I was angry with my foe," to the allegorical ending, "In the morning glad I *see* / my foe *outstretch'd beneath the tree*." Line 8, "And with *soft* deceitful wiles," can be read as literal within the preceding metaphorical story about the poet's nurturing of his wrath/"*plant*" and the following allegory of wrath as an "*apple tree*." Although this reading of the poem undermines Crisp's use of the poem in support of Fauconnier and Turner's Conceptual Blending Theory, it is otherwise consistent with the concept of allegory. It is also consistent with the allegorical naming in *Pilgrim's Progress*, in which names like "*Slough of Dispond*" refer simultaneously to geographical locations in the vehicle story and to emotional states in the topic story. However, Oakley and Crisp (2011), in an essay discussed later in this chapter, make a stronger case for including conceptual blending in a cognitive processing account of allegory.

This intermediate approach also undermines Crisp's (2008) attempt to distinguish between the cognitive processes involved in reading allegory vs. extended metaphor. For example in *Pilgrim's Progress*, when Christian falls into the "*Slough of Dispond*," or in *The Divine Comedy* when Dante, "*midway through* life's *journey*," awakes to find himself "*alone in a dark wood*," it is somewhat difficult to credit the idea that an attentive reader (who has the requisite background cultural knowledge) would not be consciously aware of the blend. Even an inattentive reader must surely notice the relationship between "*Dispond*" and Christian's decidedly despondent behavior while mired in the slough in *Pilgrim's Progress*, and Dante's opening, "*midway through* life's *journey*," clearly marks what follows in *The Divine Comedy* as metaphorical. Crisp's point probably applies to certain forms of esoteric philosophy that are presented in deliberately obscure allegorical form, but it does not seem relevant to the more familiar examples discussed earlier in this chapter.

Animal Farm. *Animal Farm* (Orwell, 1946) is presented as a novel, with a well-developed plot that satisfies all the criteria of narrative form: the characters strive to accomplish a goal, encounter betrayals and other setbacks, strive to overcome these setbacks, and ultimately fail. The plot involves a successful revolt by the much-abused animals on a farm owned by drunken and abusive Farmer Jones. After they drive off the farmer, they set up an egalitarian society, and live for a time in peace, harmony, and happiness. However the pigs assert themselves as leaders over the other animals, and the cleverest and most ruthless of these, aptly named *Napoleon*, manages through scheming and deceit to become an all-powerful dictator. Eventually Napoleon is transformed into a humanoid farmer, with all the characteristics of Farmer Jones. In the very last line of the novel, when Napoleon hosts a dinner for the human farmers in the neighborhood and the animals gather to peer in through the windows of the farmhouse, "the creatures outside looked from pig to man, and from man to pig, and from pig to man again; but already it was impossible to say which was which" (p. 128).

Animal Farm possesses few of the formal characteristics of allegory, as identified by Harris and Tolmie (2011) and defined earlier in this chapter. There are no homilies, and the nearest thing to a lesson comes from the cynical donkey, Benjamin, who comments from time to time that "things never had been, nor ever could be much better or much worse – hunger, hardship, and disappointment being, so he said, the unalterable law of life" (Orwell, 1946, p. 120). Aside from *Napoleon*, the animal names are typical of the names humans give their domestic animals – Snowball, Boxer, Clover, etc.

Many of these animals can be readily identified with figures or types from the Russian Revolution. Character traits are mapped onto specific animals, usually representing how different groups among the Russian population reacted to events, e.g., the horse Boxer is the credulous prototypical Worker who continues to believe in the Revolution in spite of all evidence, but these are not reflected in metaphorical names. Thagard (2011) refers to *Animal Farm* both as an allegory and as a "beast fable," implying that he regarded fables as a subcategory of allegory. However, as discussed in the above, it is worth distinguishing between these two genres, just as it is worth distinguishing between metaphors and analogies (which Thagard also conflates).

In *Animal Farm*, Thagard (2011) points out that the metaphorical mapping of relations among the various actors, and the mapping of the causal and explanatory relations among events, is more important than the mapping of particular persons. He argues that the vehicle in an effective analogy generates emotional responses that map onto the topic. Consequently, analysis of allegory must begin with a theory of emotion. Thagard rejects the idea that emotion is an abstract cognitive state, claiming instead that emotion integrates physiological perception of associated bodily states with appraisal (In Barsalou's terms, *interoception* and *introspection*). These responses are activated by the vehicle and associated by metaphorical mapping with the topic.

Thagard (2011) has developed a useful system for diagramming these affective mappings, which I have further adapted in Figure 4.1 to illustrate the overall plot. Positive entities and actions are shown in ovals, negative in squares. Metaphorical mappings are shown by dotted lines. Thagard argues that "effective allegories like *Animal Farm* engage neural processes for both cognitive appraisal and physiological perception" (2011, p. 139) and map the

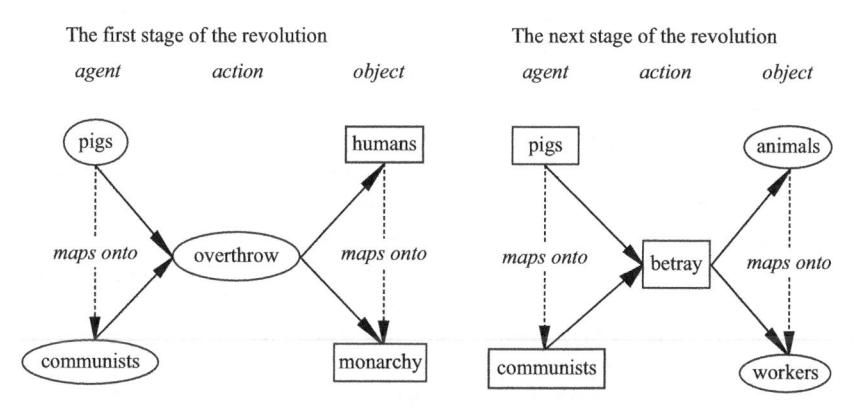

Figure 4.1 Cognitive-affective diagram of revolution in *Animal Farm*

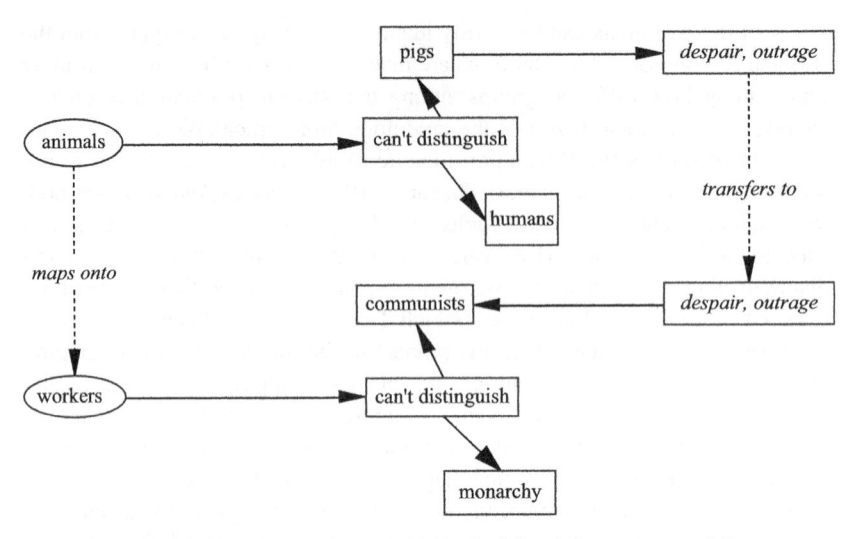

Figure 4.2. "The creatures outside looked from pig to man, and from man to pig, and from pig to man again; but already it was impossible to say which was which"

emotional responses to the source onto the target. This is consistent with Gerrig (1993) and Green (2004). Figure 4.2 illustrates the mapping of the evaluative and emotional responses conveyed by the final sentence of *Animal Farm*. Figures 4.1 and 4.2 illustrate the utility of Thagard's analytic approach; they also support his claims about the importance of both physiological and evaluative aspects of emotion in interpreting and understanding allegory.

In Chapter 11, I will discuss a political cartoon that builds on the allegorical structure of *Animal Farm* and applies it as a commentary on recent political rulings by the U.S. Supreme Court. In the next section, I will discuss a group of popular culture texts, a music video and several popular songs, that incorporate allegorical elements organized around the conceptual metaphor LOVE IS A JOURNEY.

"Third Race at the Honeymoon-Is-Over Downs." Oakley and Crisp (2011) apply conceptual integration / mental space approach to a contemporary music video, *"Third Race at the Honeymoon-Is-Over Downs,"* which bears a close resemblance to the country song "The Race Is On" by George Jones and Don Rollins (1964), recorded by George Jones in 1964 and subsequently covered by an assortment of artists ranging from Alvin and the Chipmunks (1965) to the Grateful Dead (1981). Oakley and Crisp argue that a "network of mental spaces" makes a special contribution to understand the conceptual processes involved in understanding allegory, which, they claim, cannot be explained as a simple mapping of source to target.

The video consists of an audio file by Nick Sanabria, synchronized to a video of a horse race by Marc Bolton that the authors downloaded from YouTube. A series of phrases related to a marriage that begins in bliss and ends in a nasty breakup; each phrase is converted to a racehorse name, and the whole is narrated using the rhythms and intonations of a radio sportscaster announcing a literal horse race. As the authors point out, a marriage and breakup that extends over several years is compressed into a minute and 16 seconds. The authors identify three "mental spaces": the *presentation space* (i.e., vehicle or source story) of a horse race; a *reference space* (i.e., topic or target), the marriage relationship gone sour; and a *blended scenario*, in which elements from these two "input spaces" are blended into a unified story.

The video begins with a metaphorical title, "Welcome to *the third race*, at the *Honeymoon-is-over-downs*." As the race begins, "*jumping out in the lead* is *Romance-and-Affection* with *Domestic Bliss* in *close behind*." Other "*horses*" are named "*Marriage Vows*," "*Immediate Child*," "*Nasty Attitude*," "*More Children*," and "*Drinking Heavily*." The race ends: "*At the wire, it's Up-Yours, Keep-The-Fucking-House ... and I-Am-Outta-Here*." As the authors point out, this works primarily because the use of horse-race announcement style maintains the "*horse-race*" scenario (activated by the opening line "Welcome to the *third race*") and the escalation of relationship and relationship-breakup terms maintains the relationship breakup scenario.

It is not clear what the metaphor "mental *space*" adds to the more familiar concept of *schema*, i.e., a coherent set of ideas and experiences related to a topic, or what jargon like "double-scope blend" adds, but I find the authors' claim convincing, that the idea of "*blending*" goes beyond the more familiar idea of a source-to-target (vehicle-to-topic) mapping in explaining how an extended metaphor of this sort works. It is clear that *both* the horse-race schema *and* the marriage break-up schema must be activated simultaneously for the emotional effects to be achieved; this is probably true of most truly effective metaphors.

Given the history of heartbreak metaphors in popular culture, we also need to invoke a third schema to explain the effects of "*Third Race*." A common conceptual metaphor, LOVE IS A JOURNEY or more precisely LOVE IS MOTION THROUGH SPACE, underlies "*Third Race*," and it has been developed along similar lines several times. Fauconnier and Turner (2002) initially specified a *generic space* that underlies both input spaces and links them together, but the "*horserace*" / "*movement through space*" schema doesn't fit their characterization of a generic space. (Something more like *optimism* → *wagering* → *losing the wager* → *disappointment* would better serve the role of a *generic space*.)

Preceding "*Third Race*" by several decades is Rollins's (1964) "*The Race Is On*," which has been covered by a series of artists since its initial release. The chorus begins

> Now the *race is on* and *here comes Pride up the backstretch*
> *Heartaches* are *going to the inside*
> *My Tears* are *holding back*

And ends

> *The race is on* and it *looks like Heartaches*
> And the *winner loses all*

Like "*Third Race,*" "*The Race Is On*" blends a familiar horse race announcing schema with a relationship breakup schema. It also makes extensive use of metaphorical puns (including "*going to the inside*" and "*holding back,*" which have distinct relevance in both input schemas, and thus facilitate the blend, leading to the ironic conclusion that "the *winner loses all,*" also meaningful in both schemas. Adding a synchronized video may have contributed to the effect of the contemporary version, but in 1964, many people would have been familiar with the structure and style of a horse race reported on the radio.

Casting the net slightly more widely, Ariana Grande's (2013) "Honeymoon Avenue" begins with "I *looked in my rear view mirror*" and maps heartbreak onto driving home in the rain, "*Stuck in the same old lane / Going the wrong way home.*" "Honeymoon Avenue" accomplishes its effects by blending the breakup schema with an even more familiar schema of driving in dense traffic. Her heart is "*stuck in bumper-to-bumper traffic*" and, later, "my heart is *at a yellow light, a yellow light*" (as a traffic signal, a yellow light signifies both *warning* and *transition from go to stop*). This also has a precedent, "Heartbreak Hotel" (Axton, Crudup, Durden, & Presley, 1956), which is located "*Down at the end of Lonely Street.*"

None of these examples quite qualifies as allegory, except in a very broad sense, but all of them use the tools of allegorical naming. "Honeymoon Avenue" develops JOURNEY fairly coherently as an extended metaphor, and "*The Race Is On*" develops HORSE-RACE as a coherent extended metaphor, blending JOURNEY with COMPETITION. "*Third Race*" enhances the metaphoric coherence by adopting the rhythm, tone, and timing of a radio announcer relating an actual horse race – a clear example of a musical metaphor (Forceville, 2009b). All of them assume familiarity with both "*input spaces*" or schemas; all of them are, arguably, also enhanced by familiarity with the underlying conceptual metaphors LOVE IS A JOURNEY and LOVE IS A CONTEST, and with the tradition of love poetry and love songs built on one or the other, or both, of these metaphors.

Conclusion

Based on several examples of medieval allegory, I have proposed a definition of *allegory* as displaced writing about abstract ideas in which persons, places,

Conclusion

and actions stand for abstract ideas and relations among abstract ideas, usually with a didactic or persuasive motivation. Evidence shows that, at least among college students, most are able to recognize and interpret allegory. However, a sizable minority do *not* readily recognize allegory, and those who do recognize allegory do not agree on the interpretations *or* evaluations offered. (In Chapter 11, I will discuss research on visual metaphors showing that, at least in some instances, a *majority* of readers either fail to arrive at the artist's [stated] intention or fail altogether to arrive at a coherent interpretation.)

There is considerable evidence that, when people process language generally, neural systems that would be activated by the experiences described are at least weakly and briefly activated (Bergen, 2012; Gibbs, 2008); these *perceptual simulations* apparently play a role in processing metaphors, although how central a role has yet to be determined. Similarly, research has shown that *"transportation"* into a *"story world"* – simulating the places and events described so vividly as to feel like a participant – greatly enhances both enjoyment and persuasiveness of a story. The Elaboration Likelihood Model (Petty & Cacioppo, 1981, discussed in Chapter 3) suggests that the degree to which perceptual simulations (and transportation into a story world) are experienced is likely to be a function of both motivation (including personal involvement) and ability (including background knowledge). Combining these lines of research suggests that allegories (and, by extension, other story metaphors) will be both more enjoyable and more persuasive for readers who have the background knowledge required to understand them and who are sufficiently motivated, by interest and personal relevance, to become *"immersed"* in the story to the point of experiencing it as "real." Familiarity with the genre – both with the strategy of allegoresis in general and with a specific sub-genre, such as love songs based on activities such as *"horse race," "auto race,"* and *"travel,"* will contribute to the ability to process and enhance depth of processing.

Traditional approaches to metaphor specify in effect a one-way mapping, in which attributes of the vehicle are mapped or projected onto the topic. For allegory this would imply that aspects of the vehicle story, such as *Christian*'s feelings of despondency when he becomes mired in the *Slough of Dispond* (in *Pilgrim's Progress*), will be simply projected onto the topic, in this case the despondency of an individual who has difficulty living by Christian principles. However, Fauconnier and Turner's (2002) conceptual blending model suggests that, at least for readers with sufficient background knowledge, the input space (schema) of *Christian faith* will be activated alongside the input space of this particular passage in the story, and the two blended in an output space that includes elements of both. Thagard (2011) has shown how this kind of blending can be accomplished in a mathematically and neurologically plausible way through what he calls *convolution*. Since this kind of blending is likely to require considerable cognitive effort, the Elaboration Likelihood

Model applies here as well: readers who lack either the ability to process, including the requisite background knowledge as well as familiarity with allegory as a literary device, or the motivation in terms of interest and relevance, are unlikely to process the allegorical elements sufficiently to experience this kind of blend. This may help explain why 30 percent or more of the participants in the experiments reported by Gibbs (2011) failed to furnish an allegorical interpretation for the stimulus materials in his experiments.

Allegory as a strategy includes several devices that may facilitate the process of conceptual blending or convolution. For example, the use of allegorical person and place-names tells the reader how to connect features of the vehicle and topic stories, and may also guide the activation of relevant schemas in the first place: in "Welcome to *the third race*, at the *Honeymoon-is-over-downs*," "*third race*" and "*downs*" activate a *horse-race* schema; and "*Honeymoon-is-over*" activates a *breakup* schema. Even if the listener has not personally experienced a relationship breakup, popular culture is saturated with movies, songs, novels, and other examples to draw on. However, as *Animal Farm* illustrates, allegorical names are not necessary. The opening of the story activates the *animal fable* schema, and the language in which the plight of the animals is described is likely to activate the *revolution* schema for anyone with even a cursory knowledge of recent world history. The unfolding of the story engages the reader in accessing even more elements from both schemas. From persuasion research (Petty & Cacioppo, 1981), we know that readers and listeners remember a message longer and more accurately and are more persuaded by a message when they are actively engaged in elaborating it by filling in details. The effectiveness of *Animal Farm* is in part a function of its ability to engage the reader in working out the various parallels between the animals' experience and the events of the Russian Revolution.

5 Parables and Fables

Trading Dialogue for Lodging
> There is a tradition that, in order stay in a Zen temple, a wandering monk must win a debate about Buddhism with one of the resident monks. If he loses the debate, he has to move on.
>
> Two brother monks lived together in a temple; the elder was learned and wise, but the younger one, who had only one eye, was foolish.
>
> A wandering monk, seeking lodging, challenged them to a debate about the sublime teaching. The elder monk felt tired, so he asked his younger brother to take his place, recommending that he request the dialogue in silence. The younger monk led the stranger into the shrine for the debate. After a short time the wandering monk came to the elder monk, and said "Your young brother is very wise: He quickly defeated me."
>
> "Please tell me about the debate."
>
> "I began by holding up one finger to represent Buddha, the enlightened one. In reply he held up two fingers, to signify Buddha and his teaching. I held up three fingers for Buddha, his teaching, and his followers, living the harmonious life. Then he raised a clenched fist, demonstrating how all three come from one realization. With that, I conceded defeat, so I must leave."
>
> As soon as the traveler left the younger monk ran in, asking "Where is he?"
>
> "I understand you won the debate."
>
> "Won, nothing! There was no debate. He insulted me, and I intend to beat him up."
>
> "Tell me what happened," asked the elder monk.
>
> "As soon as we were seated he held up one finger, insinuating that I have only one eye. Since he was a stranger, I tried to be polite to him by holding up two fingers to congratulate him for having two eyes. But he insulted me again by holding up three fingers, insinuating that between us we have only three eyes. So I doubled up my fist to punch him, but he ran away before I could get to him."
>
> (This and the other Zen stories related in this chapter are based on stories collected by Paul Reps [1957].)

Although its clearest expression is in artfully crafted texts like *Psychomachia* and *Pilgrim's Progress*, the allegorical impulse is also manifested in what Harris and Tolmie (2011, p. 112) describe as "an allegorical radial network" including parables and fables as well as morality plays, satires, parodies, folktales and myths, with boundaries that are "both fuzzy and mutable." Many of these originate in folktales, stories handed down from generation to generation, refined and polished in the process. These folktales often include a "moral," sometimes only implied, sometimes explicitly stated as a coda. They are also frequently picked up, reframed and reinterpreted by poets and teachers, both lay and religious. Familiar tales like "Cinderella" and "Snow White" are encountered in many different versions within European culture, and similar tales are found in other cultures.

Some of these stories, like many of the *101 Zen stories* collected by Reps (1957), are based on events represented as having actually happened, usually to Zen masters, saints, or other holy persons but sometimes to ordinary people. Others, like the fables of Aesop and the folktales collected by the Grimm Brothers, come from oral traditions of storytelling (and may appear in many different versions in different regions). Some, like the stories of Hans Christian Andersen, have been created according to the pattern of folktales. Many, like *The Little Engine That Could* (Piper, 1930), are initially invented by one author, then shaped and reshaped through several narrations by different authors.

In this chapter, I will focus on parables and fables, which share a similar format and both have an apparent and usually overt didactic purpose. Both are shorter and less complex than the allegories discussed in Chapter 4, and they lack features such as allegorical person and place-names. Parables are closest to the prototypical allegory, in that they have a specifically religious meaning, often within a particular doctrinal tradition – but sometimes easily generalized to other traditions. Fables tend to emphasize issues and concerns that are more psychological and social than spiritual or religious. Parables always have human characters in realistic human situations; fables sometimes have human characters but often involve animals or other nonhumans, often in quite unrealistic situations.

Parables

Religious teachings are often presented in the form of stories. In many cases, these are stories about the gods and their relationships, which can be either interpreted allegorically or understood as literal accounts of transcendent beings. But most religious traditions also present stories that exemplify or illustrate fundamental teachings. A particularly obvious example of story metaphor is the parable, a fictional, often fanciful story, usually told as a generic story (set in no particular time or place, and involving no particular persons). Often the mapping is not stated, but left for the hearers to work out, as in this parable of Buddha:

A man was traveling along a path when he encountered a tiger. He ran away, with the tiger close behind, until he came to the edge of a precipice. Catching hold of a wild vine the man quickly lowered himself over the edge. Far below he could see sharp rocks ready to dash him to pieces if he fell; above him, the tiger paced back and forth, waiting to devour him if he climbed back up. Only the vine sustained him.

Two mice appeared, and began to gnaw away at the vine. The man saw a wild strawberry plant growing from the cliff near him. Grasping the vine with one hand, he plucked a ripe strawberry with the other and ate it. How sweet it tasted!

According to the principles outlined in preceding chapters we would expect a reader who engages fully with this story to experience at least partial simulations of the scene, and particularly of the man's emotional responses, including terror and heightened arousal. We might also experience a simulation of his racing thoughts as he seeks a way out of the quandary he is in, and of his dread once the mice appear. As the reader processes the final two sentences, simulations of the strawberry might be experienced, or only a simulation of the feeling of intense pleasure – heightened by the contrast with his fear and terror. Consistent with Green's (2004) findings about the persuasion-enhancing effects of transportation into the story world, we would expect also that these partial simulations would contribute to the effectiveness of the story for conveying a teaching by mapping these responses onto a topic story.

The most obvious topic story in the parable of the tiger and the strawberry is the life of a human being whose JOURNEY through life is beset with perils "*ahead*" as well as "*behind*," and whose attempts to escape these perils only lead to new and even greater dangers. Faced with such a dilemma, the only recourse is to savor whatever satisfactions ("*strawberries*") are there. More profoundly, the story also maps onto the topic of a spiritual JOURNEY, in which the very acuteness of the mortal dilemma presents the catalyst for enlightenment.[1] In the specific context of Zen teachings, the contrast between the man's frantic attempts to think of a way out of his dilemma and the calm centeredness represented by his ability to savor and appreciate the strawberry is also vitally important.

Parables often take the form of metonyms – even the fanciful story about the tiger and the strawberry is a metonym in the sense that the ability to appreciate the sweetness of the fruit, in the face of certain death, reflects and represents a more general ability to focus on the immediate and present. Many of Jesus's parables are more overtly metonymic. The Prodigal Son in the vehicle story leads a sinful life, repents, and is forgiven, mapping onto and at the same time providing an example of a more general topic story of sin, repentance, and forgiveness, as well as a story about the love between parent and child. The Good Samaritan in the vehicle story displays kindness and charity, mapping onto and providing an example of the topic story about kindness and charity.

The use of these scenes from ordinary life (the father-son relationship, the experience of seeing a stranger in distress) facilitates the simulations necessary for transportation into these stories and thus enhances their persuasive impact. Like the story of the tiger and the strawberry, both of these parables from Jesus merge metaphor and metonym; the situation described is a single instance of the broader more general principle and thus stands in a metonymic relationship to the teaching illustrated, but it also stands as a metaphor for a more abstract concept that cannot be readily explained in literal language.

Other parables of Jesus can only be understood as story metaphors, without apparent metonymic qualities:

Everyone then who hears these words of mine and does them will be like a wise man who built his house on the rock. And the rain fell, and the floods came, and the winds blew and beat on that house, but it did not fall, because it had been founded on the rock. And everyone who hears these words of mine and does not do them will be like a foolish man who built his house on the sand. And the rain fell, and the floods came, and the winds blew and beat against that house, and it fell, and great was the fall of it. (Matthew 7:24–27, English Standard Version)

Like the parable of the tiger and the strawberry, this vehicle story can map onto at least two topic stories, one about life generally and one about spiritual life and religious faith in particular. In contrast to the more typical LIFE / SPIRITUALITY IS A JOURNEY, this parable is based on LIFE / FAITH IS A STRUCTURE (combined with TROUBLES ARE A STORM). The organization of this parable is interesting for at least two other reasons. Unlike the parable from Buddha, here Jesus provides the metaphor mapping in the opening phrase, "Everyone then who hears these words of mine and does them." Second, the parable presents contrasting stories, which underscores the mapping and makes it even more explicit. The example from Hillary Clinton's concession speech (Chapter 1) also relies on a blend of conceptual metaphors and on contrasting stories, but in her case the contrast is between the story of the 2008 nomination, which she lost, and a *future* campaign in which she or some other woman will find that "*the path will be a little easier.*"

A common form of parable is a story from real life that is told in a way that it can be readily mapped onto a generic story so that it illustrates a general principle. These stories often blend metaphor and metonym.

A great Zen teacher, Keichu, was the head of a large temple in Kyoto. Calling on him for the first time, the governor of Kyoto handed the attendant his card, which read "Kitagaki, Governor of Kyoto." When his attendant presented the card to Keichu, the Master read the card and sent it back.

"I have no business with such a fellow. Tell him to leave."

When the attendant returned the card, with apologies, the governor smiled, and said "That was my mistake." He took a pencil and scratched out the words Governor of Kyoto. "Please ask your teacher again."

Upon reading the altered card, the teacher exclaimed, "Oh, is that Kitagaki? I want to see that fellow. Please show him in."

Hearing or reading this story the audience is likely to experience simulations from the perspective of Kitagaki, the governor: the sense of self-importance, taken so much for granted that it is hardly noticed until Keichu's response makes it salient. We might experience a flash of annoyance but if so it is quickly resolved by simulating the governor's humble acceptance of the rejection, and possibly his chagrin at having committed such a *faux pas*. An audience member might also enter into the story from the perspective of the attendant – along with feelings of embarrassment at having to deliver the rejection to the governor. Either way the story maps metonymically onto general situations in which a person's identity-related feelings of importance interfere with communication. From the story we do not know the purpose of the governor's visit – it may be an official visit in his capacity as governor, in which case the initial calling card was not inappropriate, or it could be a personal visit, seeking instruction from the Zen Master, or it could be both. Keichu's initial response makes it clear that he has no interest in an official visit, and his second response makes it clear that he is completely welcoming of a personal visit. Either way, the vehicle story also maps more specifically onto a spiritual story about putting off the preoccupations and achievements of ordinary life in order to engage more fully with spiritual seeking – a topic that is closely bound up with the metonymic story about unthinking self-importance.

A somewhat similar story comes from Jesus, although in this case it is clearer that the interlocutor's interest is personal and not in any sense official:

A wealthy young man came to hear Jesus preach. After the sermon he approached the Master, and asked, "What can I do to be saved?"
Jesus replied, "You know the commandments, Do not commit adultery, Do not kill, Do not steal, Do not bear false witness, Defraud not, Honour thy father and mother." The young man answered, "Master, all these have I observed from my youth." Then Jesus said, "One more thing is lacking. Sell all that you have and distribute it to the poor, and you will have great treasure in heaven. Then come, take up your cross, and follow me." The man did not reply, but just walked away sadly.
Watching the man leave, Jesus remarked to his disciples, "It would be easier for a camel to pass through the eye of a needle than for a rich man to enter the Kingdom of Heaven." (Matthew 19:17–25)

This is told as a story of an actual event, an actual interaction between Jesus and a wealthy young man who is unable to bring himself to make the kind of commitment that is required to achieve his objective. Like the parable of the Prodigal Son, it also maps onto all similar situations. A reader/listener who is "*transported into*" the story might experience a simulation of the interaction and the emotions it arouses from the perspective of one of the disciples who witness the interaction, or from the perspective of the wealthy young man. It is clearly the intention of the writer that readers experience it from the perspective of the wealthy young man – that readers experience the young man's religious aspirations as well as his attachment to his worldly wealth, and the contradictions between these aspirations and desires. Individual members of the audience will then map these aspirations, attachments, and contradictions onto their own contradictory aspirations and attachments, and understand the need to sever their attachments in order to achieve their religious aspirations.

Members of the audience who identify with the disciples who witnessed the interaction may experience very different simulations, including satisfaction with the choices they have made, and possibly even a kind of smug superiority in comparison with the wealthy young man. (This is apparently *not* the intention of the author.)

Parables often resolve apparent contradictions between rules. An example from the Zen tradition:

Two monks were traveling together when they came to a river bank. Beside the river stood a young woman wearing an expensive kimono who was crying bitterly. The first monk asked her what was troubling her.
"I need to cross the river to travel to another village where I am to be married, and there is no ferry. If I wade the river my beautiful kimono will be ruined."
Without hesitation the first monk picked her up and carried her across the river, set her down on the far shore, and continued down the road with his companion.
The second monk was silent for some time, then, after they had gone a few miles, scolded the first monk as follows: "You know that we are not supposed to touch a woman! Why did you violate your vows?"
The first monk replied, mildly, "I left the woman beside the river. You carry her still in your heart."

Here we are invited to experience the distress of the young woman and the sympathy felt by the monk; perhaps we will also feel the woman's warm, soft flesh through her kimono as she is carried across the stream. Those knowledgeable about the monastic life are likely also to experience concern about the first monk's violation, especially when reminded of it by the second monk. This sets up a contradiction that is rechanneled and resolved in an unexpected way by the first monk's reply. Here, as with Jesus's parable of the Prodigal Son, the story serves as an example of how to resolve contradictions between following the rules of religious life and responding to human needs. It also serves as a metaphor, expressing a more enlightened attitude toward the relationship between rules of religious practice and the religious feelings they are supposed to support.

A similar point arises from another story in which Jesus turns a real-life incident into a parable:

On one Sabbath, Jesus was walking through the grainfields with his disciples, who began to pluck and eat heads of grain. And the Pharisees said to him, "Why are your disciples doing what is not lawful to do on the Sabbath?" And Jesus said until them, "Have you never read what David did, when he was in need and was hungry, he and those who were with him: how he entered the house of God ... and ate the bread of the Presence, which it is not lawful for any but the priests to eat, and also gave it to those who were with him? The Sabbath was made for man; man was not made for the Sabbath." (Mark 2:23–28)

Here the Pharisees play the same role as the second monk in the Zen parable, by reminding the protagonist of the rules and scolding him for violating the rules. Both parables can be read as metonymic examples of how to resolve contradictions between religious rules and human needs; both can also be read as metaphorical statements about living the spiritual life: again, metonym and metaphor are closely bound up with one another.

In yet another example, a group of religious leaders sought to test Jesus's understanding of Mosaic Law:

The scribes and the Pharisees brought a woman who had been caught in adultery, and placing her in the midst they said to him, "Teacher, this woman has been caught in the act of adultery. In the Law, Moses commanded us to stone such women. So what do you say?" And Jesus said to them, "Let him who is without sin among you throw the first stone." When they heard it, they went away one by one, beginning with the older ones, and Jesus was left alone with the woman standing before him. Jesus said to her, "Woman, where are they? Has no one condemned you?" She said, "No one, Lord." And Jesus said, "Neither do I condemn you; go, and sin no more." (John 8:3–11)

Told as a literal story about Jesus, this story seems to illustrate his capacity for empathy and forgiveness. But it also serves as a parable, a metaphorical story that maps readily onto any situation in which self-righteous people seek to invoke harsh punishment against others. It also serves on a more abstract level to illustrate Jesus's teachings about redemption, and to contrast the ideal of forgiveness and redemption with legalistic ideas of adherence to a code of laws.

The parables discussed previously are about peripheral (although important) aspects of the spiritual life but the story of the woman taken in adultery can be interpreted both as a metonymic story about a peripheral aspect of spiritual life and as a metaphorical parable that deals with spirituality, salvation, or enlightenment more directly. Other parables deal exclusively with the nature of spirituality or enlightenment. A nice example is the story "No Water, No Moon":

When the nun Chiyono studied Zen under Bukko of Engaku she was unable to attain the fruits of meditation for a long time.

At last one moonlit night she was carrying water in an old pail bound with bamboo. The bamboo broke and the bottom fell out of the pail, and at that moment Chiyono was set free.

In commemoration, she wrote a poem:

> *In this way and that I tried to save the old pail*
> *Since the bamboo strip was weakening and about to break*
> *Until at last the bottom fell out.*
> *No more water in the pail!*
> *No more moon in the water!*

In "No Water," the mapping is clear. "*The old pail*" maps onto the linear intellectual striving for understanding by way of language, and Chiyono's repeated attempts to "*save the old pail*" maps onto her reflexive attempts to break through to enlightenment by use of language and reasoning. Only when "*the bottom fell out*" (her attachment to reasoning gave way) did the "*water*" (illusion and striving) "*run out.*" The role of the moon is particularly interesting in this poem; the image of the moon reflecting on the surface of the water in the pail is both quite lovely and totally illusory, since it was only the *image* of the moon in the pail – an image often used as a symbol of illusion. This illusory image ran out with the "*water,*" leaving Chiyono's mind (the "*pail,*" now "*bottomless*") empty and free of illusion.

The story with which I opened this chapter, "Trading Dialogue for Lodging," also comes from the same collection as "No Water, No Moon," characterized by Reps as "based on actual experiences" (Reps, 1957, p. xiii) but it has the quality of a humorous folktale, a "good story" that has been repeated and polished many times. Most of the stories in the Reps collection map explicitly on the pursuit of enlightenment, but "Trading Dialogue for Lodging," like the parable of the tiger and the strawberry, also supports a more direct mapping onto ordinary experience, in this case the experience of miscommunication. The younger monk believes the "silent debate" concerns his own physical imperfection – the fact that he has but one eye – whereas the visitor believes it concerns the nature of the sublime teaching: the gestures can be readily interpreted in either topic. The younger monk's egocentricity is also contrasted with the visitor's focus on spirituality, but that does not appear to be the central theme. "Trading Dialogue for Lodging" can be read simply as a bit of humor or as a parable about communication. (At a more abstract level it can also be read as a parable about the impossibility of expressing Zen insights through language *or* gesture.)

Metaphorical stories often express or expand on common conceptual metaphors. This is clear in several of the allegories discussed in Chapter 4: *Pilgrim's Progress* and *Divine Comedy* are both based on LIFE IS A JOURNEY / SALVATION IS A JOURNEY. A central feature of Zen teaching is to confront and contradict commonly accepted conceptual metaphors in a way that creates contradiction that can lead to understanding and enlightenment. A clear example is a story from Reps titled "The True Path."

Just before Ninakawa passed away the Zen master Ikkyu visited him. "Shall I lead you on?" Ikkyu asked.

Ninakawa replied: "I came here alone and I go alone. What help could you be to me?"

Ikkyu answered: "If you think you really come and go, that is your delusion. Let me show you the path on which there is no coming and no going."

With his words, Ikkyu had revealed the path so clearly that Ninakawa smiled and passed away.

A *path* on which there is no coming or going is itself a contradiction, which highlights the master's contradiction of Ninakawa's use of the JOURNEY metaphor. However, it is also interesting that the conceptual metaphor is so deeply imbedded in our language about (and presumably our understanding of) life and death that the translator used the idiom *"passed away,"* which can only be understood in terms of a JOURNEY metaphor and thus contradicts the central point of the story by echoing Ninakawa's use of "I *go* alone." This (probably inadvertently) reinforces part of the message in the story at the beginning of this chapter, by demonstrating how language customs constrain the expression of meaning. Zen parables and aphorisms often address this and other weaknesses of language, as in the story "Trading Dialogue for Lodging," discussed in the preceding.

Fables

Like religious and spiritual teachings, folk wisdom, including an understanding of human motivations and responses in ordinary interactions, is often expressed in parable-like stories. A number of these come down to us from the classical Greek era, reputedly collected and written down by a slave named Aesop; several of Aesop's fables are so familiar that their titles, or other associated expressions that index the underlying story have become commonplace aphorisms. I will discuss some of these fables in this section; I will discuss the aphorisms based on them in Chapter 7.

The Fox and the Grapes

One hot summer day a fox came across a grapevine on a high trellis, from which hung one bunch of grapes, ripening in the sun. "That's just what I need to quench my thirst," said the fox to himself. Realizing that the grapes were too high to reach from a standing position, he drew back a few paces, took a running start and jumped as high as he could, but just came short of the grapes. Again and again he tried, but each time he just missed the grapes. At last, hot, tired, and quite cross he turned his back and walked away with his nose in the air. "I am sure those grapes are too sour," he told himself.

Even readers who don't believe foxes really eat grapes are likely to process this story in some detail, with simulations of the heat and the sun beating down, the trellis with its grapevine, and the fox running and jumping

114   Parables and Fables

Thirsty fox	→	Individual with needs or desires
Grapes	→	Desired object or situation
Fox trying to get grapes	→	Individual trying to achieve desired object
"Sour grapes"	→	"I didn't want it anyway."

Figure 5.1 Concept map for "The Fox and the Grapes"

repeatedly but just failing to get the grapes. (In this age of anthropomorphized cartoon animals, the simulation fox may be running on two legs like a human.) The topic story, about people disparaging something they wanted but were unable to achieve, may not be processed at all – even if the storyteller explicitly states a moral. However, if the story is told in the context of a conversation in which a speaker has recently denigrated a previously sought object or opportunity, it is more likely that hearers will experience both the vehicle and topic stories in parallel and blend them into a single story. Figure 5.1 shows how the vehicle story maps onto a typical topic story.

Some fables are not as familiar as the aphorisms derived from them. "*Dog in the Manger*" a fairly common way of criticizing someone who needlessly interferes with another person's needs or plans, is used in a wide variety of situations, not all of which track very closely with the canonical version of the story, as retold below:

The Dog in the Manger
A sleepy dog came across the manger of an ox, filled with loose hay. "That will make a comfortable place for a nap!" he thought, "and the ox won't mind if I borrow it for a while." So he jumped in and lay down to sleep. After a while the ox returned from its afternoon labor and approached the manger to feed on some of the hay. The dog, enraged at having his lovely nap disturbed, began barking and growling at the ox, and threatened to bite it until the ox gave up and went away hungry.

As with "The Fox and the Grapes," a person hearing or reading this story with no external context is likely to experience simulations of the sleepy dog crawling into the manger and lying down in the soft hay, the hungry ox, and the dog's barking and growling when his sleep was disturbed. The hearer or reader may also experience simulations of the dog's irritation at having his sleep disturbed or the ox's hunger and disappointment, and possibly both. Again, even if the teller explicitly states the moral of the story, the audience may not map it onto a topic story in any detail unless the conversational context provides an already-activated and salient topic story.

Unlike "The Fox and the Grapes," "The Dog in the Manger" includes two characters with contradictory needs and desires. Consequently, it is possible to process the story from the perspective of either the sleepy (and presumably tired) dog who needs a comfortable place to rest or the hungry ox who needs to eat the hay the dog is lying on. According to the story the manger belongs to the ox, a fact that might dispose listeners to experience the story from the ox's perspective, as a story about a rude dog obstructing a hungry ox from its dinner. However, the dog with his need for a comfortable bed is introduced first, which could lead listeners to experience the story, from the dog's perspective, as a story about a rude ox interrupting a pleasant nap. The visual and motor simulations may be similar, but the emotional simulations experienced are likely to depend very much on the perspective from which the hearer interprets the story.

Another of Aesop's fables, "The Ant and the Grasshopper," provides an even more interesting ambiguity.

The Ant and the Grasshopper
In a field one summer day a grasshopper was hopping about, chirping and singing gaily. An ant passed by, bearing a kernel of corn twice its size back toward the anthill.

"Mr. Ant, come play and sing with me. The day is too lovely for such weary toil!"

"I am helping to lay up food for the long winter," the ant replied, "and I dare not take even a minutes rest. The winter will be long and cold, and I recommend that you do likewise."

"Why do you bother about winter?" the grasshopper asked. "There is plenty of food at present, and tomorrow is soon enough to think about that!" But the ant continued its toil, leaving the grasshopper to his singing and dancing.

When winter came, the grasshopper had stored up little food and soon found himself starving, while he saw the provident ants distributing corn and seeds from what they had stored up during the summer.

The canonical story contrasts the improvident and lazy grasshopper with the hardworking and provident ants, and implicitly maps these onto members of human society who either play and enjoy life ("*grasshoppers*") or anticipate future hardships and work hard to prepare for them ("*ants*"); see Figure 5.2.

Listeners will readily experience simulations of the actions and particularly of the emotional responses of the two characters. However, like "The Dog in the Manger," "The Ant and the Grasshopper" presents two contradictory sets of needs. Listeners may be expected to simulate the story from the perspective of the hard-working and serious-minded ant, but they might well experience it from the perspective of the playful grasshopper. This possibility is nicely realized in the cartoon version of the story,

Anthill	→	Community
Ant	→	Hardworking member of community
Grasshopper	→	Lazy and improvident outsider
Summer	→	Time of plenty
Winter	→	Time of need

Figure 5.2 Concept map for "The Ant and the Grasshopper"

prepared by Disney Studios and released by United Artists in 1934 as part of its *Silly Symphonies* series.

The cartoon shows the grasshopper playing a merry tune on a fiddle and singing "the world owes us a living." He convinces some of the ants to dance and play with him, but the queen shows up and puts them all back to work. When winter comes, just as in the Aesop version, the grasshopper is unable to find food or shelter from the cold. Starving and blue with cold, he knocks on the ants' door; they let him in and feed him. But instead of throwing the grasshopper out into the cold to starve, the queen offers to let him stay if he will play his fiddle to entertain them. The cartoon ends with the grasshopper singing, "We owe the world a living," while the ants dance and make merry. On one level, the Disney version reinforces the message of the Aesop version – it is important to work hard during times of plenty to prepare for times of scarcity. But on another level, it subverts the "work hard" message by *also* celebrating the virtues of music and merriment. In the Aesop version, the grasshopper contributes nothing and so starves. In the Disney version, the grasshopper is able to contribute according to his own talent (music and play) to enrich the lives of all.

A number of writers have invented metaphorical stories following the general pattern of the fable. A very well-known example is Hans Christian Andersen's story "The Emperor's New Clothes":

A certain emperor was famous for his vanity and his love of fine clothing, which he showed off on every possible occasion. One day a couple of rascals who were passing through the country heard of the emperor's vanity, and of the vast sums of money the emperor spent on new clothes. So they let it be known that they were weavers of the finest cloth that could be obtained anywhere. Not only were the colors of the most brilliant hues and the textures so light that they could scarcely even be felt against the skin; the cloth they wove also had a very special property, that they became invisible to anyone who was incurably stupid or otherwise unfit for the office they held. Hearing of this, the emperor summoned the two weavers of such marvelous cloth, and ordered a new suit of clothing from them. After the passage of some time, the emperor sent his first minister to see how the work progressed. When he was shown the loom and the cloth already completed, the minister could, of course, see nothing. "This will never do," he said to himself. "If I report that I cannot see the cloth, the emperor will think me unfit and turn me out of my post." So he reported to the emperor that the cloth was even more splendid than he had expected. And so the work progressed, until finally the two weavers presented the new clothing to the emperor. Like the first minister before him, the emperor could see nothing, but having put it out that the clothing was invisible only to fools and those unfit for their positions, he pretended to see and admire the clothing as the two weavers pretended to dress him in it. Then the emperor went forth, leading a procession of his courtiers, all of whom feigned admiration for the splendid clothing. All the citizens who saw them pass, having heard of the cloth's magical qualities and fearful of having their own inadequacies exposed, also exclaimed loudly over the beauty of the new clothes. Only one young child, too young to be concerned about what others might think about him, looked at the emperor and exclaimed to his mother: "But Mum! He is wearing nothing at all!"

This story presents a complex blending of characters, motives, and plot-lines. There are the two con artists with their scheme to turn the insecurities of the emperor and his staff into their own profits. There are the emperor, his ministers, and his subjects, all of whom are confronted with a contradiction between what they see and what they have let themselves be led to believe. And finally there is the young child, who may be dismayed that he cannot see what everyone else can see – or perhaps dismayed that others cannot see what is obvious to him. The reader or hearer can experience – simulate – the events of the story from any of these perspectives. Most of us will wish to identify with the child – and stop there. But it is not difficult to map the vehicle story onto topic stories of our own, stories about gullible and vain people we have known. More difficult is to enter the story world through the perspective of the first minister – or of the emperor himself, and map the vehicle story onto topic stories regarding times when we ourselves have accepted patently absurd claims as a result of pluralistic ignorance (Miller & McFarland, 1991).

Especially in the past 150–200 years, many fables have been written for the moral or emotional instruction of children. A good example is *The Little Engine That Could*, adapted by Piper (1930) from a story that had been told in several earlier versions by a series of writers.

There was once a little engine, employed about the railroad yard for small tasks such as switching freight cars from one track to another and assembling long lines of cars to be pulled by the larger, more powerful engines. One morning a long train, made up of heavy and dirty ore cars, asked for an engine to pull it up over a long, high grade. Looking at the extreme length of the train and the weight of the cars, one after another of the large freight engines made an excuse why it could not undertake the job. Finally, in desperation, the train asked the little yard engine if it would try. "I think I can," puffed the little engine as it connected itself to the long, heavy train, and as it began to pull the train up the grade it kept puffing, "I think I can. I think I can. I think I can." As it entered the steepest section of track, nearing the top of the grade, it slowed down: "I ... think ... I ... can. I ... think ... I ... can. I ... think ... I ... can." Then, as it pulled over the top and started down the other side, it puffed "I ... thought ... I ... could. I ... thought ... I could, I thought I could, I-thought-I-could, I-thought-I-could, I-thought-I-could!"

Unlike many of the classic fables and even what are now called "fairy tales," *The Little Engine That Could* was originally written for a young audience. The "little / big" contrast encourages identifying with the little engine. It is uncertain whether humans are capable of simulating the actions of a machine – the frequency with which children pretend to be automobiles, airplanes, and other mechanical contrivances suggest they can readily do so. Certainly they can enter into the story world to the extent of simulating the little engine's emotions, beginning with the feelings of inconsequentiality and inadequacy, continuing through the frustration, fear of failure, and ultimate accomplishment and elation.

Many other fables have been invented over the years. Rudolf, the reindeer whose red nose is a liability until a dense fog on Christmas Eve turns it into an asset, comes immediately to mind, along with Hans Christian Andersen's "Ugly Duckling" who turns into a lovely swan. Indeed, the general theme is a staple of children's literature, and many new examples appear every year. Their intent is partly entertainment, but as with *The Little Engine*, there is also often a strong instructional, persuasive intent, in this case to persuade children not to shrink from taking up difficult tasks or give up too easily. Their effectiveness as implements of persuasion and instruction is likely to depend at least in part on the degree to which the young children in their audience are *"transported"* into their *"story worlds,"* i.e., the degree to which children experience detailed and intense simulations of the actions but especially the emotions and thoughts of the characters in the fables.

Summary and Discussion

Like allegory, parables and fables have an overtly instructional content and function. Parables and fables are usually shorter than allegories, with a simpler narrative. They are also presented in a more realistic manner, as a story that might actually have happened. Even animal fables are presented in a realistic manner, with the animals displaying humanlike characteristics. The metaphorical and/or metonymic mapping is usually only implicit, although fables sometimes include a moral that specifies the mapping, and parables may include references to the topic story within the narrative. Allegories often include extended homilies to drive the point home; these are rarely seen in fables and, if they are present in parables they are much shorter. All three forms create a compelling story world and invite the audience to enter into the story world and experience the events as if they really happened.

Allegorical stories are usually literary creations with formal and elaborate structure of persons and places. Fables often derive from folktales; they have been shaped through a process of telling and retelling; invented fables usually imitate the qualities of folktales. Parables may also build on folktales, although real events are often shaped into parables as well.

These categories are not sharply defined, although various scholars have attempted to arrive at definitions that would support a clear distinction among the different literary forms. The different categories shade into one another, and into other literary forms like plays and novels on one end of the spectrum, and into spontaneous storytelling at the other end. They all present a vehicle story that is interesting enough to invite the audience to *"enter into"* the story and experience it as if they were participants, and at the same time to imply a topic story that is blended with the vehicle story in such a way that the events and outcomes of the vehicle story explicitly or implicitly provide information about possible or probable events and outcomes in the topic story. However, the genres also differ in the degree to which they are presented, and interpreted, primarily as instruction or as entertainment. Allegories and parables are more overtly instructional; fables, like fairy tales and other folktale forms, are presented and interpreted primarily as entertainment.

All of these genres include examples, consistent with the discussion in Chapters 1 and 3, that can be interpreted as metaphors, metonyms, or both at once.

6 Metaphorical Stories

Ordinary discourse, including political and marketing discourse as well as casual conversation, is full of stories, some quite short, some quite long. Many of these stories report actual events from the teller's experience, or from someone else's experience. Stories are often used *metaphorically*, in much the same way that religious teachers and social commentators use allegories and fables, as a way of commenting on actual events or making a point. Sometimes these everyday metaphorical stories resemble parables or fables, in that the teller develops the vehicle story fairly elaborately, but in other cases the vehicle story is sketched quite briefly, and the audience is left to fill in the details. As with allegories and parables discussed in Chapters 4 and 5, the mapping of vehicle onto topic may be explicitly stated, but it is often only implied. Metaphorical stories are particularly common in persuasive discourse such as political speeches and advertising, but they appear in many contexts including scientific writing and ordinary casual conversations.

In the *"glass ceiling"* story from her 2008 concession speech near the end of the Democratic Presidential primary campaign, discussed in detail in Chapter 1, Hillary Clinton built on a now common metaphor for the way covert sexism can limit women's career opportunities (now extended to all disfavored classes). She expanded the metaphor into a story about attempting to *"smash through the glass ceiling"* as a vehicle for characterizing her own campaign and for expressing both the frustration felt by her and her supporters and her own hope for future success. She did not explicitly map the vehicle story onto the topic of her campaign, but by shifting to a JOURNEY metaphor (*"the path will be a little easier next time"*) and by directly addressing her supporters (*"thanks to you, it's got about 18 million cracks in it"*), she made the mapping clear.

A similar example comes from Tony Blair's speech to the 2005 British Labour Party conference at Gateshead. In the opening segments of the speech, Blair used several expressions based on the commonplace JOURNEY metaphor for politics, which was already implied by the Labour Party theme, *"forward, not back"* (for a detailed discussion, see Ritchie, 2008; for a detailed comparison of Blair's use of these and other key terms with other metaphorical uses found in ordinary English discourse, see Deignan & Semino, 2010). Blair briefly introduced an ORGANIZATION metaphor for government, asserting that his role is that of a "*servant* of the people," then asserting that his "*boss*" is, *not* the Labour party or its dissident members, but "the British people." This metaphor served indirectly to address an incipient revolt among members of the party who, along with a large portion of the British electorate, had become disaffected with Blair's leadership, in part because of some of his economic policies but particularly because of his support of the war in Iraq. After musing about the early days of his tenure as prime minister, Blair explicitly addressed this disaffection by developing the NATION IS A FAMILY metaphor (Lakoff, 1996) into a "*marital spat*" story that resonates both with a common plot of comic strips and situation comedies and with a scenario common to political rhetoric (Ritchie, 2008; Deignan & Semino, 2010):

So after the euphoria, came the *steady hard slog* of *decision-making* and *delivery*. And the events that *tested* me. And the media *mood turning*, and friends sometimes being *lost* as the *big* decisions *mounted*, and the thousand little *things* that *irritate and grate*, and then all of a sudden there you are, the British people, thinking: you're *not listening* and I think: you're *not hearing* me. And before you know it you *raise your voice*. I *raise mine*. Some of you *throw a bit of crockery*. And now you, the British people, have to *sit down and decide* whether you want the relationship to continue. If you decide you want Mr Howard, that is your choice. If you want to *go off with* Mr Kennedy, that's your choice too. It all *ends in the same place*. A Tory Government not a Labour Government. (Blair, 2005, lines 30–36)

Several of the words and phrases marked as metaphorical in this passage imply stories that are not elaborated; like the allegories discussed in Chapter 4, metaphorical stories often accompany or include other metaphors. "*Steady hard slog*" develops the common WORK IS A JOURNEY conceptual metaphor in a way that characterizes it as a particularly tedious and unpleasant "*journey*." "*Decision-making* and *delivery*" builds on the conceptual metaphor DECISIONS ARE OBJECTS and characterizes executive work in terms of a story about making and delivering some kind of object.

"The media *mood turning*" is somewhat ambiguous; it suggests the conceptual metaphor POLITICS IS A JOURNEY or perhaps NEWS REPORTING IS A JOURNEY, in which case the media (as a single institution) is a '*traveler*' who '*changes direction*.' However, the word "*turning*" is also used to describe a process in which milk or some other food-stuff begins to spoil ('*turns* sour,' literally sour in the case of milk, but mood, including the collective mood of the media, is also frequently characterized as '*sour*'). This usage of "*turn*" is itself based on an implied JOURNEY metaphor, but it suggests a richer meaning for "the media mood *turning*," with much more intense perceptual simulations. "The *big* decisions *mounted*," based on IMPORTANCE IS SIZE and MORE IS UP, implies a story about large objects piling up. All of these small metaphorical stories contribute perceptual simulations to the larger story about the early years of Blair's leadership, and establish the background for the story-metaphor that begins about halfway through the passage.

"The thousand little *things* that *irritate and grate*" presents actions or habits as OBJECTS, specifically, as '*objects with a rough and pain-inducing texture.*' This marks a transition from a brief history of Blair's relationship with the voters into a metaphorical vehicle story about an *interpersonal* disagreement, by implication a fight between spouses, which serves as a metaphor vehicle to express something about the *political* disagreement (the topic of the metaphor).

"The thousand little *things* that *irritate and grate*" could fit easily into a story about either a political or a domestic relationship (or in a literal usage, into a story about camping in the desert or wearing uncomfortable clothing). Similarly, "there you are, the British people, thinking: you're not listening and I think: you're not hearing me" can be interpreted as a *literal* statement about Blair's meetings with constituents as well as his addresses to "the British people." It can also be interpreted as a metonym or metaphor based on ATTENDING TO IS LISTENING / UNDERSTANDING IS HEARING – which can be applied either to the topic story about political discourse or to the ensuing topic story about a bit of domestic violence. The transition to an interpersonal dispute is implied by "you *raise your voice*. I *raise mine*" (MORE / LOUDER IS UP), and the transition to a story about a domestic dispute becomes explicit with "Some of you *throw a bit of crockery*" (INSULTS ARE OBJECTS).

In contrast to the typical allegory or fable, Blair provides an explicit mapping of the vehicle story (a marital fight with the potential ending of divorce and remarriage) onto the topic story (the dispute within the Labour Party with the potential ending of electing a new party leader) by referring in several places to "you, the British people," culminating in "you, the British people, have to *sit down and decide* ... If you want to *go off with Mr. Kennedy*." He then brings it back to the context of the political meeting by adding as a coda "It all *ends in the same place*. A Tory Government not a Labour Government."

There is an interesting contrast between Blair's earlier use of the ORGANIZATION metaphor, in which the people are his "*boss,*" and his use of the FAMILY metaphor, in which he presents the '*wife*' with an ultimatum: "*sit down and decide.*" Popular culture typically represents the *wife* as throwing dishes; this implied mapping of *citizens* onto '*wife*' is reinforced by "*go off with* Mr. Kennedy." In any event, Blair *explicitly* states that the decision about continuing the relationship is up to "you, the British people." The prime minister / '*husband*' whose actions led to the fight clearly has no intention of changing, contradicting the implications of the "*boss*" metaphor and at the same time reinforcing the traditional model of gender roles that is implied by the pop culture *"throwing crockery"* story, and mapping these onto the party leader's relationship with citizens in general and the party in particular.

The passage ends with a transition from a metaphorical story based on POLITICS IS MARRIAGE to a metaphorical story based on POLITICS IS A JOURNEY, with "It all *ends in the same place.*" As with the opening phrases, *"things* that *irritate and grate"* and "you're *not listening,"* this transition is immediately preceded, and facilitated, by an ambiguous phrase that can apply to either vehicle or topic story. A wife thinking about leaving her errant husband might decide literally to *"go off with* Mr. Kennedy," but if the voters elect Mr. Kennedy as prime minister, they will *"go off with* Mr. Kennedy" metaphorically but not literally.

It is likely that most members of the audience were familiar with the pop culture depiction of a marital spat that includes throwing dishes, which was at one time a staple of a certain genre of comedy. Those who were familiar with the scenario are likely to have experienced a simulation in which Blair is blended with and seen as a firm (or perhaps stubborn and self-righteous) husband facing an angry and perhaps somewhat hysterical wife. Mapping *changing leaders* onto *"going off with* ..." would also be likely to activate simulations of divorce and adultery, complete with the attendant emotions – anger, bitterness, etc. Metaphorically expressing the challenge to his leadership as a pop culture *'marital spat,'* with the comic overtones reinforced by characterizing fundamental political disagreements as *"throwing a bit of crockery,"* discredits the political opposition and belittles their concerns (Deignan and Semino arrive at a similar conclusion). Comparing Blair's use of terms like *"crockery"* and the phrase *"passion and hunger"* with the appearance of these words and phrases in a large collection of English discourse, Deignan and Semino found that Blair's usage, while drawing on themes or *scenarios* familiar enough to be recognizable by members of his audience, was also rather atypical, which could have the effect of enhancing attention to both his wording and the implied metaphorical stories.

This set of interwoven metaphorical stories has a coda: Ritchie (2008) observes that Blair's use of the *'marital squabble'* scenario (and his somewhat atypical use of *"throwing crockery"*) and his casting the dissident party members in the role of a discontented housewife effectively denigrated their legitimate concerns about the direction his leadership was taking and belittled the importance of the political issues involved. Deignan and Semino reach a similar conclusion. A few months after the 2005 general election, which the Labour Party won, Blair was ousted from his position as party leader and prime minister; Labour suffered a resounding defeat at the next general election. It is entirely plausible that Blair's use of the *"throwing crockery"* story to disparage the concerns of dissatisfied voters and backbench Labour

Party members, and the political attitudes implied by this story, both contributed to these subsequent defeats.

Metaphors Expanded into Stories

Contrary to the view that familiar metaphors become completely lexicalized, so that the metaphorical meaning is processed directly as a secondary meaning of the word or phrase, speakers are often quite inventive in transforming common metaphors into stories, sometimes quite elaborate stories. One example appears in an informal focus group conversation among scientists (at a daylong meeting about communicating science to the general public; for details, see Ritchie & Schell, 2009). The participating scientists worked in the same lab and were on quite friendly terms, as demonstrated by teasing and joking throughout the session. In response to a comment about the need to be continually alert to the power of public officials over research funds, one participant, Jack,[1] remarked, "Ya. There really is *no more ivory tower.*" This remark itself implies a story in which there once was an *"ivory tower"* and maps it onto a story in which it was once but is no longer possible to conduct basic research with no worries about funding. About a minute later, another participant echoed this metaphor, and a complex collaboratively developed story ensued:

LARRY: Jack said something, one way of ... of *capturing* part of that, ah, *change of role* is ah, *no more ivory tower.* It's probably, we're, we're *not there now* ... it's probably *not too far in the future.*

JIM: I've never really *seen the ivory tower.* (Laughter)

LARRY: You haven't. They never did *let you in* did they?

JACK: Is that *what you dream about, in the night,* Jim? *Ivory tower* you just go to sleep and the first thing you get is the *seven million dollar grant* from ... to do whatever you want from the *MacArthur Foundation?* and you *go up into the ivory tower.* What the, *open pit, unstable wall*

JAN: Ya the *unstable.*

LARRY: Ya, *instead of the ivory tower, we're in an unstable foundation.*

This passage contains several brief metaphorical stories blended into a whole. Larry's initial statement expands TIME IS SPACE and CHANGE IS A JOURNEY into a story in which these scientists (and by implication the entire science community) are *'traveling'* toward a time/*'place'* where scientists will no longer be free to pursue topics that interest them without worrying about funding. Jim's quip builds on this story, but implies that the conditions expressed by the *"ivory tower"* metaphor have already vanished. Larry's comeback picks up on the *"tower"* metaphor to construct a different story, about Jim's attempt to gain entry into the privileged status of doing *'pure science.'* Jack then develops a third story, a story within a story in which securing a prized research grant is contained within a story about Jim's dreams. Finally Jack transforms the STRUCTURE metaphor implicit in "*ivory tower*" as a critique of the group's shared dependence on unreliable ("*unstable*") funding (Ritchie & Schell, 2009).

Larry's initial statement appears to have been intended to elaborate the story-metaphor mapping implied by "*no more ivory tower*" by layering the implied JOURNEY and TIME IS SPACE metaphors ("we're *not there* now ... it's probably *not too far in the future*") and mapping it onto a story about the way government and other external support for research is changing: the vehicle story implies a '*journey*' both toward the "*ivory tower*" and toward a time (metaphorically, a '*place*') where the "*ivory tower*" has disappeared. But Jim's quip altered the vehicle story by implying that, by the time he '*began the journey*,' the "*ivory tower*" had already '*disappeared*,' with the implication that he had never experienced a situation in which he did not have to struggle for research funds.

Larry's reply has the overt quality of a teasing put-down: "never did *let you in*" implies that Jim had perhaps sought '*admission*' and had been found unworthy or unqualified. The language, "*let you in*," literally refers to entry into a place (the "*ivory tower*") but is also consistent with being admitted to or excluded from some exclusive or elite place or organization (A GROUP / STATUS IS A LOCATION IN SPACE). Jack's question "Is that *what you dream about, in the night*," appears initially to have been intended as an elaboration of Larry's teasing put-down. However, he continued the story about Jim's dream, blending the vehicle and topic stories into a "*dream*"/aspiration story in a way that is possible only in dreams, and extended the resulting fantasy as a metaphor for the situation they all face as scientists trying to do basic research in a government-funded laboratory, and bringing Jim back into the group (Ritchie & Schell, 2009). It is likely that these transitions were accompanied by and facilitated by perceptual simulations – a visual simulation of an ivory tower, accompanied by activation of factual knowledge about science funding, a visual simulation of Jim, standing forlornly in front of the locked door of a tower, accompanied by a simulation of relevant emotions, simulations of dreaming and of the experience of receiving a '*no-strings*' research grant, and finally simulations of a tower built on crumbling foundations.

Another example of a transformed idiomatic metaphor appeared in a conversation among a group of four African American men about public safety and police-community relations (for details, see Ritchie, 2010). The speaker, Willard, had made several remarks critical of lax child discipline in homes and schools, and about the failure of community members to hold adolescents accountable for their anti-social activities. After another speaker made a long speech critical of police officers' rough treatment of people they arrest on suspicion of committing a crime, Willard replied with a story metaphor based on a creative transformation of a commonplace idiom, *'we're all in the same boat'*: "it's like someone in a boat and saying, 'Well look I'm just gonna *put a hole in the boat* so I can *get me some water.*' No, *everybody goes down. Everybody goes down.*"

In this passage the vehicle story is abbreviated; listeners are expected to fill in the result of knocking a hole in the boat and understand why *"everybody goes down."* The topic story and the vehicle-topic mapping are also left unspoken, to be filled in by the listeners: If juvenile delinquents are allowed to disrupt (*"put a hole in"*) the moral, legal, and social norms and institutions that make civil life possible (*"the boat"*), then everyone in the community will suffer the consequences (*"go down"*). The ability of audience members to enter into the story world of the vehicle story (a person sitting with other people in a boat and deliberately putting a hole in the boat) and blend it with the topic story is vital to the effectiveness of this story.

In a 2003 public meeting about an incident in which police officers shot and killed Kendra James, an unarmed African American woman (Ritchie, 2011a; Ritchie & Cameron, 2014), a participant created a metaphorical story by ironically contrasting the meaning of the conventional metaphor, *"blind justice,"* with the literal meaning of *blind*. The speaker had just criticized the district attorney for failing to seek an indictment of the police officer who shot Ms. James, and contrasted the district attorney's aggressive presentation of incriminating evidence in other criminal cases with his neutral presentation of evidence in the James case as well as in other recent excessive use of force cases. He wrapped up this criticism as follows:

Somebody said that 'justice is *blind*,' but we as Portland citizens, we need to know, or I need to know, that our elected and sworn officials are not *taking advantage of her* or us just because she's blind.

Here the speaker contrasted the customary idiomatic understanding of the metaphor *"blind"* as implying a disregard for irrelevant individual characteristics with a very different understanding of the metaphor as implying that one ignores or refuses to *"see"* blatantly manifest faults or crimes, and develops the literal meaning of *blind* into a story about officials who *"take advantage of"* the visually disabled goddess – and, by implication, get away with crimes that she is unable to see. The potential simulations, with the ironic contradictions and negations, are illustrated in Figure 6.1.

An example of a different sort comes from Cameron's (2007) analysis of the "Reconciliation dialogues" between Pat Magee, a convicted IRA terrorist, and Jo Berry, whose father was killed by a bomb planted by Magee. Berry read a poem she had written, based on a conventional *"building bridges"* metaphor in reference to their collaborative attempt to overcome the *'gaps'* between the Irish Catholic and Protestant communities. Magee transformed the *"bridge as*

Metaphors Expanded into Stories 127

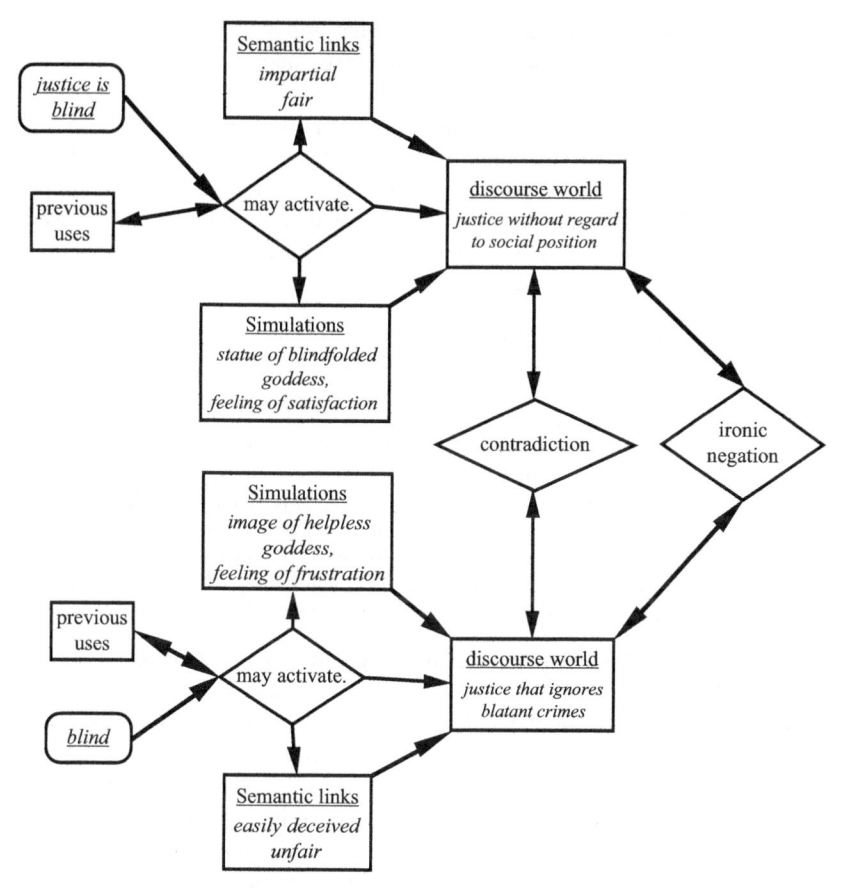

Figure 6.1 *"Blind Justice"*

connector" metaphor, with its implied story, into a very different sort of story. In immediate response to the poem he pointed out that a bridge has *"two ends"*; later he further transformed the metaphor by pointing out that bridges can *"create distances"* and *"become barriers"* (Ritchie, 2013; more detailed discussion in Chapter 7).

People often collaborate in developing metaphorical stories. In the *"ivory tower"* example, one person introduced the metaphor in a way that implied but did not elaborate a metaphorical story and other participants quickly picked up on the idea and developed different aspects of the story. A similar example comes from another conversation about police-community relations from the same series. The participants in this conversation were four "new left" activists, apparently good friends before they were brought together for this conversation. All four exhibited a somewhat subversive sense of humor; one participant in particular, Tyler, made jokes and teases throughout the conversation.

In this conversation, as in the other conversations in the series, the talk turned several times to situations in which police officers injured or killed unarmed civilians, often apparently as a result of failing to follow proper procedures. Several times during the conversation, police officers were described as "public servants." On one occasion, Tyler elaborated on this metaphor, leading to the following exchange:

TYLER: "Cops are more like a *servant*, like a *waiter or waitress*, right? So if they *fuck up*, they say, oh, I'm really sorry. You want to talk to my boss or manager?"
DEKE: "If you're a cop and you *screw up* at work, like you *pepper spray a baby*, or you shot someone who didn't deserve ... it is just weird. *Stakes are a lot higher* than they are in our jobs."
TYLER: "I'm sure. If a waitress approached you with saying, oh I'm really sorry, you said 'over medium', but I got you 'over easy'. Cops just fucking *pepper sprayed your baby*, even more so, right? [Laughter] ... They *feel a sense of 'it's a tough job*,' but fuck, you know, we all have *tough* jobs. You should be held accountable *at all levels.*"

Here, a commonplace story about working/eating in a short-order café is introduced as a metaphor for the expectation that people, including police officers, should be accountable for their mistakes. (From the transcript it appears that at least one of the participants had worked as a food server.) Although it is possible that a baby has, at one time or another, been the victim of police use of pepper spray, there is no evidence in the transcript that Tyler was referring to any actual incident. "*Pepper spray a baby*" could be understood as a blend of hyperbole with metonym, or it could be understood as a metaphor for any and all forms of police violence. The story about the waitress's rather mild mistake is contrasted here with an exaggerated (and potentially also metaphorical or at least metonymic) story about accidental police violence, with the two stories tied together by the unifying metaphor "we all have *tough* jobs" and the discriminating metaphor "*at all levels,*" which recognizes the status and responsibility difference between food servers and police officers while insisting on their similarity with respect to accountability.

This passage continues with a disruption by another participant, Celeste, that leads into a collaborative transformation of the metaphorical story into an absurd fantasy:

MICHAEL: Of course, the fallacy of that assumption ... the waitress is doing something blatantly crazy unethical,
CELESTE: Some places you get tipped more for that.
MICHAEL: Like, I love that sauce. [Laughter]

TYLER: You guys have the best soup. [Laughter]
CELESTE: We do.
DEKE: Think about that next time you order from the W——.

Here it appears that Michael intended the first statement as a continuation of the serious discussion. However, by violating the story frame and treating the metaphorical story as a literal story, Celeste opened an amusing fantasy story. Demonstrating that he did not resent the sudden shift from serious to playfully irreverent, Michael joined and built on the fantasy story, followed by the other participants.

This segment is one of several in which this group shifted abruptly between serious talk about the topic, police-community relations, and lighthearted banter. Here, the banter involved treating a metaphorical story as true. In another exchange from the same conversation, the banter involved role-playing and treating the conversation as something entirely different (Ritchie, 2010).

TYLER: Are you a cop? Are you a cop?
CELESTE: No.
TYLER: Are you a cop?
CELESTE: No.
TYLER: That's *three times*, okay. *We're cool.*

In this exchange, Tyler initiates a minidrama in which the group is engaged in a dangerous and subversive conspiracy and Celeste is suspected of being an undercover agent. The sequence ending with Tyler's closing comment about "three times" is based on the common belief among political radicals (and users of illegal drugs) in the United States, that testimony of an undercover police officer will not be admitted in a criminal trial if the officer has denied being a police officer three times. Ritchie and Zhu (2015) show that this is a type of GM (Chapter 3 and Halliday, 1998), in which one type of interpersonal interaction (jocular teasing) is "transcategorized" into and presented as another type of speech act, a hostile test of identity.

Metaphors Based on Truncated Stories

Sometimes speakers tell stories in a more or less canonical form, providing details about motivation, objective, setbacks encountered and overcome, and ultimate accomplishment of the objective. More often, part or all of this is either well-known by the listeners or can be easily inferred: speakers frequently omit large parts of a story, relate events out of time order, or merely allude to the narrative implications of a metaphor (see Chapter 7).

During the 1988 U.S. presidential campaign, Texas Agricultural Commissioner Jim Hightower asserted that "George Bush was *born on third base* (but) *he thought he had hit a triple.*" This remark blends two metaphorical stories from the game of baseball, in which a *triple* refers to a hit that allows the batter to run all the way to third base. "*Hit a triple*" metaphorically maps onto Bush's frequently repeated story about how he made his own fortune, consistent with the story, commonplace in the United States, about 'working one's *way up from the bottom.*' Being "*born on third base*" maps onto a story topic about being born in a family with substantial resources in wealth and social and political connections and relying on all of that 'social *capital*' to have a successful career. The contrast between the two metaphorical stories maps onto contrasting career success stories; together they blend into a single implicit story about a member of the moneyed elite pretending to be an "ordinary person" for the sake of political advantage.

As Jim Hightower's quip illustrates, a phrase is often used deliberately to index a story in a way that contrasts with or comments metaphorically on another story, which is either the topic of the metaphor or associated with the metaphor. Both Presidents Bush liked to characterize themselves as '*self-made* men' (a central metaphor in U.S. politics since the founding of the republic), even though both actually came from quite privileged backgrounds (George Bush Sr. was the son of former Senator Prescott Bush, a wealthy banker and son of a wealthy industrialist: the family has enjoyed a position of social, political, and financial privilege for several generations). It is reasonable to assume that the business successes of each were greatly abetted by "social capital" (the family name and social connections) and probably by financial capital – money invested by or borrowed from family members. Thus, George Bush was metaphorically "*born on third base,*" although he claimed to have "*hit a triple,*" i.e., to have made his own way by moving to Texas and earning millions in the oil industry. This is an example of a vehicle story that metaphorically maps onto a topic story.

Just as the "*knock a hole in the boat to get me some water*" story discussed earlier transforms the stock metaphor "*we're all in the same boat,*" "*born on third base*" exploits and transforms a familiar metaphor field, in this example LIFE IS BASEBALL, which provides the basis for many common metaphorical expressions. Someone who failed entirely (at courtship or other endeavors) '*struck out*' or alternatively, 'didn't even *make it to first base.*' Adolescents commonly refer to different stages in sexual activity as '*bases,*' leading to actual intercourse ('a *home run*'). A person who achieves a great success at anything is said to have '*hit a home run*' or '*hit it out of the park.*' A person who achieves a slightly less than complete success may be said to have '*hit a triple*' or '*hit a double.*' The harsh criminal laws passed in California and other states during the 1970s and 1980s that sent people to prison for life after the third felony offense were labeled '*three strikes and you're out,*' implying a metaphorical story in which a series of successful pitches (in a baseball game) is mapped onto a series of minor felony convictions (in law enforcement).

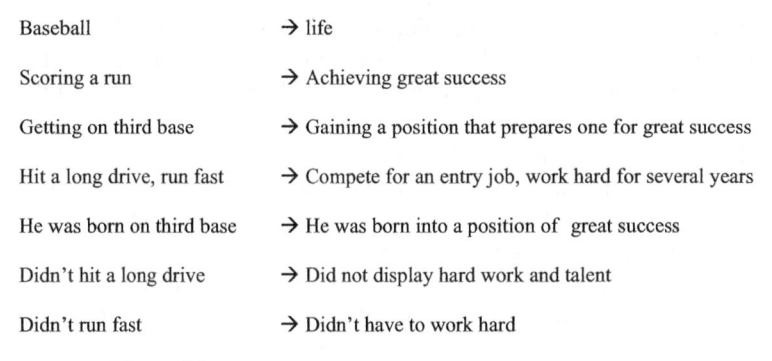

Baseball	→ life
Scoring a run	→ Achieving great success
Getting on third base	→ Gaining a position that prepares one for great success
Hit a long drive, run fast	→ Compete for an entry job, work hard for several years
He was born on third base	→ He was born into a position of great success
Didn't hit a long drive	→ Did not display hard work and talent
Didn't run fast	→ Didn't have to work hard

Figure 6.2 LIFE IS BASEBALL

The literal baseball story of getting to third base (where the player is prepared to score a run relatively easily) involves *skillful and effortful play*: hitting the ball quite far and in a way that is difficult to catch, and running fast enough to reach third base before the outfielder can throw the ball in to the infield. The LIFE IS BASEBALL metaphor maps this story onto the ordinary story of career advancement, which involves competing for a good entry-level position and working hard so as to work one's way up into a position (such as a senior management position) in which it will be relatively easy to take the next step to complete career success (Figure 6.2). Being *"born on third base"* in Hightower's quip maps onto being born into a position from which success can be obtained with little effort, and *"thought he'd hit a triple"* maps onto *claims to have worked hard like everyone else*.

In addition to mapping a political story onto a familiar sports story, Hightower's quip also accomplishes a complex bit of metaphorical framing. *"Hit a triple"* metaphorically expresses the autobiographical frame preferred by the Bush campaign (Bush achieved his success through hard work and skill); *"born on third base"* reframes the Bush autobiography in terms of inherited privilege. Moreover, the reframing itself, using the phrase "he thought he had ..."), reframes the Bush autobiographical claims as both inflated and delusional.

Metaphorical stories can also help to explain technical or complex concepts. The passage about Alzheimer's disease from *TIME*, quoted by Steen (2015) and briefly discussed in Chapter 3, is a good example.

Imagine your brain as a house filled with lights. Now imagine someone turning off the lights one by one. That's what Alzheimer's disease does. It *turns off the lights* so that the *flow* of ideas, emotions, and memories *from one room to the next* slows and eventually ceases. And sadly – as anyone who has ever watched a parent, a sibling, a spouse succumb to the *spreading darkness* knows – there is no way to *stop the lights from turning off*, no way to *switch them back on* once they've *grown dim*. At least not yet. (Nash, 2000, quoted in Steen, 2013, 182)

As pointed out in Chapter 3, the opening sentence, "Imagine your brain ..." draws attention to the fact that what follows is a metaphor, and also guides the mapping. The vehicle story tells about a house in which someone turns off the lights one by one, so that the house gradually becomes darker. There is no way to stop the person from turning the lights off, and no way to turn them back on. The sentences that tell the vehicle story are intermixed with sentences that explain how it maps onto the topic story; the middle sentence inserts another topic story about a person watching a loved one "succumbing *to the darkness*." This metaphorical story is based on a blend of two conceptual metaphors, CONSCIOUSNESS IS LIGHT / UNCONSCIOUSNESS IS DARKNESS and THE BRAIN IS A HOUSE. "The *flow* of ideas, emotions, and memories *from one room to the next* slows and eventually ceases" suggests yet a third conceptual metaphor, something like COGNITION IS LIQUID. In this example, although "*spreading darkness*" carries some negative emotional valence, most of the emotional impact seems to be provided by the topic story, that is, by "anyone who has ever watched a parent ..."

Summary

Metaphorical stories take many forms and serve many purposes. Sometimes, as in the "*throwing crockery*" example, they serve to characterize the social valuation of an event or, as in the "*born on third base*" example, to contradict and discredit an opponent's story. Often metaphorical stories are told as a way of explaining an abstract concept, as in the Alzheimer's example. Metaphorical stories also serve to establish or reinforce shared identity or values, as in the "*glass ceiling*" example from Hillary Clinton's 2008 concession speech, discussed in detail in Chapter 1. Metaphorical stories are often elaborated and embellished as a way of enhancing their entertainment value (and contributing to social bonding), as in the "*waitress*" example.

Metaphorical stories told in detail appear in many communicative contexts – in this chapter relatively detailed metaphorical stories from political speeches, health communication, and a casual conversation were discussed. Briefer metaphorical stories are probably more common in all of these contexts, if only because the more detailed stories may not hold perceivers' attention as well. Metaphorical stories are often only implied, or only the bare bones are related, as in the "*born on third base*" example. At the margins these shade into story metaphors, discussed in Chapter 7, metaphors that merely suggest or index metaphorical stories.

7 Story Metaphors and Aphorisms

As pointed out in Chapter 2, often a single word or phrase (a *story index*) is enough to activate an entire story. For example, for many people including most social scientists, *Stanford Prison Experiment* indexes a story about an oft-criticized experiment in which Stanford Psychologist Phil Zimbardo demonstrated that ordinary people, put into positions of power, will abuse that power. *Abu Ghraib* similarly indexes and activates a real-life story about a U.S. military prison during the recent Iraq war, in which Zimbardo's results were, unfortunately, confirmed. Both the experiment and the wartime incident have become metonymic representations of the broader theme.

Single words can also index, or activate, metaphorical stories. Some metaphorical words and phrases seem to invite activation of a metaphorical story – many others, which I will call *story metaphors* – either require activation of a metaphorical story in order to make sense, or become much more meaningful if a metaphorical story is activated. In this chapter, I will begin with story metaphors from some recent political speeches and other campaign material, followed by discussion of story metaphors from other discourse. Then I will discuss story metaphors implied by aphorisms, including aphorisms that, themselves, are derived from and index parables and fables. Finally, I will address the question of which metaphors do and which do not invite or require activation of a metaphorical story, and what factors influence whether a metaphorical story is activated. That is, what makes a metaphor a *story metaphor*?

Metaphors That Allude to, Invite, or Require Stories

During one of the 2012 Republican Presidential primary debates, Governor Rick Perry referred to Mitt Romney as a "*vulture capitalist.*" On the surface this is a nominal metaphor, simply associating Romney with a culturally disfavored bird, and it is quite possible that some of those who heard the comment processed it as a simple nominal metaphor. By way of comparison, when U.S. Civil War General McClellan repeatedly called Abraham Lincoln

a. Simple transfer of qualities

"*Vulture*"	→	Romney
Ugly	→	Ugly
Smelly	→	Smelly

b. Transfer of qualities after metaphorical interpretation

"*Vulture*"	→	Romney
'*Ugly*'	→	undesirable outcomes
'*Smelly*'	→	immoral or unethical

Figure 7.1 "*Vulture Capitalist*" as transfer of qualities

a "*gorilla*," presumably his intention was to map qualities associated in the popular imagination with that animal, such as ugliness and ungainliness, onto Lincoln. Similarly, Perry's metaphor could be understood as a simple transfer of qualities associated in popular culture with vultures, such as ugly, smelly, and ungainly. More likely, these qualities would be metaphorically interpreted and mapped onto metaphorically-implied personality characteristics (Ritchie, 2003a).

The mapping, shown in Figure 7.1, would draw on conventional metaphors: '*ugly*' is often applied to a policy or action proposal with the implication that it is either difficult to implement or is likely to have undesirable consequences. '*Smelly*' is often used, along with the related vehicle, '*rotten*,' to imply moral or ethical '*corruption*,' i.e., that a particular action is unethical or that a person is prone to unethical or immoral behavior. Compare "Something's *rotten* in the State of Denmark" (Shakespeare, *Hamlet*, act I, scene 4) and "I *smell a rat*," attributed to Patrick Henry and Big Mama Thornton, among many others.

Although the interpretation as a simple nominative metaphor is plausible, "*vulture*" also indexes a culturally familiar story, in which vultures spot a dying animal, circle around, then descend and strip the flesh off the animal's bones. The ready accessibility of this vehicle story, along with the political and historical context, invites a more elaborated interpretation of the metaphor.

A major theme in Romney's campaign was his claim to managerial competence, based on his role in managing the 2002 Winter Olympics in Salt Lake City and his career as a co-owner of Bain Capital, a venture capital firm. One of the primary ways Bain Capital makes money is by purchasing companies that are failing; usually these companies have assets worth much more than the market value of outstanding stock so that, if the acquiring firm is not able to turn the company around and make it profitable within a short time, a large profit can still be made by simply closing the company down, laying off its workers, and selling ('*stripping*') its assets.[1] The acquiring firm often burdens

"Vulture"	→	Romney, venture capital firms like Bain
"Looks for dying animals"	→	looks for failing businesses
"Descends on the dying animal"	→	Buys up the company's stock
"Strips off and eats their flesh"	→	Sells off their assets and keeps the money
"Hastens the animal's death"	→	Hastens the company's failure
"picks their bones clean"	→	Leaves no productive assets for future use
"Leaves babies motherless"	→	Leaves workers without jobs
"Physically cruel"/"heartless"	→	Morally and economically damaging

Figure 7.2 *"Vulture Capitalist"* as story metaphor

the company with debt to repay the purchase price of the stock, then sells the now debt-ridden and financially weakened company to other investors. Under any of these topic stories the results often include massive layoffs of the company's employees, leaving them and their communities impoverished.

The vulture is a common and widely feared symbol of death. Vultures circle in the sky above a weak or dying animal, and it is widely believed that vultures, impatient for their meal, will sometimes hasten an animal's death by starting to feast on it before it is completely dead, thereby increasing the animal's suffering (and – relevant to Perry's metaphor – leaving the animal's babies motherless in order to feed its own chicks). The image of a vulture often appears in political cartoons, sometimes as a token of death, but often as an index to a story involving vultures' reputed treatment of weak and dying animals (or prospectors).

This vehicle story about actions associated with vultures is easily mapped onto the topic stories about venture capitalists (Figure 7.2), and this mapping is supported by Perry's statements during the South Carolina primary debates, when he described two South Carolina companies purchased and closed down by Bain Capital, and summed up with the declaration that Romney and his company had *"picked their bones clean."* Interpreting the metaphor as a story metaphor greatly adds to the meaning, and makes far more sense in the context of the political debates in which it was used. Compared to the simple attribute transfer interpretation, the story metaphor interpretation is also more consistent with the commonplace role of the vulture in the popular culture of the United States, especially the popular culture of the western United States.

This mapping, shown in Figure 7.2, is reinforced (and may have been initially suggested) by the alliteration of *venture* with *vulture*; this alliteration certainly renders the metaphor more memorable, and it probably contributed to its rapid spread by making it more interesting to repeat and discuss. Later in the campaign, during the South Carolina primary, Governor Perry described two South Carolina companies that Romney's venture capital firm, Bain Capital,

"Vulture"	→	Romney
'Clears away rotting corpses'	→	Clears away weak and failing enterprises
'Recycles nutrients'	→	Frees capital and labor for other enterprises

Figure 7.3 *"Vulture Capitalist"* – extended mapping

had bought and closed down; Perry claimed that Romney and his company had *"picked their bones clean."* This phrase can only be understood as a metaphorical reference to a *'predator'* or *'scavenger'* of some sort, and supports the claim that Perry intended the phrase *"vulture capitalism,"* not as a simple nominal metaphor but as the index to a metaphorical story.

Considering the actual role of vultures in an ecosystem potentially leads to an interesting extension of the metaphorical story. In the natural environment, vultures play an important role by disposing of rotting corpses, which might otherwise spread disease, and recycling their nutrients. Apologists for venture capitalists claim that they play an analogous role in the economy, disposing of failing companies and freeing their resources for more productive uses. This would lead to something like the mapping shown in Figure 7.3. It is interesting (but not particularly surprising) that Romney's defenders did not exploit this extension of the metaphorical story. To have made this extension would have required making the story itself even more salient – and Romney's campaign staff no doubt preferred to *'let sleeping dogs lie.'*

I will take up the topic of aphorisms, including *'let sleeping dogs lie,'* later in this chapter.

Another example of a political put-down that implied a metaphorical story occurred in 1984, when Senator Gary Hart and former vice president Walter Mondale were competing for the Democratic presidential nomination. Throughout the campaign, Hart repeatedly claimed to have a large list of specific policy proposals – but he always described them in vague terms, without providing any specific details. During two televised debates prior to the New York and Pennsylvania primary elections, Mondale referred to Hart's repeated claims about the policies he would champion and his repeated failure to provide any details, then asked Hart, *"Where's the beef?"* In the United States, *'meaty'* and *'substantial'* are common metaphors for detailed and well-reasoned ideas, consistent with A DETAILED ARGUMENT IS MEAT and IDEAS ARE OBJECTS / THOUGHT IS SUBSTANCE. Like *"vulture capitalist,"* a satisfying interpretation of Mondale's metaphorical question is possible on this basis alone – but for viewers familiar with the contemporary culture of TV advertising, the question activated a story metaphor that greatly enriched the meaning.

In the months immediately prior to the Democratic primary debates, a humorous and highly successful television commercial for the Wendy's chain of hamburger restaurants featured an elderly lady played by actress Clara Peller, sitting at a fictitious competing restaurant and looking at a very small hamburger patty on a massive hamburger bun. She lifts the top of the bun, looks with an expression of dismay at the tiny beef patty, then turns toward the camera and exclaims, "Where's the beef?" Mondale's question activated the story from the Wendy's commercial as a metaphor vehicle, and mapped it onto an imagined story of voters looking for '*meat*' in Hart's policy proposals. The near absence of meat in the competing restaurant's hamburger maps onto the lack of details in Hart's proposals, implying that Peller's angry rejection of the hamburger would also map onto an equally angry rejection of Hart by the voters.

Gamson (1992, p. 23) reports another example of a conventional metaphorical idiom developed into a truncated story then transformed into a tease. At the end of a modified focus group conversation, the participants (a group of middle-aged men who knew each other quite well prior to the focus group) were chatting about their feelings about the focus group experience:

BILL: I've been *enlightened*.
PAUL: I enjoyed it.
KEN: I didn't *pull any punches* anyways ...
JOE: You didn't *throw any* either.

Ken's assertion that he didn't "*pull any punches*" implies a truncated story based on a standard idiom from boxing. While sparring (practicing) with a person of lesser ability, a skilled boxer will often "*pull* his punches," reduce their force to avoid seriously injuring the sparring partner. To "*pull one's punches*" is to reduce the force of something, such as a criticism, in order to avoid another person's feelings (see also Ritchie, 2008; Ritchie & Negrea-Busuioc, 2014).

Ken's remark implied a metaphorical mapping of the vehicle story from boxing onto the story of his own performance in the focus group discussion, implying a mapping of the expert boxer's skill and the '*power*' of the boxer's punches onto his own rhetorical skill and '*power*,' implying that he '*threw powerful punches*,' i.e., expressed strong opinions. Joe's reply, "You didn't *throw any* either," altered the vehicle story and by implication altered the topic story: Ken the '*boxer*' did not "*throw* any *powerful punches*," so Ken the focus group participant did not *express powerful or uncompromising opinions*. This takes the apparent form of a serious criticism but it is typical of spontaneous jibes among close friends, usually not to be taken seriously (Norrick, 1993; Ritchie, 2008).

In a conversation about police-community relations among a group of middle-class neighbors in an urban neighborhood (Ritchie, 2011b), one of the participants, referring to recent incidents in which police shot and killed unarmed civilians, characterized a typical alibi as follows:

whenever I hear a an officer say .. it seems like the *magic words*.. like the *get out of jail free card*.. is.. 'I felt.. that.. my life was in.. that I was being threatened or..' like these *magical phrase* that police officers it's like .. they're trained that's the word like if anything bad ever *goes down* say.. 'I felt you know I felt that my life was in jeopardy.'

The first metaphor, "*magic words*," might be construed as a straightforward descriptive metaphor, except that the word "*magic*" denotes not just a quality but an entire process. For most people it will also activate one or more stories – of stage magic performances, of passages from fairy tales and novels where a character uses some "magical" phrase to accomplish an objective. The speaker's intention was obviously to map a story of this kind onto the police officer's use of the stock phrase, "my life was in jeopardy."

The second metaphor, "*get out of jail free card*," makes sense only in reference to the popular game, *Monopoly*, in which it figures in a subplot within the larger narrative of the game, a subplot in which a player is suspended from participation ("*in jail*") and uses the card to "*get out of jail*" without paying the usual penalty. (The word "*jail*" and the phrase "*get out of jail free*" are themselves metaphors of course. Within the game, temporary suspension from participation is metaphorically described as being "*in jail*," a metaphor reinforced by a visual metaphor, a drawing of a barred window, metonymically evoking a jail cell, on the game board.) The phrase is widely used in application to any situation in which a person invokes some principle or status to excuse some logically unrelated act in an overtly nonsensical way. Any or all of these cultural stories may be activated as the metaphor vehicle in addition to or even in place of the *Monopoly* story.

Several examples of metaphors that refer to and potentially activate story metaphors can be found in Cameron's (2007) analysis of the "Reconciliation Talks," a series of conversations between Jo Berry, whose father, a Member of Parliament in the Thatcher government, was killed by a terrorist bomb and Pat Magee, the IRA operative who planted the bomb. One such example, mentioned in Chapter 6, began when Jo read a poem she wrote about "*building bridges*" between communities, a metaphor that activates a story about building physical bridges so that members of two communities previously separated by a barrier such as a body of water can communicate with each other and participate in common activities. This story maps readily onto a story about learning and developing ways to understand the perspective of members of other, previously hostile, groups (i.e., build empathy between groups) in order to communicate with each other. In response, Pat pointed out that a bridge has "*two ends*," implying that the perspectives of both groups must become part of the bridge.

At a different point, Pat developed the *"bridges"* metaphor into a fairly complex metaphorical story:

Pat: there's an inverse, to that er, (1.0) you know, er, (2.0) figure of speech you know, *bridges*. *Bridges* can be *built*. and that is if you, actively – er, create, er, .. *distances* ... *barriers* ... or what are they? they are exclusions ...(1.0) and er, .. a thing I believe absolutely fundamentally, 1652 is that er, ...(1.0) if you exclude anybody's *voice*, ... (1.0) you know, ... you're ... you're *sowing the seed* for later violence. (1.0) the way to counter that, ...(1.0) is to *build bridges* ...(1.0) the way to ensure it doesn't happen, is to *build bridges*. (Cameron, 2007, pp. 213–214)

Pat began by pointing out that a (physical) bridge can become a barrier as well as a connection. Then he introduced a different metaphor, *"sowing the seed* for later violence." This is also a fairly common metaphor, and appears in various versions throughout the Bible, for example in Galatians 6:7–9, "whatever one sows, that will he also reap." Understanding the metaphor requires activating a vehicle story about planting seeds in a field or garden. Following the *"sowing"* metaphor, Pat returned to the *"building bridges"* metaphor.

The Reconciliation talks began with Jo's desire to understand the motives that would lead someone to plant a bomb like the one that killed her father. It appears that Pat's initial motive for participating in the talks was to get Jo to understand his – and the IRA's – view of British-Irish history. However, the talks quickly developed their own logic, and both participants became committed to reconciling and bringing about peace between the two groups, a prospective story for which a story about *"building bridges"* is a conventional – and apt – metaphor.

Aphorisms

Aphorisms are short, pithy statements that capture some accepted bit of wisdom, usually in a metaphor. In most cases, the metaphor implies a metaphorical story, or requires activation of a metaphorical story to make sense. In fact, aphorisms are often based on a well-known metaphorical story such as a parable or fable, so that the aphorism indexes the parable or fable. I will begin this section with *'let sleeping dogs lie,'* introduced in regard to the situation apparently faced by Mitt Romney's staff with respect to potential positive implicatures of *"vulture* capitalist."

'Let sleeping dogs lie.' Even more than *"vulture capitalist,"* this common aphorism seems to require at least a weak activation of a story that implicitly goes something like this: a person, walking down a path or sidewalk, comes to a place where a dog lies asleep in the middle of the path, making it difficult to pass by. If the person awakens the dog in order to move it off the path, the

'Sleeping dog'	→ Implications of *"vulture capitalist"* metaphor
'Disturb the dog'	→ Argue about the interpretation of the metaphor
'Be attacked by the dog'	→ Attract more unfavorable attention to the metaphor
'Let the dog sleep'	→ Wait for people to get bored with the metaphor
'Detour around the dog'	→ Focus on other campaign issues

Figure 7.4 *'Let sleeping dogs lie'* (situation facing Romney's staff)

person might be attacked and bitten. If the person lets the dog sleep and detours around the dog, it is possible to continue onward without the risk of being bitten. This maps onto a situation, such as that faced by Romney's campaign staff, as shown in Figure 7.4.

I would not propose that the implied story is activated in this level of detail every time someone encounters a parable or aphorism of this sort; it seems plausible that sometimes a phrase like *'sleeping dog'* is processed as a lexical unit with a direct link to lexical meanings, along the lines of *it's best not to mention a disagreement if no one else does*. However, when the stories indexed or summarized by these metaphors *are* activated, the increment to processing effects is sufficiently large to justify a fairly large increment to processing effort – the stories are highly relevant.

The painting by Bruegel reproduced on the cover of this book illustrates another common saying, "*The blind leading the blind*," which is the title of the painting. The metaphor is based on KNOWING IS SEEING or UNDERSTANDING IS SEEING. So "*blind*" is often used as a metaphor for *not knowing* or *not being aware of*, as in the familiar statue of the goddess of justice wearing a blindfold (see Chapter 11). "*The blind leading the blind*" blends this metaphor with the JOURNEY or MOTION metaphor, implying that a person who is instructing someone else about a topic is equally ignorant about the topic. This implies a vehicle story about the consequences of a blind person leading another blind person that maps onto a topic story about ignorant people receiving direction from someone who is equally ignorant. As I will discuss in more detail in Chapter 11, Breugel's painting fleshes out the vehicle story and makes it explicit.

Aphorisms based on fables and parables. A familiar form of story metaphors is the fable or parable, discussed in Chapter 5. Many aphorisms refer in one way or another to a well-known story. A speaker might refer to an errant offspring as a "*prodigal son*," indexing Jesus's story with the same name. However, it is also possible that people who hear – or even people who use – this phrase may not think of or may not even know the parable, in which case they might be referring only to an offspring who behaves irresponsibly, with none of the implications of repentance and forgiveness. (A person who does not know the meaning of "prodigal" might confuse it with another word like "prodigious," and misunderstand the comment entirely. This kind of misunderstanding probably happens much more frequently than most of us realize.)

"*Sour grapes,*" indexing the story of the fox and the grapes, has also become a commonplace in ordinary speech. It is also possible to process this phrase as a metaphor without activating the fable on which it is based. One expects grapes to be sweet, and will be disappointed if they are sour; "*sour grapes*" could refer simply to a person's disappointment with an outcome that had been desired, without activating the resolution of cognitive dissonance by devaluing the outcome, as is implied by the moral of the fable.

Jesus's parable of the woman taken in sin is often indexed by simply repeating the punch line, "Let one who is without sin cast the first stone." Although the parable refers to a harsh punishment prescribed by certain religious traditions for the sin of adultery, it is routinely mapped onto criticizing anyone for any fault whatsoever. '*Adultery*' maps readily onto any socially disapproved act, and "*casting a stone*" maps onto criticizing as well as punishing. Indeed, a common variant of the metaphor is to '*cast* aspersions' regarding someone else's suspected actions or motives.

Much the same idea has also been captured by an aphorism that is apparently independent of the parable: '*People who live in glass houses should not throw stones.*' This aphorism implies, and probably requires, activation of a story about someone who throws a rock at a neighbor's house and hits his own house, or the neighbor retaliates by throwing a rock back. This metaphorical story vehicle then maps readily onto any topic story in which a person, who is vulnerable to criticism, criticizes someone else. However, the fact that all of those who had brought the woman to Jesus for judgment in the story silently slipped away strongly implies that *everyone* is guilty of some sin (everyone '*lives in a glass house*'), while '*people who live in glass houses*' seems to suggest, or at least can be interpreted as suggesting that (1) not everyone is necessarily guilty (most people do *not* live in houses made entirely of glass), and (2) only those who are guilty of some sin or fault need refrain from criticizing others.

It is common for aphorisms to abstract away from the richer meaning of the parable or other story on which they are based. Jesus's story of the Good Samaritan has to do not only with kindness to strangers, which is how the phrase "*Good Samaritan*" is often used. In the parable it is also important that several people who were supposedly holy men passed by the stricken man, ignoring his need, and that the Samaritan was not only a stranger but also a stranger from a different, and much despised, social group – who had thus every reason to ignore the needy victim. This "despised outsider" part of the story is only occasionally part of the meaning implied by use of the metaphorical aphorism in a particular context.

Another example, discussed by Moscovici (1961), comes from the Greek story about King Oedipus, as told by Sophocles. In the story, Oedipus is abandoned by his parents as an infant because of a prediction that he will kill his father. He grows up, encounters but does not recognize his father and kills him, then proceeds to his father's city, where he meets and marries his mother. Freud adapted *"Oedipus* complex" as a metaphor for the sexual and emotional maturation of boys who, Freud claims, have an innate sexual attraction to their mothers and competition with their fathers. Moscovici shows how the specific term *"Oedipus complex"* as well as the more generic term *"complex"* was taken into popular culture during the 1950s as a metaphor for all sorts of emotional difficulties, often with no identifiable relationship to Freud's actual theories or to the underlying Greek myth.

This kind of abstracting is also nicely illustrated by the common usage of *"a dog in the manger."* This is often applied to people who spoil or otherwise deprive others of objects or situations for which they themselves have no use or desire. In the fable, the dog actually does make use of the hay, but as a soft place to sleep and not as something to eat. The fable seems to be about appropriating for one's own use something that belongs to and is needed by someone else, but this aspect is often missing from the idiomatic use of the phrase.

Aphorisms in political and commercial discourse. A rather earthier example of an aphorism comes from President Lyndon Johnson's remark about J. Edgar Hoover, the controversial director of the FBI. Hoover had used his position to gather potentially embarrassing and in some cases incriminating information (*'dirt'*) about almost every public figure in the United States, including most politicians, and it was widely claimed that he had abused this information to discredit opponents and in some cases, destroy careers of people he did not like, and generally to wield a dangerous amount of power over public affairs. When he was asked why he didn't fire Hoover, Johnson commented that "It's probably better to have him *inside the tent pissing out,* than *outside the tent pissing in*" (*New York Times*, October 31, 1971).

This aphorism elaborates a relatively conventional metaphor. To *'piss on'* something or someone is to *show extreme disrespect*. In New Zealand, as exemplified in the title of an article by Fine and DeSoucey (2005), *"Taking the piss"* refers to something that might be expressed as *reacting with good humor when subjected to jocular abuse*. In the United States an exchange of vitriolic insults (in a political campaign but also in other contexts) is often referred to as a *'pissing contest'* or *'pissing match.'* 'Pissing contest' itself has a strong potential to activate a set of vivid and disgusting perceptual simulations (two 10-year-old boys urinating on each other, a scene sometimes observed during recess in elementary school). This in itself qualifies as a story index: The school-yard *pissing match* is part of a more extended narrative that may have begun with name-calling or other acts of belligerence, and is likely to end with the boys rolling around on the ground pounding on each other, then sitting in opposite corners of the principal's office. This story maps onto a political *'pissing match'* in which opponents exchange disrespectful and insulting accusations in a sequence that *"degrades"* both of them. (A related political story metaphor, also traceable to preadolescent boys, is *'mudslinging.'*)

Johnson's aphorism expands this metaphor image and locates it in a tent which, depending on what is most salient to the hearer, may be simulated as a camping tent at night or as a shade tent during the day. In any event, *"inside the tent pissing out"* may be disgusting to the other inhabitants of the tent, but not nearly as disgusting as the opposite, *"outside the tent pissing in."* These two phrases together have the effect, or at least have a strong potential to have the effect of constructing a story world (Gerrig, 1993; Green, 2004) in which Johnson and the other members of his team are together in a tent, with Hoover either inside the tent with them (hence *"pissing out"*) or outside the tent (*"pissing in"*). This story world is blended with the actual story with its own literal alternatives: either Hoover is retained as part of Johnson's government, making accusations and releasing embarrassing information about people who are *not* part of the government, or Hoover is fired from Johnson's government, and begins to make accusations and release embarrassing information about people who remain in the government (presumably including Johnson himself). Among the implications: Hoover's actions are diminished to the level of spiteful schoolboys, and by implication his political importance is also diminished. Hoover is going to be *"pissing"* in one direction or another, and Johnson can't control that. The best he can do is to control the *'direction'* of the *"piss,"* i.e., who *'gets pissed on.'* It would be difficult to understand Johnson's aphorism without activating some simulation of this sort, and it seems likely that the strength and rawness of the language promotes the hearer's *"transportation"* into the story world, thereby increasing the persuasive power of Johnson's explanation (Green, 2004; Green & Brock, 2000).

Johnson's aphorism is an example of a metaphor that may be processed through purely semantic connections, through the activation of perceptual simulations, or both. In American slang, as well as apparently in the slang of Australian and other English-speaking cultures, *'piss'* is extensively connected with a number of meanings that are likely to have been activated in the minds of those who heard or read about it. But the contrasting phrases, *"inside the tent pissing out"* and *"outside the tent pissing in,"* also have the potential to activate strong story schemas and perceptual simulations. Activation and partial simulation of these contrasting stories add a rich layer of meaning to Johnson's explanation of why he did not fire Hoover, and it would be difficult to understand the aphorism at all without at least partially activating these story schemas and accompanying simulations. At the same time, the semantic connections with other vernacular uses of *"piss"* adds to the meaning, in particular by linking Johnson, the president of the United States at the time, with many other speakers in many other social contexts.

When the vehicle is a word or phrase. According to traditional definitions a metaphor is a single word. This raises the question, to what extent does the activation and blending of stories contribute to processing metaphors in which the vehicle is a single word, or a short phrase? Since most verbs identify actions, they are probably the easiest case to deal with. When President Obama, in his Georgetown speech on the environment, declared, "It's just time for Washington to *catch up with* the rest of the country," "*catch up*" activates the idea, and most likely a simulation, of motion. In the context, it seems quite likely that a story is activated in which one person or group of persons hurries after a large group (POLICY-MAKING IS A JOURNEY); this is easily blended with the story of public opinion polls that favor a more active approach to climate change while political leaders dither.

It seems evident that the story metaphor account does not fit *some* metaphor vehicles at all well. That hoary old standard, 'Achilles is *a lion*,' is usually assumed to activate only some of the qualities associated with a lion, such as its strength, and not necessarily its activities. It is possible to think of a story about '*a lion*' that might map onto a story about *Achilles* (for example, if Achilles was accused of having killed his lover's children by a previous lover), but in the absence of a specific context there is very little to activate either the story-vehicle or the story-topic. Even more to the point '*beanpole*,' as a description of a tall, thin child activates only the physical qualities, specifically the shape, of a bean pole, and '*willow*-waisted' activates only the slenderness and suppleness associated with willows. It seems highly unlikely that any of these metaphors would activate a metaphorical story line. Similarly, 'the eagle is the *lion* among birds' (Tourangeau & Rips, 1991) has been interpreted primarily in terms of the lion's culturally-imputed qualities of "nobility" and top-of-the-food-chain dominance. But consider a different bird and a different mammal: 'the crow is the *coyote* among birds.' Although one might focus on a culturally imputed quality such as *wiliness*, that quality itself implies action, for those familiar with both animals, a story about *doing something* in a "wily" way. If the metaphor is interpreted according to Native American mythology, stories must almost inevitably become activated; similarly, if it is interpreted according to observation of actual coyotes and crows, these observations are likely to involve stories of typical behavioral sequences that can be blended.

Another of the old standards, 'cigarettes are *time bombs*,' can only be understood by activating a story-schema, or script, for *time bombs*. (As much is implied by the typical explication of this metaphor.) Growing up in the 1950s, when lung cancer research was beginning to ring the alarm bells, I more frequently heard '*cancer sticks*' and '*coffin nails.*' '*Coffin nails*' appeared as slang for cigarettes as early as the late 19th century and was a commonplace by the 1930s; it has appeared as an image in many antismoking cartoons, and is likely to activate a "still picture" perceptual simulation of a coffin with cigarettes sticking out all around the edges, but it also activates a more dynamic script in which some entity nails down the lid of a coffin, and blends it with a script of chain-smoking.

Similarly, 'some jobs are *jails*' has been explained in terms of 'unpleasant and *confining*,' but *confining* implies a story, and any way in which someone might actually utter the metaphor ('this job is *a jail!*') almost demands activation of a detailed story about the speaker's work life (the exclamation is unlikely to have any meaning otherwise) and blending it with a *jail* script. Again, I have more often heard *'dead-end job,'* which taps into A CAREER IS A JOURNEY, a conceptual metaphor that is implicitly a generic *career* script. The underlying story of MOVING ALONG A PATH also implies the possibility of *'meeting obstacles,' 'taking a wrong turn,'* and *'coming to a dead-end.'* As with other examples encountered earlier, it is conceivable that these expressions could be understood through simple lexical connections, e.g., "a job with no possibility of promotion." However, if it is encountered in a conversation that includes a topic story about the speaker's actual career, the meanings will be richer if the vehicle story is also activated.

Some nominal metaphors seem to *require* activation of a vehicle story. For example, *'bulldozer'* (discussed by Wilson & Carston, 2006; see also Ritchie, 2009) is a massive, heavy piece of construction equipment. As a metaphor for a demanding boss or obstinate negotiator, it only makes sense in terms of a story that can be blended with the story of the topic person's actions in a staff meeting or negotiation. Associated metaphors like *'push people around'* and *'run over* people' likewise require at least partial activation of a vehicle story in order to make sense. Similarly, 'a *bull in a china shop,'* without activation of a vehicle story, merely transfers a sense of *'being out of place'*. With activation of a vehicle story of wanton and possibly unintended destructiveness, it has much richer meaning.

Near the other end of the power spectrum, the rhetorical question 'are you a man or *a mouse*?' is only meaningful in the context of a story in which the topic person confronts some challenging, probably dangerous situation. Here, it is not the size, quick movements, or temperament of the mouse that is relevant. Rather it is the culturally imputed behavior of a mouse in the face of danger, and the resultant vehicle story of *'fleeing and hiding'* that blends with the topic story to produce the blended story about the disfavored behavior.

Framing Effects and Conflicting Story Metaphors: An Example from Health Communication

Thibodeau and Boroditsky (2011) argue that metaphors embedded in metaphorical stories can influence how people think about and search for information about a topic, and what solutions they deem appropriate. Mattingly (2011) identifies three metaphors widely used in medicine. Healing is '*sleuthing*,' the body is '*a crime scene*,' and the doctor is a '*detective*'; healing is '*battling disease*,' the body is '*a battlefield*' or '*war zone*,' and the doctor is a '*warrior*'; healing is '*mechanical repair*,' the body is '*a machine*,' and the doctor is a '*mechanic*.' Each of these implies a vehicle story that maps onto the topic story about treating a disease. The first maps onto a story from the familiar detective genre; the second onto a familiar genre of war stories, and the third onto the everyday story about experiencing automotive problems and taking the vehicle to a mechanic. A very different kind of story is implied by the use of '*vegetable*' and '*vegetative state*' to describe a patient who has experienced severe damage to the brain. At a surface level, this metaphor does not necessarily imply a story; it is just a descriptive metaphor that compares the person to a plant, which is biologically alive, but does not have a functioning nervous system. Indeed, the fact that plants do not appear to "behave" in the ordinary sense of the word would seem to rule out a story. However, ordinary people can be quite creative in using language to accomplish their objectives, and that creativity often includes transforming metaphors, even static metaphors like '*vegetable*,' into dynamic stories.

Mattingly (2011) tells a story about an infant born with severe spinal bifida who was kept alive solely by technology that sustained several of her vital biological functions. The medical staff wanted to withdraw artificial support and allow the infant to die a natural death, but the deeply religious parents wanted to keep the infant alive at all costs.

The BODY IS A MACHINE metaphor in this case was somewhat ironic because in many senses, the child was part of and kept alive by a *literal* complex of machines; the medical intervention had turned her into a kind of "*artificial baby*," more machine than person. In an attempt to convince the parents to allow them to disconnect the child from these machines, the medical staff compared her to "an *old car with a bad engine, too broken down to repair*." However, to the parents, the fact that this supportive technology was available fit within a very different story, a narrative about God's creativity, a miracle in which God used the scientists to create the technology that could save their baby and keep her alive. When a nurse warned the parents that "Your daughter's going to *be a vegetable*," the child's mother extended and developed this static metaphor into a dynamic counternarrative: "That's okay, we're going to be her *garden*. We will *water her* and she will *grow*."

What Metaphors Index or Activate Stories – and When?

How important is the activation and blending of stories in comprehending a single word or short phrase as a metaphor? Do all or even most metaphors activate associated stories or do metaphors differ with respect to their potential to activate stories associated with vehicle, topic, or both? In most of the examples in my own data, verbs used as metaphors imply actions, and these are often either sequences of actions or actions that typically occur as part of a sequence.

On this basis it seems reasonable to infer that metaphors based on action verbs have at least the potential to activate a story. Returning to the previously-quoted passage from Tony Blair's (2005) party conference speech at Gateshead, "events that *tested* me" seems to imply a narrative – an encounter with (personified) "*events*" that opposed Blair's skillful execution of plans and had to be overcome. "Media *mood turning*" presents the mood of the media as either a '*vehicle turning onto the wrong street*' or '*milk turning sour*,' itself a metaphor based on CHANGE OF STATE IS CHANGE OF DIRECTION. Both metaphor layers imply at least a brief narrative. "Friends ... being *lost*," and "decisions *mounted*" also seem to suggest metaphorical narratives that map onto subnarratives within the overall story of Blair's early years in office. On the other hand, the canonical form '*X is a Y*,' as in '*Achilles is a lion*' often implies a static state.

Counterexamples are easy to come by. Also from the Blair speech, "*irritate*" and "*grate*" both suggest a single continuing action, and map readily onto a topic verb such as *annoy*, with no obvious story implied. Nouns and adjectives also vary in the degree to which they seem likely to activate or invite activation of stories. As pointed out in the foregoing, at least in the context of a political debate, Rick Perry's metaphor "*vulture capitalist*" seems almost to demand activation of stories associated with both topic and vehicle. In contrast, when U.S. Civil War General McClellan repeatedly referred to President Lincoln as "*a gorilla*," there is no indication that he intended to activate any associated story, or anything beyond a simple descriptive insult. 'Cigarettes are *time bombs*' and '*coffin nails*' both demand activation of stories associated with both topic and vehicle – without the stories they make no sense. '*Dead-end* job' and '*dead-end* relationship' both seem likely to invite metaphorical stories (about a JOURNEY) to complete their meaning, but '*dead* battery' and '*deadly* bore' do not.

Some metaphorical words and phrases refer to or index well-known metaphorical stories such as parables and fables – "*sour grapes*," "*prodigal son*," "*Good Samaritan*." Others, like '*coffin nails*,' "*glass ceiling*," and "*vulture capitalist*," imply vehicle stories that are not necessarily spelled out, but are necessary to understand the metaphor. Conversely, communicators, including speakers, writers, and cartoonists, frequently develop metaphorical stories out of commonplace metaphors, as in the example "if she's a *vegetable*, we'll be her *garden*."

Steen's (2015) ideas about *intentionality* (discussed in Chapter 3) is helpful here. If the metaphor is novel, or has been transformed in a way that makes it seem novel, or if it is developed in more than one metaphorical phrase within the same passage or the surrounding context calls attention to the metaphorical potential of a word or phrase, hearers or readers are more likely to recognize and process it as a metaphor. By extension, if these same factors call attention to the narrative potential of a word or phrase, hearers or readers may be more likely to process it as a metaphorical story. The use of grammatical metaphor (Halliday, 1985; see Chapter 3) may also provide a cue to metaphorical intention – again, if the context calls attention to the grammatical transformation it may be recognized and interpreted as a metaphorical story, as in the example in which then Senator Obama used both the word "*divide*" and the phrase "*racial divisions*" in the same passage, thereby allowing the concept of "*divide*" to assume causal agency.

Petty and Cacioppo's (1981) Elaboration Likelihood Model (see Chapter 3) provides a more general account. They show that the degree to which people think about and elaborate on a message is influenced by both their motivation and their ability. Perceptions about the intention of the speaker, as addressed by Steen's concept of intentionality, are only part of motivation. Perceived personal relevance is also important, as is a factor Petty and Cacioppo call *need for cognition*. They described need for cognition as a kind of mental drive, but it can be conceptualized more broadly as a response to the *entertainment* or *amusement* value of an idea. A phrase like Rick Perry's "*vulture capitalist*" or Lyndon Johnson's "*outside the tent pissing in*" may motivate elaboration and further processing simply because it is amusing and may provide a rhetorical resource for subsequent conversations (or for use in a book about metaphorical stories).

Ability to process also merits closer examination. In Petty and Cacioppo's initial formulation, it included mental capacity (intelligence and verbal ability), freedom from distraction, available energy (is the person tired or fresh), and access to relevant background contextual knowledge. In the case of metaphors, contextual knowledge would include knowledge about both vehicle and topic – in the example of "*vulture capitalist*," knowledge about vultures and their culturally imputed behavior and about venture/equity capitalists and their culturally imputed behavior. Contextual knowledge also interacts with motivation; for example, a voter who favored Romney would have had a motivation to process and elaborate the metaphor that would be very different from that of a voter who favored Perry.

Petty and Cacioppo's discussion of the Elaboration Likelihood Model tacitly assumes a "*code*" model of communication, in which speaker and hearer potentially have access to the same context, the same background knowledge. This assumption is rarely true, and it is probably never true with respect to public discourse such as political speech. Ritchie and Cameron (2014) analyze a public meeting held to discuss an incident (one of a series of such incidents) in which a police officer shot and killed an unarmed African American during a routine traffic stop. They showed how both the representatives of the Police Bureau and the representatives of the African American community addressed multiple audiences, and how failure to account fully for the differences in context salience among these audiences led to the breakdown and failure of the meeting. These differences in context salience led to different interpretations of several metaphors used by both sets of speakers, and sustained the lack of mutual understanding and empathy that motivated the meeting in the first place. Generalizing from this example, it appears that access to particular contextual knowledge is at least as important as general contextual knowledge in determining whether and how metaphors will be processed. Even when metaphorical stories are elaborated and processed, they will not necessarily be the same stories, or processed in the same way, by various members of the audience. (Here again, motivation interacts with background knowledge: hearers can and often do actively *choose* which of the available contexts to consider when processing a metaphor.)

To sum up, it seems that the potential of a metaphor to activate a metaphorical story might be influenced by several factors: Is a story *necessary* for the metaphor to make sense? Are there indications in context that a speaker may have intended for a story to be activated (e.g., Governor Perry's contention that Romney's company had bought two companies and "*picked their bones clean*")? Does the metaphor have richer or deeper meaning that reward the extra processing effort if a story is activated? Is the metaphorical story enjoyable or entertaining in its own right – and does it have the potential for repetition and re-use in other communicative contexts? Finally, even when all these conditions are satisfied, it may still be difficult to predict how diverse members of an audience may interpret and elaborate the metaphorical story. I will return to this question in Chapter 11.

8 Story-Metaphors in Journalism and Public Affairs

Metaphors, including metaphorical stories as well as story metaphors and static metaphors, are abundant in public discourse, where they serve to explain complex concepts, render arcane processes in more familiar language, persuade audiences, and provide a *"frame"* to connect issues and events within an overall cultural and political theme. Chapter 9 will discuss metaphorical stories in a political speech, Chapter 10 will discuss metaphorical stories in discourse surrounding the politicized issue of climate change, and Chapter 11 will discuss metaphorical stories in editorial cartoons. This chapter will focus on metaphorical stories and story metaphors in journalism, including their potential framing effects.

Framing

As discussed in Chapter 3, understanding of discourse is influenced not only by the *"content"* but also by context, which includes the audience's understanding of what is going on – what kind of interaction is this, what kind of topic is it, and so on. Many researchers and commentators have addressed the ways journalists and other communicators use language, including metaphors, to influence the salience of a particular context, using a metaphor based on *"framing,"* which can be understood in at least two ways. A structure such as a house is built around a *frame*, which provides support for the structure and determines its general shape. A photograph, painting, or other picture is often presented within a *frame*, which separates it from both the implied scene surrounding it and the surface on which it is displayed, and draws attention to the images included within the frame. By extension, the *"framing"* of a news story or other piece of discourse such as a conversation may refer to how the parts of the story or discourse are organized (*"structured"*) or it may refer to how certain parts are made more salient and given greater importance, and other parts are excluded or downplayed.

Gamson (1992) argued that journalists present issues within *story frames* that reflect journalistic news values, which in turn represent widely accepted ideas about what kind of story will induce customers to buy and read print news, tune in to electronic news, and attend to the sponsors' ads. Iyengar (1991) distinguished between *episodic* and *thematic* frames, arguing that news media prefer to frame crime stories as *episodes*, for example, by focusing on particular crimes and confrontations between police officers and civilians and de-emphasizing *thematic* issues such as economic and social factors that exacerbate criminal activity and institutional policies and procedures that exacerbate police-civilian confrontations. Price, Tewksbury, and Powers (1997) examined media framing of issues in terms of relevant *values* such as human interest vs. financial impact and demonstrated that the values implied by language in a headline can strongly influence what readers attend to and recall as well as their subsequent opinions about the topic. In the context of interpersonal communication, Tracy (1997) analyzed interlocutors' discourse frames in 911 calls. She found that, when interlocutors frame a social interaction in divergent or contradictory ways, these frame conflicts can lead to miscommunication and failure of a communicative interaction.

Ritchie and Cameron (2014) examined the transcripts of a public meeting about a controversial incident in which police officers killed an unarmed civilian, and found that representatives of the community and the police understood and described the incident and the underlying issues through contradictory frames, leading to total failure of the meeting. From the transcript of the meeting as well as from subsequent news accounts it appears that the contradictory frames were neither acknowledged nor addressed by public officials, community leaders, or the professional facilitators hired to conduct the meeting; it is likely that these people in leadership positions were so deeply committed to their own frames that they failed even to recognize the frame conflicts. Ritchie and Cameron conclude that unacknowledged frame conflicts undermine a basic condition for accomplishing empathetic understanding, which requires that one recognize and be willing to enter into the experiential world of the Other in order to understand how the Other experiences the underlying context and events. Analyzing and identifying the Other's frames, including metaphorical frames, is an important tool for establishing the conditions for empathetic understanding in any situation of potential conflict.

These and many other studies support the claim that frames exist independently of language, but are readily activated by language. Schön (1993) argues that metaphors create frames that can influence how people understand an issue and shape public discourse (see also Lithwick, 2016; Thibodeau & Boroditsky, 2011). To the extent that they invite readers and listeners to enter into the story world, metaphorical stories and story metaphors would be expected to create particularly strong framing effects.

Story Metaphors in German and British News Coverage of the EU[1]

Musolff (2006) has proposed that metaphor use in public discourse is shaped by a particular type of story frame that he calls *scenarios*, shared by members of a discourse community. A scenario is often based on a conceptual metaphor, and includes assumptions about typical aspects of situations that provide both vehicle ("*source*") and topic ("*target*") of metaphors: participants, roles, story lines, outcomes, and conventional evaluations. Metaphors in journalism and public discourse are often based on a small number of thematic scenarios. Musolff identifies 12 broad groups: (1) building and construction; (2) social class and clubs; (3) economy and business; (4) games and sports; (5) geometry and geography; (6) life, health, and strength; (7) love, marriage, and family; (8) nature and weather; (9) performance and shows; (10) school and discipline; (11) war, fortress, and battle; and (12) way, movement, and speed (2004; 2006, p. 26). Although each of these produces static descriptive metaphors, most of the examples discussed by Musolff imply metaphorical stories.

Musolff (2006) focuses on one group of scenarios that are expressed in metaphors in recent German and British news coverage of the European Union, those based on LOVE, COURTSHIP, MARRIAGE, and FAMILY. Accordingly, these story frames implicitly establish value frames, based on values associated with family life, blended with the love and marriage story frame. The European Union is a "*family*" that is based on "*marriage*" and, in some news articles, has multiple "*parent / partners*," is shown in the following examples.

The reality behind the will-they-won't-they, *pre-nuptial dances* among aspirant members of Europe's monetary union *club*. (*The Guardian,* January 27, 1996)

This passage is initially based on an implicit descriptive metaphor "an international treaty is a *marriage*," followed by "a treaty organization is a *club*." However, the actual phrase, "will-they-won't-they, *pre-nuptial dances*" implies a vehicle story about courtship in which the couple engages in a dance or series of dances, mapping onto a topic story about prenuptial negotiations in which one or another of the partners repeatedly calls off the engagement, then says it's on again. This topic story is itself cast as a vehicle story that maps onto the negotiations about the monetary union, made explicit by the phrase "Europe's monetary union *club*":

The economic *marriage* that the eleven partners are about to *embark upon* would have needed a longer *engagement period*. This was not to be. Let's hope this *marrying in haste* does not lead to regrets at leisure. (*Suddeutsche Zeitung,* February 27, 1998; translation by Musolff, 2006, p. 29)

Here the "treaty is a *marriage*" metaphor is more explicitly stated – again implying a static descriptive metaphor. However, the passage beginning with "would have needed a *longer engagement period*" implies a story about a courtship in which the participants allow themselves insufficient time to get to know each other and be certain of their mutual suitability. The phrase "*marrying in haste*" is a version of a common idiom, "*marry in haste, repent at leisure,*" which originates in a line from William Congreve (1693), "Thus grief still *treads upon the heels* of pleasure: / Married in haste, we may repent at leisure." This line itself incorporates a metaphorical story in which Grief is personified as a person who follows another person (Pleasure) much too closely – and steps on Pleasure's heels. This story about overly hasty courtship and the subsequent *interpersonal* conflicts is mapped onto a hypothetical topic story in which the partners to the proposed Union encounter *international* conflicts. It may also be noted that "*embark upon*" is a story metaphor from an entirely different domain; it implies a metaphorical story about a person beginning a long sea voyage – a common metaphor for both marriages and political arrangements (cf. 'their marriage is *on the rocks*' and the ubiquitous '*ship of state*').

Continuing the COURTSHIP / MARRIAGE conceptual metaphor, aspirant members of the Union are described as "*lovers*," the negotiations over membership as "*courtship*," and members of the union are described as "*spouses*":

the euro, symbol of Italy's *romance* with the European Union. (*The Independent*, June 15, 1998)

Turkey must now be *wooed* to accept EU membership. (*The Independent*, December 11, 1999)

"*Marital difficulties*" are also mapped onto *political disagreements*:

Labour's *honeymoon* with the EU *appeared* to have *come to an abrupt end*. (*The Times*, December 2, 1998)

The possibility that Britain's *separation* from the European exchange rate mechanism will *end in divorce*. (*The Financial Times*, January 4, 1993)

In the "*honeymoon*" example, a story about a newlywed couple whose "*honeymoon*" (a '*sweet* month' of concord and happiness following the wedding) abruptly ends as they face the reality of irritating personal habits, financial stresses, and so on, is mapped onto the period in which the Labour Party was fully supportive of the EU, and its abrupt end in political discord. The second example activates a story about a troubled marriage in which the partners agree to a separation, fail to reconcile their differences, and eventually divorce; this is mapped onto Britain's abstention from the exchange-rate agreement and a potential outcome to the story in which Britain leaves the Union altogether. Throughout all of these examples, both marriage (the vehicle phrase and story) and international politics (the topic) are expressed in terms of the generic conceptual metaphor, JOURNEY – e.g., in "*come to an abrupt end*," the honeymoon is represented as a "*journey*" and the story of a honeymoon that "*ends in*" discord is presented as the story of a journey. This complex blend of story metaphors characterizes several of Musolff's examples.

France and Germany are often portrayed as a *"married couple,"* and Britain sometimes as a *"lover"* in a *"ménage à trois."* In their own right, these may be analyzed as static descriptive metaphors, but they often appear within a metaphorical story or a context that implies a metaphorical story, as in the following examples:

Like a *couple* whose *relationship* is *on the wane*, these *two partners* [France and Germany] feel that they have to *reassert their love for each other* ever more frequently in order to *bridge the gulf* between them. (*The Times*, September 8, 1994)

Do we want to *get into bed with* two countries whose recent record has been so *retrograde*? (*The Daily Telegraph*, February 19, 2004)

The first of these examples tells a story about a married couple in a troubled marriage and maps it onto the diplomatic relationship between France and Germany as leading partners in the EU. As with several of the other examples, both topic and vehicle stories include story metaphors from other domains entirely. *"On the wane"* presents the romantic/political relationship as an object (most familiarly the moon) that becomes or seems to become *"smaller."* *"Bridge the gulf"* is based on the conceptual metaphor DISAGREEMENT IS PHYSICAL DISTANCE: it also implies a story about building a bridge to provide a way across a great distance in space.

Member states other than "the big three" (France, Germany, and Britain) are often referred to as *"siblings / children"*:

Slovakia remains the *problem child* of the European *family*. (*Die Welt*, March 13, 1998)

How Western Europe's *grown-up* democracies treat the *foundling*-states *appearing on their eastern doorstep*. (*The Economist*, December 7, 1991)

Britain's European Union partners yesterday feted the new government's *return* to Brussels with a *warmth* which would not have *disgraced* the *biblical welcome accorded the prodigal son*. (*The Guardian*, May 6, 1997)

All of these phrases, *"problem child," "foundling-states,"* and *"prodigal son"* refer to well-known metaphorical stories that are part of the cultural context. The first two in particular have a playful tone that might invite deeper processing and extended development of the implied story, even from a reader with limited interest in the topic story.

Several of the metaphors Musolff cites refer directly to stories that have been abbreviated and indexed as aphorisms. "A *warmth* which would not have disgraced the *biblical welcome accorded the prodigal son*" directly refers to the parable, discussed in Chapter 5, which has itself achieved the status of a commonplace aphorism. "The *foundling*-states *appearing on their eastern doorstep*" is a truncated version of a familiar story about a desperately poor woman who abandons her infant on the doorstep of some well-to-do family – which has appeared as the basis for many humorous cartoons, including political cartoons. Most of these aphorisms have been applied to a wide variety of contexts, which has two potential consequences. On the one hand, their familiarity may decrease the probability that a reader will process them in any depth. On the other hand, the other contexts in which a reader has encountered them may contribute to a richer and more complex meaning if they are processed in any detail. Most of these examples also create a level of incongruity that many readers will find humorous, or at least entertaining – this may serve to motivate deeper processing and greater elaboration of the metaphor.

Citing Turner and Fauconnier (2003), Musolff argues that these scenarios blend elements of the vehicle and topic stories. His examples also illustrate another kind of blending – many of the passages he quotes blend conceptual metaphors from several domains into a single coherent scenario. "A *warmth which would not have disgraced* the *biblical welcome accorded the prodigal son*" activates the "*prodigal son*" parable, and blends FAMILY with TEMPERATURE. "*Pre-nuptial dances* among aspirant members of Europe's monetary union *club*" blends the COURTSHIP / MARRIAGE scenario with an EXCLUSIVE SOCIAL CLUB scenario. "*End in divorce ...*" and "Labour's *honeymoon* with the EU *appeared* to have *come to an abrupt end*" blend the COURTSHIP AND MARRIAGE scenario with a JOURNEY scenario. "Like a *couple* whose *relationship* is *on the wane*, these *two partners* feel that they have to *reassert their love for each other* ever more frequently in order to *bridge the gulf* between them" blends the MARRIAGE scenario with a DISTANCE metaphor for the emotional aspects of relationship – a metaphor that applies with equal ease to the vehicle, MARRIAGE, and the topic story about political arrangements. The vehicle story implies an almost pathetic attempt by two spouses to keep their passion alive through repeated verbal assurances, and the metaphorical story maps this pathos onto the political relationship.

In addition to the LOVE – MARRIAGE – FAMILY conceptual metaphor domain, the passages discussed above draw on NATURE, SPACE, and particularly the JOURNEY conceptual metaphor. In most cases these metaphors are already blended in the vehicle metaphor – they are all common in discussion of love, marriage, and family. Given that the EU was originally conceived in part as a way to put an end to more than 1,000 years of chronic warfare, the absence of WAR metaphors and the abundance of MARRIAGE, SPACE and JOURNEY metaphors in Musolff's examples is not surprising. In a different context, we might expect a quite different mixture of conceptual metaphors. In particular, in news coverage and commentary about an inherently contentious field such as law or environmental policies we might expect to see fewer FAMILY metaphors and more metaphors based on WAR and COMPETITIVE SPORTS.

The focus on MARRIAGE and FAMILY metaphors provided a resource for some very amusing visual images as well as entertaining metaphorical stories, but these metaphors and the metaphorical stories they imply also have potential consequences for how readers (as well as the commentators themselves) think about the topic. Inevitably, it implicates ideas related to the vehicle concept itself, ideas about monogamy and gender roles, and engages emotional and social commitments in a way that competes with the more '*cold-blooded*' political and economic calculations that motivated and justified creation of the EU in the first place.

Over the decades the EU story has played out in the press as a kind of political "*soap opera*," complete with "*courtship*," "*marriage*," "*children*," and finally a "*divorce*," as summed up in a CNN story under the headline "Brexit: An Often Rocky Marriage Ends in Sudden Divorce":

London (CNN) As *marriages go*, 43 years is not bad. But ever since Britain and Europe *tied the knot* in 1973, the relationship has been a *tortured* one – with arguments about money, accusations of *infidelity* and *seeping* exasperation *on both sides*. (Lister, 2016)

What role this conflation of personal and social with economic and political may have played in the Brexit vote, and what role it will play in the complex negotiations required to complete Britain's exit from the EU remains to be seen, but it seems quite likely that the emotional, social, and even legal entailments of the MARRIAGE metaphor has had and will continue to have an effect on how people think about and react to these more abstract issues. It is also likely that the domestic "*soap opera*" scenario may have helped shape the attitudes of many Brexit voters as well as their expectations of how the "*divorce*" will play out. Even as the "*marriage*" metaphor renders political union more readily understandable it also oversimplifies it and trivializes the economic and legal dimensions.

A cartoon by John Cole in the *Scranton Times-Tribune*, June 30, 2016, headlined "The Dog That Caught the Bus," uses a very different story metaphor, based on an old joke comparing an older man courting a younger woman to a dog chasing a car: "He wouldn't know what to do with one if he caught it." The cartoon shows a London double-decker bus, labeled "Britain," lying on its roof, wheels still spinning and exhaust coming out its tailpipe, dozens of eye staring out the windows. A disheveled looking dog with a tag labeled "Boris Johnson" is dangling from a loose bumper, "Brexit now" and "Vote leave" fliers dropping from his paw, with a thought bubble "Bloody 'ell ... Now what do I do?" The immediate metaphorical story compares a dog chasing a bus to Boris Johnson chasing Britain's exit from the EU, but the underlying "*marriage*" / "*soap opera*" scenario is implicit in the cultural context of the more traditional use of the metaphor as a disparaging comment on an aging roué.

In the next section, I will examine a recent article about a topic of quite a different sort, Justice Kagan's first term on the U.S. Supreme Court (Lithwick, 2011). Then I will return to the question of how these metaphorical stories might interact with their topics in the actual unfolding of events.

Story Metaphors and Metaphorical Stories in Legal Journalism

In a 2011 article in the *New York Magazine*, legal journalist Dahlia Lithwick summed up and evaluated Justice Elena Kagan's first year on the U.S. Supreme Court. Perhaps because Lithwick was trying to give a sense of the qualitative contrast between Kagan and the other justices, on the one hand, and between her own assessment of Kagan and that of other court observers on the other, the article provides a rich vein of static/descriptive lexical metaphors as well as dynamic story metaphors and short metaphorical stories.

Among the static, descriptive metaphors, the justices are described as "*tiny titans*," an ironic juxtaposition that expresses the justices' importance in terms of the race of powerful giants in Greek mythology, who ruled the world before the gods – then contrasts that figurative importance with the descriptor "tiny." In context, *tiny* could be a reference to the visual contrast between the human justices and the high bench in a very large, high-ceilinged room where they sit; it can also be read as a reference to the contrast between their frailty as individual humans and the (*"Titanic"*) importance of their office. The court is described as fostering an image of itself as "an American *oracle at Delphi*, the *closest thing* this country has to a *national church*." The suspected partisan basis for the justices' votes is characterized as evidence of "*naked* ideology." Kagan is described as *not* having been "a *frothing* ideologue" – an idiomatic descriptive metaphor apparently referring to the froth that comes from the mouth of a rabid animal. The questions she asks are described as "*incisive*," another idiomatic metaphor based on A PROBLEM IS AN ORGANISM / ANALYSIS IS DISSECTION.

Many of the otherwise static metaphors in "Her honor" appear in the context of stories, some within metaphorical stories and some in combination with metaphorical stories. The "*tiny titans*" "preside from a high bench" in a "ceremonial courtroom ... with a ceiling that *rises to the heavens*," a SPACE / MOTION story metaphor that reinforces the mythological implications of "*titans*." In another reference to Greek myth, the architecture of the Supreme Court building plus the rules barring television cameras and limited seating for spectators "reinforce the impression that the high court is *an American oracle at Delphi*, the closest thing this country has to a national church." This string of mythological metaphors almost but not quite adds up to a story about the Supreme Court as a quasi-religious institution, which maps onto an implied story about the author's (and by implication any other citizen's) experience of the court. Beyond this opening LAW IS RELIGION metaphor, Lithwick primarily employs metaphors based on WAR / VIOLENCE AND SPORTS / GAMES to characterize the Court. Some of these conceptual metaphors also show up in her characterization of Kagan, and of Kagan's actions and interactions with the court, but SPACE, JOURNEY, MOTION, and TUNING metaphors appear frequently in relation to Kagan but scarcely at all in relation to the court itself. These differences reflect Lithwick's overall focus on contrasts – between Kagan and the previously constituted court, and between how she and other observers assess Justice Kagan.

WAR AND VIOLENCE. Lithwick uses several metaphors based on a commonplace conceptual metaphor, LEGAL PROCESS IS WAR, a subset of the more general ARGUMENT IS WAR, which has been central to CMT from the outset (Lakoff and Johnson, 1980). The WAR metaphor is introduced and extensively developed immediately after the "*national church*" metaphor:

> When they agreed this month to hear the challenge brought by 26 states to President Obama's signature health-care-reform law, the justices *stepped into a defining battle* over the meaning of the Constitution, the nature of freedom, and the role of the courts.

The initial phrase introduces the topic story – the challenge to the Affordable Care Act. "*Defining battle*" is a story metaphor – it implies but does not tell a story about a violent struggle and blends it with another implied story about providing a definition for something, which is spelled out in the subsequent three phrases. "*Stepped into a defining battle*" completes the story metaphor, turning it into a metaphorical story in which someone enters violent struggle – "*stepped into*" suggests something like a warrior-hero in premodern times, armed with sword or spear, who steps forward into or in some cases ahead of a line of battle to confront a foe. The entire sentence has the potential to evoke a story about the ancient custom of trial by combat, in which a principle of law (usually guilt or innocence of an accused person, but sometimes principles of sovereignty or authority) was decided by a one-on-one battle between champions for the two sides, with the expectation that God will intervene on behalf of the Truth. The final sentence in this passage continues the WAR metaphor, then blends it with a very different conceptual metaphor, LAW IS THEATER: "The *fight* over the Affordable Care Act ... will *push* the nine justices into a *political spotlight* they say they try to avoid." Here the image, the perceptual simulation, is of a reluctant thespian pushed forward onto the stage and into the spotlight to perform; this brief story is mapped onto the Supreme Court reluctantly "*stepping forward*" to "*play a role on the national stage.*" The two metaphors blend together into a story of the Supreme Court reluctantly "*playing a role*" by participating in a "*defining battle.*" A similar blend appears in another passage, along with yet a third metaphor: "Like the confirmation process itself, *attacks on cartoon versions* of villainous justices are mostly just *theater.*"

The outcome of the Affordable Care Act case poses "the risk of *damaging* the Court's *hard-fought appearance* of *cool* judicial *detachment.*" This is another complex blend of metaphors. "*Cool*" and "*detachment*" are both idiomatic descriptive lexical metaphors, based, respectively, on EMOTION IS

HEAT and COMMITMENT IS A PHYSICAL BOND. *"Appearance"* is also an idiomatic lexical metaphor, based on TO KNOW OR BELIEVE IS TO SEE, a conceptual metaphor that also provides a basis for *"naked* ideology," but *"hard-fought"* (also idiomatic) converts it into a story about a fight to win or accomplish something, in this case a fight about the court's reputation (HAVING A REPUTATION IS BEING SEEN). The sentence blends all of these into a single story about a fight to be seen as cool and detached, which maps onto the Court's endeavors to have others believe that it approaches each case with no prior emotional commitments.

If the justices do vote on the basis of *"naked* ideology," it is feared that the result will be "a partisan *outcome* that may make Bush v. Gore *look like a fight over unpaid traffic tickets."* "[New event] will make [extreme event] look like [trivial event]" is a common idiomatic construction used to emphasize the extremity of some anticipated [new event]. In this case, the vehicle is a story about a legal dispute over the relatively trivial offense of failure to pay traffic tickets, so the expression is more accurately regarded as a metaphorical metonym – using a story about one kind of legal action to express the enormity of another kind of legal action.

Describing the style of argumentation typical of the Supreme Court, Lithwick notes that "many of the greatest judicial stylists have used rhetorical *brickbats* to *mark their territory,* to *brutalize* opponents." *"Mark their territory"* seems to refer to the proclivity of wolves, bears, cats, and other predators to claim home territory by urinating or defecating, scratching marks into tree trunks, or otherwise leaving signs of their presence in conspicuous locations around the boundaries. Humans similarly use piles of rock, posts, signs, and fences. In this version of the story the justices mark their territory by throwing pieces of brick to brutalize anyone who might dare enter in. This story is mapped onto a justice who lays claim to an area of legal expertise through insults, put-downs, and other forms of verbal arguments. The current group of justices, in particular, have come to "use the hourlong oral-argument sessions to *showcase* their own brilliance or to *batter* a colleague or the lawyer," through "rhetorical *brickbats"* and cleverly phrased legal arguments.

Explaining why justices sometimes write individual opinions instead of joining a collective deciding or dissenting opinion, Lithwick writes that "Lone opinions are a way for a justice to *lay philosophical markers,* to signal future *battles,* to *send up a flare* to like-minded justices." A *"philosophical marker"* might *"mark their territory"* but it might also *"mark the place for a future battle."* All of this tells a story of a warrior marking the place for an expected battle and shooting a flare to alert allies as to the site and summon them to join the battle. This vehicle story is mapped onto the topic story of a Supreme Court justice, writing an opinion about a current case, stating possible grounds for future arguments on the same or related topics. These ideas are then on record for the same justice or another justice (or, potentially, lower court judge or attorney arguing a future case) to use in discussing the merits of a future case.

WAR also serves as a metaphor for groups advocating a particular position on a matter before the court, and for criticism of the court itself. Lithwick relates how a *"tea-party"* group has "explicitly *targeted* the new health-care law," mapping a vehicle story about a soldier aiming a weapon at an opponent onto the tea-party group directing criticism at the health-care law. Similarly, "the health-care case has *put the high court in the national crosshairs*. Just as the country is *locked in* partisan indecision, the high court is being *attacked from all sides*." Here, the soldier is aiming a weapon by directing it so that the image of the enemy is in the crosshairs of the rifle sight. But it is not just one soldier: the attack is coming from all sides – many soldiers are aiming their weapons at the enemy. Moreover, the protagonist is locked in a space in which it is impossible to escape. Locked in is mapped onto the persistent inability of the political system to make a decision about important issues; being *"in the crosshairs"* and *"attacked from all sides"* are mapped onto criticism of the court (*"in the cross-hairs"*) from both left and right (*"from all sides"*). The effect of all these uses of the WAR metaphor is not merely to dramatize the arguments, but to present them as if they were *physically* violent, aggressive, and dangerous.

SPORTS and GAME metaphors about the court. Using a familiar GOLF metaphor, Lithwick describes the "cases *teed up* before the Court." This can be interpreted as a simple static lexical metaphor, but, especially in context, it also implies a story in which the golf ball is placed on a tee, then the golfer steps up with a driver and hits the ball more or less well; this story is mapped onto a story in which a case is placed on the Supreme Court docket, the Court considers the case, using constitutional principles, and decides the case more or less well.

Another sports metaphor implies so much violence that it almost merits inclusion in the section on WAR metaphors: "new justices ... often *go silent* during their first few weeks and months at the *verbal roller derby*." This comes two sentences after a phrase characterizing the current Court as "an extremely '*hot* bench'," a court in which "justices ask so many questions ... that counsel can't get a word in" (ACTIVE IS HOT or perhaps INTIMIDATING IS HOT). Roller Derby is an extremely rough game, involving deliberate hard physical contact between players. By itself, the phrase works simply as a lexical metaphor mapping the physical aggression of the sport onto the verbal aggression during arguments before the court. However, the early phrases, "new justices ... often go silent," map back onto the *"roller derby"* metaphor in a way that implies a story about a new member of a Roller Derby team who hangs back and refrains from entering the rough-and-tumble of the game until they have more experience, a story that then maps back onto the topic story of new justices, explaining *why* they remain silent for the first few weeks on the Court.

A third sports metaphor is attributed to Tom Goldstein, a lawyer with extensive experience arguing before the court: "You don't *snooker* Supreme Court justices." The vehicle term comes from billiards, 8-Ball pool, and other games in which balls must be sunk in a certain order. A *snooker* is when a player leaves the cue ball in such a position that the opponent's shot at the next ball is blocked, so that the only option is to play the cue ball off a cushion; "*snooker*" has come to be used as a general idiom for any action that leaves another person (usually an opponent in a game or argument) in a particularly difficult situation. The metaphorical story refers to a skillful action in pool or billiards; it maps onto a story about making an argument that would trap a justice into supporting a position he might otherwise oppose. In the context of the article, it is not clear whether Goldstein was implying that the justices are too clever and too learned to be trapped in this way, or that it would be very unwise to make an argument such that a justice believes one is attempting to lay such a trap. The metaphor can be read either way – or both.

WAR and GAME metaphors with respect to Justice Kagan. In contrast to Lithwick's treatment of the court in general, the WAR metaphors applied to Kagan are either about someone else attacking her or contrasting her *un*warlike approach with the warlike approach of other justices. For example, "one of her most vocal critics on the left, Salon's legal columnist, Glenn Greenwald, *blasted* Kagan in the spring of 2010" (EXTREME CRITICISM IS AN EXPLOSION). Similarly, "the *caricatures* of her as an *unhinged lefty bomb thrower* ignore over a year's conduct as a justice." "*Unhinged*" activates a minor story about a door that swings in an uncontrollable and unpredictable way because it is partly off its hinges; it is used colloquially to describe a mentally unstable person. "*Unhinged lefty bomb thrower*" blends this story into a larger story, familiar from newscasts and movies, of a fanatical (Communist, New Left, etc.) activist during a riot, a political demonstration turned violent, or a revolution, throwing bombs at the police or other targets. "*Caricature*" activates a story about an editorial cartoonist or a sidewalk artist who draws portraits of people – celebrities or paying customers – with certain features exaggerated for humorous effect. These two stories are blended into a single story about a caricature artist drawing exaggerated portraits showing Kagan as a mentally unstable rioter throwing bombs, and maps it onto a story about news commentators reporting on Justice Kagan in a way that greatly exaggerates her beliefs and actions in a way to make her resemble a mentally unstable political radical. The story activated by "*caricature*" reinforces the final phrase, the claim that critical columnists "ignore over a year's conduct" when they "*draw* these *caricatures*."

The same point is underscored by pointing out that Kagan has been "giving no *inflammatory* speeches ... and *setting no fires.*" Based on PASSION IS HEAT, a common conceptual metaphor, CONFLICT IS FIRE provides the basis for several idiomatic metaphors, including "*inflammatory rhetoric*" and "*setting fires*"; these are also related to "*throwing bombs.*" "Setting (no) *fires*" activates – and negates – a story about an arsonist; "giving no *inflammatory* speeches" facilitates mapping the story onto the radical rhetoric that has marked much of the recent discourse about a variety of public issues, including health care.

In contrast to more ideological approaches to discourse about controversy, Kagan is "interested in *working through* the argument ... and appealing to readers to *weigh in*, instead of *beating them down.*" Here again, several idiomatic metaphors with the potential to activate metaphorical stories are blended into a single story. If a path or road has rough and steep places, it may require considerable work to get through it; an agricultural field may also require work to get through. LOGIC IS WORK and AN ARGUMENT IS A JOURNEY combine these vehicle stories and map them onto thinking about a legal issue. Boxers and other athletes are commonly weighed before a match. Containers with more material in them weigh more than empty containers. From these common experiences come conceptual metaphors like EVIDENCE and REASONING ARE WEIGHTY and INTELLECTUALLY VALID IS PHYSICALLY SOUND. Finally, "*beating them down*" potentially activates a story about physically assaulting people who have objected to something in order to silence them. All of these common idiomatic story metaphors are blended in this passage into a contrast between a metaphorical story about cooperating with readers to "*work through*" facts and reasoning about an issue and a metaphorical story about dominating readers by "*beating them over the head*" with a volley of facts and reasons. "For her, the work of the Court isn't a matter of *crushing the opposition*; it's a matter of *finessing* it." "*Crushing*" activates an even stronger story than "*beating them down*"; however, in contrast to "appealing to readers to *weigh in*," "*finessing*" potentially activates a story schema about cleverness and persuasiveness. Both of these metaphors contrast sharply with the violence of "*crushing*" and "*beating down.*"

Two particularly interesting and rather odd contrasting stories are suggested by "Kagan seems to have *brought a Bic pen to a quill fight.*" A "*quill fight*" calls to mind both the framers of the Constitution with their quill pens, as memorialized in several paintings, and the quote, "The pen is mightier than the sword." So the story has something to do with WAR, in particular, war waged with quills. Given the emphasis among Conservative jurists on deciding cases according to the intentions of the original framers, it is reasonable to interpret a "*quill fight*" as an argument about what those intentions – the intentions of the people who used quill pens – must have been. But what about a "*Bic pen*"?

Inexpensive, common, serviceable, not at all fancy. Perhaps the intended contrast is one of class, middle-class Bic users vs. aristocratic quill users, or perhaps the contrast is between modern and functional Bic pens and old-fashioned, fussy quill pens. The context doesn't quite support either reading: "a mix of her second-person narrative and appeals to collective wisdom" seems rather to suggest a contrast between a common-sense appeal to ordinary realities and a more esoteric appeal to literal doctrines handed down over two centuries. This example shows how the basic ambiguity of metaphors can often expand their field of possible meanings even while blurring the precision of intended meanings.

Although Lithwick does mention that Kagan "logged time at the shooting range with Scalia and hit the DC opera scene with Ginsburg," she uses only one metaphor based on sports or games to describe Kagan, referring to Kagan as playing "close-to-the-vest," a common idiom based on card games in which players may hold their cards close to their chests to keep from revealing what cards they hold.

SPACE, JOURNEY, AND MOTION THROUGH SPACE. Metaphors based on WAR and SPORTS are applied to the Court as an institution, but metaphors based on SPACE and MOTION are applied to the Court in only one complex passage – blended with metaphors from at least three entirely different domains.

It's an impossibly *fine line* Supreme Court justices are expected to *walk*: They're supposed to interact with the public, yet do nothing to show that they have prejudged a dispute; to *live out in the sunlight*, but convey the impression that nothing matters to them but their *holy connection* to the constitutional text; to think and write *deeply* about important legal questions, but to *approach each case with the innocence of a newborn kitten.*

"*Walk a fine line*" can be understood as a variation on "*walk the strait and narrow path*": Along with the following explanatory phrases it tells a story about a person (a Supreme Court Justice) walking a narrow line, a passage between two hazards such that deviating to either side would be disastrous; this story maps onto a topic story about the expectation that their conduct satisfy two apparently contradictory sets of expectations. "*Walk a fine line*" might also activate a story about a test for sobriety that is often used by a police officer during a late evening traffic stop. "*Live out in the sunlight*" is also ambiguous and allows at least two different (but mutually compatible) interpretations. Based on KNOWING IS SEEING, to "*live in the sunlight*" is to "*live in the open*" where one's actions (and perhaps one's thoughts) can be "*seen*," i.e., known by all. But "*sunlight*" also contrasts with "*dark*," and can suggest a *happy* life, a *moral* life, or both. "Their *holy connection* to the constitutional text" sustains the RELIGION metaphor for the law and the Constitution that appears in several other passages. "Think and write *deeply*" uses a conventional idiomatic lexical metaphor for detailed and careful reasoning. The passage closes with a phrase that blends a JOURNEY metaphor with a very different metaphor: "*approach each case with the innocence of a newborn kitten.*" A "*kitten*" is a conventional metaphor for "cute" and "playful," but a *newborn* kitten is blind and helpless. "*Innocence*" suggests that it also lacks knowledge or preconceptions. In any event, the entire phrase seems to imply a story about a blind, helpless kitten exploring its environment – and to map this onto the story of a Supreme Court justice exploring a new case with a lack of prior knowledge, perhaps with an attitude of playful curiosity but perhaps in a state of helplessness. Again, the metaphor seems obvious on the surface but upon closer examination it is ambiguous and open to multiple interpretations, activating multiple possible metaphorical stories. In any event, the entire passage tells a complex metaphorical story about how justices should ideally present themselves.

SPACE and MOTION metaphors are applied to Kagan in several ways. She "*had a rough ride* as solicitor general" (A CAREER IS A JOURNEY; CRISES ARE BUMPS IN THE ROAD). She has expressed a "concern for civil discourse across ideological divisions" (DISAGREEMENT IS SEPARATION IN SPACE). "She is deciding her cases one at a time, without hints or promises about where she may be *moved down the road*" (AN OPINION IS A POSITION IN SPACE; ARGUMENT IS A JOURNEY). Her process of legal reasoning includes "*triangulating against* the words of the Constitution and the *constraints* of prior precedent." "*Triangulating*" is based on a practice in navigation, in which bearings are taken on at least three landmarks (or stars, in celestial navigation) and drawn on the navigational chart; the position is assumed to lie within the triangle formed by these three lines. "*Constraints*" is an idiomatic metaphor based on ARGUMENT IS MOTION IN SPACE; LIMITING ARGUMENT IS LIMITING MOTION.

A different application appears in a passage comparing Kagan's language skills to Justice Scalia, who "has been acknowledged as the Court's greatest *wordsmith*": "Kagan *nudged her way* into his literary *stratosphere*." Since the stratosphere is very high above the ground level where ordinary humans live and work, the "literary *stratosphere*" is "*very high above*" (GOOD IS UP) the level of ordinary language use. Kagan did not "*rocket into*" Scalia's "*level*" of language skill, she only "*nudged her way into*" it, a metaphor suggesting a slow, delicate, and gentle entry in contrast to the aggressive and violent motion of a rocket – consistent with the non-aggressive way she has been portrayed throughout the article.

"**Social** *tuning*." Another SPACE / MOTION metaphor interacts with a different set of metaphor vehicles: Kagan has "something that *comes from a higher –* almost *subconscious – level.*" Since "*sub*conscious" literally suggests "*below* *the level* of conscious awareness," this phrase seems self-contradictory. The contradiction is partially resolved by interpreting *"higher level"* in terms of a conceptual metaphor like GOOD IS UP and *"subconscious"* in terms of CONSCIOUS IS UP. In any event, that "something" is her *"social sonar,"* her *"highly attuned* sense of *political survival,"* her *"finely tuned* social and situational sense that allows her to *pick up* everything that's going on in a room." Sonar is a technology that uses reflected sound waves to detect underwater objects like submarines (in a military setting), schools of fish, or old shipwrecks. These three *"tuning in"* metaphors imply that Kagan has something like a *"sixth sense."* However, her *"social sonar"* occasionally fails her, leading her to act too informally or make a humorous quip that other justices do not appreciate.

As one example, Lithwick quotes a metaphorical story from Justice Kagan herself: "Kagan accused the majority of *looking for 'smoking guns,'* but in the end, *'the only smoke here is the majority's, and it is the kind that goes with mirrors.'"* In this passage, Kagan used two contrasting metaphorical stories to chide the other justices. A *"smoking gun"* refers to a story about a homicide investigation: smoke coming from the barrel of a gun is evidence that the gun has recently been fired; possession of a smoking gun is evidence of guilt. This story conventionally maps onto looking for conclusive evidence of any crime – or any other devalued action. The second phrase refers to an idiomatic metaphor, *"smoke and mirrors,"* a reference to magic shows and other performances in which mirrors are used to create an illusion and smoke is used to conceal actions performed to achieve mystifying effects. This idiom has been frequently used to express many forms of deception, including deceptive accounting practices used to conceal certain aspects of a company's performance and evasive use of language by public officials (Ritchie, 2011a; Ritchie & Cameron, 2014).

Summing up: Contrasting Justice Kagan with her colleagues. Throughout the article on Justice Kagan, Lithwick uses metaphors of WAR and VIOLENCE to characterize the other justices on the court, and contrasts them with metaphors that imply a more subtle and delicate, but firm and steadfast approach. Lithwick's metaphors for both Kagan and the other justices are active, with the singular and rather stark exception of the rather ambiguous *"newborn kitten"* metaphor for the way justices are *expected* to approach their work. Lithwick contrasts Kagan with the other justices by applying violent metaphors to the other justices and metaphors of motion and restraint to Kagan; she also explicitly states that the violent metaphors do *not* apply to Kagan. These contrasts create a *"framing story"* about Kagan's entry into and expected effect on the culture of the Court, within an overall framing story about the court itself as a turbulent and even violent place.

Like the metaphors based on Musolff's LOVE / FAMILY scenario, many of the metaphors in Lithwick's article on Justice Kagan blend story frames with value frames. The article as a whole blends story frames based on WAR, SPORTS, and JOURNEY into an overall scenario, familiar from novels and movies about topics ranging from "the teacher who tames an impossible secondary school" to "the sheriff who tames a lawless town": the mild-mannered and peace-loving but firm outsider who enters and calms a turbulent situation. The Supreme Court *before* Kagan "*stepped into a defining battle*"; the other justices use "rhetorical *brickbats* to *mark their territory*, to *brutalize* opponents" in a "*verbal roller derby*"; the Court hands down decisions that put it "*in the national crosshairs.*" By contrast, Justice Kagan is "interested in *working through* the argument," "*triangulating against* the words of the Constitution and the *constraints* of prior precedent." She displays her writing talent, not by "*rocketing into*" Justice Scalia's "*level*" of language skill, she only "*nudged her way into*" his literary *stratosphere*." Justice Kagan is not "a *frothing* ideologue," contrary to the claims of other court observers; rather she has been "giving no *inflammatory* speeches … and *setting no fires.*" In contrast to the aggressive brilliance of the other justices, Justice Kagan relies on her interpersonal and social skills, her "*social sonar,*" her "*highly attuned* sense of *political survival,*" her "*finely tuned*" social and situational sense.

Metaphorical Framing

In a 2016 commentary on journalistic use of metaphors, Lithwick observes that public discourse about crime is "*saturated* with metaphor" (METAPHOR IS A LIQUID). She explains her own use of metaphor in her writing, "sometimes to *tamp down* some of my own horror" and acknowledges the "temptation to *dip into the rich well* of metaphor" (p. 7). "*Tamp down* my horror" implies a vehicle story in which Lithwick uses metaphor as an instrument to push an unpleasant "*substance*" into the container and maps that story onto a topic story about controlling her own emotional response to crime. "*Dip into the rich well* of metaphor" expresses metaphor as liquid in an underground reservoir, a variation on a familiar metaphor for the "*sub*conscious" as a "*source*" of inspiration.

Summing up the powerful effects of metaphor, Lithwick (2016) concludes that "our job as journalists is to *probe* the '*tedious*' metaphors we have used about '*thugs*' and '*monsters*' as well as to *push back on* the facile images of victims as *china dolls and angels.*" This metaphorical story about journalists uncovering the meaning "*inside*" a metaphor expresses another familiar metaphor in which meanings are "*hidden* objects" (cf. Reddy, 1993; see Chapter 3). "*Push back on*" implies a metaphorical story in which journalists defend society against the "facile images" that are "*aggressively pushing*" against society. Throughout her essay Lithwick uses a series of metaphorical stories to characterize metaphors as active and potent – but in a hidden way that is not apparent until they are *"smoked out"* through journalistic *"probing."* Her overall claim is that metaphors are particularly potent, more than literal language, as a way of framing issues in a certain way. This claim is consistent with, and supported by, a series of experiments recently conducted by Thibodeau and Boroditsky (2011).

In a series of experiments Thibodeau and Boroditsky (2011) asked participants to read a brief story about a fictitious city of Addison. In one version, crime was presented as a *"beast preying on"* the city. In another version, crime was a *"virus infecting"* the city. Otherwise the two versions of the story were identical, and both versions included exactly the same statistics about crime in Addison. Thibodeau and Boroditsky found that the metaphorical framing had a significant influence on participants' views about the most appropriate remedy for crime as well as on their subsequent search for information about crime. When asked about the reason for their policy recommendations, most of the subjects referred to the statistics and few referred to or even seemed aware of the framing metaphor.

This study seems to support the claim that metaphors, along with other aspects of language, can have powerful framing effects. Lithwick (2016) claims that it does, and accordingly recommends that journalists select the metaphors carefully, taking responsibility for the way their metaphors will shape subsequent public debate. However, Steen, Reijnierse, and Burgers (2013) performed a replication of Thibodeau and Boroditsky's experiment, and did not find a metaphorical framing effect. They concluded that "there is another process at play across the board which presumably has to do with simple exposure to textual information" (p. 121). However, in conjunction with a replication of the 2011 study Thibodeau and Boroditsky (2015; Thibodeau, Iyiewaure, & Boroditsky, 2016) conducted two norming studies to determine how people interpret the response options used in both studies, Thibodeau and Boroditsky (2015) and Steen et al. They discovered that one item, "neighborhood watch programs," was ambiguous, and its meaning to the research participants seems to have changed between 2011 and 2015. They claim that this change in meaning explains the failure of Steen and his colleagues to replicate their original findings, and emphasize the importance of using current norming studies in experiments of this sort.

In sum, Thibodeau and Boroditsky's series of experiments found consistent and significant metaphorical framing effects, but Steen et al.'s replication of these experiments casts doubt on the conclusions and suggests a simpler and more conventional explanation for the results of the original series. Steen et al. do not claim to have proven that framing effects do not exist; rather they conclude that, if framing effects do exist, they are part of a more complex and subtle set of comprehension processes. The more elaborately developed and repeated story scenarios discussed by Musolff and the kind of metaphorical stories discussed in previous chapters of this book have yet to be experimentally tested.

The effects studied by both groups, Thibodeau and Boroditsky and the Steen group, are short-term effects observed relatively soon after exposure to a single message. The WAR and SPORTS metaphors used by Lithwick (and other journalists who cover legal issues in the United States) and the FAMILY / MARRIAGE metaphors that appear in coverage of the EU have become part of the cultural background, and may be expected to have an effect that is more subtle as well as more persistent because it becomes part of the context we use to understand future messages and future issues.

The scenarios described by Musolff, based on MARRIAGE AND FAMILY, provide a familiar and coherent framework for thinking about the European Union; many of the examples he quotes are also intrinsically amusing. Similarly, many of the metaphors in Lithwick's (2011) article on Justice Kagan and her 2016 commentary on crime reporting suggest amusing metaphorical stories, and provide entertainment that reward the reader independently of what she has to say about these topics. One function of metaphorical stories is to increase motivation to process a message and elaborate on it. If the metaphor is apt, this additional processing and elaboration may lead to a more nuanced understanding of the topic. On the other hand, if the metaphor is not apt, it may simply distract the audience from the central message. Another function of metaphorical stories is to shape and reshape the cultural context of communication about a topic in a way that influences audience expectations of and consequently their understanding of future messages about the topic.

Summary

In journalistic writing about the EU, Musolff (2006) found that metaphors were frequently based on COURTSHIP, MARRIAGE, AND FAMILY conceptual metaphors. Among other functions, these metaphors serve to personalize and in a sense humanize the participating states (and their leaders, who are often portrayed in family member roles). In her essay on recently appointed Supreme Court Justice Kagan, Lithwick drew on three other conceptual metaphors from Musolff's list of 12 broad groups. She used metaphors based on WAR / VIOLENCE and SPORTS / GAMES largely to characterize the Supreme Court as an institution, and to characterize the behavior of the *other* justices. When these metaphors appear in regard to Kagan, they appear as *contrasts* – as descriptions of what Kagan does *not* do. She is not a *"lefty bomb thrower,"* she does not *"set fires"* or *"crush the opposition."* Even her approach to rhetoric is gentle and non-violent: she did not *"rocket into"* Scalia's *"level"* of language skill, she only *"nudged her way into"* it.

Summary

In discussing Kagan, Lithwick used many JOURNEY metaphors. In addition to the *"rocket into"* / *"nudged her way into"* contrast, Lithwick tells us that Kagan "had a *rough ride* as solicitor general" and that she does not give many clues *"where* she may be *moved down the road."* To handle the complex relationships within the court she relies on her *"social sonar."*

An interesting exception to the reliance on WAR / VIOLENCE and SPORTS / GAMES to characterize the Court and the other justices is a passage in which Lithwick describes the role and identity pressures on the justices. Under constant media scrutiny, they are expected to *"live out in the sunlight."* They are expected to deliver incisive legal opinions, but they are also expected to *"approach each case with the innocence of a newborn kitten."* These metaphorical stories contrast sharply with the aggressive tone of the WAR / VIOLENCE metaphors used to characterize the behavior of the other justices. They also contrast sharply with the metaphors used to describe Kagan: having a *"social sonar,"* and a *"highly attuned* sense of *political survival"* are hardly characteristics we would associate with *"the innocence of a newborn kitten."*

These contrasts tell us something about how Lithwick sees Justice Kagan – they also say much about how she sees the Supreme Court before Kagan, and about how Kagan might change the tone of the court. Lithwick weaves a literal story about Kagan's personal and career history in with the metaphorical stories implied by these metaphor groups, but she does not tell us how the story will end.

How metaphors in general and metaphorical stories in particular affect public discourse is uncertain. Past research suggests that language can have powerful framing effects independent of content. However, experimental research on possible short-term framing effects of metaphors has yielded mixed results, consistent with the conclusion of Steen et al. (2013) that metaphorical framing effects are complex and subtle. To my knowledge no experimental researcher has yet focused on either framing effects or more general persuasive effects of metaphorical stories. Lithwick (2016) ends her essay with the conclusion that journalists "have a responsibility, when we report on crime, to place it in within a context, and locate it in the larger trends." Regardless of how the controversy over the potency of metaphorical framing plays out in future research, this seems like excellent advice.

9 Barack Obama Talks about Race

Barack Obama's campaign speech *A More Perfect Union*, from the 2008 Presidential primary campaign, provides a rich vein of metaphors. About half the metaphorical phrases in Obama's speech can be readily interpreted as static and descriptive, but the others invite, and some seem to demand, activation of a metaphorical story. Most of Musolff's metaphor scenario categories are represented: WAY – MOVEMENT – SPEED, JOURNEY AND SPACE: GEOMETRY, GEOGRAPHY, CONTAINER are particularly important to the organization of the speech. However, many of the most important metaphors in the speech do not fit any of these categories. This fact is not surprising, since the Obama speech occurred in a political and cultural context quite different from the contexts studied by Musolff and discussed in Chapter 8. The JOURNEY metaphor appears throughout Obama's speech, and SPACE is only slightly less prominent. In addition, three groups of metaphors, RELIGION, FIRE, and INHERITANCE, are particularly important to the organization of Obama's speech. Even though they are each represented by a relatively small number of metaphorical phrases, they each express ideas, and activate metaphorical stories, that are central to Obama's argument. A fourth category, "BLOOD," is represented by only one solitary – but very important – phrase. Two other categories not included in Musolff's list, OBJECTIFICATION and PERSONIFICATION are represented by several metaphors in Obama's speech – but most of these examples are relatively conventional metaphors; only a few seem uniquely important to this speech.

As with many of the other examples discussed in this book, in particular Hillary Clinton's *"glass ceiling"* metaphor discussed in Chapter 1 and the EU metaphors discussed in Chapter 8, the metaphors in Obama's speech seem even more pertinent in the light of recent events in the United States, including a spate of incidents in which African Americans were killed by police officers and police officers were attacked by African Americans, and the controversy over "political correctness" that appeared early in the 2016 presidential campaign.

Background and Audience

A More Perfect Union is an example of the importance of context for metaphor analysis and comprehension; it also provides an example of how consideration of metaphorical stories and story metaphors can contribute to understanding a sample of discourse. Although issues related to race inevitably played a role in the campaign, Obama had sought to downplay those issues and focus on more traditional political themes, particularly the economy and widespread disenchantment with the war in Iraq and other recent military engagements. On the one hand, many leaders of the African American community openly speculated on whether Obama, the child of an African man and a White woman, raised in a mostly White community by his White grandparents, was "Black enough," i.e., whether he really understood the issues confronting racial minorities in the United States. On the other hand, Reverend Jeremiah Wright, the pastor of Obama's church in Chicago and a personal friend, had made a number of statements, some during church sermons, that many observers and commentators regarded as unpatriotic. Some of these, taken out of context according to Rev. Wright's supporters, had been widely circulated via electronic media, as well as in national news broadcasts. The controversy thrust issues related to race relations to the fore of the Democratic primary, and Obama was forced to address these issues.

Obama's primary rhetorical task was to address the controversy over Rev. Wright's public statements while being fair to his longtime pastor and friend (Ritchie, 2012). He also needed to reassure African Americans that he truly understood their situation and their concerns well enough to deserve their full support during the election – and at the same time reassure mainstream White voters that he understood the problems and issues facing all Americans, and that he was campaigning to be the president of *all* citizens, not just those who belong to ethnic minorities. In brief, he had to address several distinct audiences, audiences with radically different cultural and economic experiences and issues, audiences that have experienced a shared history but experienced it from radically different perspectives.

Structure of the Speech

The speech has four distinct sections. It begins with the historical, political, and personal context. The second section details the controversy over Rev. Wright's comments, and Obama's relationship with Wright and with Wright's church. The third section details the history of economic and political struggles that underlies the current status of race relations, and the fourth section lays out an agenda for overcoming these problems and for unifying the country.

The first section opens with a brief story of the compromises required to unify the nation around a Constitution, compromises that included the *"original sin"* of including a formal recognition of slavery in the Constitution itself. It progresses to a brief personal history, relating Obama's personal story to the broader story of race relations, and culminating in a brief story of his campaign for president. The second section summarizes the controversy over Rev. Wright's statements, details the nature of his relationship with Rev. Wright and his membership in Wright's church. The third section begins with a detailed account of the *"legacy"* of slavery and racial discrimination and how it leads to the kind of bitterness reflected in Wright's controversial comments – then transitions to a parallel account of the economic and political basis of the frustrations and resentments experienced by middle-class White Americans. He then connects all of this with Wright's controversial comments, and with a critique of radical rhetoric on both sides. In the fourth section, he lays out a social agenda for empathy and unity and a political agenda for resolving the underlying economic and political problems. This section closes with a personal story of a White campaign worker, contrasting with the opening story about the Constitutional Convention.

Context

The speech was given in Philadelphia, in a convention center across the street from the historic meeting place where the U.S. Constitution was written, debated, and adopted. Obama opened his speech with a quotation from the Preamble to the Constitution, "We the people, in order to form a more *perfect union*," and referred back to the "more *perfect union*" metaphor throughout his speech. He then referred to the story of the founding of the nation, and introduced several metaphorical themes, at least three of which, RELIGION, JOURNEY, and SPACE (particularly DISTANCE / UNITY) that provide crucial frames for the entire speech:

The document they *produced* was eventually signed but ultimately *unfinished*. It was *stained* by this nation's *original sin* of slavery, a question that *divided* the colonies and *brought* the convention to a *stalemate* until the founders chose to allow the slave trade to *continue* for at least twenty more years, and to *leave* any final resolution to future generations.

The central metaphor in this passage is *"stained by ... original sin,"* a RELIGION metaphor grounded in Christian theology (see Chapters 2 and 3). *"Divided"* belongs to the SPACE group, which also arguably includes *"union."* *"Brought"* and *"continue"* belong to the group JOURNEY / MOTION THROUGH SPACE. *"Produced,"* *"unfinished,"* and *"leave"* are all OBJECTIFICATION metaphors that treat abstract concepts as physical objects; *"leave"* also implies MOTION. I will discuss these and other metaphors Obama used to frame the *history* of race relations in the United States in the next section; then I will expand the discussion to metaphors he used to discuss the controversy over Rev. Wright's remarks and, more generally, his own presidential campaign.

"The Past Isn't *Dead*"

Near the beginning of the third section of the speech, as a way of introducing the history of racial discrimination, Obama quoted William Faulkner, "The past isn't *dead and buried*. In fact, it isn't even past." Anyone who would deal with issues related to race in the United States, particularly issues concerning the status of African Americans, must address the nation-defining issue of slavery that, as Obama pointed out, was recognized and protected in the Constitution itself and ultimately led to the Civil War, and the ensuing decades of legally sanctioned racial oppression ("*Jim Crow*" laws; see Chapter 11). By a perhaps inevitable irony, the first "Black" president of the United States was not a descendant of slaves, but rather the child of a White mother and an African father. The first several paragraphs address this irony and the history of Obama's candidacy, and develop a series of framing metaphors.

"***Stained by* the *original sin* of slavery.**" About a third of the way through the speech, in the second section of the speech, Obama devoted several paragraphs to a description of Rev. Wright's church, including a long paragraph quoted from Obama's autobiographical book *Dreams from My Father*. The speech itself was in large part a response to a controversy over remarks made by Rev. Wright – many of them, as Obama explains, originally spoken in a religious context. However, in spite of the importance of religion to the speech, only two overtly religious metaphors appear in the speech. One is a reference, late in the speech, to one of Jesus's parables: "Let us be *our brother's keeper*, Scripture tells us. Let us be *our sister's keeper*." The other is the phrase quoted above, which appears at the very beginning of the speech, in which Obama tells us that the U.S. Constitution was "*stained* by this nation's *original sin* of slavery."

As I pointed out in earlier chapters, "*original sin*" is potentially ambiguous. It could easily be interpreted as referring simply to the sin committed at the time when the nation was originated, in which case the phrase is, arguably, not metaphorical but literal. *Original* also has a conventional meaning of something like "unique and creative," according to which the nation's "*original sin* of slavery" would be a sin unique to this nation – an unlikely reading, since slavery has existed throughout recorded history, in almost every culture. However, the term has a particular significance in Christian theology, as a reference to Adam and Eve's sin of disobedience (or rebellion) that led to their eviction from the Garden of Eden (see Chapter 5). It was the *first* sin committed by humans, and it was the sin that set the stage for all subsequent sin. In this sense, as it appears in the speech the phrase *is* metaphorical.

Original sin has an even more specific meaning in Christian doctrine: the guilt of disobedience is passed on from Adam and Eve to all future generations, so that even a new-born baby is a sinner by inheritance. This doctrine itself takes two different forms: For Roman Catholics in particular, original sin is a state not an act, so original sin implies that the child is already guilty at birth, but for many Protestant denominations, sin is an act not a state, and original sin merely implies that the infant is born with a *propensity* to commit sin. For the members of Obama's audience who understand the more elaborate aspects of the doctrine, "*original sin*" would activate the entire Garden of Eden story, along with the subsequent story of guilt (the Roman Catholic version) or of propensity to sin (the Protestant version), that is passed on through all subsequent generations. In Christian doctrine, original sin can be expiated only through Jesus's sacrifice on the cross. "The *original sin* of slavery" maps this story of Adam and Eve's disobedience to God onto the founding fathers' sin of recognizing the institution of slavery in the constitution itself: An entailment of this metaphorical story is that modern Americans, who have not themselves owned slaves, have inherited the guilt of slavery (the Roman Catholic version) or the propensity toward the sin of racism (the Protestant version) from previous generations. A further implication that Obama does not explicitly discuss: just as, in Christian doctrine, the original sin of Adam and Eve can be expiated (or overcome) only through Jesus's sacrifice on the cross, the original sin of slavery may require a metaphorically similar sacrifice/expiation.

"*Stain*" and the verb form "*stained by*" can, by itself, be interpreted as an idiomatic descriptive lexical metaphor, based on a conceptual metaphor that might be expressed as IMMORAL IS DIRT or perhaps more generally IMMORALITY IS MATTER OUT OF PLACE. In the context, it also activates a story in which performing some action or handling some substance causes something to become dirty or stained. This vehicle story maps onto the topic story of the Constitutional Convention compromising over slavery and including clauses that recognize a right to own slaves in the Constitution.

A person who denies that slavery was integral to Southern culture and a primary cause of the Civil War (or who does not believe that early American slave owning was morally wrong) would not understand this metaphor. Moreover, a person who lacks detailed knowledge of the traditional Christian doctrine of original sin would not experience the complete story (and might not experience any of the story) and consequently would not understand the implications of the metaphorical story for contemporary race relations. The audience can be divided into several groups with respect to this metaphor. First, not all Christians know and accept the "inherited sin" implications of the doctrine of original sin, and Obama's audience quite likely included many non-Christians as well as many people who identify as Christian but lack detailed knowledge of the theological entailments of original sin. Second, those who understand original sin as an inherited *state* of sinfulness and guilt, and those who understand it as an inherited *propensity* to commit sin would understand the metaphorical mapping in quite different ways. Third, although it seems reasonable to assume that most if not all of Obama's audience recognize slavery as a wrong, even among people who thoroughly understand the doctrine of original sin, many would protest that modern-day Whites are not in any way responsible for actions of slave-owners that took place a century and a half ago. For example, in a recent op-ed piece in the *New York Times*, Rockmore (2015) pointed out that history textbooks adopted by the state of Texas discuss slavery in passive voice, as "something that happened," obscuring the fact that individual citizens *actively* owned, exploited, and brutally abused other individual human beings. The "question that *divided* the colonies" still "*divides*" the nation, and where people are '*located*' with respect to this "*division*" is likely to have influenced how they understood this (and other) passages in the speech. To the extent that this is an accurate description of the situation, fruitful discussion about the nation's heritage of slavery and the related topic of race relations is inherently complicated and very difficult.

"*Legacy.*" In the introductory, context-setting part of the speech, after a paragraph discussing the civil rights–era struggle to realize the Constitution's promise of equal citizenship under the law (in which he introduced several metaphorical themes I will address later in this chapter), Obama gave a brief synopsis of his own personal story, including the following sentence: "I am married to a Black American who *carries within her the blood of slaves and slaveowners* – an *inheritance we pass on* to our two precious daughters." "*Blood*" is a conventional idiomatic metaphor for *genes*. It can be traced to the ancient belief that the male sperm carries the father's physical and personality traits in a bit of blood that mixes with the blood of the mother. From this ancient belief we have phrases like "*full-blooded*" and "*bloodlines*," as well as sayings like "*blood is thicker than water.*"

So what does it mean to say that Obama's wife "*carries within her the blood of slaves and slaveowners*"? This can best be understood as a reference to the story of rape and exploitation of Black women by White men that was part of the culture of slavery and persisted well into the 20th century. Like the "*original sin*" metaphor, this metaphorical story is embedded in cultural and historical knowledge (and perspectives) that are very likely *not* common to all contemporary citizens of the United States (and indeed may be unknown to many). But even among those who do know about this history, the perspectives are likely to differ quite radically. It is likely that many White members of the audience would be inclined to doubt that the sexual exploitation of slave women, and subsequently of nominally free Black women, was as widespread as it in fact was. First- and second-generation citizens might be totally unaware of the history – but immigrants who came as refugees from political oppression might understand it in terms of very different stories of sexual exploitation and oppression.

The metaphor *"an inheritance we pass on"* is also ambiguous. *"Inheritance"* implies something of value – a potential resource. In many cultures, especially traditional cultures, rape is a source of shame and stigma – not just for the rapist, but often even more for the victim. With this metaphor, Obama seems to be nullifying the shame and stigma of sexual victimization and converting it to a story of strength and survival. *"Legacy"* appears in three other passages, all three with decidedly negative valence, as I will discuss below.

The phrase "I am married to a Black American" – more precisely, the fact that Obama does not name his wife in this passage – has potential metaphorical and metonymic import. Unnamed, she potentially stands metonymically for *all* Americans who are descended from slaves. This passage also underscores the fact that Obama is *separate from* this heritage, African American by parentage but not "a descendant of slaves and slaveowners"; this is part of the reason for questions about whether he was "Black enough," and why he is not "the most conventional candidate."

Midway through the speech, in the third section of the speech Obama refers to "inequalities *passed on from* an earlier generation that suffered under the *brutal legacy* of slavery and Jim Crow." A couple of paragraphs later, he refers to a *"legacy of defeat"* that "was *passed on* to future generations" then again, to the need for the White community to acknowledge that the *"legacy* of discrimination" is real and must be addressed. This complex use of *"inheritance"* and *"legacy"* underscores the narrative and metaphorical implications of *"original sin."*

Journey

JOURNEY and MOTION metaphors have a central place in African American post-slavery culture. Slaves' only hope of freedom was to escape to the north via the *"underground railroad,"* ideally to Canada where they were out of reach of their former masters, a long and perilous journey. The story of Moses leading the Israelites out of their captivity in Egypt resonated with this story of perilous escape from bondage. More recently, the various "freedom rides" to integrate interstate buses and "freedom marches" for voting rights and other civil liberties were important and powerful features of the Civil Rights movement that led to passage of the Civil Rights and Voting Rights acts during the Johnson administration (as dramatized in the movie *Selma* [DuVernay, 2014]).

Journey 177

The passage in the first, context-setting part of the speech, in which Obama first describes the beginning of his campaign for the Democratic nomination for president, must be read in the context of this history of literal journeys and marches in pursuit of freedom and justice:

This was one of the tasks we *set forth* at the beginning of this campaign – to *continue the long march* of those who *came before us*, a *march* for a more just, more equal, more free, more caring and more prosperous America. I chose to *run* for the presidency at this moment in history because I believe *deeply* that we cannot solve the challenges of our time unless we solve them together – unless we perfect our union by understanding that we may have different stories, but we *hold* common hopes; that we may not look the same and we may not have *come from the same place,* but we all want to *move in the same direction – towards* a better future.

This passage opens and closes with apparent references to the story of civil rights marches: "*continue the long march* of those who *came before us*" and "we all want to *move in the same direction – towards* a better future." "Those who *came before us*" refers to a standard idiom for both ancestors and people who have previously been engaged in the same activities or project as the speaker, based on LIFE IS A JOURNEY and SOCIAL CHANGE IS A JOURNEY. "We may not have *come from the same place*" is a standard idiom that can be understood either literally, as referring to one's place of birth or childhood residence, or metaphorically, as referring to social class, cultural group, ideology, or other aspects of identity. As a metaphor it blends a MOTION metaphor (LIFE IS A JOURNEY) with a SPACE metaphor (IDENTITY IS A PLACE). Either way it implies a story of maturation and change along with a possible literal story of migration. "*Move in the same direction*" can be analyzed much the same way, although it is more frequent as a metaphor than as a literal statement. ("Go west, young man" and the slave spiritual "follow the *drinking gourd*" both famously advocated literally *moving in the same direction*.)

In several places throughout the speech, Obama used JOURNEY and MOTION metaphors to refer to political, economic, and social improvements ("*progress*"). In the third section of the speech he spoke admiringly of African Americans who "were able to *make a way* out of *no way* for those like me who would *come after* them." Here "*way*" is a static lexical metaphor for the opportunities and achievements – job, home, family – that constitute a fulfilling life. The vehicle in "*make a way* out of *no way*" tells a story of creating a road or path in a wilderness, where there is no apparent suitable location; it maps onto a story of creating a living – a job, home, community, and family – under circumstances where these successes appear to be impossible. There was "*no way*" because all ordinary '*paths toward*' creating a satisfying life were '*blocked*' by legal discrimination. "For those … who would *come after* them" continues the vehicle story to include future travelers who are able to use the same road; it maps onto future members of the Black community who are able to benefit from these apparently impossible achievements.

The *"path"* metaphor appears in several places, e.g., "the *path* of a *more perfect union*," often but not always in a context that implies a story, for example following the related metaphor *"continue on ..."* At the end of the speech, continuing this same metaphorical story, Obama describes a story of mutual recognition and support, which is not, in itself, enough to accomplish all that needs to be done, "But it is *where we start*."

Obama also used MOTION as a metaphor for shirking issues. Referring to the controversy over Rev. Wright's statements (near the end of the second section of the speech), he states that "the politically *safe thing* would be to *move on* from this episode and just hope that it *fades into the woodwork*." *"Move on from* this episode" activates a vehicle story about a person who experiences difficulties – an accident, getting robbed – and continues walking or driving without resolving or even addressing the problem; it maps onto a topic story about a person who experiences difficulties such as an argument or embarrassment and continues with previous activities without resolving the problem. In the following paragraph, Obama predicts that "if we *walk away* now, if we simply *retreat into our respective corners*, we will never be able to *come together* and solve challenges like health care." *"Walk away"* activates basically the same metaphorical story as *"move on from."* *"Retreat into our respective corners"* is more ambiguous. It seems to suggest a sports metaphor in which boxers or wrestlers, at the end of each round, return to opposite corners of the ring to rest and prepare for the next round (POLITICS IS A BOXING MATCH). But the vehicle story can also be interpreted in terms of a common parenting strategy: When two children are fighting, they are sent to sit in opposite corners of the room until tempers subside. (Consistent with the SPORTS metaphor, parents often refer to the practice as a *'time-out.'*)

In other passages, Obama combines JOURNEY with STRUCTURE to get *"ladders of opportunity"* (and in a different passage he refers to women who are *"struggling to break the glass ceiling,"* a metaphorical story analyzed in detail in several other chapters). He refers to both Whites and Blacks who *"feel* their *dreams slipping away"* and in two different passages, combines MOTION with COMMERCE / BUSINESS in "your dreams don't have to *come at the expense of my dreams."* In the beginning of the speech, he refers to the authors of the Constitution, who *"launched* America's improbable *experiment* in democracy,"* expressing JOURNEY as a specifically *ocean* journey; he uses the same maritime metaphor again when he speaks of people *"embarking* on a program of self-help."

Space, Distance, Direction, Container

Motion and journeys both imply space. Motion implies moving through space, from one place to another and a journey begins in one place and ends in another. Not surprisingly, these two metaphor groups are blended in several phrases in Obama's speech. In the third section, after describing and comparing the resentment of White working-class people in a stagnant economy with the anger of Blacks about continuing discrimination, Obama concludes that "to *wish away* the resentments of White Americans, to label them as *misguided* or even racist, without *recognizing* they are *grounded in* legitimate concerns – this too *widens the racial divide*, and *blocks the path* to understanding."

"*Wish away*" activates a fanciful story in which an undesired object can be made to disappear by means of a wish; *resentments* are metaphorically transformed by the metaphorical mapping into objects (OBJECTIFICATION) that can be removed by wishing. "*Misguided*" activates a vehicle story in which a person (or vehicle) is guided in the wrong direction, so does not travel toward the desired place; this vehicle story is mapped onto a topic story about White Americans who wish to improve their own situation but are "*guided*" toward thoughts and actions that will not contribute to their objectives. "*Widens the racial divide*" activates a vehicle story in which two groups of different race are moved farther apart in space and maps it onto a topic story about disagreements between two groups. "*Blocks the path* to understanding" activates a story of a journey toward a particular place; the metaphorical mapping represents *understanding* as a "*place*" and the attempt to understand others as a "*journey*" that is "*blocked*" by dismissing others' concerns.

Obama summarizes the situation at the end of the third section with a blend of three metaphors: "This is *where we are* right now. It's a *racial stalemate* we've been *stuck in* for years." In the same passage he acknowledges that we cannot "*get beyond* our *racial divisions* in a single election *cycle*." "*Where we are*," "*stuck in*," and "*get beyond*" continue the POLITICAL SITUATION IS A PHYSICAL PLACE metaphor theme. "*Stalemate*" activates a CHESS metaphor describing a situation in which no possible move will lead to either victory or defeat – a different metaphor expressing the same idea as "*stuck in*" ("*unable to move*"). "*Racial divisions*," as discussed in Chapter 3, converts the verb *divide* into a noun, representing it as an entity capable of entering into a causal relation, and continues the DISAGREEMENT IS PHYSICAL SEPARATION metaphor. These metaphors are blended into a complex metaphorical vehicle story in which the protagonists are attempting to travel to a desired place but are stuck in a situation where they are blocked by something that divides them (a fence, wall, or ditch, perhaps); this story is mapped onto the American public (or political system) and its unsuccessful attempts to achieve racial harmony and equality of opportunity.

DISAGREEMENT IS PHYSICAL DISTANCE appears in several other metaphors throughout the speech. Some of the controversial *"views"* expressed by Rev. Wright "have the potential ... to *widen* the racial *divide*." "The *brutal legacy* of slavery and Jim Crow" includes segregated and inferior schools that help explain the achievement *"gap"* between Black and White students. Legalized discrimination in property ownership, lending, and employment help explain the "wealth and income *gap between* black and white, and the *concentrated pockets* of poverty." Ignoring the basis for Black anger "only serves to *widen the chasm* of misunderstanding ... between the races."

Fire

Although only a few examples appear in the speech, metaphors based on PASSION IS HEAT play an important role in organizing the speech. In the second section, describing the controversy, Obama tells us that his former pastor, Rev. Wright, used *"incendiary* language" to express his views about race relations; some of his remarks caused a *"firestorm"* of criticism. Although these are common idiomatic metaphors for describing extremely emotional and controversial language, for many in the audience they may also have activated vehicle stories of an arsonist starting fires that quickly got out of control. Given the history of race riots that resulted – sometimes deliberately and sometimes more or less accidentally – in fires that destroyed entire communities it is also likely that some members of the audience will have experienced memories of these literal *"firestorms,"* in which case Rev. Wright's rhetoric might be *"incendiary"* in a metonymic sense (as an incitement to others to start actual fires) as well as in a metaphorical sense (as an incitement to extreme and passionate anger).

In the context-setting first section of the speech, Obama relates his personal story and the story of his wife, who *"carries within her the blood of slaves and slaveowners,"* discussed in a previous section. This story "has *seared into my genetic makeup* the idea that this nation is *more than the sum of its parts* – that *out of* many, we are truly one." *"My genetic makeup"* maps onto *fundamental beliefs and personality*. *"Seared into"* can be understood as an expression of PASSION IS HEAT in which case the passage might be paraphrased as something like "has led me to believe passionately ..." However, *"seared into"* also potentially activates a story of coming into contact with something very hot, which creates indelible scar tissue – i.e., a process of *branding* by creating scar tissue, a very painful process that is still used with cattle and, during the slave era, was commonly used to mark ownership of slaves. This story of *"branding"* by *"searing with a hot iron"* then maps onto a story about a painful process through which Obama formed beliefs that are permanent and unchanging. *"Seared into,"* along with *"incendiary"* and *"firestorm"* are, arguably, all examples of *hyperbole* (exaggeration for effect – see Chapters 1 and 3) blended with metaphor. Here their effect is to emphasize the intensity of Obama's feelings about these topics, and potentially to increase the intensity of perceptual simulations stimulated by them.

Battle, War, Struggle

Other than the FIRE metaphors, Obama used very few metaphor vehicles based on WAR or VIOLENCE, although he used several based on STRUGGLE. A notable example, midway through the speech, in the third section, blends two powerful metaphors of struggle with two other metaphors from entirely different domains: "for all those who *scratched and clawed their way* to *get a piece* of the American *Dream*, there were many who didn't make it – those who were *ultimately defeated*, in one way or another, by discrimination." "*Scratched and clawed their way*" combines a JOURNEY metaphor ("their *way*") with a metaphor vehicle based on the frantic struggles of an animal such as a cat and maps it onto a typical African American's struggles against discrimination. "*Ultimately defeated . . . by discrimination*" is a WAR metaphor in which discrimination is personified as an enemy. "The *American Dream*" is an idiomatic metonym for an idealized life of comfort and prosperity; "*get a piece of*" objectifies the "*Dream*" as an object, like a pie that can be sliced up and partitioned out. The entire passage tells a story of a person who struggles like a desperate animal to reach and secure a portion of some desired object, but is defeated by a more powerful enemy, and maps it onto the story of African Americans attempting to gain access to education, housing, and employment but failing because of discrimination.

WAR-based metaphors also appear in "*move beyond* some of our old racial *wounds*," "*succumb* to despair or cynicism," and "*pounce on* some gaffe," each of which implies a vehicle story about battle that is mapped onto a topic story about past struggles against racial discrimination in the first two examples, and about rhetorical nit-picking in the third example. In reference to health care, Obama describes poor people who "don't *have the power* on their own to *overcome* the special interests in Washington, but who *can take them on*." Toward the end of the final section of the speech he tells a story about one of his campaign workers, Ashley Baia, who "*sought out allies in her fight* against injustice."

Nature, Landscapes, Biology

In the third section of the speech, after describing the bitterness of Black citizens because of various form of racial discrimination and the matching grievances of working-class Whites who have seen factories close and jobs disappear, Obama described how these grievances have been exploited by politicians; "these resentments ... have helped *shape the political landscape* for at least a generation." The implied vehicle story about a construction project that changes and reshapes a landscape is mapped onto a topic story about political ideologies and loyalties. (The entire third section of the speech serves to describe "the *political landscape*.")

Metaphors based on NATURE and LANDSCAPE appear in a more pungently evocative form in a trio of metaphors based on implied stories about wetlands and marshes. Describing some of the race-based accusations and counter-accusations that preceded and led to the speech, in the second section of the speech, Obama described how "we saw *racial tensions bubble to the surface*"; later in the speech, he referred again to the "issues that have *surfaced* over the last few weeks." "*Bubble to the surface*" suggests a story about rotting organic material in a swamp emitting noxious gas. "Racial *tensions*" (itself a metaphor or perhaps a metonym based on a physiological response to conflict) map the implied "*noxious gas*" onto the recent spate of rumors and accusations. Again, in the third section of the speech he referred to "an era of *stagnant* wages," an idiomatic metaphor that could be interpreted simply as a descriptive metaphor or as implying a story about a body of water with no current, no motion, which maps onto a "*pool*" of labor that experiences no changes in earnings.

Several other NATURE and BIOLOGY metaphors appear throughout the speech. Rev. Wright's views about the Middle East are described as seeing the conflicts there as "*rooted* primarily in the actions of stalwart allies like Israel." Obama describes his political convictions as "*rooted* in my faith," and declares the importance of "understanding the *roots*" of bitterness and resentment. All of these express causal relationships in terms of a story about the function of a plant's roots in both anchoring the plant to the soil and providing nutrients. Elsewhere in the speech Obama criticizes "a politics that *breeds* division, and conflict, and cynicism" (POLITICS IS PROCREATION) and a view that treats race as "*fodder*" for the nightly news (NEWS IS A HUNGRY ANIMAL).

In the third section, Obama explains how legalized discrimination and the continuing lack of employment opportunities for Black men has "contributed to the *erosion* of Black families." Similarly, continuing discrimination in housing and the lack of community services in Black neighborhoods has helped "*create a cycle* of violence, *blight*, and neglect that continue to *haunt* us." The overall story is literal, but it employs idiomatic metaphors that imply metaphorical stories. "*Erosion*" implies a vehicle story about how landscapes are worn away by wind and water and farming soils are blown and washed away and maps this onto a topic story about the disintegration of family life. The final metaphor, "continue to *haunt* us," presents a story of unseen spirits that cause trouble for ordinary people, familiar from countless movies and campfire stories, and maps it onto a topic story abstract sociological trends that cause trouble for society.

In the final section, Obama offers "continuation of the status quo" story in which we "*pounce on* some gaffe by a Hillary supporter as evidence that she's *playing the race card*, or we can speculate on whether white men will all *flock* to John McCain." "*Pounce on*" implies a metaphorical story based on NEWS COMMENTATORS ARE PREDATORY ANIMALS, and "*flock to*" implies a metaphorical story based on something like MEN ARE SHEEP, or perhaps GEESE – both animal metaphors have other cultural associations that may resonate with Obama's use of the phrase here.

Games, Economics, and Commerce

"*Playing the race card*" is an idiomatic metaphorical story from an entirely different group of metaphors, POLITICS IS A GAME. It also potentially activates stories of Southern politics during much of the 20th century, when politicians would routinely pander to the racist sentiments of many White voters in order to win elections. "*Stalemate*," used in the first section to describe the situation of the Constitutional Convention and in the third section ("racial *stalemate*") to describe the present lack of progress on race relations, and "a *zero-sum game*," used to describe the belief that increased opportunity for one group inevitably means decreased opportunity for others come from the same metaphor group.

By way of game theory, "*zero-sum game*" has also become a core metaphor in discussions of economics and business. Several other metaphors are also drawn from this group. Closely related to "*zero-sum game*" are the concerns, described in several places in the third section, that "your *dreams come at the expense of my dreams*." At the end of the first section, in the transition to the second section, Obama describes apparent concerns that his campaign is based on "the desire of *wide-eyed* liberals to *purchase* racial reconciliation *on the cheap*." Here a story vehicle about naive ("*wide-eyed*") shoppers looking for bargains is mapped onto a topic story about naive political liberals who believe electing a Black president will automatically bring racial reconciliation without need of further "*expenditure*" of effort.

Personification and Objectification

Metaphors based on personification and objectification of abstract qualities and processes are scattered throughout the speech. In the first, context-setting section, Obama tells how "we *saw* how *hungry* the American people were for this message of unity" (A MESSAGE IS FOOD; DESIRE IS HUNGER). In the transition to the second section, Obama admits that, even after he condemned

Rev. Wright's radical statements, "*nagging* questions *remain*" (QUESTIONS ARE AN INSISTENTLY SCOLDING PERSON). In the third section, the bitterness lingering from the years of legal racial discrimination "*finds voice*" in conversations "in the barbershop or around the kitchen table." The "*real culprits* of the middle-class *squeeze*" are "a corporate culture rife with *inside* dealing ..." (CORPORATE CULTURE ETC. ARE CRIMINALS). Early in the fourth section Obama insists that African Americans must "*embrace the burdens* of our past without *becoming victims of* our past" (PAST DEPRIVATIONS ARE HEAVY OBJECTS and THE PAST IS AN AGGRESSOR).

In the fourth section Obama tells us we need to change the conversation, and "talk about the *crumbling* schools that are *stealing* the future of Black children." "*Crumbling*" here is both literal (the buildings where many children attend school are in need of repair, with plaster walls and concrete foundations and walls literally crumbling) and metaphorical (the educational practices, teacher training and supervision, and other abstract aspects of K–12 education are depicted as "*substances*" that are "*crumbling*"). The literal vehicle story of buildings falling apart is mapped onto the topic story of failing educational processes. "We want to reject the cynicism that *tells us* that these kids can't learn ..." (CYNICISM IS A PERSON).

Optics/Vision

Metaphors based on VISION are also scattered throughout the speech. In the opening, context-setting section Obama refers to "the temptation to *view* my candidacy *through* a purely *racial lens.*" The vehicle refers to an optical lens that filters out all but a certain wavelength of light, maps it onto the topic of race; including "the temptation to *view*" expands the vehicle to a story about looking through a filtering lens in order to see only a certain wavelength and maps it onto a topic story about seeking to understand his candidacy solely in terms of race. In the following paragraph he refers to two "*ends*" of a "*spectrum*" of political commentary (AN OPINION IS A COLOR OF LIGHT).

At the beginning of the second section, in which Obama describes Rev. Wright's controversial comments, he says that these comments "*expressed a profoundly distorted view* of this country." In "*distorted view*" the vehicle can be '*looking through a low-quality lens*' or it can be '*looking in a fun-house mirror*'; either way the image is distorted; this vehicle story is mapped onto a topic story of how Rev. Wright understands the country. At the end of this section, where he makes the transition into the third section, Obama cautions us not to "make the same mistake that Reverend Wright *made* ... to simplify and *stereotype* and *amplify* the negative *to the point* that it *distorts* reality." "*Distorts* reality" operates the same here; the "*lens*" metaphor is blended with an objectification metaphor for a mistake ("*made*") and a JOURNEY metaphor for Wright's argument. *"Amplify"* can be interpreted in terms of sound but it also applies directly to the metaphor of negative ideas as *"distorted light."* Finally, at the end of the third section, Obama refers to scripture's call to "be *our brother's keeper"* and pleads that we *"find that common stake* we all have in one another, and let our politics *reflect* that spirit as well." This blends an ECONOMIC (or GAMBLING) metaphor, *"stake"* with an OPTICAL metaphor, *"reflect."*

Summary

Obama's speech *A More Perfect Union* can be interpreted as a single, long, complex story about his campaign, within the context of U.S. racial politics, or it can be viewed as a series of complex stories about race relations in America, about his campaign, and about his troubled relationship with his former pastor and friend, Rev. Wright. Either way, it is constructed of a number of shorter stories and many metaphors. Some of the stories are literal and some are metaphorical; some of the metaphors are simple descriptive metaphors but many imply metaphorical stories. These metaphors are drawn from a remarkably large array of conceptual metaphor groups, and many of the metaphor groups are represented by metaphors in two or more of the four sections of the speech.

Some of the metaphors are conventional idiomatic expressions that might readily escape notice – the stories implied by many of these are easy to overlook, and their contribution to the effect of the speech is arguably rather negligible. However, many of the metaphors, including some that are based on quite conventional idioms, are reinforced in the context of the speech in ways that demand attention and activation of an implied metaphorical story.

The speech was motivated by the long history of racial discrimination and conflict in this country, as well as by a very particular incident or rather series of incidents in which Obama's former pastor, Rev. Wright, made pungent statements about that racialized history. The first section of the speech summarizes the history of race relations and his own personal relation to that history; the second section summarizes the story of Rev. Wright's controversial utterances and Obama's personal relation to Rev. Wright – and to Wright's statements. The third section begins by laying out the basis of Wright's anger and bitterness in the long history of racial oppression and discrimination. Then, consistent with the fundamental requirement for empathy, that groups be able and willing to "'enter into' the experiential world of the Other" (Ritchie & Cameron, 2014), Obama detailed a parallel set of experiences and concerns of middle-class White Americans, and shows how these experiences and concerns lead to an equally justified, and parallel, kind of anger and bitterness. In the final section, he attempted to build a case, based on these parallels, for "*coming together*" to solve the economic and political problems that underlie *both* groups' anger and bitterness.

Unfortunately, as I discussed with respect to the "*original sin*" and "*blood of slaves and slave-owners*" metaphors, "*entering into the world*" of the Other" seems to require either a shared cultural background and a shared set of assumptions, or a sophisticated understanding of the differences. If members of both groups, African Americans and White Americans, insistently see their own experiences and cultural assumptions as unique and special, and their own stories as uniquely "true," then entering into the world of the Other may prove unachievable.

Obama used a series of powerful and evocative stories, some literal but many metaphorical with the potential and apparent intention to facilitate people on both sides of the divide, Whites and African Americans, to enter into the world experience of the other and hence to establish the conditions for empathy. However, subsequent history suggests that this was unsuccessful: Obama's political enemies (including the Republican elected to succeed him as U.S. president) continued to allege that he was neither a Christian nor even a natural-born U.S. citizen. Political polarization over issues related to race relations has, if anything, increased, and fruitful discussion of issues related to relations between police forces and the African American citizens within their jurisdictions remains as elusive as it ever was.

Throughout this chapter, I have repeatedly drawn attention to potential and apparent differences in contextual knowledge including knowledge and beliefs among the various audiences for Obama's speech. It appears from several passages in the speech that Obama was aware of these differences, and he attempted to address the differences, for example, by telling stories of the struggles and disappointments faced by working-class White citizens that parallel the stories of the struggles and disappointments of Black citizens. However, it does not appear that he adequately allowed for magnitude and valence of the differences in contextual knowledge and salience.

An alternative explanation for the failure of this speech to catalyze a fruitful and unifying conversation about race has been suggested by several political commentators who criticize Obama for failing to follow up on the speech. In retrospect, once elected he *might have* convened a commission on the legacy of slavery or in some other way lent the power and prestige of his office to sustaining the conversation that his speech had begun. It is impossible to know whether that kind of follow-up would have been successful, whether it might have interfered with other priorities of the Obama administration, or even whether it would have been possible.

In this chapter, I have attempted to show how Obama's metaphors may potentially activate metaphorical stories, and in several places I have discussed alternative metaphorical stories that might be activated. There is no way to know how various members of the audience actually understood these metaphors and stories, or whether they were understood at all. However, the political events subsequent to this speech are quite consistent with the conclusion that, especially with respect to an issue as complex and as deeply embedded in history as this, differences in knowledge, understanding, and salience of relevant social, cultural, and political context are likely to result in very different understanding of the same facts and the same stories. It would contribute considerably to our understanding of the state of interracial empathy in contemporary America if we could understand better what contextual knowledge is salient to members of various audiences and what, if anything, members of various audiences experience when they hear these metaphors and these stories.

10   Metaphorical Stories about Climate Change

> Everybody talks about the weather but nobody does anything about it.
> – Attributed to Mark Twain

The weather is commonly regarded as fickle and unpredictable, in contrast to the longer-range weather patterns often summarized as the *climate* of a locale, and long thought to be stable over relatively long periods. However, recent research has led to the realization the climate also changes, sometimes quite rapidly, and for reasons that are poorly understood and probably quite complex. With respect to climate as well as weather, variability, not stability, is the norm (Hulme, 2009). The role of human activity (such as agriculture and deforestation) in local climate variability has been recognized for 2,000 years, but in recent years the nature and extent of human influence on climate at a larger, global scale has become more evident, even as it has become, at least in the United States, politically controversial.

Factors contributing to climate variability include changes in solar radiation, composition of the Earth's atmosphere, and albedo, the reflectivity of the Earth's surface. Human activities such as agriculture and industrial activity influence the composition of the atmosphere and the reflectivity of the surface, although the significance of human activities relative to "natural" processes such as changes in solar radiation and volcanic activity have been hotly debated. Much of the recent debate has centered around the concentration of CO_2, methane, and other "*greenhouse* gasses" in the atmosphere, which have been rising rapidly as a result of agricultural and industrial activity. In this chapter, I will examine some of the metaphors, particularly story metaphors and metaphorical stories that have been used in this debate. I will begin with a brief summary of the issues involved; for a more complete and nuanced discussion, see Hulme (2009).

Climate and Climate Change

Although the ability of human activities such as burning forests and draining swamps to alter local climate patterns was recognized as early as the third century BC, the long history of large-scale variations in global climate, including ice ages, was not recognized until the early 19th century (Hulme, 2009). During the following century, scientists considered several possible explanations for past climate variations, and their implications for future climate patterns. Solar radiation appears to vary on a long cycle, and is currently entering a period of decrease which, by itself, would predict the eventual onset of another ice age. The increased concentration of aerosols (smog) in the atmosphere, by reflecting solar radiation before it reaches the ground, also has a potential cooling effect. As recently as the 1970s some climate scientists were predicting that these two factors together could lead to a cooling period and possibly to another ice age (Hulme, 2009).

An opposite *warming* effect results from the increase of CO_2, methane, and other "*greenhouse* gasses" in the atmosphere. Complicating processes include volcanic activity, which releases CO_2 but also releases sulfur aerosols and copious amounts of ash that can block much of the sunlight, with significant short-term cooling effects. Atmospheric warming reduces snow and ice, which reflect sunlight back into space, and exposes water and soil, which absorb more heat. Thawing of arctic permafrost releases methane. Warmer water can lead to more clouds – which reflect light back into space. Ocean currents, which can be affected by surface warming, have huge effects on weather patterns. All of these systems are interrelated in complex ways that are still poorly understood; as a result, it is possible for two equally qualified scientists to look at the same data and come to quite different predictions, depending on the assumptions they make about how these various processes interact.

Over the past several decades, the increase in computer capacity and speed has enabled scientists to develop increasingly complex models to represent the relationships among the relevant variables including the concentration of CO_2 and other "*greenhouse gasses*" as well as aerosols, clouds, etc., and the degree to which each absorbs, transmits, or reflects radiation at various wavelengths, the chemical breakdown of these chemicals and their absorption into water, soil, etc. As new relationships are discovered and new data become available they are incorporated into the models. The models can sometimes be tested by determining what they would predict for recent, present, or near-future values and comparing these predictions with actual observations. Most climate scientists agree that these models have become sufficiently refined, and their short-term predictions agree sufficiently with actual observations, that their long-term predictions should be taken seriously. However, some reputable scientists continue to dispute the value of the models, because of the simplifying assumptions built into the models and the high level of variability in the data.

Potential effects. Initially, the expected effects of increasing CO_2 in the atmosphere were summarized as *environmental warming*. More recently, climate scientists have emphasized that the interaction of complex systems may result in cooler and wetter weather in some regions, hotter and drier weather in other regions, and greater volatility – more severe storms, greater extremes in temperature and rainfall – in most regions. Accordingly, *environmental warming* has fallen out of favor, and climate scientists increasingly refer to *climate change*. Warming may lead to milder climates and longer growing seasons in some latitudes (arguably a good thing for people who live in the cooler "*higher*" latitudes), but to hotter and drier summers in other latitudes, potentially rendering marginal agricultural areas closer to the equator unusable and possibly even making some regions uninhabitable. A warming atmosphere and warming oceans are likely to lead to rising sea levels, both because ocean water will expand as it warms and because of melting glaciers; at the extreme, if significant portions of the glaciers in Greenland and Antarctica melt or slide into the ocean, sea levels could rise by tens or even hundreds of meters. Sea level rises of this magnitude would flood huge coastal areas, potentially displacing billions of people.

Other potential effects include turning the oceans more acid as they absorb more CO_2, which could destroy coral reefs and damage other ocean habitats. Longer summers and milder winters may extend the range of parasites and diseases, including malaria and sleeping sickness. Conversely, increasing concentrations of CO_2 may foster more growth of green plants, including both crops and weeds.

Adding to the uncertainties associated with these complex effects are the differences in time scales. The effects of CO_2 and other "*greenhouse* gasses" are predicted to occur over an extended time frame. Sea levels may rise enough within the next few decades to increase the risk of flooding in low-lying coastal areas such as New York City, the Pacific Island nations, and most of Bangladesh, but truly catastrophic sea level rises of tens of meters are predicted to take much longer, possibly several centuries. On the other hand, the "*greenhouse* gasses" vary in the length of time they endure in the atmosphere: CO_2 builds up slowly but also dissipates slowly. Actions to avert dangerous increases must be taken in the short term (within the next decade or two at the most), but the effects of large increases in CO_2 are expected in the long term, with the worst effects likely to show up late this century or early in the twenty-second century.

Cultural factors. As if the scientific issues were not complex enough, the discussion of climate variability and the possible contribution of human activity to climate change is greatly complicated by the influence of different religious and philosophical beliefs, moral and aesthetic commitments and preferences, economic interests, and so on. Some religious doctrines hold that God alone has control over aspects of the environment such as weather; thus, in both popular and legal discourse tornados, floods, earthquakes, and so on, are "*acts of God*." The idea that human activities could cause or even influence, much less control, these processes contradicts these religious beliefs. Conversely, other religious doctrines hold that God has delegated to humans the responsibility to care for the natural environment, which to many entails preserving so much as possible the natural purity and "innocence" of lakes, woods, and so on. According to yet another set of religious beliefs, advanced societies that have achieved wealth and comfort have an obligation to help poorer and less fortunate people, thus the industrialized world has an obligation to help less developed nations to achieve similar standards of living, on the one hand, and protect vulnerable citizens of less developed nations from the destructive effects of climate change, on the other. Thus, the view that the faithful are required to behave charitably toward those less fortunate itself provides a basis for opposing views about climate change: are we responsible for slowing the pace of climate change in order to mitigate its effects on impoverished societies that inhabit coastal lowlands, or are we obligated to share the wealth-producing benefits of fossil fuels with impoverished societies, even at the risk of accelerating climate change? Each of these views has different implications for how one might view both the possibility that human action has an influence on the climate and the kind of corrective actions that might be taken.

Economic interests are also important. A majority of climate scientists claim that the use of fossil fuels – carbon compounds created during earlier geological eras – is a major factor in the increase in environmental CO_2 and other "*greenhouse* gasses" during the past few hundred years. However, extracting and selling fossil fuels is a primary source of income for a number of large and powerful corporations – and for a number of nations, including less developed nations for whom petroleum may be the primary source of wealth. People whose livelihood depend on coal or petroleum are more likely to be skeptical about claims that the use of carbon-based fuels will lead to disastrous climate changes. On the demand side, petroleum in particular has provided the basis for relatively inexpensive and portable energy sources necessary to transportation and other sectors of the economy. Most of the current world economy is heavily dependent on the use of carbon-based fuels. Economic interests are also frequently cited as a basis for *ad hominem* attacks on the credibility of people whose opinions differ with those of the speaker.

The culture of science itself is also a complicating factor. Scientific knowledge is never truly settled for once and for all – new evidence and new ways of using old evidence always has the potential to overturn even well-accepted theories. With respect to complex and poorly understood processes like weather and climate, this is even truer. Science thrives on disagreement, argument, and an attitude of openness to new evidence and new ideas. Unfortunately politics (and journalism) need certainty or at least clarity. Political and economic leaders are required to make decisions in the present, based on the best knowledge they have (and the best balance among competing interests they can achieve) – and the consequences of their decisions always happen in the future, when new knowledge, not available now, may make their present decisions look foolish.

These two cultures often become intertwined. When scientists see conditions that may have adverse long-term consequences, and when they find reason to believe that these consequences can be alleviated by changing present policies, they are often drawn into advocating for those policy changes. If they fear that their warnings are not being heeded and the evidence they present not being taken seriously, there may be a temptation to exaggerate either the magnitude or the immediacy of the risk in order to gain the attention of policy makers; these "rhetorical excesses" often introduce yet another element of dispute within the culture of science, even as it alters the relationship of scientist to policy maker from advisory to advocacy (Hulme, 2009).

All of this has taken place in the debate over climate change, and it has affected the use of stories and metaphors – including metaphorical stories – in some quite interesting ways. In this chapter, I will examine a series of speeches by a scientist, Jim Hansen, in two addresses to the U.S. congress, given in 1988 and 2008, twenty years apart, and one address to the general public, a 2012 TED talk. Then I will examine a speech by Senator James Inhofe before the U.S. Senate. Finally, I will look at the stories and story metaphors in a key 2013 environment speech by President Barack Obama.

Metaphors and Story Metaphors of Climate Change – General

Because the processes involved in climate patterns are so complex, scientists and others involved in the debate over climate change use a variety of metaphors. Metaphors are used to describe and explain the scientific theories involved, to explain possible consequences and proposed remedies, to establish frames for the discussion, and to persuade others. In this section, I will discuss some metaphors that are used by almost all participants in the debate.

Almost everyone who discusses climate change refers to the buildup of CO_2, methane, and other "*greenhouse*" gasses in the atmosphere. The metaphor vehicle is based on an implicit story about the greenhouses used by farmers and gardeners to extend the growing season and grow plants that are vulnerable to cold nights. These greenhouses are constructed of glass or another material that is transparent to radiation in the visible spectrum but opaque to infra-red radiation. Light enters a greenhouse and warms the soil. The soil warms the air by contact, and also emits heat as infra-red radiation, which is reflected back by the glass, further warming the air and preventing the soil from cooling off during the night. This process is metaphorically mapped onto the atmosphere. The carbon in coal and petroleum ("fossil fuels") is converted to CO_2 that is released into the atmosphere; industrial activities and particularly large-scale agriculture also releases significant amounts of methane. CO_2, methane, and water vapor are all transparent to visible light but not to infrared, and therefore function much like the glass panes in a greenhouse. CO_2 is taken out of the air through several processes including absorption into water and conversion into organic compounds and oxygen by plants. As industrial use of fossil fuels has increased over the past few hundred years, the rate at which CO_2 is released into the atmosphere has increasingly exceeded the rate at which it is removed through photosynthesis and absorption, leading to a steadily increased concentration of CO_2 in the atmosphere, and a consequent increase in the *"greenhouse"* effect.

Virtually everyone uses conventional metaphors including MORE IS UP and MORE IS BIG, both for the concentration of CO_2 in the atmosphere and for observed effects of CO_2; these as well as STRENGTH are used to characterize cause-effect relationships. VISION and PERCEPTION metaphors are also used by most commentators, e.g., *"clear* signs . . ."' Conventional metaphors such as *"high* latitudes" (farther from the equator) are also used by virtually everyone. Most commentators use *"impact"* to emphasize the importance of effects.

Jim Hansen, NASA scientist

Dr. James Hansen is an astrophysicist who was employed by NASA in the 1980s, when he was given the assignment of conducting research on changes and potential changes in Earth's climate as a result of the *"greenhouse"* effect. He was invited to testify about his research to Congress in 1988, then again in 2008. Between these appearances, he gave a number of public talks about his research, was ordered by the White House to make no further public statements on the topic, but after an article about it appeared in the *New York Times* the ban was lifted. In 2012 he gave a TED talk about his career and his research. In this section, I will examine Hansen's use of stories and metaphors, with particular attention to story metaphors and metaphorical stories.

James Hansen's 1988 testimony. In his 1988 testimony, Hansen began by showing that the previous 25 years had been unusually warm, showed that this series of unusually warm years was unlikely to have resulted simply from random fluctuations, then compared this trend to observed increases in the concentration of CO_2 in the atmosphere to show that the pattern of atmospheric warming matched the predictions of what would result from the *"greenhouse* effect." Finally, he presented estimates of future extreme weather events such as prolonged heat waves to argue that the increased frequency of extreme heat waves due to the *"greenhouse* effect" will be sufficient to be noticed by the average person. He closed by emphasizing the need for more observational data from around the world, as well as improved global climate models.

In the 1988 testimony, Hansen relied primarily on conventional metaphors: "*draw* three main conclusions," "*high* degree of confidence," "*magnitude* of warming," "*level* of detail." He described a "*clear* tendency" for greater than average warming, which "*seems* to *arise*" because the ocean warms more slowly than land. The metaphors he used for emphasis were also conventional. He described a scenario based on no attempt at all to reduce CO_2 emissions as "*business as usual*" and a scenario based on strict emission controls as "*Draconian*" cuts. He referred both to the "effect" and the "*impact*" of the "*greenhouse* effect" on patterns of extreme weather.

"*Business as usual*" implies a metonymic story, in which a vehicle story about an organization that continues its established practices, by implication in spite of changing circumstances, is mapped onto a topic story about continuing established national energy policies in spite of new knowledge about the environmental effects. For those familiar with the story of the Athenian lawgiver, "*Draconian*" potentially imply a metaphorical story about the imposition of unusually harsh measures; however, it is unlikely that many in Hansen's audience were familiar with the vehicle story. Both of these phrases are conventionally used as simple descriptive metaphors, as are most of the other metaphors in Hansen's 1988 testimony. In general, Hansen's 1988 testimony to Congress was delivered in measured tones, with only a handful of implicit story metaphors and no dramatic metaphorical stories. There are traces of advocacy in Hansen's 1988 testimony, but the overall tone is restrained and objective, consistent with the ideal of objective scientific discourse.

Jim Hansen 20 years later – Hansen's 2008 testimony. During the following 20 years, in response to accumulating evidence about the potential effects of "*greenhouse* gasses," Hansen increasingly began to advocate for changes in energy and industrial policies that would reduce the amount of CO_2 released into the atmosphere. This shift toward an active advocacy is apparent in his use of dramatic story metaphors and metaphorical stories that saturate the 2008 testimony, in contrast to their almost total absence in 1988.

Hansen's 2008 testimony began with a reference to the 1988 testimony, in which he described the "*striking* similarities" (TO BECOME ABRUPTLY AWARE IS TO RECEIVE A PHYSICAL BLOW) between the two times. "Again a *wide gap* has *developed between*" what scientists and nonscientists understand (DISAGREEMENT IS PHYSICAL SEPARATION). Analysis of scientific data "*yields* conclusions that are *shocking* to the *body politic* . . ." (AN UNPLEASANT SURPRISE IS A SHOCK). Hansen described crucial differences between the situation in 1988 and that in 2008, and concluded that the situation has become much more urgent. He then described several particular aspects of the global environment that are particularly under threat, followed by a discussion of the economic and political obstacles to effective policy response. He ended with a long section in which he advocated a detailed proposal for a change in energy policy to reduce use of carbon-based fuels. Although descriptions of the situation, descriptions of needed remedy, discussion of obstacles, and advocacy of a particular policy solution are intermixed in the speech, I will discuss them in order.

The Situation. Immediately after describing the *"widening gap"* between scientists and nonscientists, Hansen used two strong story metaphors to describe the difference between the situation in 1988 and the situation in 2008: "now we have *used up all* slack in the *schedule* for actions needed to defuse the global warming time bomb." As an adjective, *slack* refers to a rope or chain that is loose. As a grammatical metaphor converted to a noun *"slack"* identifies a condition of slackness, a condition in which there is no *"force"* (urgency) applied to either end of the rope. If the rope tethers a horse or other animal, this slackness is a *resource* that allows a certain freedom of movement, but if the animal runs to the end of the rope so that it becomes taut, the animal has *used up* the "slack," and consequently is no longer free to move in any direction except sideways or backward. (Other possible vehicle stories might involve a mountain climber who *"reaches the end of the rope"* or other similar scenarios, activating different simulations, but the effects are likely to be quite similar.) As a metaphor here, the *"rope"* maps onto the amount of time available to respond to a risk of a destructive event before it actually happens (the *"schedule"*). In 1988 there was still ample time to respond (*"slack in the rope"*). The story of an animal (or mountain climber) that has reached the end of a rope and is no longer able to move maps onto a story about the situation in 2008, in which we have *"used up"* all the time and are may not have time to prevent the damaging event.

"Defuse the global warming time bomb" specifies what the dangerous situation is. *"Bomb"* is a conventional metaphor for a sudden and unexpected destructive event. As a grammatical metaphor, time converts a noun referring to duration or sequence to an adjective (also, implicitly, a verb) that describes how the bomb is made to explode – it explodes at a certain unpredictable time (noun →adjective) or it explodes as a result of a device that times it (verb). Combined with *"bomb"* this grammatical metaphor yields a conventional metaphor, *"time bomb"* that describes a situation in which a destructive event may happen at an unpredictable time, and implicitly activates a story about such a destructive event. As a grammatical metaphor, *"defuse"* converts a noun referring to a device that causes a bomb to explode (at a certain preset time in the case of a time bomb) to a verb meaning to remove a fuse or otherwise disable a bomb so that it will not explode. As a grammatical metaphor, "warming" converts an adjective referring to temperature to a verb referring to a process of increasing temperature, then to a noun (modified by "globe, transformed to the grammatical metaphor global") referring to a process in which the temperature of the entire globe is increased.

The phrase blends all of these metaphors into a single metaphorical story; the vehicle story about disabling a time bomb so as to prevent a damaging explosion maps onto a topic story about the damage that may be caused by a rise in the temperature of the entire globe. "*Defusing*" then maps onto the adoption of policies that will prevent global warming. The sentence as a whole blends these two story metaphors into a single story about a person or group who has enough time to defuse (disable) a bomb but delays action ("*uses up the slack*") until it is almost too late and the bomb is about to explode; this vehicle story maps onto the political delays in adopting policies to reduce the emission of "*greenhouse* gasses" and slow the pace of environmental warming. The contrast between these dramatic and frightening metaphorical stories and the calm, measured tones of the 1988 testimony is striking.

In the next paragraph, Hansen introduced two more dramatic metaphors to characterize the result if we fail to "*constrain*" the concentration of CO_2 "to a *level* that prevents the climate system from *passing tipping* points that *lead to* disastrous climate changes that *spiral* dynamically *out of* humanity's control." As a grammatical metaphor, tipping transforms a verb describing a motion in which an object moves to some angle away from a vertical position into an adjective and blends it with "*point*" to yield a metaphor vehicle literally describing a position at which, if the object tips any further, it will fall over entirely. The metaphor "*tipping point*," popularized in a book by Malcolm Gladwell (2006), refers to the idea that complex systems will often remain "*stable*" as long as key variables remain within a certain range, but when one or more variables exceed a certain value, just as the object in the vehicle story falls over on its side, the system "*collapses*" into a totally different state. (Hansen used both "*tipping point*" and "*collapse*" again later in the speech.) As a grammatical metaphor "spiral" transforms a noun describing a three dimensional geometric figure into a verb expressing a process in which a system undergoes a repetitive series of ever more extreme changes, in this particular cases changes that lead the system "*out of*" the "*space*" within which it is possible to control it. This metaphor first maps a vehicle story about a physical object that spirals outward to the point that it can't be controlled onto a topic story about a system – in this case the Earth's climate system – that undergoes a series of increasingly extreme changes (e.g., warm to cold to even warmer to even colder). All of these metaphors are blended into a single vehicle story about an object that tips so far that it becomes unstable, falls over in a way that causes another object to become unstable and move in an uncontrollable spiral; this blended vehicle story maps onto a story about Earth's climate system changing in a complex and uncontrollable series of processes.

A little later in the speech Hansen asked, "What is *at stake*," a conventional metaphor with the potential to activate a story about gambling with something of value and maps it onto an implied topic story about "*gambling* with the future of Earth." He admits that the atmospheric warming to date has been so slight that it "seems almost innocuous," then blends several metaphorical stories and story metaphors to explain why it is not innocuous.

But more warming is already "*in-the-pipeline*," *delayed* only by the great *inertia* of the world ocean. And climate is *nearing dangerous tipping points*. *Elements* of a "*perfect storm*," a global cataclysm, are *assembled*. Climate can *reach points* such that *amplifying feedbacks spur large rapid* changes.

"*In the pipeline*" is a conventional metaphor based on an implied story about a liquid such as oil or water that is certain to arrive soon because it has already started. The progress of the substance has been "*delayed*" by "*inertia*," the tendency of objects or substances at rest to remain at rest. "*Pipeline*" maps onto the "*greenhouse* effect" process; "*inertia*" maps onto the tendency of a large body of water such as an ocean to maintain a relatively constant temperature and chemical composition. The vehicle story about a substance moving through a pipeline toward speaker and audience maps onto a topic story about a process of atmospheric warming that has already begun. By including "*in-the-pipeline*" and "*perfect storm*" within quotation marks Hansen drew attention to their metaphoricity. This use of a "*tuning device*" to mark these phrases as metaphorical may have increased the probability that they would be recognized as deliberate (Steen, 2015); it may also have increased cognitive processing attention to the entire passage.

Following this, Hansen repeated the "*tipping point*" story analyzed above, then referred to "*elements of a perfect storm*." "*Perfect storm*" entered popular culture in a book by Sebastian Junger (1997) about a powerful and destructive 1991 Halloween nor'easter that resulted from what meteorologist Bob Case described as "the perfect situation" to generate a powerful storm, a confluence of a low-pressure system, a high-pressure system, and a large mass of tropical moisture. The vehicle story here maps onto a topic story about how the confluence of factors, including increased levels of CO_2, methane released by melting permafrost and reduced albedo due to receding glaciers, will lead to rapid atmospheric warming. The use here can be interpreted as both metaphorical and metonymic, inasmuch as extremely violent storms are expected to result from this process. "*Amplifying feedbacks*" potentially activates a vehicle story about sound engineering in which a microphone is exposed to a loudspeaker, such that the microphone picks up sound waves and "*feeds* them *back into*" the amplifier, creating a closed circuit that rapidly increases the sound volume and can cause serious damage both to the sound equipment and to auditors' eardrums. This maps onto a topic story about how the effects of increased concentrations of "*greenhouse* gasses" such as melting permafrost and releasing methane can lead to further concentrations of "*greenhouse* gasses" and further warming that causes serious damage to the climate system. "*Spur*," of course, refers to the use of a sharp object attached to a rider's boot that is used to stimulate a horse to run faster; this maps onto a topic story about abruptly accelerating the process of environmental warming.

The remedy. Hansen used several metaphors based on JOURNEY to describe how the worst effects of climate change can be averted. He claimed that "a *path yielding* energy independence and a *healthier* environment is, *barely*, still possible. It requires a *transformative* change of *direction* in Washington in the next year." The ORGANISM metaphors implied by "*yield*" and "*healthier* environment" appeared again when Hansen proposed a carbon tax as a way to "*wean* us off fossil fuel *addiction*." "*Addiction*" has become a conventional metaphor for a range of activities, including television (see Chapter 11). Later in the speech, Hansen asserted, "We must *move beyond* fossil fuels eventually. Solution of the climate problem *requires* that we *move* to carbon-free energy promptly." He later said, "Building code and vehicle efficiency requirements must be improved and *put on a path toward* carbon *neutrality*" (JOURNEY).

Obstacles. Beginning early in the speech, Hansen assured listeners that the needed changes are "*clear*" (KNOWING IS SEEING). However, "the changes have been *blocked* by *special interests, focused on short-term* profits, who *hold sway* in Washington and other capitals." "*Blocked*" continues REFORM IS A JOURNEY and "*focused*" applies the VISION metaphor to the topic of *purpose*. "*Special interests*" has become a conventional metonym for *groups of people who advocate policies that benefit themselves even if they are bad for everyone else*. (These tropes are repeated several times during the speech.) Similarly, "*hold sway*" is a conventional metaphor for dominating a debate over policy decisions. Later in the speech he expressed the same idea with an even stronger metaphorical story, asserting that "the fossil-industry *maintains* its *strangle-hold* on Washington *via demagoguery*," helped by "*swarms* of high-priced lobbyists *in alligator shoes*," a common colloquial metonym suggesting *highly paid*.

Midway through the speech, Hansen compared fossil fuel companies to tobacco companies during the 1960s and 1970s, who (falsely) "*discredited the smoking-cancer link*." Because CEOs of fossil energy companies pursue "*short-term profits*" even though they "know what they are doing and are aware of long-term consequences of continued *business as usual*," they "should be *tried for high crimes* against humanity and nature." However, "conviction of ExxonMobil and Peabody Coal CEOs will be no consolation, if we *pass on* a *runaway climate* to our children." Here the vehicle story of a horse or team of horses that is running out of control is mapped onto the topic story about environmental warming.

Finally, continuing the ANIMAL metaphor, Hansen advocated that "Americans *turn out to pasture* the most *brontosaurian* congressmen." The vehicle story of a racehorse who, at the end of its racing career, is sent to spend the rest of its life in a pasture is mapped onto a topic story of terminating congressmen's careers. *"Brontosaurian"* is simply a variation on *"dinosaur,"* a conventional hyperbolic metaphor for someone who is ignorant about current science (*"out of date"*) and advocates discredited ideas and policies. The blend of these two metaphors yields a metaphorical story about an animal that is both (extremely) archaic and no longer able to perform its normal functions that is placed in a locale where it is well-fed and out of the way; it maps onto a topic story about voting politicians out of office.

Jim Hansen's TED talk. Hansen's TED talk covered much the same ground as his 2008 testimony, and used many of the same metaphors. However, he introduced a few new metaphors, which I will explain in this section. The speech was structured around a rhetorical question, posed at the beginning and answered at the end of the speech: "What do I know that would cause me, a reticent, Midwestern scientist, to get myself arrested in front of the White House protesting?" After posing this question (posed in reference to a dramatic literal story) he gave a brief history of his career, up to his first (1988) testimony. He told a brief hypothetical story about his worry that his grandchildren might criticize him in the future for failing to speak out about what he knows, then explained the scientific evidence for human contributions to climate change, with a brief mention of climate change deniers, and closed with a summary of the action that is needed and the costs associated with delay.

Describing the *"greenhouse"* effect, Hansen explained that "gasses such as CO_2 absorb heat, thus *acting like a blanket* warming Earth's surface"; later he compared adding CO_2 to the atmosphere to *"throwing another blanket on the bed."* The vehicle story refers to adding blankets to a bed in order to stay warm; this vehicle is more familiar than *"greenhouse,"* although it is also less accurate (blankets only limit the conduction of heat and retain warmth already underneath). He then repeated the *"noise level"* metaphor explained in the previous section. He repeats the "energy *balance / imbalance"* metaphor several times.

In order to explain how much total energy is added to the atmosphere because of the imbalance between energy entering and energy leaving the atmosphere, Hansen compared it to *"exploding 400,000 Hiroshima atomic bombs per day 365 days per year."* By itself this is an odd comparison, since few nonphysicists have a clear idea how much energy is released by an atomic bomb. However, as a vehicle story, *"exploding 400,000 Hiroshima atomic bombs per day"* has potentially terrifying implications. Only the heat from the bombs can be mapped onto the topic story, of course, but the other, irrelevant attributes of an atomic bomb, in particular the destructive force of the blast itself and the radioactivity, are the most salient parts of the *Hiroshima* vehicle story, and they add emotional intensity to the metaphor.

Another rhetorical question about his own involvement in the controversy introduced another set of metaphorical stories: "How did I get *dragged deeper and deeper* into an attempt to communicate, giving talks in 10 countries, getting arrested, *burning up* the vacation time that I had *accumulated over 30 years?*" First we have a vehicle story about Hansen being dragged into a deep pit, or perhaps into deep water, which maps onto the topic story of his being convinced to travel and give so many talks. Then we have a vehicle story about burning a substance of value; this is mapped onto a topic story of using his vacation time to give lectures. This is meshed with a story about some substance (such as snow) accumulating over a long period of time, that maps onto the story of adding to a record of earned vacation time. All three of these stories are blended into a single complex vehicle story that maps onto the topic story about Hansen's political activism.

Finally, after additional uses of the *"tipping point"* and *"spiraling out of control"* metaphors, Hansen introduced another apocalyptic metaphorical story based on a vehicle story about a giant asteroid:

increasing intensity of droughts and floods will severely *impact breadbaskets* of the world, causing massive famines and economic decline. *Imagine a giant asteroid on a direct collision course with Earth* ... Yet, we dither, t*aking no action to divert the asteroid,* even though *the longer we wait,* the more difficult and expensive it becomes.

"*Impact*" is used by everyone who discusses policy issues, but here it is echoed by and interacts with the "*giant asteroid*" vehicle story in a way that lends substance and intensity to both. This interaction greatly intensifies the quality of careless irresponsibility implied by second phrase, "*taking no action to divert the asteroid.*" For those who follow science news, the metaphor vehicle will gain greater power from recent discussion of the risk from the damage that could be caused by future asteroid strikes and the need to work out measures to detect and divert dangerously large objects that are on a collision course with Earth.

Summary. Each of these speeches responded to a different situation, a different social and political context. In the first speech, Hansen used few metaphors, and the metaphors he used tended to be conventional and static, with limited potential to activate dramatic stories. The 2008 testimony was almost the exact opposite: It is filled with dramatic and frightening metaphorical stories. He also used many dramatic story metaphors, lexical metaphors with the potential to activate metaphorical stories, which I did not discuss in detail. The 2008 speech in particular illustrates the tendency, discussed by Hulme (2009), for scientists who are particularly concerned about an issue such as climate change to respond to apparent public (and policy makers') indifference by exaggerating and dramatizing the threat. In addition to alarming "doomsday" metaphors like "*asteroid*" and "*Hiroshima* *atomic bomb*," some scientists also distort the time scale, speaking and writing about, for example, large sea level rises that may happen in a few hundred years as if they are likely to happen within a few decades. Other scientists worry that this kind of exaggerated rhetoric may undermine credibility and inadvertently support the arguments of those who deny the scientific evidence entirely.

Many of Hansen's metaphors and metaphorical stories express a strong disdain for members of the audience who might disagree with him ("*turn out to pasture*," "*brontosaurian*"), reinforced by accusations that politicians who fail to accept and act on the evidence for human contributions to climate change are merely responding to the self-interested influence of energy company executives. Given the story he told about his career in the TED talk, it appears that between 1988 and 2008 Hansen grew cynical and pessimistic about the prospects for the kind of action he regards as necessary; this is reflected in the quality of the metaphors he used. Whether it is a useful rhetorical strategy, I will take up again at the end of this chapter.

Senator Jim Inhofe, Republican (Oklahoma) – Speech before the Senate, September 25, 2006

One of the leading critics of attempts to address concerns about potential climate change through political action and changes in energy policy is Senator Jim Inhofe, Republican from the oil-producing state of Oklahoma. In this section, I will discuss one of his speeches on the topic, delivered before the U.S. Senate on September 25, 2006. In this speech, Inhofe focused primarily on a critique of media coverage, but he also provided a critique and rebuttal to the claims of scientists like Jim Hansen, accompanied by a personal criticism of Hansen himself.

Inhofe began the speech with a history of media coverage of climate during the previous century, then reviewed some of the most important evidence offered in support of the global warming hypothesis. He pointed out that the predictions of catastrophic levels of warming, melting of polar ice caps, and sea level rises are based on computerized models that are themselves based on (necessarily) simplifying assumptions and incomplete data. He cited several scientists and groups of scientists who have disputed the validity of the climate models; he also cited research that has discredited some of the specific evidence that seems to support the global warming hypothesis. He devoted several paragraphs to a critique of the potential economic consequences of overreacting to the predictions of catastrophic climate change, beginning with the observation that industrialization has produced the greatest increase in human welfare in history, but there are still millions of people in poverty. He then cited a group of Nobel Prize–winning economists who ranked climate change much lower than a long list of other spending priorities. Finally he returned to his critique of the media, including a detailed criticism of both Al Gore and Jim Hansen.

Critique of media coverage. Inhofe began with a critique of media coverage of the climate, which "has alternated *between* global cooling and warming *scares* during four separate and sometimes *overlapping* time periods." The grammatical metaphor "*scares*" transforms a verb meaning *to induce fright* into a noun designating media coverage as *an entity that induces fright*; "*between*" and "*overlapping*" blends this metaphor with TIME IS SPACE and locates the *fright-inducing* entity in space/time. In the following sentence, Inhofe told us that "*from* 1895 until the 1930s the media *peddled* a *coming* ice age." "*Peddle*" is colloquially used as a belittling metaphor; it potentially activates a vehicle story of a person going door to door (or standing on the street) trying to sell some minor consumer product. Applied to the topic story of media reporting on scientists' speculations about the possibility of a long-range cooling trend, it implies a lack of seriousness and objectivity. This implication is reinforced by "*fourth estate's* fourth *attempt to promote* opposing climate change *fears*" and "*advocates of alarmism* have *grown increasingly* desperate" immediately following. "*Promote ... fears*" activates a story quite different from *warn of risks* and "*advocates of alarmism*" activates a story quite different from *people concerned about potential risks*.

Inhofe characterized a letter from the vice president of London's Royal Society to the media as a "*chilling*" letter "encouraging them to *stifle* the *voices* of scientists skeptical of *climate alarmism*." Finally, Inhofe claimed that the media have "*served up* a *parade of environmental alarmism*." "*Alarmism*" (which Inhofe used repeatedly) implies a story in which people attempt to arouse fear in others when there is in fact nothing to be afraid of. "*Stifle*" implies physical violence (ARGUMENT IS WAR). "*Parade*" is a vehicle referring to a story about a long line of entities, usually costumed and/or performing in some way; mapped onto a story about scientists warning about the potential effects of increased levels of CO_2 it implies a distracting "*performance*" that need not be taken seriously. "*Served up*" is a conventional metaphor for repetitive and tiresome rhetoric.

Disputing the evidence. Inhofe began his critique of evidence for the "*greenhouse* effect" with the "*hockey stick*" graph, initially produced by Mann, Bradley, and Hughes (1999) by combining recent measured (mean global) temperatures with estimates based on tree rings and other evidence from earlier periods. To smooth out fluctuations in the data, they produced a 30-year moving average, which shows a slowly declining mean global temperature from the year 1000 to 1900 (the "*shaft*" of the "*hockey stick*"), when the moving average began a rapid upward movement (the "*blade*"). Inhofe claimed that "the '*hockey stick*' was completely and thoroughly *broken* once and for all in 2006. Several years ago, two Canadian researchers *tore apart* the statistical *foundation* for the *hockey stick*."

The vehicle story in the first sentence implies a piece of equipment rendered totally useless; it maps onto a topic story about a series of papers that claimed to have found fatal flaws in the analysis used by Mann, Bradley, and Hughes (McIntyre & McKitrick, 2003; Soon & Baliunas, 2003). The second sentence combines a STRUCTURE metaphor with the *hockey stick* visual metaphor) and a vehicle story about the destruction of a structure; it maps onto a story about two independent research studies that claimed to refute Mann, Bradley, and Hughes's findings. In one, Soon and Baliunas (2003) claimed to have found evidence that mean temperatures were greater during the medieval warming period than in the 20th century. In another, McIntyre and McKitrick (2003) disputed the data used by Mann, Bradley, and Hughes. Inhofe did not mention that the Soon and Baliunas paper was immediately criticized by other scientists and its findings widely dismissed. McIntyre and McKitrick's paper also aroused considerable controversy, but several other replications have supported Mann, Bradley, and Hughes's method and findings; other researchers have also found parallel patterns using different data (e.g., Huang, Pollack, & Shen, 2008; Juckes et al., 2007; Kaufman et al., 2009; and Lee, Zwiers, & Tsao, 2008). In sum, Inhofe's criticism of Mann et al. was consistent with some of the information available at the time, but it was stated in exaggerated, absolute terms that betray a lack of understanding of scientific process – and he failed to note the controversies surrounding the evidence he used.

In several other places Inhofe implied or stated that scientists who study climate change ignore past fluctuations in global temperatures, e.g., "<u>Climate alarmists</u> have been attempting to *erase* the inconvenient Medieval Warm Period *from* the Earth's climate history for at least a decade." The vehicle is a story about someone erasing a passage from a history book; it maps onto a story about people who are concerned about climate change trying to get other people to ignore a set of historical facts. However, an examination of the controversy over the Mann, Bradley, and Hughes research shows that these researchers included the best data they had from the "Medieval Warm Period," and later researchers using better data did not find evidence that it was warmer then than during the 20th century.

Inhofe cited a number of scientists who have expressed disagreement with part or all of the climate change forecasts, most notably a 2006 open letter from Ian Clark and 60 other prominent scientists to the Canadian prime minister in which they recommend that he convene a national discussion of the issue. Clark et al. claimed, "If, *back in* the mid-1990s, we knew what we know today about climate, *Kyoto* would almost certainly not exist, because we would have concluded it was not necessary." However, the letter did not provide any details about "what we know today."

A little later, Inhofe stated:

> One of the *ways alarmists* have *pounded* this *mantra* of "consensus" *on* global warming *into* our pop culture is *through* the use of computer models which *project* future calamity. I now believe that the *greatest* climate threat we *face* may be coming from *alarmist* computer models.

"*Pounded ... into*" suggests a vehicle story of a muscular person with a sledgehammer driving a large stake into the ground, or perhaps a wedge into a block of wood; "*mantra*" activates a story of repeating a phrase over and over as a way of silencing a stream of thought. Blended with each other and with the "*alarmist*" metaphor previously discussed, they map onto a story of climate scientists attempting to convince others to become fearful about the damaging effects of "*greenhouse* gasses" and silence any other thoughts by repeating the same phrases over and over again with increasing emphasis. "The *greatest* climate threat we *face*" implies a story in which computer models somehow create severe damage or injury. He later claimed that these threatening models are "installed on the *hard drives* of the *publicity and grant seeking climate modelers*." The effect is simultaneously to impugn the motives of the climate scientists who warn of the danger of climate change and imply that these warnings are more dangerous than any of the effects they are warning us about.

Priorities. In several places Inhofe criticized the economic priorities implied by the proposal (in the Kyoto Protocol) to restrict emission of "*greenhouse* gasses" from the developing world as well as from the developed world: "The Kyoto Protocol is a lot of economic *pain* for no climate *gain*." He claims that the emission reduction targets are primarily symbolism, which "may be *hiding a dark side*" – the effect on poor people in the developing world who would be deprived of the advantages of access to clean water and labor-saving energy resources. "*Dark side*" can be interpreted in terms of either KNOWLEDGE IS LIGHT or GOOD IS LIGHT. "*Hiding*" implies KNOWING IS SEEING; the vehicle story of concealing the fact that an object is dark on one side maps onto a topic story of lying or keeping silent about known adverse effects of a policy, in this case known adverse effects on poor people in developing countries – a metaphorical story that implies bad faith on the part of climate scientists who favor implementation of the Kyoto Protocol.

A little later in the speech, Inhofe described a 2004 meeting of Nobel Prize–winning economists (the "Copenhagen Consensus") that organized the spending targets listed by the United Nations in a priority list, based on the potential return on investment for each proposal. Inhofe notes that they "*placed* global warming at the *bottom of the list in terms of our planet's priorities*," below "*combating* disease, *stopping* malaria, *securing* clean water, and building infrastructure to help *lift* the developing nations *out of* poverty." Inhofe overlooked the following excerpt from the 2004 Copenhagen Consensus report:

The panel recognised that global warming must be addressed, but agreed that approaches based on too abrupt a shift toward lower emissions of carbon are needlessly expensive. The experts expressed an interest in an alternative, proposed in one of the opponent papers, that envisaged a carbon tax much lower in the first years of implementation than the figures called for in the challenge paper, rising gradually in later years. ... The panel urged increased funding for research into more affordable carbon-abatement technologies.

In brief, the reason the committee ranked addressing global warming at the bottom of the list is that the proposal put before them was judged to be too costly for the prospective benefit, not because they considered the issue unimportant.

Back to the critique of media and media figures. Toward the end of the speech, Inhofe repeated the series of quotations from major newspapers and magazines, dating back to the late 19th century, in which the media predicted climate disasters – of opposite valence. "By the 1930s, the media *took a break* from reporting on the *coming* ice age and instead *switched gears* to *promoting* global warming." "*Took a break* from" implies a story in which a person is working on an extended project and pauses for rest before resuming work; mapped onto the topic it implies that the media regarded reporting about an impending disaster (as opposed to reporting on what climate scientists have to say) as their primary job; this interpretation is reinforced by "*promoting*," which maps public relations practices onto media reporting. "*Switched gears*" maps a story about driving a motor vehicle onto the topic story of news reporting.

Focusing his attention on Jim Hansen, Inhofe noted that a *60 Minutes* report on climate change "made no mention of Hansen's partisan *ties* to former Democrat Vice President Al Gore," the grant Hansen received "from the *left-wing* Heinz Foundation" or the fact that Hansen later endorsed John Kerry for president. "So it *appears* that the media makes a distinction between *oil money* and *ketchup money*." This bit of word play is an apparent reference to criticisms of the lobbying and political contributions by representatives of the petroleum industry. Finally he noted that "Hansen *appeared* to concede *in* a 2003 issue of Natural Science that the use of 'extreme scenarios' to dramatize climate change 'may have been appropriate *at one time*' to *drive* the public's attention to *the issue*."

Inhofe used several other dramatic story metaphors and metaphorical stories in his critique of media coverage. "A*s the dog days of August rolled in*, the American people were once again *hit* with more *hot* hype regarding global warming, this time *from The New York Times* op-ed pages." It isn't clear whether he meant that the hype was "*hot*" or that the *Times* coverage was hyping stories about *hot* weather – which is consistent with "*dog days of August*" that "*rolled in*" (TIME IS MOTION THROUGH SPACE). Toward the end of the speech the quotes "a British group called the Institute for Public Policy Research ... a *left leaning* group" who characterized exaggerated reports of potential negative results of climate change as "*climate porn*" then notes with approval that "the media's *addiction* to so-called '*climate porn*' has failed to *seduce* many Americans." "*Climate porn*" suggests both that climate reporting is irresponsible and exaggerated in a way similar to the way pornography exaggerates sexual behavior and that exaggerated reports of climate change effects appeal to a prurient impulse similar to sexual voyeurism. "*Addiction to*" implies a story about drug addicts who are so dependent on a drug that they will do anything to secure more of it, and maps it onto the news media's need for dramatic stories. "Failed to *seduce*" reinforces the sexual story implied by "*porn*," activates a story about how pornography leads to sexual arousal and maps it onto readers' responses to climate change stories – they are not aroused by them.

Summary. Senator Inhofe's speech was presented primarily as a criticism of news media coverage of climate research and as a refutation of the evidence produced by scientists like Jim Hansen to support the claim that human activities have led to a radical increase in the concentration of "*greenhouse gasses*" in the atmosphere and that this will lead to atmospheric warming and climate change. Some of the evidence he produced has been discredited, and he presented some of it in a clearly distorted way. Like Hansen in his 2008 testimony to congress and his TED talk, Inhofe used a series of frightening metaphorical stories, enhanced by grammatical metaphors, but he used them primarily to discredit the metaphorical stories used by Hansen and others concerned about climate change, while intensifying simulation of a different set of catastrophic outcomes predicted to result from the actions advocated by Hansen.

Inhofe's use of phrases like "left-*leaning*" and his treatment of Jim Hansen's political relationship with Al Gore and John Kerry, as well as his reliance on conservative and business-oriented media (like Bloomberg News) is likely to reinforce the political polarization over this question, in which people who believe that the evidence supports the conclusion that increased concentration of "*greenhouse* gasses" will lead to atmospheric warming and eventually to ecological crises are called "climate change *promoters*" and people who are not convinced by the available evidence are called "climate change *deniers*." I will return to this issue later in this chapter.

Barack Obama's 2013 Address at Georgetown University

In June 2013 President Obama gave a major address on climate change at Georgetown University. He began and ended the speech with a literal story about the Apollo 8 lunar orbit mission; this story underscores the "*fragility*" of

Earth, and frames the issue simultaneously in terms of American scientific prowess and shared religious heritage (the astronauts read from the book of Genesis as they looked back on Earth from moon orbit on Christmas Eve). Within the body of the speech he framed the topic of climate change in terms of three contrasts, peace / violence, active / passive, and past Republican bipartisan cooperation / present Republican partisanship (Ritchie & Thomas, 2015). Like Obama's speech on race relations (Chapter 9), this speech is also laced with metaphors, drawn primarily from JOURNEY / MOTION, SPACE / CONTAINER, WAR, OBJECT and PERSON; he also drew on CONSTRUCTION, BUSINESS, SPORTS, and VISION.

Immediately after the Apollo 8 story, Obama summarized recent changes in the atmosphere using a combination of dramatic metaphors, e.g., "worry that *rising levels* (MORE IS UP) might someday *disrupt* the *fragile balance* (CLIMATE IS AN UNSTABLE OBJECT; EQUILIBRIUM IS A BREAKABLE OBJECT) that makes our planet so *hospitable* (HUMANS ARE GUESTS ... Science ... *tells us* (PERSONIFICATION) that our planet is changing in ways that will *have profound impacts* ... (AN EFFECT IS A BLOW) ... The potential *impacts go beyond* (JOURNEY, MOTION) rising sea levels." He linked these *"impacts"* first to the recent storm-surge flooding in New York City, then to droughts that *parched* and subsequent heavy rains that *drenched* Midwest farms, wildfires that *scorched* a large area of the West, and "a heat *wave* in Alaska" that *"shot* temperatures *into* the 90s" (WAR). He continued with several more examples of recent weather-related disaster, then referred to recent arguments over whether the evidence for human contributions to climate change is sufficient to justify a potentially quite expensive response and asserted that "Ninety-seven percent of scientists, including ... some who originally disputed the data, have ... acknowledged the planet is warming and human activity is *contributing to* it."

Shifting to his action plan, Obama asserted "I refuse to *condemn* your generation and future generations to a planet that's *beyond fixing*." "A planet that's *beyond fixing*" blends a metaphor that presents Earth as an object (machine or structure) in need of repair with a JOURNEY metaphor to produce a story metaphor mapping onto a topic story about reducing or reversing the effects of climate change. "I refuse to *condemn* your generation to a planet" implies a vehicle story in which a judge sentences a group of people to exile in a remote location; the blend of these two vehicle stories produces a topic story in which Obama is a judge being asked to sentence an entire group of people to the punishment of living in an environment that is subject to irreparable damage from climate change.

Obama then picked up the WAR metaphor again: "I'm here to *enlist* your generation's help ... *in the fight against* climate change." These metaphors activate a vehicle story about WAR (in which the United States is a leader) and maps it onto Obama's proposed environmental policies. He then blended two new metaphors into a different story metaphor: "This plan *builds on progress* that we've already *made*. Last year, I *took* office. ... And we *rolled up our sleeves* and we *got to work*." "*Builds on*" and "*rolled up our sleeves ... and got to work*" activate a story about a group of workers on a construction project; "*progress*" activates a JOURNEY metaphor. The blended vehicle story maps onto a topic story about the Obama administration's attempts to convince Congress to pass needed environmental legislation. The following passage details some results of these efforts, and sums them up with another series of metaphors: "These *advances* [MOTION] have *grown* our economy [ORGANISM], they've *created* new jobs [OBJECT], they can't be *shipped overseas* [MOTION] – and, *by the way*, they've also helped *drive* [FORCE] our carbon pollution to its *lowest levels in* [MORE IS UP, LESS IS DOWN] nearly 20 years."

Obama then turned his attention to the political obstacles to action: "But this is a *challenge* that does not *pause* for partisan *gridlock*. It *demands* our attention now." Here climate change is presented as a PERSON who "*challenges*" the nation; then the challenge is presented as PERSON who is MOVING forward in spite of the "*gridlock*" (a traffic condition in which no vehicles are able to move in any direction – ACCOMPLISHMENT IS MOTION) and "*demands*" attention. All of this is consistent with "climate change is *the enemy*," a WAR metaphor explicitly picked up again at the end of this passage: "a plan to *lead* the world in a coordinated *assault* on a changing climate." At this point Obama followed up on the "*gridlock*" metaphor by relating a story about a previous time, 43 years earlier, when Congress passed the Clean Air Act almost unanimously and it was signed by a Republican president, contrasted the bipartisan spirit of that time with the partisanship of the present time, and called on the present Congress to act in a similar bipartisan way.

In further follow-up, Obama repeated several objections to new environmental regulations that "you'll *hear* from the *special interests* and their *allies in* Congress." Everyone involved in this discussion uses "*special interests*" to describe those who disagree with them, with the implication that their opposition is based solely on (usually financial) self-interest. Obama used it several times in this speech. "*Allies in* Congress" implies the ARGUMENT IS WAR metaphor, with "*special interests*" as the "*enemy*." Many of the expected objections are expressed as story metaphors (i.e., they imply metaphorical stories): "this will *kill* jobs and *crush* the economy, and basically *end* American free enterprise." "*At the time* when we passed the Clean Air Act to try to *get rid of* some of this smog, some of the same doomsayers were saying new pollution standards will *decimate the auto industry*. ... they said our electricity bills would *go up*, the lights would *go off*, businesses around the country would *suffer* – I quote – '*a quiet death*' ... When we phased out CFCs ... it didn't *kill off* refrigerators or air conditioners or deodorant." Each of these metaphor vehicles activates a vehicle story about death and destruction – consistent with a WAR metaphor, but with *environmental regulations* rather than *pollution* as the "*enemy.*" As he listed these predictions that were made about previous environmental regulations, Obama refuted each one, pointing out that each set of regulations had the intended effect ("Our air got *cleaner* ... we *cut* acid rain *dramatically* ... American chemists *came up with* substitutes ... American workers and businesses figured out how to do it better without harming the environment as much").

Obama named companies who were taking action to reduce carbon emissions and change to renewable energy, and mentioned a Climate Declaration in which a large group of businesses called "*action on* climate change 'one of the *great* economic opportunities of the 21st century,'" and concluded that "A *low*-carbon, *clean* energy economy can be an *engine of growth* for decades *to come*. And I want America to *build that engine*. I want America to *build* that future." "*Growth*" implies an economic metaphor based on FINANCIAL AMOUNT IS PHYSICAL SIZE; this passage further embeds it in a metaphorical story based on JOURNEY, in which "*low-carbon energy sources*" is represented as an "*engine, pulling* the economy *forward on its journey.*" This is further embedded in a metaphorical story based on CONSTRUCTION in which the United States "*builds*" the "*engine of growth.*"

A few paragraphs later, Obama repeated the WAR metaphor: "last year, Republican governors in Kansas and Oklahoma and Iowa – Iowa, by the way, a state that *harnesses* almost twenty-five percent of its electricity from the wind – helped us in the *fight* to *extend* tax credits for wind energy manufacturers and producers. Tens of thousands good jobs were *on the line*, and those jobs were *worth* the *fight.*" "*Harness*" is an ORGANIC metaphor ("*wind is a team of horses*") and "*extend*" a SPACE metaphor; otherwise the metaphors and metaphorical stories in this section are all based on POLITICS IS WAR. After repeating the war metaphor, Obama introduced a metaphorical story based on SPORTS: "countries like China and Germany are *going all in in* the *race* for clean energy. ... I want America to *win that race*, but we can't *win it* if we're not *in it.*" Another metaphorical story based on sports comes a few paragraphs later, blended with a CONTAINER metaphor for investment: "We'll also encourage private capital to *get off the sidelines* and *get into* these energy-saving investments."

After describing his proposal for new energy efficiency standards, Obama admitted that they "don't sound all that *sexy*" (EXCITEMENT IS SEX), then compared the proposal to "planting 7.6 billion trees and letting them *grow* for ten years – all *while doing the dishes.*" This metaphorical story contrasts a simple routine domestic chore with a common scheme for offsetting carbon fuel use by planting trees – expanded by a very large factor. He then returned to another metaphorical story based on JOURNEY / MOTION, preceded by a conventional DIRTY / CLEAN metaphor for pollution: "So using less *dirty* energy, transitioning to *cleaner* sources of energy, wasting less energy *through our economy* is *where we need to go*. And this plan will *get us there faster*. But I want to be honest – this will not *get us there overnight*." After explaining that "even if we Americans *do our part,* the planet will *slowly keep* warming for some time to come," he used another metaphorical story reinforcing the JOURNEY metaphor: "It's like *tapping the brakes of a car before you come to a complete stop and then can shift into reverse*. It's *going* to *take time* for carbon emissions to *stabilize*."

Obama used several other JOURNEY / MOTION metaphors. After acknowledging the special needs of developing countries, he proposed that we need to "help more countries *skip past* the *dirty* phase of development." Contrasting current attitudes of congressional Republicans with past Republican leaders, he pointed out, "It wasn't that long ago that Republicans *led the way* on new and innovative policies." Referring to Gina McCarthy, who he had nominated to head the EPA, he said, "She's being *held up in* the Senate. She's been *held up* for months, *forced* to *jump through hoops*" (treated like a TRAINED CIRCUS ANIMAL).

Near the end of the speech, Obama used three more metaphorical stories to criticize people who disregard or dispute the evidence that human activities have contributed substantial to the increase in "*greenhouse* gasses" like CO_2 and thus have contributed to the growing risk of climate change: "Nobody *has a monopoly on* what is a very *hard* problem, but I don't have much patience for anyone who denies that this challenge is real. We don't *have time* for a meeting of the *Flat Earth Society*." "*Flat Earth Society*" is based on a vehicle story about a group of people who deny that the Earth is a globe; it idiomatically maps onto any group of people who resist the progress of science or deny established knowledge. "*Sticking your head in the sand* might make you feel safer, but it's not going to protect you from *the coming storm*." "*Sticking your head in the sand*" activates a common folk belief that ostriches, when they perceive something dangerous, don't run away but just hide from it by burying their heads in the sand; this has become an idiomatic story metaphor for any situation in which someone ignores a threat that could have been averted. "*The coming storm*" activates a story about seeing signs such as a mass of clouds that indicate that there will soon be a serious storm; this is a common idiomatic story metaphor mapping onto any situation in which serious trouble seems likely. The two stories blend into a single metaphorical story about ignoring the signs of trouble by "*looking away*." These two metaphorical stories together convey a belittling and dismissive, even contemptuous attitude toward "climate change deniers," which is summed up in a final metaphorical story: "And ultimately, we will be *judged* as a people, and as a society, and as a country *on where we go from here,"* which continues the JOURNEY metaphor used throughout the speech, and integrates it into a story about being *"judged."*

At the end of the speech, Obama returned to the WAR metaphor: "this is the *fight* America can, and will, *lead in* the 21st century. And I'm convinced this is a *fight* that America must *lead*. But it will require all of us to *do our part*." *"Do our part"* fits readily into a number of very different metaphorical stories, but in a story about the duty to *"lead a fight"* it suggests a total mobilization of workers as well as soldiers. Then, just before returning to the Apollo 8 story, he wrapped up with another series of metaphorical stories: "The challenge we must *accept* will not *reward* us with a *clear moment of victory*. There's no *gathering army* to *defeat*. There's no *peace treaty* to sign." Each of these phrases indexes a different feature of the standard WAR metaphorical story, which begins with the gathering of an enemy army, which is defeated in a way that yields a *"clear"* victory and leads to signing a peace treaty. Each of these standard features is negated, leaving an implicit contrast with the *"war against* climate change," in which everything will be ambiguous and uncertain, and with no obvious completion. All of this explains why, in contrast to a literal war in which the gathering enemy army and hope of a clear victory to maintain morale, in this case "the politics will be *tough*."

Discussion. In addition to the metaphorical stories and story metaphors described in the foregoing, Obama used a series of tricolons and alliterative phrases both to describe the recent and forecasted effects of climate change and to rally support for his policies. Forests and farms are being *parched*, *drenched, and scorched*. Crops are *wilted* one year, *washed away* the next. Industries *pump* and *dump* carbon pollution into the air. Those in power "are elected not just to serve as *custodians* of the present, but as *caretakers* of the future." Americans do not *"look backward"*; we *"look forward."* We do not *"fear* what the future *holds*; we *shape* it." Citizens are urged to *"stand up," "speak up,"* and *"compel* action" (Ritchie & Thomas, 2015).

Repeatedly in this speech, Obama called for an end to partisanship and the resumption of the kind of bipartisan approach to environmental issues that led to passage of several other environmental protection laws during the late twentieth century. However, his contrast between "Republicans then" and "Republicans now," along with the implications of several of his metaphorical stories, seem more likely to aggravate the political polarization than to reduce it (Ritchie & Thomas, 2015).

Conclusions

There is growing evidence that human activities, particularly the use of carbon-based fuels for industry and transportation, as well as industrialized agriculture, are causing an increase in concentrations of CO_2 and other "*greenhouse* gasses" in the atmosphere, and that these changes are likely to lead to a significant increase in global temperatures accompanied by rising sea levels and other disruptive changes to the environment. The climate systems involved in these predicted effects are complex and poorly understood, and the economic stakes for several industrial sectors are quite high; the result is that both proposed policy responses and the underlying science itself have become the focus of intense political debate.

Participants in the debate, including both scientists and politicians, have used both conventional metaphors and metaphorical stories. As the analysis of Jim Hansen's series of speeches on the topic demonstrates, as the intensity of the debate has increased, the use of dynamic and dramatic metaphors has also increased, and many of these seem more likely to increase than to ameliorate the polarization. In his 2008 speech Jim Hansen used many metaphors of violence when talking about human contributions to climate change ("*time bomb*," "*giant asteroid*," "*Hiroshima bombs*," "*perfect storm*") in contrast to the much milder, even peaceable metaphors he used to discuss his proposals for ameliorating these effects ("a *path yielding* energy independence and a *healthier* environment," "*wean* us off fossil fuel *addiction*," "*put on a path toward* carbon *neutrality*").

Obama referred to people who dispute the scientific evidence for the "*greenhouse* effect" as the "*Flat Earth Society*" and implicitly accused them of "*sticking their heads in the sand.*" Using a common populist metonym, Hansen referred to "*swarms* of high-priced lobbyists *in alligator shoes*" who are working to discredit scientific evidence of climate change. Jim Inhofe used belittling story metaphors such as "*peddle*," "*fear-mongering*," "*parade*," and "*climate porn.*" Advocates for both positions use metaphors like "*addiction*" and "*special interests*" to impugn the motives of others.

Citing Ritchie and Cameron (2014), Ritchie and Thomas (2015) observe that empathy requires both the willingness and the ability to "*enter into the world of the Other*," which requires as a precondition a respect for the beliefs and concerns of the Other. As Ritchie and Thomas observed about President Obama's belittling comparison of earlier Republicans' bipartisan cooperation on environmental issues and current Republicans' obstructionism, this kind of amplified rhetoric undermines rather than builds the conditions for empathy. President Obama's ironic, even sarcastic contrast between "Republicans then" and "Republicans now," and the shift in tone between Hansen's 1988 and 2008 testimony both suggest that they have simply given up on the attempt to achieve empathetic understanding of the Republican Other, much less convince them. At the other end of the political spectrum, Inhofe also relied heavily on belittling and sarcastic story metaphors to discredit the advocates of policy action to address the rapid buildup of "*greenhouse*" gasses in the atmosphere, while presenting a distorted account of evidence against human contributions to climate change. Based on these samples of recent rhetoric on the topic, the prospect for an open and candid discussion of how to balance the potential damaging effects of *"greenhouse"* gas emissions with the economic needs of the world population do not seem very promising.

Inhofe's criticism of climate science is consistent with a recent and growing concern about public distrust of science (Gauchat, 2012). Some observers (e.g., Mooney, 2005; 2012) have claimed to identify a psychological difference between liberals and conservatives, claiming that conservatives are more likely than liberals to distrust and reject scientific findings that contradict their belief systems. However, Nisbet, Cooper, and Garrett (2015) show that both liberals and conservatives tend to engage in "motivated reasoning" (Kunda, 1990), discredit and even distort scientific findings that contradict their worldviews. The primary difference is that conservatives are more likely to reject science that focuses on environmental and health impacts of social and economic activities; liberals are more likely to reject science that focuses on industrial production. Both liberals and conservatives tend to resist or ignore messages that challenge deeply held beliefs and values. With respect to climate science in particular, conservatives have been faced with a steady stream of dissonance-producing messages in recent years, while the messages from climate scientists have been more consistent with liberal beliefs. When some climate scientists, such as those cited by Senator Inhofe, present evidence that contradicts the prevailing wisdom, liberals are just as likely to discredit or dismiss the evidence they present as conservatives are to dismiss the evidence that supports the claim that human activities are affecting the climate.

The use of story metaphors and metaphorical stories by both Hansen and Obama (on the liberal side) and Inhofe (on the conservative side) are symptomatic of the political polarization on this issue. Far from contributing to an ability to enter into the experiential world of the Other and thus help establish conditions of empathy and genuine conversation, these dramatic metaphorical stories and the simulations they evoke are more likely to undermine the conditions of empathy and block meaningful conversation.

The contrast between Obama's 2008 speech on race and his 2013 speech on climate change is particularly instructive. In the 2008 speech, he told stories about the frustrations faced by working-class African Americans in their attempt to achieve middle-class economic security, then connected these to parallel stories about the struggles and frustrations of working class White Americans, implicitly acknowledging the separate experiential worlds and inviting both groups to enter into the experiential world of the Other. In the 2013 speech, by contrast, he made no attempt even to recognize much less enter into the experiential world of conservatives. In both speeches he combined hyperbole with metaphorical stories in a way that enhanced the potential simulations, but in the 2008 speech he used this simulation-enhancing technique to open the experiential world of White Americans as well as that of Black Americans. In contrast, in the 2013 speech the hyperbole and metaphorical stories enhanced the experience of predicted climate change effects and the evidence supporting these predictions, but denigrated and dismissed the concerns of those who question either the evidence or the proposed remedies.

In sum, the dramatic metaphorical stories used by advocates on each side of the debate over the contribution of human activities to climate change have the potential to activate vivid perceptual simulations including complete stories that increases the intensity of belief and commitment among those who are already convinced of the advocated position – but they are likely to be ignored, discredited, and dismissed by those who are convinced of the opposite position. The result is to render the experiential world of each side even more opaque to those on the other side, decrease rather than increase the potential for empathy and genuine conversation, and increase the polarization over the issue, both the facts represented by the evidence and the policies proposed to address the complex problems associated with it.

11   Metaphorical Stories in Visual Communication

Until recently *metaphor* was regarded as exclusively a feature of language. However, subsequent to the introduction of CMT (Lakoff & Johnson, 1980), the scope of the concept, *metaphor*, has inevitably expanded. If metaphors exist as relationships between embodied experience and abstract concepts, as Lakoff and Johnson argue, or even as relationships among abstract concepts (e.g., between war and argument), then it follows that metaphors can be expressed in modes other than language (Forceville & Urios-Aparisi, 2009). Forceville (2009a) further argues that a complete theory of conceptual metaphor must account for a wider range of metaphors including, at the very least, metaphors expressed visually in gesture and images, and sonically, including music and vocal qualities.

Forceville's discussion implies two separate distinctions. The first and perhaps most obvious distinction is between language, in whatever mode it is expressed (e.g., spoken, written, or signed), and all other kinds of communicative exchange. But it is also important to distinguish among perceptual modes within language. Spoken and written language afford different opportunities (or risks) of ambiguity and misperception, and they also afford different opportunities for combining signals in different modes. Spoken language combines readily with music and gesture; written language with pictures and diagrams – even typography affords opportunities for visual metaphor, as when **bold print** is used to express an idea *'forcibly.'*

Most of the research to date on metaphors in modes other than language has focused on *visual* metaphors, in particular the metaphorical images in editorial cartoons and advertising and, more recently, metaphorical gestures. Visual metaphors in editorial cartoons and advertisements appear both with and without accompanying language. Often the visual metaphor simply illustrates a metaphor that is already familiar in language; these examples may appear alone or they may be accompanied by a linguistic expression of the same metaphor. Sometimes language appears as an anchor to guide interpretation of the visual metaphor; sometimes it appears as a contrast or comment on the visual metaphor. Although they usually present a single "moment in time" image, visual images may also suggest or imply a story; for example, Edwards

(1997) argues that political cartoons have the effect of narrative because they invite viewers to complete a story suggested by the depicted moment. Visual advertisements and visual art also have the potential to invite viewers to enter a "story world" and complete the story that includes the depicted scene.

Earlier chapters have focused on metaphorical stories (stories apparently intended to map metaphorically onto unrelated topics or, occasionally to map metonymically onto a different aspect of a related topic) and story metaphors, words or phrases that potentially activate metaphorical stories. Visual images that either depict or suggest story metaphors and metaphorical stories, such as the cover image, a 16th-century painting titled *The Blind Leading the Blind* by Pieter Bruegel the Elder, have been discussed in connection with some of these examples; this chapter will examine metaphorical stories in visual media in more detail.

Editorial Cartoons

An editorial cartoon consists of an image, alone or in combination with language, presented as a comment on some aspect of current public life. Cartoons are similar in some ways to comic strips, and use some of the same conventions, including visual metonyms such as lines to indicate speed and motion and stylized indications of emotion and response. However, comic strips usually include a sequence of panels representing the progress of a story line; political cartoons are usually confined within a single panel. Even if multiple panels are used in a political cartoon, they more frequently represent comparison or contrast rather than the progress of a story line. Editorial cartoons usually address a current public (political or social) issue, event, or personality in a way that represents a particular point of view. Political cartoons are often but not always humorous or at least ironic; they usually juxtapose images, stories, or ideas in a way that is incongruous or surprising.

Lin and Chiang (2015) argue that visual metaphors are comprehended through multimodal fusion of verbal, visual, and conceptual elements from both vehicle and topic. An example they cite is a cartoon about the controversy over importation of U.S. beef into Taiwan. The image shows a statue of a bull made of wood with a partially open door in its side, on wheels before the gates of a walled city. The body of the bull is labeled "U.S. Beef." A figure standing between the bull statue and the barely open city gates is quoted as saying, "Open the door, your commander's rewards are coming." Lin and Chiang argue that the concept of the Trojan Horse (from the *Iliad*) is blended with the concept of beef importation, the language with its ambiguous mention of "reward," and the image, which itself blends the Trojan Horse (a statue made of wood with a door in it) with a wooden statue of a bull, metonymically representing U.S. beef. Examining this example from the present perspective, the Trojan horse activates the story of the insertion of Greek troops into Troy inside a wooden statue, presented as a prize recognizing the Trojan victory, which led to the actual defeat and destruction of Troy. The wording guides mapping this vehicle story onto a projected topic story about allowing beef to be imported into the country (the *"Trojan bull"*) with consequent damage to Taiwanese consumers and markets.

Because cartoons often use familiar images and symbols, researchers often treat editorial cartoons as straightforward and transparent, with self-evident and easily discerned meaning. However, interpretation of editorial cartoons requires a familiarity with cartoon conventions in general (e.g., speech balloons; the use of wavy lines to represent fire and curved lines to represent motion), and the particular cartoonist's style along with a broad knowledge of current events, politics, history, and cultural themes such as the Trojan horse (El Refaie, 2009a; 2009b). Political cartoons often combine real and imaginary elements, or present real elements in a fantastic or imaginary way. Although they are not always metaphorical, the image they present often suggests an imaginary story in a fictional world which refers, at a more abstract level, to real-life events and persons. "This relationship between the two levels of meaning is essentially metaphorical, inviting people to map properties from a more tangible area of reality onto one that is more abstract" (El Refaie, 2009b, p. 186).

Although we often associate editorial cartoons with commentary on political issues, they also comment on many other aspects of public life and culture. A cartoon by El Roto (2003), "La Gran Droga," depicts the plunger of a syringe, with the image of a television broadcast tower located in place of the needle. This cartoon visually represents a common conceptual metaphor, MASS MEDIA IS A DRUG, which has appeared in many forms, including book titles such as *The Plug-in Drug: Television, Children, and the Family* (Winn, 1977). The syringe activates a vehicle story about injecting a drug and the broadcast antenna activates a story about broadcasting a television signal; the blend maps the vehicle story onto a topic story about '*addiction*' to television.

Political cartoons. Editorial cartoons frequently comment on political issues, leaders, or candidates. Sometimes the images simply refer to a literal story but often the cartoonist uses images to create a metaphorical story. An example is a cartoon by Nicholas Garland (2004; reproduced by El Refaie, 2009a, p. 178), "Playing with Matches," in which the cartoonist uses a metaphorical story to comment on the reelection of George W. Bush. A toddler (with the face of President Bush) is shown crawling away from a set of wavy lines apparently intended to depict a large fire toward a matchbox, next to several loose matches. The label on the matchbox says, "4 more years." These are the only words in the cartoon; they serve to anchor the topic as Bush's second term. The fire is "*behind*" the President / toddler and the matchbox and loose matches are *"in front"* of him (PAST IS BEHIND / FUTURE IS IN FRONT).

The apparent intent is to activate a familiar metaphor *"playing with matches,"* or *"playing with fire."* The wavy lines (*"fire"*) in the background implies a vehicle story in which the toddler / Bush has already started one huge fire; the matchbox suggests a continuation of that story into the future, when Bush will start yet more fires. The topic is implied by the label "4 more years" – but it is left to the viewer to determine whether the *"fire"* in the background is intended to refer specifically the war in Iraq or to more general effects of Bush's presidency (DESTRUCTION IS FIRE, CHAOS IS FIRE). Fire is not easy to draw in a cartoon and it is possible that some readers, even with the cue of the matchbox, might not have understood that the curvy lines in the background were intended to represent fire.

In the case of *Playing with Matches*, the cartoonist based the metaphorical story on an idiomatic metaphor for reckless risk taking. Cartoonists also frequently transform a real episode into a metaphor vehicle. An example is a Bagley (2007) cartoon commenting on the second Iraq War. In this cartoon, a wrecked and burning military jet with the word *Iraq* on its fuselage is depicted on the left, a man in a flight suit, holding his right arm aloft with the "V for Victory" gesture, is running toward a podium bearing what appears to be the U.S. presidential seal. The podium is directly in front of the bridge of an aircraft carrier. The banner on the bridge of the aircraft carrier with the words "MISSION ACCOMPLIS ..." and the man wearing a pilot's uniform, with George W. Bush's face, running from the plane toward the podium with its presidential seal evokes the 2003 incident when President Bush flew (as a passenger) onto the aircraft carrier USS *Abraham Lincoln* to give a speech celebrating the victory over Saddam Hussein in the second Iraq War. The celebratory incident was later heavily criticized as rather premature because of the guerilla insurgency that broke out shortly afterward. The plane is labeled "IRAQ," underscoring the reference to the Iraq War; it is depicted as a wreck in flames, in a position suggesting that it nosedived into the deck of the carrier.

These elements imply a fictional story about a crash-landing on the carrier deck (in fact, President Bush rode as a passenger and the jet landed safely on the deck of the carrier). The word "IRAQ" on the fuselage of the aircraft maps this vehicle story onto the topic story about how the victory in Iraq turned into the *"wreckage"* of a disastrous prolonged guerilla war, a war that left Iraq itself in flaming ruins (literally as well as metaphorically). The wreckage could refer to the U.S. war effort, to Iraq as a nation, or both. To understand this metaphorical story, the reader would have to know about the controversy over Bush's 2003 flight and speech, and about subsequent events in Iraq.

The basic vehicle story suggested by the "Mission Accomplished" incident has been reused many times. David Fitzsimmons (2014) blended the basic

Figure 11.1 David Fitzsimmons (2014) *Arizona Daily Star Mission Accomplished: Iraq.* Used with permission.

"mission accomplished" story with a funeral story (Figure 11.1). The funeral wreath with its banner reading "Mission Accomplished" and the image of a U.S. flag activates a conventional *"funeral"* story schema. The headstone with its inscription activates the story of Iraq as a modern nation; the dates "1920–2014," which conventionally refer to a deceased person's birth to death life span, implies that "Modern Iraq" was born in 1920 and died in 2014. For readers familiar with Middle Eastern culture, the minarets on the tombstone reinforce the association with the Middle East.

The brown areas within curved lines suggest heaps of fresh dirt, implying a just-completed burial, but the skulls and bones sticking out of the fresh dirt imply multiple past deaths, marking the grave site as a "killing field" where many dead people have been buried without ceremony. The man in the background, wearing the red, white, and blue top hat that conventionally symbolizes "Uncle Sam" (the United States) has *"turned his back on"* the grave site and is *"walking away,"* potentially activating a story about insouciance and casual neglect. The cracks on the headstone also suggest a story of destruction and decay that underscores the ironic implications of the "mission accomplished" banner. The implied reference to the disastrous outcome of the second Gulf War, seven years earlier, and its ironic contrast with the rest of the image can be read as an indictment of both the previous and the current administration's policies with respect to Iraq. Even more than the Bagley version of "Mission Accomplished," Fitzsimmons's version requires an extensive and detailed application of historical and political background knowledge of its readers.

Further afield, Kirk Walters (2011) showed the U.S. Capitol building on end, half submerged in water (like a sinking ship) with two speech balloons. The top speech balloon reads, "Captain Boehner, we've run aground and are sinking fast." A second balloon, just below the first speech balloon (suggesting it is Boehner's reply), reads, "Mission accomplished." Here the basic "mission accomplished" story is blended with a sinking ship story; "Boehner," the name of the Republican Speaker of the U.S. House of Representatives at the time, maps the blended vehicle story onto a topic story in which the Republican majority, under Boehner's leadership, "*sinks*" the U.S. government. (The image of a sinking ship or some other object positioned like a sinking ship is frequently used in editorial cartoons to activate a familiar vehicle story script like "The Titanic" or "running aground.")

Visual images imply metaphors through many devices. The combination of a jet plane and the "mission accomplished" banner evokes the story of Bush's premature victory speech; after many uses in editorial cartoons the banner alone came to be sufficient. Cartoonists develop caricatures to represent public figures, usually settling on an accepted image based on an exaggeration of some feature, which also becomes sufficiently familiar that a label is no longer needed. The big ears and silly-looking smile on the figure in the Bagley cartoon had by 2007 become a familiar symbol of President Bush; Bagley apparently saw no need to label the figure running from the wrecked plane to the podium. The striped top hat on the "Uncle Sam" figure in the Fitzsimmons cartoon is even more familiar, readily recognized in most parts of the world.

Law and justice. Both the U.S. Statue of Liberty and the statue of Justice that stands in front of many courthouses are depicted wearing a draped robe, symbolizing them as Roman goddesses. The goddess Liberty holds a tablet inscribed with the date of the American Declaration of Independence in one hand and an uplifted torch in the other hand, evoking the metaphor vehicle "*light*," implying both KNOWLEDGE IS LIGHT and FREEDOM IS LIGHT. A broken chain lies at her feet, activating a generic story of "*breaking the chains*" that maps metaphorically onto the story about gaining freedom from oppression and servitude, and in particular about abolition of slavery.

The goddess of Justice that stands in front of many courthouses and courtrooms also makes use of the "draped garment" symbol to signify a goddess. Typically she is blindfolded – thus unable to "*see*" social status and other personal characteristics of those brought before her (TO SEE IS TO KNOW). She carries a scale in one hand, to "*weigh*" the evidence presented to her (IMPORTANCE IS WEIGHT), and a sword in the other, with which to administer justice. These symbols blend into a vehicle story in which evidence is *"weighed"* by someone who is *"blindfolded"* so she cannot see the social status or other irrelevant personal attributes of those brought before her, and she decides cases solely according to the *"weight"* of the evidence. (An ironic transformation of this conventional metaphor in a discussion about incidents in which unarmed African American citizens are killed by police officers, is discussed in Chapter 6.)

Because they are familiar to almost everyone, at least in the United States, these two images are frequently modified to create metaphorical stories that comment on a variety of issues, particularly issues related to the U.S. Supreme Court. For example, Toles (2012) shows a statue of a *naked* goddess of Justice, standing on a pedestal labeled "Supreme Court" with her arms crossed, the left arm (holding the sword) covering her pubic area and her right arm, holding the scales, covering her breasts; her blindfold has been removed and she is in a cowering position with a dismayed and embarrassed expression (evocative of a woman who finds herself unexpectedly naked in public); her robe is lying on the ground next to the pedestal. The word "partisanship" is written along her exposed thigh; the cartoon is labeled "strip search." A tiny figure representing the cartoonist, seated at a drawing table, comments "look in the scales." This blends a story about a strip search of a young girl who was accused of carrying a restricted medication to school with the story implied by the standard version of the *"Blind Justice"* image into a vehicle story of *"laying bare"* the partisanship with which the Supreme Court was accused of having decided several recent cases.

Nate Beeler (2014) combined these two metaphorical vehicle images, *"Liberty"* and *"Justice"* to celebrate the Supreme Court decision striking down the Defense of Marriage Act (DOMA). The Statue of Liberty stands, leaning slightly backward, with the goddess Justice in her arms, clutching a paper reading "DOMA Ruling." Liberty's sword is stuck in the ground, her scales lying next to it as if dropped in haste. The two are out of balance, with Liberty leaning back slightly, holding Justice in her arms; Justice's legs are off the ground as if she had just jumped into the arms of Liberty. The image suggests two lovers passionately embracing after a long separation – it also resembles contemporary news photos of lesbians embracing in celebration after the DOMA decision was announced. In the background, soft yellow (suggesting sunlight) behind Justice fades into soft blue behind Liberty. The image suggests a vehicle story in which Justice saw the ruling, dropped her sword and scales, and leaped passionately into the arms of Liberty. It maps both onto the celebratory joy of the gay and lesbian community and, potentially, onto a more abstract story about resolving the tension between freedom and equality by permitting the *"marriage"* of Liberty to Justice.

222   Metaphorical Stories in Visual Communication

> All Americans are equal but some Americans are more equal than others.

SCOTUS

CITIZENS UNITED AND McCUTCHEON RULINGS

P. JAMIOL

Figure 11.2 Jamiol (2014): Animal Farm. Used with permission.

Cartoonists often draw on metaphors originating in entirely different realms of experience to comment on political issues. Jamiol (2014) developed a comment on the Supreme Court rulings in two cases that effectively eliminated controls on political contributions by extremely wealthy individuals (Figure 11.2). The pig is wearing the robes of a Supreme Court justice and seated on a dais labeled "SCOTUS" (Supreme Court of the United States); together these anchor the reference to the Supreme Court. The pig is holding a tablet referencing two recently decided cases, Citizens United and McCutcheon, both of which removed restrictions on the ability of very wealthy individuals and corporations to influence elections.

The statement in the speech balloon is a transformation of a line from the novel *Animal Farm* (discussed in Chapter 4). The novel tells a story about a group of farm animals who rebel against the tyrannical farmer, drive him away and take over the farm, a story that is usually interpreted as an allegory about the Russian Revolution. The pigs (apparently representing Communists) assume leadership of the revolution, and one of the pigs, named Napoleon (representing Stalin) co-opts the revolution. At a crucial point, the original slogan "All animals are equal" is modified to "All animals are equal – but some animals are more equal than others." It is significant that the cartoon shows the Supreme Court justice who speaks the slogan as a pig, i.e., as one of the "more equal" animals, with the potential additional identification of the chief justice as Napoleon, the self-installed dictator in the novel. In order to understand the vehicle story in this cartoon, a reader would need to have a fairly detailed knowledge of the novel. In order to understand how the vehicle story maps onto a topic story, the reader would also need to have a detailed knowledge of these two rulings and the surrounding controversy. Without this background cultural and political knowledge, a reader might not be able to interpret the cartoon at all, or might simply fall back on the conventional association of *"pig"* with greed and untidiness.

Pat Oliphant (2011) developed a vehicle story based on the early 20th-century melodrama series *Perils of Pauline* to comment on the same rulings and their potential effect on U.S. politics. Each episode of the series *Perils of Pauline* ends with the heroine put into severe danger by villains. The series is most commonly associated with an image of the heroine, Pauline, tied to a railroad track with a train bearing down on her. Oliphant activates this story by a drawing of the woman (in slacks and high-heeled shoes) tied to railroad tracks as several dark, shadowy figures run away from her down what appears to be either a railroad tunnel or a grade cut. "The electoral process" is written on her shirt, and she holds a book labeled "Almanac of campaign financing." These clues guide mapping the vehicle story onto the topic story about the Citizens United decision. She is quoted in a speech balloon: "These folks from the Roberts Court are so thoughtful – they left me a nice, violent video game to play while I wait for the train." The tiny figure of a bird in the lower-right-hand corner (representing the cartoonist) comments, "They didn't want you to be bored." This apparently refers to a separate topic story about the continuing controversy over violent media content. For many viewers, both the violent video game detail and the shadowy figures retreating in the background may have the effect of confusing the metaphoric mapping.

The vehicle story requires at least some familiarity with the melodrama series, although the title and the idea have been used hundreds of times in various contexts, including a divorce blog titled "Perils of Divorced Pauline." As with the Jamiol cartoon, Oliphant's cartoon also requires current political and cultural knowledge about the Supreme Court and the potential effects of the Citizens United and McCutcheon decisions. The viewer also needs to connect the shadowy figures retreating in the background with the Supreme Court justices.

In a 2011 cartoon Clay Bennett developed the *"coffin nails"* metaphor for smoking addiction as a comment on extreme partisanship. The image shows a cigarette pack with the design of a popular brand, with the word "unfiltered" and, where the brand name would ordinarily be, the word "Partisanship." An open, partly used book of paper matches is to the left of the pack, to the right and above, an ashtray overflowing with cigarette butts. At the top left: "President Obama has quit smoking." At the bottom right, next to the cigarette pack: "Speaker Boehner has not." A potential implication is that partisanship is an addictive habit; a secondary implication is that Obama has broken the partisanship habit, but Boehner is still engaging in partisanship – the overflowing ashtray suggests a long series of partisan actions.

A common story metaphor for short-sighted and ultimately self-defeating actions is *"digging our own grave."* Fauconnier and Turner (2002) claimed that this expression requires a complex cognitive process involving activation of a "double scope network" on the grounds that death is not caused by merely digging a grave. The metaphor blends a "causal, intentional, and internal event structure" with an "unwitting failure" scenario and, separately, with the "concrete structure of graves, digging and burial." They overlook the possible origin of the phrase in commonplace events including tragedies such as mine and tunnel cave-ins, in which a hole dug for a different purpose (extracting coal or valuable minerals; completing a railroad or highway route) unintentionally become the workers' *"grave."* Less tragically, people sometimes become trapped in a hole they have dug for other reasons, and require assistance to get out of it. These commonplace stories are readily transformed as metaphor vehicles for vehicle stories in which people borrow excessively and thus *"digs themselves into a hole"* or in which they invest heavily in dubious schemes that lead to their financial ruin, and thus *"dig themselves into a hole"* which *"collapses around them"* so that it turns out they have been *"digging their own graves"* (Ritchie, 2004).

In a comment on the decision of Republican Congressional leaders to *"shut down"* the activities of the U.S. government by refusing to pass a needed budget bill, McKee (2004) extended this story metaphor further, illustrating the then common expectation that the Republican strategy would lead to electoral defeat (Figure 11.3). The image of an elephant wearing slacks and a necktie identifies the protagonist as Republican; the label "GOP" on the tombstone makes that even clearer. The yellow diamond-shaped sign in the background (a road sign conventionally used to warn motorists of a potentially hazardous situation such as a construction project) guides the reader in mapping the story onto the then-current news stories about the Republicans' "govt. shutdown strategy." The trees in the background position the *"grave"* out of doors.

Although simple on the surface, the cartoon requires the reader to blend vehicle stories about a potentially hazardous road construction project, a

Figure 11.3 (2013). "Digging your own grave"
Rick McKee / *The Augusta Chronicle*, September 18, 2013. Used with permission.

person digging a grave, and the grave caving in so that it becomes the digger's own grave, then map them onto a topic story that blends the Republican's actions in the budget crisis with a (predicted) subsequent electoral defeat. Interpreting the cartoon requires a series of fairly complex cognitive processes, beginning with activating the "*digging your own grave*" story metaphor. The visual interest in the cartoon provides some motivation, which may be reinforced by the symbols of the Republican Party for readers who have strong feelings (one way or the other) about current politics. A reader with less interest in politics, or who fails to activate the vehicle story, is unlikely to make much sense of the cartoon. (In retrospect the outcome of these events, which led to the takeover of Congress by even more radically conservative "*Tea Party*" Republicans, lends a heavy but unintended irony to the cartoon.)

Cartoons about race relations and civil rights. A cartoon by John Darkow (2014) commented on the Supreme Court's recent decisions that severely restricted enforcement of voting rights in southern states (Figure 11.4). The white object in the foreground appears to represent an iceberg; along with the ship in the background it apparently refers to the story of the *Titanic*. The labels imply a topic story about the Supreme Court heading toward a disastrous encounter with racism. The "*iceberg*" has five pointed tips showing above water, labeled "stop and frisk," "Sterling," "Cliven Bundy," "Treyvon

226 Metaphorical Stories in Visual Communication

Figure 11.4 Darkow (2014): Racism in America. Used with permission.

Martin," and "Paula Deen," referring to five recent controversies. The oval shadows in each of the pointed tips resemble the eye holes in Ku Klux Klan hoods.

The labels imply a mapping of the Titanic story onto a story about the Supreme Court and, by implication, the U.S. judicial system, ignoring the racism that is *"hidden beneath the surface"* of American life, a story that contrasts ironically with the proclamation emerging from the ship that "Except for a few outliers ... Racism is over!" The eye holes suggesting Klan hoods imply that the referenced incidents express sentiments typically associated with the KKK for these incidents. The KKK hoods also imply that Sterling, Bundy, and Deen are associated with the KKK – but labeling one of the KKK hoods Trayvon Martin muddles this aspect of the story, since Martin was a *victim* of alleged racism, not a perpetrator. As with the other cartoons discussed in this chapter, extensive cultural, political, and current events knowledge is necessary to make sense of the cartoon.

John Cole (2014) blended a conventional metaphor with a slang term to comment on a recent state court decision that invalidated a Pennsylvania state law requiring a photographic voter ID card. The cartoon includes two images and a label at the top reading "warning signs ..." The figure on the left, a miner holds a birdcage with what appears to be a dead bird in the bottom; the label says "canary in a coal mine." The bird and the label refer to a vehicle story about miners who carry a small bird into a mine. The bird is more susceptible to poisonous gas, so if the bird loses consciousness or dies the miners will be warned of the hazard in time to escape. Next to the miner is a man in a suit, resembling Governor Tom Corbett (and labeled "Corbett"), who is holding a birdcage with a dead crow, labeled "PA Voter I.D." The label at the bottom says, "Jim Crow in a courtroom." *Jim Crow* began as a pejorative term for African Americans and a reference to segregated railroad cars but in the 1940s was broadened to refer to all legal segregation. Here it is blended with the "*canary*" story into a vehicle story in which a dead bird signals danger to the person holding its cage; it maps onto a topic story about the attempt by Republicans, led by Governor Corbett, to suppress minority voting with a stringent ID law. In this case, readers need to know about the "canary in a coal mine" story metaphor as well as details about the voter ID law and Corbett's role in it. Since "*Jim Crow*" historically referred to African Americans, the cartoon can be also potentially be read as implying the demise of African American voters rather than of the voter ID law, which is probably *not* what the cartoonist intended.

Cartoons about climate change. A cartoon by Toles (Figure 11.5) blends three idiomatic metaphors, including the "*canary*" metaphor discussed in the

Figure 11.5 The canary in the coal mine
TOLES © 2013 *Washington Post*. Reprinted with permission of UNIVERSAL UCLICK. All rights reserved.

previous section, into a complex image that activates a vehicle story in which "Uncle Sam" (the striped top hat again) is a coal miner who ignores the warning sign – the "*dead canary.*" Uncle Sam's response, "kick it down the road," apparently refers to young boys who walk along a country road kicking a can just to keep it moving down the road. It has become a metaphor for leaders who adopt a short-term solution to a crisis, leaving a permanent resolution for later – ideally for someone else to deal with. The cartoonist's comment, lower-right-hand corner, refers to the idiom, "*going to Hell in a hand-basket.*" The loaded coal cart anchors the entire story in the carbon economy. These elements blend into a story about two coal miners who ignore the warning sign of poison gas and defer action on it.

The "canary in a coal mine" story has been frequently used to comment on the lax administration of safety standards in the coal industry; this cartoon can be interpreted as a comment on that controversy. However, the label, "CLIMATE," on the roof of the mine also connects the story to another current controversy, the story of the neglect and outright denial of evidence that rising CO_2 levels are leading to potentially catastrophic climate change (Chapter 10). The vehicle story about young boys kicking a can can refer to both the climate change crisis and to the mine safety crisis. This story is blended into a second vehicle story about miners ignoring the warning sign of a dead canary, with potentially deadly consequences. This complex blended story maps onto a topic story about politicians (the man in the "Uncle Sam" hat) who ignore obvious signs of danger from CO_2 and other "*greenhouse*" gasses. It also potentially maps onto a topic story about politicians who ignore the repeated disasters that result from lax enforcement of laws governing mine safety. The cartoonist suggests "put it in a handbasket," apparently to make it easier for the problem(s) to "*go to Hell in a hand-basket.*" "*Hell*" is a popular idiomatic metaphor for extreme heat, e.g., "hot as *hell*," "not until *Hell freezes over*," which, by implication, will soon describe the climate.

Magazine covers also frequently feature images that refer to or activate a metaphorical story. One cover on *TIME*, April 28, 2008, depicts a group of soldiers in black and white raising a redwood tree, shown in full color, with the headline "How to Win the War on Global Warming." The name of the magazine, TIME, is shown in green instead of the usual red, and the magazine is also bordered in green instead of red. The group of soldiers looks exactly like the famous photograph of raising the flag after the victory at Iwo Jima during World War II (and the statue based on the photo), with the tree in the place of the flag. The "raising the flag" story potentially activates an underlying vehicle story of victory at the end of a long and hard-fought battle; the tree and the headline guide mapping this story onto a topic story about a long and difficult struggle to overcome global warming. The image could be understood as a simple illustration of the idiomatic metaphor, "War on ...," which has been applied to a multitude of causes (poverty, drugs, illiteracy, etc., discussed in Chapter 10). However, readers who are not familiar with the iconic photo and statue may miss the point entirely. For readers who are aware that the initial Iwo Jima photo was actually staged after the battle was over, the image might activate an entirely different – and probably unintended – metaphorical story implying that the environmental crisis is also "*staged.*"

The April 9, 2001, cover of *TIME* has an image that is even more complex. A series of 1980s antinarcotics commercials featured the image of an egg frying in a cast-iron skillet, with a voice-over saying, "This is your brain on drugs." The 2001 cover of *TIME* featured the same image, except that the golden-yellow yolk of the egg bears the image of North and South American continents and the headline "Global Warming." Below the headline is a series of short sentences: "*Climbing* temperatures. Melting glaciers. Rising seas. All over the Earth we're feeling the heat. Why isn't Washington?" These sentences activate a vehicle story about being uncomfortably hot and map it onto a topic story about politicians who (are not) hearing demands for action from their constituents ("*feeling the heat*"). The image – an Earth frying in a metal skillet – reinforces the *heat* trope, but it also, for those who recall the antinarcotics campaign of a decade earlier, activates the topic story about drug addiction and turns it into a vehicle story that maps onto an unspoken topic story about addiction to carbon fuels and other activities that contribute to global warming.

How Do People Actually Process Visual Metaphors?

El Refaie (2009b) observed that metaphor interpretation depends in part on knowledge of sociocultural background information as well as the specific context. In two pilot studies she explored how people make sense of cartoons. In each study she showed editorial cartoons to participants one at a time and asked a series of questions to elicit information about how they processed the images as well as their own interpretation. She also interviewed the artist who drew each cartoon, so she could compare her own interpretation and those of her participants with the artist's stated intentions.

In the first study, El Refaie (2009b) recruited a group of well-educated middle-class people (five British and three non-British), all employed in a university setting, regular newspaper readers with good knowledge of current affairs. She showed them a series of cartoons about an investigation, headed by Lord Butler, of Tony Blair's decision to join the United States in the Iraq War. The report of the Butler Commission had exonerated Blair from charges of having lied about the justification for the war. One of these showed a man in Middle East clothing, standing next to a field full of fresh graves and holding a newspaper with the headline "Butler Report." Several minarets show on the skyline behind the man. The man is quoted as saying, "Guess what, everyone? Nobody's to blame." A second cartoon shows a series of images of a cat with a face that vaguely resembles Tony Blair, in poses that suggest he is falling from a high place and landing on his feet, walking toward the edge of the picture ("*a cat always lands on its feet*").

In the third (and most complex) cartoon, a naked man (with the big ears associated with Tony Blair in contemporary editorial cartoons) stands in a bathtub, dripping a thick white substance and looking angry; on the floor next to him is something that could represent a wadded-up towel, or possibly a pair of underwear. Standing in front of the tub with his back to it is a man (with a caricature of Lord Butler's face), dressed as a butler, wearing a wide grin, holding a paint can labeled, "Nice 'n' neutral full color White with the merest hint of Raspberry." It appears that the image was intended to activate a vehicle story about a butler dumping a can of whitewash over a naked man who was taking a bath while his underwear lie burning on the floor. The "hint of *raspberry*" refers to a mocking sound. The topic story refers to the Butler Report, which exonerated the Blair government of wrongdoing in the events leading up to the Iraq War (an alleged "*whitewash*").

Among the well-educated group, native English speakers all got references to "whitewash" and "raspberry," but non-native speakers had trouble with these idioms, leading to an array of divergent interpretations. Even among well-educated native English speakers, a drawing of Y-front underwear (associated by some cartoonists with Tony Blair) with what was intended to be flames and smoke to invoke the saying "Liar, liar, pants on fire" was not easily interpreted: Several of these participants weren't sure if the underwear was supposed to be soiled or burning.

In the second study, El Refaie (2009a) recruited a group of young people, ages 16–19, including 6 White native-born British, 13 Muslims, and 6 with other Asian backgrounds. She showed them two cartoons about the 2004 U.S. presidential election, including the cartoon discussed in a previous section of this chapter, in which George W. Bush's face is drawn onto the body of an infant crawling away from a large fire toward a box of matches labeled "4 more years."

Only a handful of the informants in the second study arrived at an interpretation similar to the cartoonist's stated intention. Some participants found it difficult to give any interpretation at all, and became quite frustrated with the task, but most of them gave reasonable interpretations. For example, one participant concluded, from the blend of President Bush's face with the body of a toddler, that the cartoonist intended to impute childishness to the president. Virtually all of the participants in both studies identified symbols and images based on conceptual metaphors that are familiar in many cultures, such as A TIME OF DECISION IS A CROSSROAD and FUTURE IS IN FRONT.

However, the participants who were not native English speakers interpreted the less universal metaphors and symbols – and constructed metaphorical narratives – based on their own background culture. This was particularly true of the Muslim participants in the second study, who interpreted both Bush cartoons according to their own cultural preoccupations and their perspective on the Iraq War.

All of these cartoons are relatively complex visually. The cemetery and "*whitewash*" cartoons require knowledge of the controversy surrounding the Butler report. All of the examples include potentially distracting elements. Unless the viewer understands the vertical lines as indicating motion, it is not clear whether the cat drawing is intended to show the same cat in a series of poses or several cats next to each other. The angry expression of the figure representing Blair in the "*whitewash*" example is consistent with the vehicle story, but inconsistent with the topic story about Blair receiving a complete exoneration (a "*whitewash*") on the charge of lying to Parliament about the Iraq war.

El Refaie (2009b, p. 191) concludes that "in the case of political cartoons, even achieving 'reference' requires a mixture of general visual literacy – in the sense of being able to identify 'a tank' or 'flames and smoke' – and more specific cultural and political literacies." The style of representation and the inclusion of distracting details are also important. In the falling cat, it is not very clear that the face is supposed to be that of Tony Blair. Similarly, the heap on the floor next to the bathtub in the "*whitewash*" cartoon is supposed to represent flames coming out of a pair of men's underwear – and thus evoke the folk saying "Liar, liar, pants on fire." This extra little detail is not essential to understanding the main point of the cartoon, and respondents found it confusing. The four British respondents recognized the article as "Y-front" underwear and understood the connection with Major (a reference to another cartoonist's work) – but they were unable to determine whether the garment was supposed to be on fire or soiled (wavy vertical lines are used by cartoonists to represent both noxious fumes and flames).

The examples used by El Refaie seem rather too detailed and potentially confusing – as do many other examples discussed in this chapter. Editorial cartoons often blend several vehicle stories in a way that can map onto the topic story in a complex variety of ways, and seem to require a very detailed knowledge of the topic. To cite just one example, as previously mentioned, the eye holes in the *Titanic*/iceberg cartoon that make the visible bits of ice look like Klansmen, which fits three of the names but not the fourth. In sum, the stimuli used in El Refaie's two studies do not seem any more complex or esoteric than other editorial cartoons, which supports the generalizability of her findings.

The implications of El Refaie's research are important: Many readers of newspapers, including fairly well-educated readers, are often unable to get the point of metaphorical images in political cartoons. The examples discussed in this chapter, like the examples used in El Refaie's experiments, require extensive and detailed knowledge of topic stories and related context and the ability to blend multiple conceptual metaphors into a coherent metaphorical story. It appears that this knowledge and interpretive ability is available, with respect to any given topic, only to readers with detailed background cultural knowledge – and sometimes even they may be mystified. That leaves an unanswered question, what *do* people get from editorial cartoons?

Summary

If metaphor is understood as experiencing or expressing one concept in terms of another concept from a completely different domain, then metaphors can be expressed in images, gestures, sounds, and potentially other perceptual media as well. The perceptual mode that has been most extensively studied by researchers and scholars is visual, including images and gestures. Visual images often simply depict or evoke a lexical metaphor. For example, a recent ad for Comcast showed a potato lying on an overstuffed sofa with the caption "get comfortable," based on the common metaphorical idiom "*couch potato*." However, the painting *The Blind Leading the Blind* by Bruegel the Elder (cover image) uses a row of figures to illustrate a vehicle story about blind men following other blind men; the topic story is left for the viewer to fill in. Visual images and music that refer to or illustrate metaphorical stories, fables, parables, and allegories are common in music, paintings and sculpture. Video cartoons often illustrate common metaphors, as when a cartoon character is shown with smoke coming out of its ears (ANGER IS HEAT); sometimes entire metaphorical stories are depicted, as in Disney's (1934) version of "The Ant and the Grasshopper," discussed in Chapter 5.

There is evidence that lexical metaphors activate partial simulations of the perceptions and motions associated with the metaphor vehicle, and that these simulations at least contribute to comprehending and interpreting the metaphor. There is less evidence regarding metaphors in other modes, but pending more extensive research it is reasonable to extend these findings to metaphors in other modes besides language. Research by Green (2004) and her associates suggests that stories, including metaphorical stories, also have the potential to invite audience to "*enter the story-world*" and experience more or less detailed simulations of the story. However, Relevance Theory and other computational approaches offer a very different approach to multimodal as well as to lexical metaphors (Yus, 2009) and, by extension, to metaphorical stories and story metaphors.

In principle, visual depiction of metaphorical stories should facilitate activation of relevant perceptual simulations and consequently increase both the extent of cognitive processing and the degree to which the metaphorical story is understood. However, El Refaie's findings renders this uncertain. El Refaie's research challenges a basic assumption common to virtually all theoretical approaches to metaphor. Her research suggests that differences in cultural background can lead to quite different interpretations and, at the extreme, to an inability to interpret a visual metaphor at all. Even people from very similar cultural backgrounds may interpret visual metaphors in quite different ways. Ritchie (2013) reports evidence of a similar lack of interpersonal coherence in how people interpret lexical metaphors. The accumulating pattern raises two questions that cannot be ignored. If people regularly arrive at different interpretations of metaphors, including metaphors in language and visual images, how do these metaphors function as communication?

Editorial cartoons and advertising images are usually presented in a context that includes language (news reports and written editorials, on the one hand, advertising copy, on the other) and usually appear within a context of related content; it is likely that this discursive context contributes to and helps guide comprehension. El Refaie presented her stimulus cartoons in the context – an editorial page – in which they initially appeared, but the lapse of several weeks may have rendered the larger context of current relevant news stories less salient). It is also likely that these images serve to attract visual attention and motivate processing of the entire message, including written text, by promising amusement and entertainment.

Another factor, not addressed by El Refaie, is the *motivated reasoning* (Kunda, 1990) discussed in Chapter 10. According to this theory, people attend to and interpret evidence in a way that supports their preconceptions, and denigrate or dismiss evidence contrary to their preconceptions. In understanding metaphorical stories, including those implied by visual images, people may be more likely to activate background contextual knowledge based on and consistent with their own prior beliefs and values – leading to very different interpretations by different segments of an audience, even when (to the researcher as well as to the communicator) the message seems straightforward and obvious.

None of this is to dispute the potential expressive power of visual images to evoke and illustrate metaphorical stories that activate detailed and extensive cognitive processing and simulations. Attention to potential metaphorical stories are vitally important in analyzing visual as well as textual messages. However, it is also important to consider differences in knowledge, activation, and application of relevant background contextual knowledge in assessing how these metaphorical stories might affect and be used by various members of an audience.

12 Metaphorical Stories and Their Place in Discourse

I opened this book with a quote from a concession speech by Hillary Clinton, given at a crucial point in the 2008 Democratic presidential primary. In the quoted passage, Clinton developed a metaphorical story by blending several familiar metaphors, including the "*glass ceiling*" metaphor, coined several decades earlier by another woman, Gay Bryant, to express her frustration with respect to the effect of gender bias on her own career. Metaphorical stories are a familiar feature of literary genres, notably allegory, fables, and parables. The central claims in this book are that metaphorical stories are also a common feature of ordinary language use, and that complete understanding of many ordinary metaphors requires attention to the metaphorical stories they potentially reference or activate. I also argue that metaphorical stories, blending narrative with metaphor, provide an avenue to deeper understanding of the interaction of language with thought, culture, and social interaction. In this final chapter, I will reprise the argument of the book, discuss its contribution to a theory of metaphor comprehension, and then discuss some implications for communicators.

Communication, Language, and Cognition

Traditional theories of communication have emphasized transmission of factual knowledge in the form of propositions that are either true or not. In this view cognition – thinking – consists of computer-like manipulation of abstract symbols in *mentalese*, a biological equivalent of the "machine language" used by digital computers. According to the signal transmission or "*conduit*" metaphor (Reddy, 1993), language use is accomplished by encoding propositions from mentalese into a natural language such as English for transmission to an audience. Language comprehension is accomplished by the "*receiver*" of the transmission through a process of decoding the abstract symbols back into the original propositions in mentalese.

According to the transmission/conduit model, language consists of abstract symbols with an exact and shared correspondence to entities and actions plus syntactic rules with an exact and shared correspondence to relations among entities and actions. The primary function of language, in this view, is to maintain an accurate (and shared) representation of the environment and to coordinate action in the world, such as finding food and shelter, detecting and evading or overcoming predators and other threats. Stories are useful when they represent and transmit true facts, including causal relationships. Stories that do not represent true facts, and all metaphors, are at best decorative and entertaining, at worst misleading and deceitful.

Communication as embodied and social. In the past few decades a different view of communication has emerged from research in several disciplines. Dunbar (1996; 2003; 2014) has shown that communication is more often about social relationships than about factual information; Dunbar argues that the evolution of abstract thought and early language was driven by the emergence of complex social structure within large social groups. McNeill (2005; 2012) argues that gesture is an inseparable part of language, and sign language developed first, replaced only later by vocal languages we know today. Dunbar (2014) suggests that language may have initially developed from music and dance, moving and vocalizing in unison, as a means of developing mutual trust and strengthening social bonds. He further suggests that the informational uses of language may have initially developed in service of storytelling during social encounters, and for coordinating future social encounters. In this view, exchanging information about and coordinating food gathering and other actions in the ecological environment would have come later.

Stories and storytelling are a central feature of discourse in every known culture, both in casual conversation and in public discourse (Norrick, 2010). Stories are important to both individual and collective identity, and are a primary means for sustaining and transmitting cultural knowledge, beliefs, and values. Stories also have an important, possibly central role in memory and reasoning (Schank & Abelson, 1995; Schank & Berman, 2002). Both the enjoyment of stories and the persuasiveness of stories are enhanced by "*transportation* into the story world" (Gerrig, 1993; Green, 2004).

Metaphors were long regarded as a surface feature of language, a source of rhetorical effects and little more, misleading or deceptive as often as they were illuminating. However, recent work in cognitive linguistics has shown that metaphors are fundamental to both thought and language. Lakoff & Johnson (1980; 1999) argue that metaphors (defined as relations between concepts, not between words) provide the underpinning of most of our abstract conceptual thought, including the basic structure of logical reasoning (Lakoff & Johnson, 1999) and mathematics (Lakoff & Nunez, 2000). Although these claims were initially based entirely on intuition and interpretive research, they have been supported by extensive experimental research (Bergen, 2012; Casasanto and Gijssels, 2015; Gibbs, 2008).

The digital computer metaphor for mind, which underlies the transmission/conduit metaphor for language, has also been challenged. Barsalou (1999; 2007) has shown that all cognitive processes including abstract reasoning can, in principle, be accomplished through simulation of neural processes associated with muscular activation and perception, including introspection and interoception. Extensive research using priming and interference experiments as well as neuroimaging has supported the claim that perceptual simulations are active during language processing and contribute to comprehension and response (Bergen, 2012; Casasanto & Gijssels, 2015). However, other evidence (e.g., Landauer & Dumais, 1997) indicates that much of our vocabulary is initially acquired and at least partially understood through relationships with other language. It appears likely that language comprehension involves a combination of embodied processes (perceptual simulations) and abstract symbols. Barsalou (2007) claims that abstract symbols predominate in surface-level processing but perceptual simulations predominate in deeper levels of comprehension. Zwaan (2014; 2015) argues that the discursive and social context determines the balance between these processes.

Context. Zwaan (2014; 2015) points out that much of the research on language processing has neglected the context of language use and focused on individual words and sentences (mostly invented for purposes of a particular experiment). The social and cultural context, as well as the immediate discourse context and surrounding language, are necessary for language comprehension; psycholinguistic research that ignores this context cannot possibly give an accurate and complete account of language use and comprehension.

The broader linguistic, social, and cultural context also strongly influences the balance between abstract and grounded symbols in both language use and comprehension. Abstract symbols will play a greater role in discourse about generalities and about remote and physically absent objects and events; grounded symbols will play a greater role in discourse about specific objects and events that are immediate and physically present. The Elaboration Likelihood Model proposed by Petty and Cacioppo (1981) predicts that the degree to which an individual elaborates on a message, the "*depth* of processing" in Barsalou's (2007) terms, will be strongly influenced by ability to process, particularly access to background contextual knowledge, and motivation to process, which includes both personal relevance and interest.

Metaphor comprehension. There is also considerable evidence that embodied cognition (simulations of perceptual and muscular action processes) and broader social and cultural context are implicated in metaphor use and comprehension (Bergen, 2012; Gibbs, 2006; 2008; Gibbs & Matlock, 2008). However, the evidence from neuro-imaging studies has been inconclusive; Casasanto and Gijssels (2015) conclude from a comprehensive review of the research that activation of mode-specific simulations is *not* implicated in metaphor comprehension, although simulations at the more abstract level of multimodal convergence zones may be.

Focusing on the communicator's (apparent) *intention*, Steen (2015) argues that, if a metaphor is presented in discourse with attributes that suggest the communicator *deliberately* used the phrase *as a metaphor*, the perceiver is more likely to process it in more detail as a metaphor. Steen recommends attention to structural elements that signal the receiver to shift attention from the topic to the vehicle. Steen gives an example from an article about Alzheimer's disease that begins with the phrase "imagine your brain ...," which alerts the reader that the writer is *deliberately* using what follows as a metaphor for the disease.

Summary. In sum, both metaphors and stories are important to all aspects of communication, including language, culture, and social interactions. Both abstract and embodied symbols appear to be involved in language comprehension generally as well as in metaphor use and comprehension and in storytelling and comprehension. Both stories and metaphors are important elements in social interaction as well as in the representation and transmission of cultural context, and both are important to both formal and informal discourse. In this book, I have focused on the interaction between these two forms of communication, stories and metaphors.

Traditional models of comprehension have assumed that context is shared – that the same background context is known and salient to message originator and audience members. More recent research has shown that this is rarely if ever the case. When assessing how communicators *intend* a message, including metaphors, stories, and metaphorical stories, to be understood and how various members of an audience actually understand it, it is necessary first to assess possible differences in knowledge of relevant context as well as factors, such as prior beliefs and motivated reasoning, that may affect the salience of contextual knowledge and how it is actually used in processing the message.

Metaphors, Stories, and Story Metaphors in Discourse

Both stories and metaphors are central in discourse, important in both thinking and communicating. Stories are as important as propositions in both communication and cognition, and probably more important to memory, especially the collective memory that is central to shared identity of social groups. Ordinary discourse often activates or refers to stories, which may extend over several speaking turns and last for several minutes, but are often quite short, and often have parts omitted if they are expected to be known and salient to listeners. Conceptual metaphors, based on correlations between different sorts of experience, provide the basis for most of the abstract concepts we use, and the metaphorical expressions that express these conceptual metaphors facilitate reference to and discussion of abstract ideas that would otherwise be difficult or even impossible to express.

The stories that appear in both formal and informal discourse may be "news" but they are often not. Stories that are known, sometimes well known, to all participants in a communication exchange may be repeated because they are amusing or otherwise entertaining or because the speaker wants to get the story "on record" as part of the current conversation (as in the brief story about Tony Stevens and the even briefer index of the story about the shooting death of Kendra James, discussed in Chapter 2). They may be repeated or mentioned as a way of affirming shared identity, or sometimes as a way for the speaker to assert a particular individual identity. Whatever else it accomplishes, telling a story, whether it is news to some participants or familiar to all, serves to establish or confirm common ground (Clark, 1996) or mutual cognitive environment (Sperber & Wilson, 1986/1995) as a basis for subsequent communication.

Metaphors are also integral to both language use and visual communication. Conceptual metaphors, based on correlations between more and less abstract experience, are a basis for conceptual thought, and the source of both innovative and idiomatic metaphors. Ordinary discourse includes many lexicalized (*'dead'*) metaphors, which eventually become so thoroughly lexicalized that their metaphorical origin is forgotten and unrecoverable to any but experts – *pedigree* and *salary* are two common examples. Even when the metaphor is not entirely *'dead'* but only *'sleeping,'* familiar idiomatic metaphors such as *'see* the point,' *'grasp* the concept,' and *'empty* rhetoric' are usually not noticed as such, but there is experimental evidence that they weakly activate neural systems associated with the metaphor vehicle, at least to the extent that processing one of these metaphors can interfere with action that contradicts the literal meaning of the vehicle (Gibbs, 2006).

Storytellers often employ metaphors to various ends, but what is of primary concern for this volume is stories that are told with apparent metaphorical intent (metaphorical stories) and metaphors, including visual metaphors, that, at least potentially, refer to or imply metaphorical stories. The interaction of story and metaphor has previously been studied in context of formal literature, focusing primarily on distinct genres such as allegory, fables, and parables. In this book I have extended this work in several ways. I began by laying out a clearer distinction among genres of metaphorical story and making the connection to theories of embodied cognition and metaphor. I then proceeded to show how metaphorical stories are developed and used in ordinary discourse, with a focus on political rhetoric and on casual conversation. I showed how metaphorical stories are often implied by ordinary metaphors (story metaphors). Not all metaphors imply stories, but some make sense only with reference to a metaphorical story. Finally, I showed how visual images such as editorial cartoons can suggest or activate metaphorical stories by blending visual elements suggesting commonly known vehicle stories with visual elements suggesting topic stories. In this section, I will briefly review each of these topics.

Much of the discussion has been interpretive, based on informed intuitive exploration of the potential entailments of visual images, metaphors, and metaphorical stories. However, interpretation is and must be constrained by evidence from experimental research and other quantitative empirical research. I have discussed much of the relevant empirical research in passing, but I will close this section with a discussion of recent research that addresses recognition and interpretation of metaphorical stories and the challenging questions posed by this research.

Metaphorical stories in literature. Metaphorical stories are common to several literary genres, including allegories, parables, and fables. *Allegories* usually present a religious, political, or philosophical idea in the form of a vehicle story that can usually be mapped onto a topic story. Often the plot of the vehicle story is based on a conceptual metaphor such as WAR / BATTLE (*Psychomachia* and *Faerie Queene*) or JOURNEY (*Pilgrim's Progress* and *Divine Comedy*). More modern (and arguably somewhat marginal) examples are built around less epic conceptual metaphors such as MARRIAGE IS A CONTEST / HORSERACE ("Welcome to the third race . . .") or around a direct one-off concept such as *class revolution* in *Animal Farm*.

Allegories are generally stylized and fictional – but accounts of real events (or events believed to have actually happened) are sometimes given allegorical meaning. As discussed in Chapter 4, many stories from the Christian Bible are presented and taught as both literally true and allegorical. The raising of the flag at Iwo Jima (staged for a news photographer) became an allegorical vehicle story – as is illustrated by the *TIME* magazine cover discussed in Chapter 11.

Parables have a more conversational form, and are presented as occurring in conversations or sermons. They sometimes present literal, or possibly literal, stories as instructional (the story about Jesus and the woman taken in sin, and the Buddhist story about the two monks and the woman at the river). Sometimes parables present overtly metaphorical stories (Jesus's contrast between the house built on rock and the house built on sand; the Buddhist story about the monk and the strawberries).

Fables have a form in between the two extremes; they are more literary and more structured than typical parables, but less stylized and more conversational than allegories. Fables often involve animals who act and talk like humans, but like parables, they usually illustrate only one concept. Both parables and fables often end with an instructional coda or "moral" that makes the metaphorical mapping explicit.

All of these literary forms provide resources for communication in non-literary contexts, including conversations, journalism, political discourse, and editorial cartoons. Well-known allegories, parables, and fables are often indexed within a conversation, speech, or news article by a related word or phrase, as discussed in Chapters 7 through 10. They are also often referenced in visual images including editorial cartoons and advertising images, either by depicting a related scene or by quoting a related word or phrase, as discussed in Chapter 11.

Metaphorical stories and story metaphors in ordinary discourse. In ordinary conversations, people often tell brief metaphorical stories, like the "*all in the same boat*" example, but sometimes they elaborate these stories for humor or other entertainment effects, as in the "police officers are like *waitresses*" story. Well-known stories and metaphorical stories, including fables, parables, and allegories, are often referenced or indexed by single words or short phrases – many aphorisms and folk sayings index familiar fables and parables ("*sour grapes*," "*prodigal son*"). In public discourse, metaphorical stories are often elaborated, sometimes with the mapping made explicit, but often not. Like ordinary conversations, political speeches and other forms of public discourse are often sprinkled with words and brief phrases that index well-known metaphorical stories or imply metaphorical stories based on elaboration of familiar metaphors.

Simple lexical metaphors, particularly nominal metaphors, are often static – they simply describe or attribute characteristics to a topic. Depending on the context, 'don't be *a pig*' characterizes certain referenced behavior as either greedy or slovenly, two attributes popularly associated with that species. But the depiction of a U.S. Supreme Court Justice as a pig in the Jamiol cartoon discussed in Chapter 11 refers, not to either of these associate attributes, but to the role played by pigs in the novel *Animal Farm*. As this example illustrates, metaphors often refer to, and potentially activate, metaphorical stories about the vehicle, which map onto implied stories about the topic. "*Vulture capitalist*" activates a culturally known story about vultures and maps it onto an almost a topic story about venture/equity capitalists. '*Bull in a china shop*' activates a rather fanciful hypothetical story about a very large animal destroying everything in a china shop and maps it onto a topic story about a person ruining a relationship or a social occasion through anti-social or socially '*clumsy*' behavior. Metaphor analysis and theories of metaphor are incomplete without consideration of these potentially activated metaphorical stories.

Story metaphors in visual images. Visual images present a somewhat unique case. Video cartoons are able to tell a complete story, but editorial cartoons and other static print images can only index or imply a story. Metaphorical stories are often indexed or implied by the juxtaposition of

Metaphors, Stories, and Story Metaphors in Discourse 241

images that are associated with well-known stories, like the modified version of "raising the flag at Iwo Jima" on the *TIME* magazine cover, discussed in Chapter 11. Words are also often used to help both with activating the vehicle story and with activating and mapping onto the topic story.

Visual images resemble language units in certain ways, probably more than has been recognized in the past. Like words and metaphors, visual images can simply refer to or describe objects, persons, or scenes in a static sense, as do typical portraits and landscapes, as well as many product images in advertising. However, images can also refer to and potentially activate stories involving depicted objects, persons, and events. Sometimes, as in the famous image of raising the flag at Iwo Jima, the image serves to activate a historical story (or, in this case, an idealized and somewhat fictionalized version of a historical story). Other images, such as many advertisements, attempt to activate an idealized hypothetical story in which the viewer / potential customer arrives in the advertised vehicle at the opera, wearing expensive clothing, or drives the vehicle along a rough mountain road in a remote and scenic part of Utah or Arizona.

Images often refer to, represent, or activate metaphors – and metaphorical stories. The previously referenced image on a *TIME* magazine cover blended a representation of the Iwo Jima picture with an image of a redwood tree to transform the *Victory in the Pacific* story originally represented by the image into a vehicle story and map it onto a topic story about "*the war against climate change*" (Chapter 11). Another editorial cartoon discussed in Chapter 11, labeled "strip search," shows the goddess Justice, naked on her pedestal with her robes lying in a heap beside her, trying to cover her breasts and pubic area with her arms, with the word "partisanship" on one thigh. This image creates a fanciful vehicle story in which the goddess's clothing is removed in a strip search, revealing her previously hidden partisanship. It maps onto a (wished-for) topic story in which an investigation reveals the partisanship hidden beneath recent U.S. Supreme Court decisions. The painting on the cover, *Blind leading the Blind*, represents a sequence of events in a vehicle story.

Classification. The discussion and examples presented throughout this book suggest a somewhat different classification of metaphors, based both on modality and on cognitive / discursive function.

Metaphors. A category of communication in which a representation of an idea or concept from one realm of experience is used to express something about an idea or concept from an entirely different realm of experience. According to CMT, the topic idea is actually experienced as the vehicle idea.

Metonyms. A category of communication in which a representation of an idea or concept from one realm of experience is used to express something about an idea or concept from a different but related realm of experience. Two common classes of metonym are part for whole ('Can you *lend me a hand*?') and whole for part, including institution for member ('The *White House* issued a statement ...'). Metaphors and metonyms are best viewed as representing ends of a continuum, and sometimes the same word or phrase can be interpreted as either a metaphor or a metonym. For example, 'a *close* relationship' may refer to *physical proximity* (a metonym), *emotional attachment* (a metaphor), or both. Each type of metaphor discussed in the following paragraphs can also be observed in the form of metonyms.

Metaphorical stories. A subcategory of communication in which a vehicle story is at least briefly narrated, such that it expresses something about, and can be mapped onto, a topic story from a totally different domain. CMT implies that the topic story is *experienced as* the vehicle story to the extent that the hearer or reader is "*transported into the story world*" (Gerrig, 1993; Gibbs, 2011).

Lexical metaphors. A subcategory of specifically linguistic communication, in which metaphors are expressed in words or brief phrases.

> **Static/descriptive metaphors**: A subcategory of lexical metaphor (a word or short phrase) in which a topic concept is experienced as a vehicle concept, and no story is implied or activated.
> **Story metaphors**: A word or phrase that implies or activates a metaphorical story.

In practice, many metaphors may be interpreted as either static or story metaphors, depending on contextual factors including perceivers' background knowledge and level of interest or motivation. On the other hand, the line between a metaphorical story and a story metaphor is also blurred: a simple phrase like "*the blind leading the blind*" seems to index a more elaborated metaphorical story, but it almost constitutes a story in itself. Lyndon Johnson's pithy phrase about former FBI director J. Edgar Hoover, "It's better to have him inside the tent pissing out than outside the tent pissing in," is only a little more fully elaborated, but it seems to contrast two metaphorical stories about Hoover.

Metaphors in other modes – visual metaphors: Visual metaphors, and multimodal metaphors in general, can imply any of the above categories.

> **Visualized metaphorical stories** (discussed in detail in Chapter 11) contain images and, sometimes, language that refers to and potentially activates a metaphorical story. But in the case of the Bruegel painting, *The Blind Leading the Blind*, the entire vehicle story seems to be represented in the sequence of blind men, beginning

at the left with two men stumbling along and culminating at the right with one man stumbling over another who has already fallen. In this example the topic story is left entirely unspecified, but in other examples the topic story is hinted by visual elements such as the image of the redwood tree that replaces the U.S. flag in the *TIME* magazine cover image based on the *Iwo Jima* story.

Visualized lexical metaphors depict or represent lexical metaphors, usually idiomatic but sometimes novel lexical metaphors.

Recognizing and Understanding Metaphorical Stories

Given the amount of research on static metaphors, in particular using experimental and neural scanning methods, it is surprising how little empirical research has examined the recognition and interpretation of story metaphors and metaphorical stories. Two sets of experiments stand out, and each of them raises disconcerting questions.

Recognizing and interpreting allegory. In one of the few empirical studies of allegory interpretation, Gibbs and Boers (2005) asked college student participants to read Robert Frost's (1969) poem "The Road Not Taken" and provide interpretations (see Chapter 4). Results suggest that participants focused on the poet's message, not their personal concerns, and more than 70 percent of the participants provided metaphorical interpretations. In another study, participants were asked to read a satirical reworking of "The Three Little Pigs," using language associated with "politically correct" ideas, e.g., "along came a big, bad wolf with expansionist ideas ..." (Garner, 1994) and provide an interpretation. Only 65 percent gave an allegorical interpretation, and 67 percent of these participants interpreted the author's intention as supporting political correctness. Only 23 percent of the participants recognized the stories as satire. Gibbs concludes that a sizable majority of his college student subjects recognize and easily interpret allegory, although they do not necessarily agree on the allegorical interpretation. However, the converse of this conclusion is that 30–35 percent of college students do *not* recognize allegory, and three-quarters do not recognize satire.

In two pilot studies about how people interpret visual images, discussed in Chapter 11, El Refaie (2009a; 2009b) found even more disconcerting results. She asked subjects to look at a series of editorial cartoons about the Iraq War, focusing on George W. Bush and Tony Blair. Her results suggest that the metaphorical stories implied by visual images may be difficult to comprehend, and may lead to ambiguity both with respect to the vehicle story and with respect to the topic. In the example of "*Playing with Matches*" (Garland, 2004, discussed in Chapter 11), the background image of swirling lines was intended to portray a *"fire"* started by President Bush during his first term in office (the Iraq War) and the open matchbox he was crawling toward was intended to portray the potential for starting more *"fires"* during his second term. Only a few of the adolescent participants in El Refaie's second study recognized either the vehicle story (*"playing with fire/matches"*) or the topic story (President Bush starting wars and engaging in other risky actions); some participants thought the cartoonist was trying to suggest that President Bush was acting like a child. Some of her participants found the task difficult and frustrating, and were able to offer no interpretation at all.

As discussed in Chapter 11, it is possible that participants were unfamiliar with the idiomatic metaphor *"playing with fire,"* that they did not see the Iraq War as a risky undertaking or did not blame Bush for it, that they were thinking of something else entirely, that they did not recognize the swirly lines in the background as a representation of fire ... the list of contextual factors that may have contributed to the ambiguity of Garland's cartoon is potentially quite long. However, other cartoons in these studies yielded similar results, so the problem was clearly not with any particular cartoon.

Ambiguity of interpretation is not restricted to allegories and visual metaphors. In my own research, I have found that people often give quite unique interpretations of familiar verbal metaphors as well. For example, when I asked them to spell "t— the line" and provide an interpretation, I have found audiences consistently divided about evenly between *"tow"* and *"toe."* Moreover, members of each group provide a variety of vehicle stories. Those who spell it *"tow"* give explanations including a tugboat, a game of tug-of-war, and an airplane with an advertising banner. *"Toe"* yields athletes lining up in a foot race and soldiers lining up for inspection.

These results, along with the mixed results of research on metaphorical framing (Chapter 8), raise questions that cannot be answered with available data. It may be that metaphors, including visual metaphors and metaphorical stories, are after all merely "decorative" embellishments to serious arguments, sometimes playful and sometimes not. Much of the research presented throughout this volume argues against such a conclusion. It does seem that metaphors rarely serve either informative or declarative functions such as expressing an unequivocal point of view in unambiguous terms. Writers and editorial cartoonists who create and use clever metaphors may use them in the belief that they present a clear idea in convincing fashion – but they clearly do not. Metaphorical stories, like President Johnson's comment about J. Edgar Hoover ("better to have him *inside the tent, pissing out*") and metaphorical images, like Beeler's (2014) drawing of the goddesses of Liberty and Justice celebrating the DOMA ruling with a passionate embrace, are attention getting and entertaining. Attracting attention, motivating more extensive cognitive processing, and activating loosely relevant emotions, images, and ideas may be the primary point of metaphors. To the extent that this is the case, metaphorical stories, including those implied by visual metaphors, may be particularly powerful – but not easily controlled. These questions all remain for future research to explore.

Directions for Future Research

Opportunities for the next generation of researchers include both theoretical and methodological issues that have been raised but not resolved by recent research and application of these ideas to analyzing discourse in general. There is a particularly urgent need to follow up El Refaie's research on viewers' comprehension of editorial cartoons, using a more diverse and representative sample of both cartoons and viewers. Similar research might usefully examine metaphorical stories in other modes as well. As El Refaie points out, it is important to examine the contribution of particular background knowledge, as well as other ability factors and motivation factors in determining whether and how people read and interpret metaphors including metaphorical stories in various perceptual modes. The influence of context on metaphor use and comprehension, suggested by both Zwaan and Steen, deserves more detailed examination generally.

There has been extensive research on cognitive processing of simple lexical metaphors. Although investigation of cognitive processing of metaphorical stories poses methodological problems, it is badly needed. Along similar lines, Gibbs (2011; Gibbs & Boers, 2005) has shown that about two-thirds of college student subjects are able to provide reasonable allegorical interpretations of both poetry and satirical fiction. Research attention might usefully be given to the other one third, the participants who are unable either to recognize or to interpret allegory. Is there an allegorical or metaphor-interpreting skill that some people have and some don't? Or is it purely situational, so that certain participants are able to recognize and interpret some allegories under some circumstances – but not others? How do Gibbs's findings generalize to other forms of metaphorical story and story metaphor?

In sum, there is clearly a need for more research, using both experimental and qualitative methods, into how people actually apply contextual knowledge to interpret and understand metaphors in general and metaphorical stories in particular. The next generation of researchers might usefully look more closely at differences in knowledge and salience of relevant contexts among members of an audience, and at the role these differences play in comprehension and response. This should include consideration of factors leading to motivated reasoning – highlighting evidence favorable to prior views and values, and discounting or disregarding contrary evidence.

As I hope to have demonstrated in the last half of this book, identifying and interpreting metaphorical stories and story metaphors that imply or potentially activate metaphorical stories can provide a useful supplement to other tools in analyzing various sorts of discourse. Metaphorical stories and story metaphors appear in ordinary conversations, political discourse, medical discourse, advertising, visual communication – and many other types of discourse. Researchers using almost any combination of methods and texts will find new worlds of interesting story vehicle – topic relationships to explore.

How People Understand Metaphors: Context-Limited Simulation Theory (CLST)

According to the initial formulation of Context-Limited Simulation Theory (Ritchie, 2006), metaphors are processed *both* by activating partial simulations of modal neural activity (e.g., vision, hearing) that would be fully activated by an actual experience of the metaphor vehicle, and by activating semantic links to other words and concepts associated with the vehicle, and to relevant knowledge of both vehicle and topic (amodal symbols). The degrees to which each system (grounded modal simulations and abstract amodal symbols) is activated, as well as the particular modal and amodal symbols that are activated, are limited by the context, including both the immediate linguistic and discursive context as well as the broader social and cultural context. According to the Elaboration Likelihood Model, the depth and extent to which a metaphor is processed is also a function of the perceiver's ability and motivation (Petty & Cacioppo, 1981). In the original formulation of the Elaboration Likelihood Model, ability includes relevant background (contextual) knowledge as well as presence or absence of distraction; motivation includes personal relevance and need for cognition – potential enjoyment of intrinsic rewards from the message.

For example, Rick Perry's assertion that Mitt Romney was a *"vulture capitalist"* potentially activates perceptual simulations including the visual appearance of a vulture feasting on a dead animal along with introspective thoughts about capitalists. For people with extensive experience with vultures, it might also have activated simulations of the sounds and smells of a feeding vulture. For people with extensive experience with certain kinds of capitalists, it might have activated simulations of interoceptive experience of elation or despair, depending on the quality of the prior experiences. The phrase may also have activated words and encyclopedic knowledge associated with both concepts, *vulture* and *capitalist*. For people with detailed knowledge of the ecological function of vultures (clearing the landscape of rotting meat and recycling nutrients) or the economic function of equity capitalists (clearing the economy of unproductive companies and redirecting resources to more productive activities), the phrase may have activated encyclopedic knowledge that would lead to a metaphorical story – and meaning – quite different from what Perry apparently intended. Finally, the receiver needs to understand the rituals and conventions of political debates in general, and the dynamics of the particular presidential primary campaign in which this metaphor appeared.

In the initial formulation of the Elaboration Likelihood Model, it was assumed that the *same* contextual knowledge is accessible and salient to originator and perceivers of a message, and need for cognition was conceptualized as a simple intellectual trait. However, both factors need modification in the light of more recent research. It cannot be assumed that the same background contextual information is equally accessible and salient to all participants in a communicative interaction; to the contrary, it seems likely that various members of an audience may have access to different (but relevant) contextual information and, even when they have access to much the same information, may apply it in quite different ways.

Motivation to process is even more complex. Hurley et al. (2011) proposed a theory of humor based on the idea that *puzzle solving* makes a useful contribution to reproductive fitness and, consequently, the experience of humor, including the socially shared experience of laughter, evolved as a reward for resolving an apparent incongruity. A similar mechanism may apply to resolving the apparent incongruity represented by a story metaphor such as "*vulture capitalist*," and in general to playful elaboration of clever messages. Moreover, it is likely that these rewards would be experienced more intensely when the topic is more relevant (and, of course, when the elaborated story is consistent with prior beliefs and values). Need for cognition – the enjoyment of language elaboration for its own sake probably varies not only among individuals, as Petty and Cacioppo hypothesized, but also within individuals over time and across topics and situations. What stimulates a playful elaboration of a metaphorical story for one person in one circumstance may be totally uninteresting to another – or may stimulate elaboration along quite different lines.

Members of the audience, both those present at the debate and those watching it on television or reading about it later, are likely to have had very different amounts and types of background knowledge about vultures, capitalists, and Mitt Romney's personal background. They certainly differed in their motivation to process and elaborate on the metaphor. As a result, they are likely to have experienced different simulations and accessed different word associations and different background knowledge. Their experiences, both of the metaphor vehicle and of its mapping onto the topic, Mitt Romney's career, are likely as a consequence to have been quite different. It is impossible for a researcher (or for the originator of a metaphor, Rick Perry in this case) to know with any certainty how perceivers will experience and understand a metaphor.

Another set of factors that may influence motivation to process is summarized by the theory of motivated reasoning, which posits a tendency to engage in biased information processing in order to reach conclusions consistent with prior beliefs (Kunda, 1990; Nisbet et al., 2015). If a metaphorical story or any other message, including a statement of research evidence, challenges the individual's prior beliefs and values, it may precipitate reactance, leading to rejection or distortion of the message. A metaphor or metaphorical story that supports prior beliefs and values is more likely to be elaborated than one that is either irrelevant to or contradicts prior beliefs and values. Perry's supports are more likely and Romney's supports are less likely to have elaborated the "*vulture capitalist*" remark in detail, and to have repeated it in subsequent conversations.

Context plays a similar role in processing metaphors and metaphorical stories implied by visual images. The *TIME* cover blending Iwo Jima with a redwood tree would make no sense to a reader who was not familiar with the "raising the flag" statue and/or the photograph it was based on. Familiarity with controversies over preserving the remaining remnants of California's once vast redwood forests is also necessary. Familiarity with the story of the battle of Iwo Jima is useful but probably not necessary. Similarly, the "*strip search*" cartoon requires knowledge about controversies surrounding extremely intrusive searches and about the allegations that recent decisions of the U.S. Supreme Court have blatantly and deliberately favored the Republican Party.

Research in the intervening years, including the research reviewed and summarized in this volume, supports the general outlines of Context-Limited Simulation Theory, but it also points to the need for some modifications, restrictions, and additions. Neuroimaging research as well as behavioral research supports the role of modal simulations in processing literal language, but it appears that metaphor vehicles may activate simulations primarily as multi-modal at the more abstract level of neural convergence zones. As Zwaan (2015) points out, this research is mostly based on metaphors presented in a very restricted context, so it is uncertain whether the same restricted results would be obtained with more vivid metaphors presented in a socially and culturally richer context.

The role of metaphorical stories in discourse comprehension also requires more detailed attention. These include metaphorical stories that are explicitly developed as in the examples from Tony Blair's 2005 Gateshead address and Hillary Clinton's 2008 concession speech, and metaphorical stories that are implicit in more conventional metaphors, *story metaphors* like "*vulture* capitalist" that refer to and potentially activate, but do not actually tell, vehicle stories. They also include the metaphorical stories implicit in visual images such as advertisements and editorial cartoons. How do perceivers process these metaphorical stories? How do contextual factors influence the extent, depth, and content of processing?

For metaphor theory and research – and, potentially, for discourse analysis more generally – the message from research such as El Refaie's two pilot studies is fairly clear. Messages that seem clear, precise, and unambiguous can nonetheless be processed in different ways by different perceivers, leading to quite different understandings. Contextual variables are clearly at play, but what they are and how they lead to such a variety of interpretations requires extensive additional research. Similar research on metaphorical stories also seems to be in order.

To sum up, the basic outlines of Context-Limited Simulation Theory still seem applicable, not just to single word or short phrase metaphors like "*stonewall* the investigation" but also to extended metaphorical stories (including full-length allegories like *Pilgrim's Progress* and allegorical novels like *Animal Farm* discussed in Chapter 4) and visual metaphors like the editorial cartoons discussed in Chapter 11. Perceptual simulations as well as lexical connections and encyclopedic knowledge are probably involved to some degree in processing most if not all metaphors, but the simulations are more likely to be multi-modal, at least in processing familiar and less vivid metaphors. The balance between embodied symbols (perceptual simulations including simulations of vehicle stories) and amodal symbols (semantic networks and encyclopedic knowledge), and the extent and depth of processing in both systems is at least in part determined by the context, including both immediate communicative context and extended cultural and social context. However, the role of metaphorical stories and the potential "*transportation*" of perceivers into the metaphorical story world deserves stronger emphasis and extensive research investigation. Moreover, the fundamental ambiguity of metaphors, including metaphorical stories and images, only briefly recognized in the initial formulation of Context-Limited Simulation Theory, deserves much greater emphasis.

Advice to Communicators on Using Metaphors and Metaphorical Stories

Although research on how people interpret metaphors in ordinary discourse is relatively limited, it is apparent that most audience members are at least able to recognize and interpret metaphors, including allegories, other forms of metaphorical story, and visual metaphors (Gibbs, 2011). However, other evidence suggests that audience members do not always process metaphors, visual or verbal, when they do recognize them, and that individual audience members often arrive at quite different interpretations of metaphors. Petty and Cacioppo (1981) show that the degree to which people elaborate on a message is influenced both by their relevant contextual knowledge and by motivation – personal relevance and interest. Personal relevance and interest are influenced by the salience of social, cultural, and political contexts. Interest may be influenced by the interaction of the individual's "need for cognition" (Petty & Cacioppo, 1981) and characteristics of the message such as novelty, perceived cleverness, and mutability, how easily it can be elaborated. Given the importance of stories in human culture and psychology, story metaphors, by activating or suggesting metaphorical stories, may be particularly inviting to further elaboration. Motivated reasoning may increase processing of metaphors and metaphorical stories that are congruent with prior beliefs and values and decrease or radically alter the nature of the processing of incongruent metaphors and metaphorical stories.

When audience members do engage in elaboration and depth processing, they may arrive at interpretations that differ markedly from those of other audience members and from the interpretation intended by the message originator. Here again context and motivation play a crucial role. Even in an apparently homogeneous audience, the message originator and various members of the audience may have access to different contextual knowledge and may have different perspectives on common knowledge (the many different perspectives on the history of race relations in the United States, mentioned in Chapter 9, and the many different perspectives on the science related to climate change, discussed in Chapter 10, are but two examples). Even when individuals have very similar knowledge and perspectives, relevant contextual information may be more salient to some than to others. In sum, it is often difficult for a message originator to know what contextual information will be accessible and salient to various members of the audience or, conversely for audience members to know what the message originator had in mind.

It is clear that context is crucial to language and image processing, and to comprehension generally. All language is inherently ambiguous (Wilson & Sperber, 2004), but metaphors are especially ambiguous; hence, context is particularly important to metaphors and metaphorical stories (Steen, 2015; Zwaan, 2014; 2015). This includes not merely what has gone before in a particular discourse event, but also the social, cultural, and political context. It is also clear that communicators and various members of an audience may know and be aware of quite different aspects of the context, and that they cannot know what other participants in a discourse event are thinking of or how they interpret a message.

As the examples throughout this book illustrate, metaphors, stories, and metaphorical stories can contribute to a number of rhetorical purposes. They can illustrate and help explain abstract concepts and complex relationships among concepts. When they succeed in drawing audience members to "*enter into the world of the Other*," they can help establish and reinforce the conditions for empathetic understanding. They can provide a '*frame*' that helps organize ('*structure*') discussion of a topic and can direct attention toward ('*reveal*') some aspects of a topic and away from ('*conceal*') other aspects. They can attract attention to a message and motivate more detailed processing and more elaboration of the message.

All of this comes with an important caveat. All language is somewhat ambiguous and context dependent, but metaphors, stories, and metaphorical stories are particularly so. It is difficult for a communicator to know, much less control, what contextual information and ideas will be accessible and salient to audience members. Hence it can be difficult for audience members to know how a communicator intended a metaphor or story to be understood and for a communicator to know how various members of the audience understand it. These considerations suggest some general guidelines regarding use of metaphors and metaphorical stories.

Attracting attention and motivating elaboration. The audience must be able to process a metaphor in the first place: contextual knowledge relevant to both the vehicle story and the topic story must be accessible and salient. Jamiol's editorial cartoon using the novel *Animal Farm* to comment on recent decisions of the U.S. Supreme Court (Chapter 11) can only be understood by a reader who has fairly detailed knowledge of both the novel and the controversies surrounding recent Supreme Court decisions. In her research on editorial cartoons, El Refaie (2009a; 2009b) found that a significant number of readers may become frustrated with the task and give up (Chapter 11). Similarly, although Gibbs and Boers (2005) found that two-thirds of their college student sample were able to recognize and provide interpretations for allegorical texts, one-third of them were not. Given that the participants had agreed to participate in the study, they had a motivation for engaging with the message over and above any intrinsic interest in the text, so it is reasonable to infer that, among ordinary readers, well over one-third would not elaborate on the metaphorical elements.

"*Vulture* capitalist" is a striking metaphor, and, in the context of a political debate, it is safe to assume that most members of the audience were somewhat motivated to elaborate on the message. Most members of the audience know enough about the vehicle, "*vulture*," to elaborate a vehicle story about these birds – it is much less certain how many members of the audience know enough about *venture* (or equity) capitalists to elaborate the topic story and map the vehicle story onto it. Perry's comment in the South Carolina debate about "*stripping the bones clean*" may have helped.

Ambiguity. As the response to the *Playing with Matches* cartoon in El Refaie's research demonstrates, it is difficult to predict how audience members will process symbolic or metaphorical elements. The cartoonist depicted President Bush as a toddler, crawling toward an open box of matches; some of the participants in the study did not process beyond the image of the toddler, surmising that the cartoonist intended no more than to imply that Bush was "childish."

Tony Blair's metaphorical story about "*throwing crockery*" may have been intended only as an amusing way of describing the disagreements with his policies – but it also had some metaphorical entailments that were likely to be quite annoying to his opponents within the party. Among other things, it belittled their honest policy disagreements, and cast them in the role of a petulant housewife. If his intention was to increase the potential for empathetic communication, this metaphorical story was probably not the best way to do it. Similarly, the "*vulture* capitalist" story metaphor allows activation of elements of the "*vulture*" vehicle, such as the role of vultures in desert ecology, that are quite contrary to the message Perry apparently intended.

The use of powerful metaphorical stories in the debate about climate change science (Chapter 10) appears likely to have actually increased polarization over this issue, leading conservatives to even greater hostility toward scientific studies that produce evidence in support of the effect of human activities on the climate, and liberals to even greater hostility toward scientific studies that cast doubt on this evidence. More attention is needed from both researchers and communicators to the way metaphorical stories – and the surrounding rhetoric – can either contribute to or block the ability of audience members to "enter into the experiential world of the Other," a crucial precondition for empathetic understanding and effective conversation about a controversial topic (Ritchie & Cameron, 2014).

We all tend to assume that the same contextual knowledge is known and salient to others as it is to us. Communicators need to resist this assumption, and think about alternative ways that a metaphor vehicle phrase or story might be understood, alternative contexts that might be more salient to some members of the audience. Obama's phrase "*original sin of slavery*" is an example. As discussed in previous chapters, there are a number of contexts that may have been salient to various audience members, leading to quite different interpretations – and many other audience members may have lacked sufficient cultural context to process the metaphor at all.

Extended metaphor – developing two or more metaphorical phrases with vehicles from the same source – can also motivate greater elaboration. An example comes from Lithwick's (2011) article about Justice Kagan, who is characterized as "giving no *inflammatory* speeches ... and *setting no fires*" (Chapter 8). Similarly, in his 2008 speech *A More Perfect Union*, Barack Obama also developed several metaphors and metaphorical stories based on FIRE and several others based on JOURNEY. On the other hand, obscure references and metaphors are less likely to be processed, and may lead to audience members avoiding the entire message. In one of the "Butler Report" cartoons studied by El Refaie (2009b), a pair of underwear is depicted lying on the floor with wavy lines rising from it. The cartoonist's stated intention was to show the underwear as "on fire," invoking the folk saying "Liar, liar ..." But many of the viewers interpreted the image as "soiled," a meaningful interpretation in context, but not the meaning intended by the cartoonist.

Lithwick's article about Justice Kagan also includes a rather obscure metaphor comparing the ideal behavior of Supreme Court Justices to "the innocence of a newborn kitten"; it is difficult to determine from the context what characteristics of a newborn kitten are relevant; the ambiguity of the message is likely to discourage elaboration. In another example, Lithwick relates that "Kagan seems to have brought a *Bic pen* to a *quill fight.*" Here, the vehicles "*Bic pen*" and "*quill*" are likely to be familiar to most readers, but it is not clear what aspects of these objects are relevant to the "*fight,*" or how they are to enter into a metaphorical story about Kagan. Again, the typical reader is likely to pass over the phrase entirely, perhaps after a brief and frustrating attempt to make sense of it.

Summary. The upshot of all this is that metaphorical stories can be very effective means to gain attention and motivate an audience to elaborate a message, but they can also be difficult to control. In order to attract attention to their intentionality (Steen, 2015) they need to seem original and creative, but in order to permit detailed elaboration they also need to draw on familiar themes and familiar conceptual metaphors. One way to accomplish this is to adapt or transform a familiar metaphor, such as "*vulture*" or "*glass ceiling*" in a way that seems fresh and new. Alternatively, a familiar story may be converted to a metaphorical story (Blair's "*throwing crockery*" story is an example). Use of a story or phrase that seems slightly but not excessively bawdy or off-color can also motivate attention and elaboration (President Johnson's "better to have him *inside the tent, pissing out*").

As with any other communication, it is important to consider the audience and the situation – what contextual information can they be assumed to have ready access to? What features in a metaphorical story will reward (hence encourage) elaboration? If the topic is a contentious issue, how can the audience be invited into, and rewarded for entering into, the experiential world of Others; i.e., how can metaphorical stories be used to encourage rather than discourage empathetic communication?

Notes

1 "SHATTERING THE GLASS CEILING"

1 Other writers use a variety of different terms, for example "source" where I use "vehicle"; "tenor" or "target" where I use "topic." I will discuss the metaphorical implications of these terms in Chapter 3.
2 The site of Napoleon's final defeat.

2 STORIES AND NARRATIVES

1 The place where General Robert E. Lee surrendered to General Ulysses S. Grant, effectively ending the U.S. Civil War.
2 The *Mercury* and *Tribune* are local community newspapers. PCC – Portland Community College – is one of several public two year colleges in the metropolitan area; one of its campuses, which had recently opened at the time of this conversation, is located two blocks from 82nd Avenue. A crosstown bus runs along 82nd Avenue where it intersects with several bus lines connecting the city center with the suburbs.
3 This section was written before the 2016 campaign rhetoric of Donald Trump, and his election as president, rendered the fantasy all too possible.

3 LANGUAGE AND METAPHOR

1 These examples all refer to a crucial battle that took place in Gettysburg, Pennsylvania, during the U.S. Civil War.
2 I will designate grammatical metaphors by underlining them.
3 For a detailed discussion of the metaphorical aspects of Fauconnier and Turner's work, see Ritchie (2004).

4 ALLEGORY

1 All quotations are taken from the Robert Hollander translation of *The Divine Comedy*, available at etcweb.princeton.edu (accessed July 21, 2015).
2 I have altered the original format of the poem in order to show more clearly the transitions from literal to metaphorical to allegorical.

5 PARABLES AND FABLES

1 In this chapter, I present several Buddhist and Christian parables and stories as examples of metaphorical stories, and comment on them from the perspective of

cognitive metaphor theory. "Those who know don't say. Those who say don't know" (Lao-tzu). I am neither a Zen master nor a theologian, and I make no claims with respect to any spiritual or religious meanings associated with these examples.

6 METAPHORICAL STORIES

1 Here and in other examples from informal conversations in which speakers are not public figures, names have been changed to preserve anonymity.

7 STORY METAPHORS AND APHORISMS

1 Strictly speaking, it is *equity capitalists*, not *venture capitalists*, who perform the kind of actions described in this story. However, "venture" is needed for the alliteration effects that help make the phrase memorable.

8 STORY-METAPHORS IN JOURNALISM AND PUBLIC AFFAIRS

1 This section was written prior to "Brexit," the June 2016 referendum in which British voters decided that Britain should leave the EU. That action is likely to change the metaphorical universe just as it has already begun to change the political and economic universe. At the time of this writing, it is impossible to say how the drama will play out, or to predict whether and how the metaphorical frames identified by Musolff will be adapted to the new circumstances.

References

Abbott, H. P. (2008). *The Cambridge introduction to narrative* (2nd ed.). Cambridge: Cambridge University Press.

Adams, D. (1979). *The hitchhiker's guide to the galaxy*. Basingstoke, UK: Pan Books.

Amsterdam, A. G., & Bruner, J. S. (2002). *Minding the law*. Cambridge, MA: Harvard University Press.

Anderson, N. (2010). Diversity on the Supreme Court (cartoon). *Houston Chronicle*, May 11.

Axton, M., Crudup, A., Durden, T., & Presley, E. (1956). *Heartbreak Hotel*. Los Angeles, CA: Unichappell Music Inc.

Bagley, P. (2007). Mission accomplished (cartoon). *Salt Lake City Tribune*, May 3.

Barsalou, L. W. (1999). Perceptual symbol systems. *Behavioral and Brain Sciences*, 22, 577–609.

—— (2007). Grounded cognition. *Annual Review of Psychology*, 59, 617–645.

Beeler, N. (2014). Lady Justice and Lady Liberty embracing (cartoon). *Columbus Dispatch*. Available at www.dispatch.com/content/cartoons/2013/06/beeler 0627.html.

Bennett, C. (2011). Coffin nails (cartoon). *Chattanooga Times Free Press*, February 10.

Bergen, B. K. (2012). *Louder than words: The new science of how the mind makes meaning*. New York: Basic Books.

Bickerton, D. (2009). *Adam's tongue: How humans made language, how language made humans*. New York: Hill and Wang.

Billig, M. (2005). *Laughter and ridicule: Towards a social critique of humor*. London: Sage.

Blair, T. (2005). A fight we have to win. A speech to Labour's Spring Conference, Sage Center, Gateshead, England.

Blake, W. (1966). *Complete writings*. Ed. G. Keynes. London: Oxford University Press.

Bruner, J. (2002). *Making stories: Law, literature, life*. New York: Farrar, Straus, and Giroux.

Brunvand, J. H. (1981). *The vanishing hitchhiker: American urban legends and their meanings*. New York: Norton.

Bryant, G. (1984). *The working woman report: Succeeding in business in the 1980s*. New York: Simon & Schuster.

Bulow, P. H. (2004). Sharing experiences of contested illness by storytelling. *Discourse & Society*, 15, 33–53.

Bunyan, J. (1678/1969). *Pilgrim's progress*. New York: Collier (Harvard Classics series).

Cameron, L. J. (2003). *Metaphor in educational discourse*. London: Continuum.
   (2006). *Procedure for metaphor analysis*. The Metaphor Analysis Project. Milton Keynes, UK: Open University.
   (2007). Patterns of metaphor use in reconciliation talk. *Discourse and Society, 18*, 197–222.
Cameron, L. J., & Deignan, A. (2003). Using large and small corpora to investigate tuning devices around metaphor in spoken discourse. *Metaphor and Symbol, 18*, 149–160.
Cameron, L., Maslen, R., & Low, G. (2010). Finding systematicity in metaphor use. In L. Cameron & R. Maslen (Eds.), *Metaphor analysis: Research practice in applied linguistics, social sciences and the humanities* (pp. 116–146). London: Equinox.
Casasanto, D., & Boroditsky, L. (2008). Time in the mind: Using space to think about time. *Cognition, 106*, 579–593.
Casasanto, D., & Gijssels, T. (2015). What makes a metaphor an embodied metaphor? Quellenangabe: Linguistics Vanguard. ISSN (Online) 2199-174X, DOI: 10.1515/lingvan-2014-1015, January.
Causley, C. (1975). *Collected poems, 1951–1975*. Boston: Godine.
Chiappe, D. L., & Kennedy, J. M. (2001). Literal bases for metaphor and simile. *Metaphor and Symbol, 16*, 249–276.
Clark, H. H. (1996). *Using language*. Cambridge: Cambridge University Press.
Clark, I. et al. (2006). Open Kyoto to debate. An open letter to Prime Minister Stephen Harper. Available at www.canada.com/nationalpost/financialpost/story.html?id= 3711460e-bd5a-475d-a6be-4db87559d605.
Clement, J. (1968). Flushed from the bathroom of your heart. From *Johnny Cash at Folsom Prison*. New York: Sony Music Entertainment Inc.
Cole, J. (2014). Warning signs ... (cartoon). *Scranton Times-Tribune*. January 19.
   (2016). The dog that caught the bus. *Scranton Times-Tribune*, June 30.
Congreve, W. (1693). *The old bachelor*. Edinburgh: Printed by and for Martin & Wotherspoon 1768.
Conrad, J. (1958). *Lord Jim*. New York: Harper.
Crisp, P. (1996). Imagism's metaphors: A test case. *Language and Literature, 5*, 79–92.
   (2001). Allegory: Conceptual metaphor in history. *Language and Literature, 10*(1), 5–19.
   (2005a). Allegory and symbol – a fundamental opposition? *Language and Literature, 14*, 323–338.
   (2005b). Allegory, blending and possible worlds. *Metaphor and Symbol, 20*(2), 115–131.
   (2008). Between extended metaphor and allegory: Is blending enough? *Language and Literature, 17*, 291.
Dante, A. (1320). *The Divine Comedy*. Translated by Robert and Jean Hollander. Doubleday: *Inferno*, 2000; *Purgatorio*, 2003; *Paradiso*, 2007. Available at http://etcweb.princeton.edu.
Darkow, J. (2014). Racism in America (cartoon). *Daily Tribune*, April 30.
Deignan, A., & Semino, E. (2010). Corpus techniques for metaphor analysis. In L Cameron & R. Maslen (Eds.), *Metaphor analysis: Research practice in applied linguistics, social sciences and the humanities* (pp. 161–179). London: Equinox.

De Mendoza Ibanez, R., & Masegosa, A. G. (2011). Going beyond metaphtonymy: Metaphoric and metonymic complexes in phrasal verb interpretation. *Language Value*, 3, 1–29.

Disney, W. (1934). The ant and the grasshopper. From *Silly Symphonies*. Beverly Hills, CA: United Artists.

Dorst, A. G., & Kaal, A. G. (2012). Metaphor in discourse: Beyond the boundaries of MIP. In F. MacArthur, J. L. Oncins-Martinez, M. Sanchez-Garcia, & A. M. Piquer-Piriz (Eds.), *Metaphor in use: Context, culture, and communication* (pp. 51–68). Amsterdam: Benjamins.

Dunbar, R. (1996). *Grooming, gossip, and the evolution of language*. Cambridge, MA: Harvard University Press.

(2003). The social brain: Mind, language, and society in evolutionary perspective. *Annual Review of Anthropology*, 32, 163–181.

(2014). *Human Evolution*. New York: Pelican Books

DuVernay, A. (2014). *Selma*. Cloud Eight Films.

Edwards, D. (1997). *Discourse and cognition*. Thousand Oaks, CA: Sage.

El Refaie, E. (2009a). Metaphor in political cartoons: Exploring audience responses. In C. J. Forceville & E. Urios-Aparisi (Eds.), *Multi-modal metaphor* (pp. 173–196). Berlin: Mouton de Gruyter.

(2009b). Multiliteracies: How readers interpret political cartoons. *Visual Communication*, 8, 181–205.

El Roto. (2003). La gran droga (cartoon). *El País*, June 6.

Fauconnier, G., & Turner, M. (2002). *The way we think. Conceptual blending and the mind's hidden complexities*. New York: Basic Books.

Federal Glass Ceiling Commission. (1995). *Solid investments: Making full use of the nation's human capital*. Washington, DC: U.S. Department of Labor.

Feirstein, B., & Trippett, L. (1982). *Real men don't eat quiche*. London: New English Library.

Fine, G. A., & DeSoucey, M. (2005). Joking cultures: Humor themes as social regulation in group life. *Humor: International Journal of Humor Research*, 18, 1–21.

Fitzsimmons, D. (2014). Mission Accomplished. *Arizona Daily Star*.

Forceville, C. (2009a). The role of non-verbal sound and music in multimodal metaphor. In C. J. Forceville & E. Urios-Aparisi (Eds.), *Multi-modal metaphor* (pp. 383–402). Berlin: Mouton de Gruyter.

(2009b). Non-verbal and multimodal metaphor in a cognitivist framework: Agendas for research. In C. J. Forceville & E. Urios-Aparisi (Eds.), *Multi-modal metaphor* (pp. 19–42). Berlin: Mouton de Gruyter.

Forceville, C. J., & Urios-Aparisi, E. (2009). Introduction. In C. J. Forceville & E. Urios-Aparisi (Eds.), *Multi-modal metaphor* (pp. 3–17). Berlin: Mouton de Gruyter.

Frenkiel, Nora. (March 1984). The up-and-comers; Bryant takes aim at the settlers-in. *Adweek* (Magazine World). Special Report.

Frost, R. (1969). The road not taken. In *The poetry of Robert Frost*. New York: Holt, Rinehart, and Winston.

Gamson, W. A. (1992). *Talking politics*. Cambridge: Cambridge University Press.

Garland, N. (2004). Playing with matches (cartoon). *Daily Telegraph*, November 2

References

Garner, J. (1994). *Politically correct bedtime stories*. New York: Wiley.
Gauchat, G. (2012). Politicization of science in the public sphere: A study of public trust in the United States, 1974 to 2010. *American Sociological Review, 77*(2), 167–187.
Gentner, D., & Bowdle, B. F. (2001). Convention, form, and figurative language processing. *Metaphor and Symbol, 16*, 223–247.
Gerrig, R. J. (1993). *Experiencing narrative worlds: On the psychological activities of reading*. New Haven, CT: Yale University Press.
Gibbs, R. W., Jr. (2000). Making good psychology out of blending theory. *Cognitive Linguistics, 11*, 347–358.
  (2006). Metaphor interpretation as embodied simulation. *Mind and Language, 21*, 434–458.
  (2008). Metaphor and thought: The state of the art. In R. W. Gibbs, Jr. (Ed.), *The Cambridge handbook of metaphor and thought* (pp. 3–16). Cambridge: Cambridge University Press.
  (2011). The allegorical impulse. *Metaphor and Symbol, 26*, 121–130.
Gibbs, R. W., Jr., & Boers, E. (2005). Metaphoric processing of allegorical poetry. In Z. Maalej (Ed.), *Metaphor and culture*. Tunis, Tunisia: University of Manouba Press.
Gibbs, R., Gould, J., & Andric, M. (2005–2006). Imagining metaphorical actions: Embodied simulations make the impossible plausible. *Imagination, Cognition, and Personality, 25*, 221–238.
Gibbs, R. W., Jr., & Matlock, T. (2008). Metaphor, imagination, and simulation: Psycholinguistic evidence. In R. W. Gibbs, Jr. (Ed.), *The Cambridge handbook of metaphor and thought* (pp. 161–176). Cambridge: Cambridge University Press.
Gladwell, M. (2006). *The tipping point: How little things can make a big difference*. New York: Little, Brown.
Glucksberg, S. (2008). How metaphors create categories – quickly. In R. W. Gibbs, Jr. (Ed.), *The Cambridge handbook of metaphor and thought* (pp. 67–83). Cambridge: Cambridge University Press.
Glucksberg, S., & Keysar, B. (1990). Understanding metaphorical comparisons: Beyond similarity. *Psychological Review, 97*, 3–18.
  (1993). How metaphors work. In A. Ortony (Ed.), *Metaphor and thought* (2nd ed.) (pp. 401–424). Cambridge: Cambridge University Press.
Glucksberg, S., & McGlone, M. S. (1999). When love is not a journey: What metaphors mean. *Journal of Pragmatics, 31*, 1541–1558.
Grande, A. (2013). Honeymoon Avenue. On *Yours truly*. Island Records.
Green, M. C. (2004). Transportation into narrative worlds: The role of prior knowledge and perceived realism. *Discourse Processes, 38*, 247–266.
Green, M. C., & Brock, T. C. (2000). The role of transportation in the persuasiveness of public narratives. *Journal of Personality and Social Psychology, 79*, 701–721.
Halliday, M. A. K. (1985). *An introduction to functional grammar*. London: Edward Arnold.
  (1998). Things and relations: Regrammaticising experience as technical knowledge. In J. R. Martin & R. Veel (Eds.), *Reading science: Critical and functional perspectives on discourses of science* (pp. 185–237). London: Routledge.

Halliday, M. A. K., & Matthiessen, C. M. I. M. (1999). *Construing experience through meaning: A language-based approach to cognition*. London: Cassel.

Hansen, J. (1988). Testimony before the U.S. Senate Energy and Natural Resources Committee (June 23).

——— (2008). Testimony before the U.S. House of Representatives Select Committee on Energy Independence and Global Warming (June 23).

——— (2012). Why I must speak out about climate change. TED Talks.

Harris, R. A., & Tolmie, S. (2011). Cognitive allegory: An introduction. *Metaphor and Symbol, 26*, 109–120.

Hemingway, E. (1987). *The complete short stories of Ernest Hemingway*. New York: Charles Scriveners' & Sons.

Hesse-Biber, S. N., & Carter, G. L. (2005). *Working women in America*. New York: Oxford University Press.

Hogan, P. C. (2003). *The mind and its stories*. Cambridge: Cambridge University Press.

Huang, S., Pollack, H. N., & Shen, P. Y. (2008). A late quaternary climate reconstruction based on borehole heat flux data, borehole temperature data, and the instrumental record. *Geophysical Research Letters, 35*, July 4.

Hulme, M. (2009). *Why we disagree about climate change: Understanding controversy, inaction and opportunity*. Cambridge: Cambridge University Press.

Hurley, M. M., Dennett, D. C., & Adams, R. B., Jr. (2011). *Inside jokes: Using humor to reverse-engineer the mind*. Cambridge, MA: MIT Press.

Hymowitz, C., & Schellhardt, T. D. (1986). The glass ceiling: Why women can't seem to break the invisible barrier that blocks them from the top jobs. *Wall Street Journal*, March.

Ijzerman, H., & Semin, G. R. (2009). The thermometer of social relations mapping social proximity on temperature. *Psychological Science, 20*(10), 1214–1220.

Inhofe, J. (2006). Speech before the U.S. Senate (September 25).

Iyengar, S. (1991). *Is anyone responsible? How television frames political issues*. Chicago: University of Chicago Press.

Jamiol, P. (2014). SCOTUS / Animal Farm (cartoon). Available at www.juancole.com/2014/04/supreme-editorial-cartoon.html.

Juckes, M. N., Allen, M. R., Briffa, K. R., Esper, J., Hegerl, G. C., Moberg, A., Osborn, T. J., & Weber, S. L. (2007). Millennial temperature reconstruction intercomparison and evaluation. *Climate of the Past, 3*(4), 591.

Junger, S. (1997). *The perfect storm*. New York: Norton.

Kahneman, D., & Tversky, A. (1982). The simulation heuristic. In D. Kahneman, P. Slovic, & A. Tversky (Eds.), *Judgment under uncertainty: Heuristics and biases*, (pp. 201–208). Cambridge: Cambridge University Press.

Kaufman, D., Schneider, D. P., McKay, N. P., Ammann, C. M., Bradley, R. S., Briffa, K. R., Miller, G. H., Otto-Bliesner, B. L., Overpeck, J. T., & Vinther, Bo M., Arctic Lakes 2k Project Members (2009). Recent warming reverses long-term arctic cooling. *Science, 325*(5945), 1236–1239.

Kintsch, W. (2008). How the mind computes the meaning of metaphor: A simulation based on LSA. In R. W. Gibbs, Jr. (Ed.), *The Cambridge handbook of metaphor and thought* (pp. 129–142). Cambridge: Cambridge University Press.

Kosinski, J. (1970). *Being there*. Toronto: Bantam.

References

Kunda, Z. 1990. The case for motivated reasoning. *Psychological Bulletin, 108*(3), 480–498.

Labov, W. (2013). *The language of life and death: The transformation of experience in oral narrative*. Cambridge: Cambridge University Press.

Labov, W., & Waletsky, J. (1967). Narrative analysis. In J. Helm (Ed.), *Essays on the verbal and visual arts* (pp. 12–44). Seattle: University of Washington Press.

Lakoff, G. (1996). *Moral politics: What conservatives know that liberals don't*. Chicago: University of Chicago Press.

(2008). *The political mind*. New York: Penguin.

(2014). Mapping the brain's metaphor circuitry: Metaphorical thought in everyday reason. *Frontiers of Human Neuroscience*, December 16.

Lakoff, G., & Johnson, M. (1980). *Metaphors we live by*. Chicago: University of Chicago Press.

(1999). *Philosophy in the flesh: The embodied mind and its challenge to western thought*. New York: Basic Books.

Lakoff, G., & Nunez, R. E. (2000). *Where mathematics comes from: How the embodied mind brings mathematics into being*. New York: Basic Books.

Landauer, T. K., & Dumais, S. T. (1997). A solution to Plato's problem: The latent semantic analysis theory of acquisition induction, and representation of knowledge. *Psychological Review, 104*, 211–240.

Lee, T. C. K., Zwiers, F. W., & Tsao, M. (2008). Evaluation of proxy-based millennial reconstruction methods. *Climate Dynamics, 31*(2–3), 263–281.

Lin, T. Y, & Chiang, W. (2015). Multimodal fusion in analyzing political cartoons: Debates on US beef imports into Taiwan. *Metaphor and Symbol, 30*, 137–161.

Lister, T. (2016). Brexit: An often rocky marriage ends in sudden divorce. CNN, June 25, 2016. Available at www.cnn.com/2016/06/25/europe/uk-european-union-divorce/.

Lithwick, D. (2011). Her honor. *New York Magazine*, November 27.

(2016). Narrative and metaphor in media depictions of crime. Presented at the Stanford Symposium on Narrative and Metaphor in the Law. Stanford, CA, January 30.

Mann, M. E., Bradley, R. S., & Hughes, M. K. (1999). Northern hemisphere temperatures during the past millennium: Inferences, uncertainties, and limitations. *Geophysical Research Letters, 26*, 759.

Mao, F. (2010). *On cognition and function of grammatical metaphor*. A dissertation presented for the degree Doctor of Philosophy. Shanghai International Studies University.

Mar, R. A., & Oatley, K. (2008). The function of fiction is the abstraction and simulation of social experience. *Perspectives on Psychological Science, 3*, 173.

Mattingly, C. (2011). The machine-body as contested metaphor in clinical care. *Genre, 44*, 380.

McIntyre, S., & McKitrick, R. (2003). Corrections to the Mann et al. (1998): Proxy data base and northern hemispheric average temperature series. *Energy & Environment, 14*(6).

McKee, R. (2013). Digging your own grave (cartoon). *Augusta Chronicle*, September 18.

McNeill, D. (2005). *Gesture and thought*. Chicago: University of Chicago Press.

(2012). *How language began: Gesture and speech in human evolution.* Cambridge: Cambridge University Press.
Miller, D. T., & McFarland, C. (1991). When social comparison goes awry: The case of pluralistic ignorance. In J. Suls and T. A. Wills (Eds.), *Social comparison: Contemporary theory and research* (pp. 287–313). Hillsdale, NJ: Lawrence Erlbaum.
Mooney, Chris. (2005). *The Republican war on science.* New York: Basic Books.
(2012). *The Republican brain: The science of why they deny science and reality.* Hoboken, NJ: Wiley.
Moscovici, S. (1961). *La psychanalyse: Son image et son public.* Paris: Presses Universitaires de France.
Musolff, A. (2004). *Metaphor and political discourse: Analogical reasoning in debates about Europe.* New York: Palgrave-Macmillan.
(2006). Metaphor scenarios in public discourse. *Metaphor and Symbol, 21,* 23–38.
Nash, J. M. (2000). The new science of Alzheimer's. *TIME,* July 17.
Nicholson, P. (2008). The class ceiling (cartoon). *The Australian,* July 20.
Nisbet, E. C., Cooper, K. E., & Garrett, R. K. (2015). The partisan brain: How dissonant science messages lead conservatives and liberals to (dis)trust science. *ANNALS, AAPSS, 658,* 36–66.
Norrick, N. R. (1993). *Conversational joking: Humor in everyday talk.* Bloomington: Indiana University Press.
(2000). *Conversational narrative: Storytelling in everyday talk.* Amsterdam: Benjamins.
Norrick, N. R., & Spitz, A. (2010). The interplay of humor and conflict in conversation and scripted humorous performance. *Humor, 23,* 83–111.
Oakley, T., & Crisp, P. (2011). Honeymoons and pilgrimages: Conceptual integration and allegory in old and new media. *Metaphor and Symbol, 26,* 152–159.
Obama, B. (2008). *A more perfect union.* Constitution Center, Philadelphia, PA, March 18.
(2013). *Remarks by the President on climate change at Georgetown University.* Available at www.whitehouse.gov.
Oliphant, P. (2011). Perils of Pauline / The electoral process (cartoon). Universal Press, June 29.
Ortony, A. (1993). The role of similarity in similes and metaphors. In A. Ortony, (Ed.), *Metaphor and thought* (2nd ed.) (pp. 342–356). Cambridge: Cambridge University Press.
Orwell, G. (1946). *Animal farm.* Harcourt, Brace & World.
Petty, R. E., & Cacioppo, J. T. (1981). *Attitudes and persuasion – classic and contemporary approaches.* Dubuque, IA: W. C. Brown.
Piper, W. (1930). *The little engine that could.* New York: Platt & Munk.
Price, V., Tewksbury, D., & Powers, E. (1997). Switching trains of thought: The impact of news frames on reader's cognitive responses. *Communication Research, 24,* 481.
Prudentius. (1723). *Psychomachia; the war of the soul: Or, the battle of the virtues, and vices.* Translated from Aur. Prudentius Clemens.

References

Ramelli, I. (2011). The philosophical stance of allegory in Stoicism and its reception in Platonism, Pagan and Christian: Origin in dialog with the Stoics and Plato. *International Journal of the Classical Tradition, 18*, 335–371

Reddy, M. J. (1993). The conduit metaphor: A case of frame conflict in our language about language. In A. Ortony (Ed.), *Metaphor and thought* (2nd ed.) (pp. 164–201. Cambridge: Cambridge University Press.

Reps, P. (1957). *Zen flesh, Zen bones: A collection of Zen and pre-Zen writings.* New York: Doubleday Anchor.

Ritchie, L. D. (1991). *Communication concepts 2: Information.* Beverly Hills, CA: Sage.

(2003a). "ARGUMENT IS WAR" – Or is it a game of chess? Multiple meanings in the analysis of implicit metaphors. *Metaphor and Symbol, 18*, 125–146.

(2003b). Categories and similarities: A note on circularity. *Metaphor and Symbol, 18*, 49–53.

(2004). Lost in *"conceptual space"*: Metaphors of conceptual integration. *Metaphor and Symbol, 19*, 31–50.

(2006). *Context and connection in metaphor.* Basingstoke, UK: Palgrave Macmillan.

(2008). Gateshead revisited: The integrative function of ambiguous metaphors in a tricky political situation. *Metaphor and Symbol, 23*, 24–49.

(2009a). Distributed cognition and play in the quest for the double helix. In H. Pishwa (Ed.), *Language and social cognition: Expression of the social mind* (pp. 289–323). Berlin: Mouton de Gruyter.

(2009b). Relevance and simulation in metaphor. *Metaphor and Symbol, 24*, 249–262.

(2010). *"Everybody goes down"*: Metaphors, stories, and simulations in conversations. *Metaphor and Symbol, 25*, 123–143.

(2011a). *"Justice is blind"*: A model for analyzing metaphor transformations and narratives in actual discourse. *Metaphor and the Social World, 1*, 70–89.

(2011b). Why the block is *the block*: Reinforcing community through casual conversation. *Metaphor and the Social World, 1*, 240–261.

(2011c). "You're lying to Jesus!" Humor and play in a discussion about homelessness. *Humor, 24*, 481–511.

(2012). Metaphor and stories in discourse about personal and social change. In B. Wagoner, E. Jensen, & J. Oldmeadow (Eds.), *Culture and social change: Transforming society through the power of ideas.* London: Information Age.

(2013). *Metaphor.* Cambridge: Cambridge University Press.

(2014). *"Born on third base"*: Stories, simulations, and metaphor comprehension. Presented at the annual conference of Researching and Analyzing Metaphor, Cagliari, Italy.

Ritchie, L. D., & Cameron, L. (2014). Open hearts or smoke and mirrors: Metaphorical framing and frame conflicts in a public meeting. *Metaphor and Symbol, 29*, 204–223.

Ritchie, L. D., & Dyhouse, V. (2008). FINE AS FROG'S HAIR: Three models for the development of meaning in figurative language. *Metaphor and Symbol, 23*, 85–107.

Ritchie, L. D., & Negrea-Busuioc, E. (2014). *"Now everyone knows I'm a serial killer."* Spontaneous intentionality in conversational metaphor and story-telling. *Metaphor and the Social World, 4*, 171–195.

Ritchie, L. D., & Schell, C. (2009). *"The ivory tower"* on an *"unstable foundation"*: Playful language, humor, and metaphor in the negotiation of scientists' identities. *Metaphor and Symbol, 24*, 90–104.

Ritchie, L. D., & Thomas, M. (2015). A *"glowing marble"*: *"brushed with clouds"* or *"parched, scorched, and washed away"*? Obama's use of contrasting metaphors and stories in framing climate change. *Metaphor and the Social World, 5*, 1–19.

Ritchie, L. D., & Zhu, M. (2015). "Nixon stonewalled the investigation": Potential contributions of grammatical metaphor to conceptual metaphor theory and analysis. *Metaphor and Symbol, 30*, 118–136.

Rockmore, E. B. (2015). How Texas teaches history. *New York Times*, October 21.

Rollins, D. (1964). *The race is on*. Sony/ATV Music Publishing LLC.

Rosch, E. H. (1973). Natural categories. *Cognitive Psychology, 4*(3), 328–350.

(1975). Cognitive representation of semantic categories. *Journal of Experimental Psychology, 104*(3), 192–233.

Schank, R. C., & Abelson, R. P. (1995). Knowledge and memory: The real story. In R. S. Wyer, Jr. (Ed.), *Knowledge and memory: The real story* (pp. 1–86). Hillsdale, NJ: Lawrence Erlbaum.

Schank, R. C., & Berman, T. R. (2002). The pervasive role of stories in knowledge and action. In M. C. Green, J. J. Strange, & T. C. Brock (Eds.), *Narrative impact: Social and cognitive foundations* (pp. 287–314). Mahwah, NJ: Lawrence Erlbaum.

Schön, D. (1993). Generative metaphor: A perspective on problem solving in social policy. In A. Ortony (Ed.), *Metaphor and thought*. Cambridge: Cambridge University Press.

Schubert, T. W., Waldzus, S., & Seibt, B. (2008). The embodiment of power and communalism in space and bodily contact. In G. R. Semin & E. R. Smith (Eds.), *Embodied grounding: Social, cognitive, affective, and neuroscientific approaches* (pp. 160–183). Cambridge: Cambridge University Press.

Senzaki, N., & Reps, P. (1957). 101 Zen stories. In P. Reps, *Zen flesh, Zen bones* (pp. 3–82). Originally published by Rider and Company, London and David McKay Company, Philadelphia in 1939.

Snaevarr, S. (2010). *Metaphors, narratives, emotions: Their interplay and impact*. Amsterdam: Rodopi.

Soon, W., & Baliunas, S. (2003). Proxy climatic and environmental changes of the past 1000 years. *Climate Research, 23*, 89–110.

Spenser, E. (1590). *The Faerie Queene: Disposed into twelue books, fashioning XII. morall vertues*. London: William Ponsonbie.

Sperber, D., & Wilson, D. (1986/1995). *Relevance: Communication and cognition*. Cambridge, MA: Harvard University Press.

Steen, G. (2013). Deliberate metaphor affords conscious metaphorical cognition. *Journal of Cognitive Semiotics, 5*, 179–197.

(2015). Developing, testing and interpreting Deliberate Metaphor Theory. *Journal of Pragmatics*. dx.doi.org/10.1016/j.pragma.2015.03.013.

Steen, G. S., Reijnierse, W. G., & Burgers, C. (2013). When Do Natural Language Metaphors Influence Reasoning? A Follow-Up Study to Thibodeau and Boroditsky. PLOS One. Available at www.plosone.org/article/info%3Adoi%2F10.1371%2Fjournal.pone.0113536.

Terrion, J. L., & Ashforth, B. E. (2002). From 'I' to 'we': The role of putdown humor and identity in the development of a temporary group. *Human Relations, 55,* 55–88.

Thagard, P. (2011). The brain is wider than the sky: Analogy, emotion, and allegory. *Metaphor and Symbol, 26,* 131–142.

Thagard, P., & Aubie, B. (2008). Emotional consciousness: A neural model of how cognitive appraisal and somatic perception interact to produce qualitative experience. *Consciousness and Cognition, 17,* 811–834.

Thagard, P., & Stewart, T. C. (2011). The AHA! experience: Creativity through emergent binding in neural networks. *Cognitive Science, 35,* 1–33.

Thibodeau, P. H., & Boroditsky, L. (2011). Metaphors we think with: The role of metaphor in reasoning. *PLoS ONE, 6*(2).

(2015). Measuring effects of metaphor in a dynamic opinion landscape. *PLoS ONE, 10*(7).

Thibodeau, P. H., Iyiewaure, P. O., & Boroditsky, L. (2016). Metaphors we think with: The role of metaphor in reasoning. *PLoS ONE, 6*(2).

Toles, T. (2012). Strip search (cartoon). *Washington Post.*

(2013). The canary in the coal mine (cartoon). *Washington Post,* February 25.

Tolkien, J. R. R. (1955). *The return of the king.* London: Allen and Unwin.

Tourangeau, R., and Rips, L. (1991). Interpreting and evaluating metaphors. *Journal of Memory and Language, 30,* 452–472.

Tracy, K. (1997). Interactional trouble in emergency service requests: A problem of frames. *Research on Language and Social Interaction, 30,* 315–343.

Turner, Mark (1996). *The literary mind.* New York: Oxford University Press.

Turner, M., & Fauconnier, G. (1999). A mechanism of creativity. *Poetics Today, 20*(3), 397–418.

(2003). Metaphor, metonymy, and binding. In R. Dirven & R. Pörings (Eds.), *Metaphor and metonymy in comparison and contrast* (pp. 469–487). Berlin & New York: W. de Gruyter.

Walters, K. (2011). Mission accomplished (cartoon). *Blade.*

Watson, J. D. (1968). *The double helix.* New York: Penguin.

Whitman, J. (1991). From the textual to the temporal: Early Christian "allegory" and early romantic "symbol." *New Literary History, 1,* 161–176.

(2003). *Interpretation and allegory: Antiquity to the modern period.* Boston: Brill.

Wilkin, M., & Loudermilk, J. D. (1959). *Waterloo.* Universal Music.

Wilson, D., & Carston, R. (2006). Metaphor, relevance and the 'emergent property' issue. *Mind & Language, 21,* 404–433.

Wilson, D., & Sperber, D. (2004). Relevance theory. In L. R. Horn & G. Ward (Eds.), *The handbook of pragmatics* (pp. 607–632). Oxford: Blackwell.

Wilson, N., and Gibbs, Jr., R. W. (2007). Real and imagined body movement primes metaphor comprehension. *Cognitive Science, 31,* 721–731.

Winn, M. (1977). *The plug-in drug: Television, children, and the family.* New York: Viking.

Yus, F. (2009). Visual metaphor versus verbal metaphor: A unified account. In C. J. Forceville & E. Urios-Aparisi (Eds.), *Multi-modal metaphor* (pp. 147–172). Berlin: Mouton de Gruyter.

Zhong, C.-B., & Leonardelli, G. J. (2008). Cold and lonely: Does social exclusion literally feel cold? *Psychological Science, 19*, 838–842.

Zhong, C.-B., & Liljenquist, K. (2006). Washing away your sins: Threatened morality and physical cleansing. *Science, 313*, 1451–1452.

Zwaan, R. A. (2014). Embodiment and language comprehension: Reframing the discussion. *Trends in Cognitive Sciences, 18*, 229–34.

(2015). Situation models, mental simulations, and abstract concepts in discourse comprehension. *Psychonomic Bulletin Review.*

Index

Abbott, H. P., 22, 29–30
Abelson, R. P., 27, 43–44
ability (cognition), 69, 73, 75, 103–104, 148, 245–246
Abu Ghraib, 133
actual event sequence. *See* event sequence
ad hoc category, 5, 52–53, 58
Adam and Eve, 25–26, 51, 173–174, *See also* Garden of Eden story
Adams, R. B. Jr., 69
Aesop, 15, 106, 113–119
Affordable Care Act, 158, 160
allegoresis, 79, 82, 94–95, 103
allegorical naming, 97, 102
allegory, 15, 19, 72, 79–106, 112, 118, 120, 222, 232, 239–240
   as literary genre, 90–92
   as political commentary, 93
   definition, 79, 82, 92–93, 102
   extended metaphor and, 79, 95, 97–98
   in antiquity, 80–82
   in late medieval and eary modern ages, 82–83
   interpretation, 79–80, 82–83, 94, 243–245, 251
alliteration, 135, 211
allusion, 17, 97
alternate world, 30
amodal symbols, 68, 246, 249
analogical mapping. *See* structure-mapping theory
analogy, 50, 71–73, 99
Andersen, Hans Christian, 106, 116, 118
Animal Farm, 93, 98–100, 104, 222, 239–240, 249, 251
   cognitive-affective diagram, 99
aphorisms, vii–viii, 6, 17, 113–114, 139–144, 154, 240
   definition, 139
   in fables and parables, 140–142
   political and commercial, 142–144

Aristotle, 19, 80
atomic bomb, 199, 201
attribute transfer, 5–6, 49–50, 53–54, 58, 135
Aubie, B., 44, 72
Augustine (Saint), 81

Bagley, P., 218, 220
Balinas, S., 203
Ballad for Katherine of Aragon, A (poem), 96
Barsalou, L. W., 8, 66–68, 73, 99, 236
Beatrice (*Divine Comedy*), 85–86, 91
Beeler, N., 221, 244
Being There, 94
Bennett, C., 224
Bergen, B. K., 67
Berman, T. R., 3, 22, 25
Berry, Jo, 126, 138
Blair, Tony, viii, 120–124, 147, 229, 231, 243, 248, 251
Blake, William, 97–98
blended space, 64, 96
blended vehicle story, 196, 200, 207, 220, 224
blending theory. *See* Conceptual Integration Theory
Boehner, John, 220, 224
Boers, E., 94, 243, 251
Boroditsky, L., 145, 167
Bowdle, B. F., 50, 72
Bradley, R. S., 202–203
Brexit, ix, 153, 156, 255
broadening, 6, 58
Bruegel the Elder (Pieter), vii, 18, 140, 232, 242
Bruner, J., 3, 22, 29
Brunvand, J., 40
Bryant, G., 9, 15
Bundy, Cliven, 225
Bunyan, John, 88, 90, 92, *See also Pilgrim's Progress*
Burgers, C., 167
Bush v. Gore, 159

267

Index

Bush, George W., 129–131, 217–220, 230, 243, 251
Butler Report, 229–230, 252

Cacioppo, J. T., 68, 73–74, 148, 236, 247, 249
Cameron, L. J., viii, 26, 49, 74, 76, 126, 138, 148, 151, 212
Carter, G. L., 13
Casasanto, D., 67, 236
Cash, Johnny, 18
categorization, 6, 52
categorization theory, 59
category formation, 51–52
Causley, Charles, 96
Chiang, W., 216
Chrysippus, 80
circularity, 53, 59, 61
Citizens United (Supreme Court case), 222–223
Clark, H. H., 31
Clark, I., 203
Clement (philosopher), 80
climate change, 28, 44, 62, 144, 188–214, 252
   cartoons about, 227–229
   cultural factors, 190–192
   potential effects, 189–190
Clinton, Hillary, 3, 6, 9–15, 18, 21, 30, 33
   2008 concession speech, ix, 1–5, 37, 42, 53, 58, 66, 108, 120, 132, 234, 248
CLST. *See* Context-Limited Simulation Theory
coda, 15, 22, 24, 26–27, 33–35, 38, 41, 84, 106, 122–123, 239
code model of language, 41, 49, 51, 54–55, 148
cognitive context, 57, 77
cognitive environment. *See* mutual cognitive environment
cognitive processing, 57, 59, 66–68, 70, 72–75, 95–96, 98, 103, 140, 144, 148–149, 154–155, 168, 197, 232–233, 236–238, 244, 247–250
Cognitive-Affective Diagramming, 72
cognitive-affective model, 71, 95
Cole, John, 156, 226
complicating action (narrative), 22, 25, 38
computer metaphor (cognition), 41, 49, 234, 236
conceptual blending, 61, 64–66, 72–74, 96, 98, 101–103, 108, 114, 117–118, 123–126, 129, 132, 140, 143–146, 155, 158, 161, 163, 177, 179, 181, 184, 196–197, 199, 202, 207, 210, 216, 218, 221, 224, 226–227, 231, 234, 241
Conceptual Blending Theory, 95, 97, *See also* Conceptual Integration Theory; conceptual blending

Conceptual Integration Theory, 64–66, 95
conceptual metaphor, vii–viii, 6–8, 14, 60, 62, 72, 74, 76, 93, 108, 112–113, 152, 185, 215, 232, 237, 253, *See also* metaphor examples (conceptual)
   generic, 75, 153
Conceptual Metaphor Theory (CMT), 6–7, 16, 60–62, 70, 74, 77, 158, 215, 241–242, *See also* conceptual metaphor
conflict (story), 23–26, 29
Congreve, William, 153
context, viii, 10, 13, 27, 44, 49, 56–59, 68–70, 74, 77, 114, 132, 148, 150, 155, 171, 177, 185, 233, 236–237, 240, 245–246, 248–253
   social and cultural aspects, 2, 5, 22–23, 32, 35, 43, 57, 68–69, 154, 156, 168, 170–171, 186–187, 200, 223, 226, 229, 231, 236, 246, 248–249
Context-Limited Simulation Theory (CLST), 74–75, 246–249
contextual knowledge, 21, 23, 148–149, 186, 233, 236–237, 245–247, 249, 251–252
convolution, 57, 71–74, 95, 103, *See also* conceptual blending
Cooper, K. E., 213
creation stories, 20, 24–25
creativity, 44–45, 70, 72, 146
Crisp, P., 15, 79, 84, 89, 92, 95, 97–98
culture of science, 191

Daffy Duck, 31
Dante (author). *See Divine Comedy*
Dante (character, *Divine Comedy*), 85, 91
Darkow, J., 225
dead metaphors, 60, 238
decoding, 49–50, 234
Deen, Paula, 226
Defense of Marriage Act (DOMA), 221, 244
Deignan, A., 123
Dennett, D. C., 69
Divine Comedy, 85, 90–91, 98, 112, 239
domain. *See* source domain
Dorst, A. G., 76
double scope network, 224
Dumais, S. T., 59
Dunbar, R., 14, 20, 29, 42, 235

editorial cartoons, viii, 14, 215–217, 220, 229, 231, 233, 239–240, 243, 245, 248, 251
Edwards, D., 215
El Refaie, E., 229–233, 243, 245, 248, 251–252
El Roto, 217

Index

elaboration, 13, 50, 64, 68, 70, 125, 148, 155, 168, 240, 247–253
Elaboration Likelihood Model, 68, 103–104, 148, 236, 246–247
ELM. *See* Elaboration Likelihood Model
embodied symbols, 237, 249
emergent structure, 64
emotion, 44, 60, 67–69, 72–73, 97, 99, 107, 109, 115, 117, 132, 142, 155, 166, 199, 216, 244
empathetic understanding, 138, 149, 151, 172, 185, 212, 250, 252–253
encoding, 49–50, 234
epic, 82–83, 85
European Union, ix, 16, 152, 168, 170
event sequence, 23–24, 28
evolution theory, 14, *See also* language, evolution of
expectation failure (story), 3–4, 22, 25
extended metaphor, 69–70, 79, 85, 101–102, 252
  allegory and, 95, 97–98

fables, 15, 17, 19, 99, 104, 106, 113–120, 147, 232, 239–240
  Ant and the Grasshopper, 115–116
    concept map, 115
    Disney version, 116
  aphorisms and, 139–142
  Emperor's New Clothes, 116–117
  Fox and the Grapes, 15, 113–114, 141
    concept map, 114
  Little Engine that Could, The, 106, 117
  Rudolf, the Red-Nosed Reindeer, 118
  Ugly Duckling, 118
Faerie Queene, The, 86–88, 90–91, 93, 239
fairy tales, 117, 119, 138
Fauconnier, G., 64–65, 97, 101, 103, 155, 224
Federal Glass Ceiling Commission, 10, 13
Fitzsimmons, D., 218
flashbacks, 28–29
folk tales, 29, 94, 106, 112, 118
Forceville, C., 215
frames (story), 27, 88, 92, 129, 131, 145–146, 151–152, 165, 250
Frenkel, N., 9
Freud, Sigmund, 78, 142
Frost, Robert, 94, 243

Galera-Masegosa, A., 8
Gamson, W. A., 18, 137, 150
Garden of Eden story, 21, 24–26, 28, 30, 33, 79, 174
Garland, N., 217

Garner, J., 94
Garrett, R. K., 213
generic space, 64, 66, 101
Gentner, D., 50, 72
Gerrig, R. J., 36, 95, 100
gestures, 48, 57, 112, 215, 232, 235
Gibbs, R. W. Jr., 8, 65, 79, 94–95, 104, 243, 245, 251
Gijssels, T., 67, 236
Gladwell, M., 196
Glucksberg, S., 17, 52, 58
Goldstein, Tom, 161
grammar. *See* syntax
grammatical metaphor, 5, 62–64, 76, 148, 206
  examples, 62, 195–196, 202
Grande, Ariana, 102
Green, M. C., 36, 95, 100, 107, 232
Greenwald, Glenn, 161
Grimm Brothers, 106
grounded modal simulations, 246
grounded symbols, 68, 236

Halliday, M. A. K., 62–63, 76
Hamlet, 134
Hansen, Jim, 28–30, 37, 192–193, 201, 205–206, 212
  1988 congressional testimony, 193–194
  2008 congressional testimony, 194–199
  TED talk, 199–200
Harris, R. A., 92, 98, 105
Hart, Gary, 136–137
Heartbreak Hotel (song), 102
Hemingway, Ernest, 22–23, 29
Hesiod, 80
Hess-Biber, S. N., 13
Hightower, Jim, 129, 131
Hitch-hiker's Guide to the Galaxy, The, 30–31
Hogan, P. C., 29
Homer, 80
Honeymoon Avenue (song), 102
Hoover, J. Edgar, 142–143, 242, 244
Hughes, M. K., 202–203
Hulme, M., 188, 200
humor, 18–19, 39–40, 42, 69, 112, 128, 154, 161, 240, 247
Hurley, M. M., 69, 247
Hymowitz, C., 13
hyperbole, 18, 128, 181, 213

idiomatic metaphor, 14, 125, 157–158, 162, 164–165, 174–175, 180, 182, 210, 227–228, 238, 243–244
Ijzerman, H., 67
Inhofe, Jim, 192, 212–213
  Senate speech, 201–206

Index

intention, 14, 69–70, 76, 94, 103, 110, 134, 138, 147–148, 186, 229–230, 237, 243, 252–253
interoception, 67, 99, 236, 246
introspection, 67, 99, 236
irony, vii, 17, 27, 39, 41, 63, 102, 126, 146, 157, 173, 212, 216, 219, 225
Iwo Jima flag raising, 228, 239, 241, 243, 248

James, Kendra, 21, 23, 33, 126, 238
Jamiol, P., 222, 251
Jesus (parables), 141
Jim Crow, 176, 180, 227
Johnson, Boris, 156
Johnson, Lyndon, 142–144, 148, 242, 244, 253
Johnson, M., 7, 60–62, 70, 72, 75, 235
jokes, 19, 35, 69, 128, 156
Jones, George, 100
Junger, S., 197

Kaal, A. G., 76
Kagan, Elena, 157–158, 168–169, 252–253
Kahneman, D., 44
Keysar, B., 52
Kintsch, W., 60
KKK. *See* Ku Klux Klan
Kosinski, J., 94
Ku Klux Klan, 226

Labov, W., 22–23, 25, 28, 32
Lakoff, G., 6–7, 16, 27, 60–62, 70, 72, 75, 235
Landauer, T. K., 59
language, 48, 56, 234
  evolution of, 14, 41–42, 45, 235
Language and Situated Simulation (LASS) theory, 68
language processing. *See* cognitive processing
Latent Semantic Analysis (LSA), 59–60, 64
layering, 31, 125
Leonardelli, G. J., 8
lexical metaphor, 14, 73, 157, 200, 232–233, 238, 240, 242, 245
  examples, 97, 159–160, 164, 174, 177
  static / descriptive metaphor, 242
  visual, 243
Liljenquist, K., 67
Lin, T. Y., 216
Lincoln, Abraham, 133, 147
Lithwick, D., 157–168, 252–253
Lord Jim, 28, 31
Luther, Martin, 83

Macbeth, 61
Magee, Pat, 126, 138
Mann, M. E., 202–203

Mao, F., 62–63
mapping, 1, 50, 74
  example, 100, 134, 136, 140
Mar, R. A., 42, 44–45
Martin, Treyvon, 225
master-plots, 29–30
Mattingly, C., 146
McClellan, George, 133, 147
McCutcheon (Supreme Court case), 222–223
McGlone, M. S., 17
McIntyre, S., 203
McKee, R., 224
McKitrick, R., 203
McNeill, D., 48
meaning, 48, 56
  types of, 56
memory, 27, 43, 45, 51, 64, 235, 237
  working memory, 44, 72, 88
mental space, 64–65, 100–101
mentalese, 49, 68, 234
metalanguage, 55
metaphor
  classification, 241–243
  definition, 4, 232, 235
  interpretation, 5, 13–15, 77–78, 82–83, 104, 229–233, 244, 249
  notation of, 7
  transcategorization, 62–63, 77
  transference, 5, 49, 53, 134
metaphor comprehension, 5, 171, 234, 236–237, 245
metaphor examples
  Achilles is a lion, 50, 52, 144, 147
  American oracle at Delphi, 157
  blind justice, 43, 126, 140, 220
  blind leading the blind, vii, 18, 140, 232, 242
  blood, 77, 170, 175
  born on third base, 129–132
  brother's keeper, 173
  building bridges, 126, 138
  bull in a china shop, 17, 145, 240
  business as usual, 194, 198
  canary in a coal mine, 227
  class ceiling, 14
  climbing the corporate ladder, 10, 12
  coffin nails, 144, 147, 224
  dead end, 145, 147
  didn't pull any punches, 18, 137
  digging one's own grave, 224–225
  enter into the world of the Other, 186, 212, 250
  Flat Earth Society, 210, 212
  get out of jail free card, 138
  glass ceiling, ix, 1, 4–5, 9–15, 61, 120, 132, 234

Index

going to Hell in a handbasket, 228
greenhouse, 28, 189, 192–193, 199
innocence of a newborn kitten, 164, 169, 253
ivory tower, 64, 66, 124–125, 127
legacy, 172, 175–176
let sleeping dogs lie, 17, 139–140
live out in the sunlight, 163, 169
marital spat, 120–124, 153
mark their territory, 159, 166
more perfect union, 61, 172, 178
Oedipus complex, 142
original sin, 47, 50, 71, 77, 172–175, 252
pepper spray a baby (police violence), 128
piss on / out / in, 142–143, 148, 242, 244, 253
playing with fire, 244
prodigal son, 154, *See also* parables, Prodigal Son
quill fight, 162, 253
sour grapes, 141, *See also* fables, Fox and the Grapes
stalemate, 50, 52, 61, 66, 71, 179, 183
stonewall, 55–56, 249
throwing crockery, viii, 122–123, 132, 251, 253
time bomb, 144, 147, 195
tipping point, 196
toe / tow the line, 71, 77, 244
Uncle Sam, 228
Vietnam, 17
vulture capitalist, 74, 133–136, 139, 147–148, 240, 246, 251
Waterloo, 17–18
whitewash, 230–231
metaphor examples (conceptual)
ANIMAL, 182–183, 198
CHANGE OF DIRECTION, 147
COMMERCE / BUSINESS, 178
CONDUIT / TRANSMISSION, 55
CONSTRUCTION, 209
CONTAINER, 7, 209
CROSSROAD, 230
DIFFICULT IS HARD, 7, 10
DIRTY / STAINED, 61, 174, 210
DISSECTION, 157
DRUGS, 217
EXPLOSION, 161
FAMILY, ix, 16, 121–122, 152, 155, 168
FIRE, 84, 162, 180–181, 218, 252
FOOD / HUNGER, 183
FORCE, 208
HEAR / LISTEN, 122
HOUSE, 132
JOURNEY, 6–7, 10–11, 60–61, 75, 86, 88, 91–92, 101–102, 107–108, 112, 120–121, 123–124, 144–145, 153, 155, 157, 162, 164, 166, 169, 172, 176–178, 181, 198, 207, 209–211, 239, 252
LIGHT, 6–7, 132, 204, 220
LIQUID, 132, 166
LOCATION, 60, 125
LOVE, 152
LOVE-MARRIAGE-FAMILY, 16, 155
MACHINE, 146
MARRIAGE, ix, 16, 123, 152–153, 155–156, 168
MEAT, 136
MOTION, 11, 61, 75, 101, 145, 157, 164, 172, 176–178, 205, 207–208, 210
NATURE, 155, 181–183
OBJECTS, 61, 121–122, 136, 172, 179, 183–184, 207–208
ORGANISM, 157, 198, 208–209
ORGANIZATION, 121–122
PERSONIFICATION, 207–208
PHYSICAL BLOW, 194, 207
PHYSICAL BOND, 159
PHYSICAL PROXIMITY, 7, 154–155, 172, 179, 194, 218, 230
PHYSICALLY SOUND, 162
PLACE, 174, 179
QUEST, 92
RELIGION, 157, 163, 172
SEEING, vii, 6–7, 140, 159, 163, 198, 204, 220
SEX, 209
SHOCK, 194
SIZE, 121, 193, 209
SPACE, 124, 155, 157, 164, 172, 177, 179–180, 202, 209
SPORT / GAME / CONTEST, 102, 130, 155, 157, 160, 166, 168, 178–179, 183, 209, 239
STORM, 108
STRUCTURE, 108, 125, 178, 203
SUBSTANCE, 136
TEMPERATURE, 7, 60, 155, 159–160, 162, 180, 232
THEATER, 158
TUNING, 157
UP, 7, 10–11, 60, 66, 75, 121–122, 164, 193, 207–208
VIOLENCE, 165, 168
VISION, vii, 184–185, 193, 198
WAR, 7, 60, 75, 84, 92, 155, 157, 160–162, 165–166, 168, 181, 202, 207–209, 211, 239
WEIGHT, 162, 221
WORK, 162

Index

metaphorical language, 6, 50, 58, 67, 79
metaphorical story, 1–2, 9, 120–132
  abbreviated, 28, 129–132
  allegory, 80, 92–93
  definition, 242
  extended, 15–16, 249
  visual, 17–19, 232–233, 238, 242–243, 248, *See also* visual metaphor
metonym, 7–8, 16, 18, 52, 60, 75, 107–108, 111, 119, 122, 128, 133, 138, 159, 176, 180–182, 194, 198, 212, 242
  definition, 7
  part-whole, 8
  visual, 216
  whole-part, 8
modal simulations, 248
Mondale, Walter, 136–137
Monopoly (game), 138
Mosaic Law, 111
Moscovici, S., 141
motivated reasoning, 213, 233, 237, 245, 247, 250
motivation (cognition), 68–69, 73–75, 103–104, 148, 155, 168, 225, 233, 236, 242, 244, 246–247, 249–253
  negative, 74
multi-modal metaphor, 232, 242
multi-modal simulations, 68, 73, 75, 237, 248–249
Musolff, A., 16, 151–156, 168, 170
mutual cognitive environment, 57, 72, 238
myth. *See* story types, fictional

narrative, 3, 10, 22–30, 32, 88–92, 96, 98, 118, 138, 146–147, 216, 231, 234, *See also* story
  definition, 3, 22–24
  literary, 42, 45
narrative gaps, 28, 31
narrowing, 6, 58
neural assemblages. *See* mental space
neural convergence zones, 66, 237, 248
Nisbet, E. C., 213
Norrick, N. R., 32, 63

Oakley, T., 98, 100
Oatley, K., 42, 44–45
Obama, Barack, 3, 54, 58, 158, 171, 224, 252
  2008 speech, 43, 47, 49–54, 58, 63, 66, 70–71, 77, 148, 170–187, 213
  2014 speech, 144, 206–214
objectification metaphor, 62, 172, 183
Odyssey, The, 29, 83, 89
Oedipus, 30, 141

Oliphant, P., 223
Origen, 79–80

parables, 15, 17, 19, 105–113, 118–120, 232, 239–240
  aphorisms and, 139–142
  camel and the eye of a needle, 109–110
  Dog in the Manger, 114, 142
  Good Samaritan, 16, 107, 141
  Jesus and, 15, 107, 109–111, 140–141, 173, 239
  Prodigal Son, 15, 107, 140, 154
  Sabbath was made for man, 110–111
  wise man and foolish man, 16, 108, 239
  woman taken in adultery, 111, 141, 239
  Zen Buddhist, 105, 107–113, 239
partisanship, 207–208, 211, 224
Paul (Saint), 81–82, 92
Perceptual Simulation Theory, 8, 73, 77
perceptual simulations, 8–9, 42, 44, 66–68, 70–73, 95, 103, 107, 113–114, 122, 125, 142–143, 145, 158, 214, 232, 236, 246, 249
perceptual symbols, 66, 68
Perils of Pauline, 223
Perry, Rick, 74, 133, 135, 147–149, 246, 251
personification, 82, 92, 147, 153, 181, 183
persuasion, 27, 36, 73, 95, 103–104, 107, 118
Petty, R. E., 68, 73–74, 148, 236, 247, 249
Philo of Alexandria, 80
Pilgrim's Progress, 15, 82, 88–90, 92, 97, 103, 105, 112, 239, 249
Piper, W., 117
Plato, 80
play (language), 18, 41–42, 154
plot, 26, 29–30, 88, 91–93, 98–99, 121, 239
Poison Tree, A (poem), 95, 97–98
political cartoons, 10, 18, 135, 154, 216–220, 232
possible worlds, 30
protagonist, 4, 24, 32–34, 87–88, 111, 160, 179, 224
prototypes, 52
Prudentius, 82–84, 92, *See also* Psychomachia
pseudo-narratives. *See* story types, generic
psychological novel, 89–90
Psychomachia, 82–85, 90, 105, 239

Race Is on, The (song), 100–101
Ramelli, I., 80
reasoning, 45, 112, 162, 164, 235, *See also* motivated reasoning
Reddy, M. J., 55

Reijnierse, W. G., 167
relevance, 24, 26, 32, 38–39, 56–59, 69, 71, 73–75, 103–104, 148, 236, 246, 249
Relevance Theory, 232
Reps, P., 105, 112
resolution (story), 2–3, 10, 22–26, 29, 34
Return of the King, The, 31
rhetorical question, 63, 145, 199–200
Ritchie, L. D., 63, 75, 123, 148, 151, 212, 233
Road Not Taken, The, 8, 94, 95
Rollins, Don, 100–101
Romney, Mitt, 74, 133–136, 140, 148–149, 246–247
Rosch, E. H., 52
Ruiz de Mendoza, F. J., 8
Russian Revolution, 99, 104, 222

sarcasm, 212
satire, 18, 30, 94, 243
Scalia, Antonin, 163–164, 166, 168
scenarios, 16, 123, 151–152, 155, 167
Schank, R. C., 3, 22, 25, 27, 43–44
Schellhardt, T. D., 13
schema, 45, 57, 59–60, 77, 101–103, 143–144, 162, 219
Schön, D., 151
script (story), 27, 29, 34–35, 144, 220
semantic association, 59–60, 66, 246
Semin, G. R., 67
Semino, E., 123
setting, 24–25, 27, 30–31, 34, 38
Snaevarr, S., 23
social bonding, 42, 45, 132, 235
Soon, W., 203
Sophocles, 141
source, 49, 55–56, 69, 71, 93, 95, 100, 252, *See also* vehicle (metaphor)
source domain, 7, 50, 55–56, 62, 75, 79, 82, 153–155, 163, 181, 232, 242
Spenser, Edmund, 86, 92–93
Sperber, D., 6, 57–58, 72–73
Spitz, A., 63
Stanford Prison Experiment, 133
Steen, G., 69, 131, 147–148, 167, 237, 245
stereotypes, 15, 30, 184
Sterling, Donald, 225
Stevens, Tony, 21, 26–30, 33, 35, 238
Stewart, T. C., 44–45, 55, 72
Stoic philosophy, 80–82
story (definition), 2–3, 23–24
story chains, 32, 39
story index, 23, 27, 113, 130, 133, 135–136, 139–140, 142, 147, 154, 211, 238, 240, 242

story metaphor, 9, 11, 19, 103, 106, 108, 125, 133–150, 195–196, 208, 216, 224, 227, 232, 238, 245, 247–248, 250, 252
abbreviated, 17
about climate change, 188–214
definition, 242
in health communication, 145–146
in journalism, 151–169
story types, 32–33
experiential, 32–33, 38
fictional, 33, 46, 80–81, 106, 218
first-person, 32, 38
generic, 2, 26, 33, 106, 108, 220
third-person, 32–33, 35
story world, 30–31, 36–37, 42, 57, 95–96, 103, 107, 117–118, 126, 143, 151, 216, 232, 235, 242, 249
story-telling, 20, 25, 28–29, 31–32, 39
cognitive aspects, 43–44
retelling, 44–45
social function of, 41–43
structure-mapping theory, 50–51
Supreme Court, 157–160, 166, 168–169, 221–223, 225, 241, 248, 251
Supreme Court justices, 159, 161, 163–164, 169, 222–223, 240, 253, *See also* Kagan, Elena
symbolic cognition, 68
syntax, 48

Tales of 1001 Nights, 31
target, 56, 71, 79, 89, 93, 100, 152, *See also* topic (metaphor)
tenor. *See* meaning
Thagard, P., 44–45, 55, 57, 71–72, 95, 99–100, 103
Thibodeau, P. H., 145, 167
Third Race at the Honeymoon-Is-Over Downs, 100–102, 104
Thomas, M., 212
Titanic, 157, 220, 225, 231
Toles, T., 221, 227
Tolmie, S., 92, 98, 105
topic (metaphor), 1, 3, 7, 56, 72
Tracy, K., 151
transcategorization. *See* metaphor, transcategorization
transmission / conduit model, 234
Turner, M., 64–65, 97, 101, 103, 155, 224
Tversky, A., 44

urban legends, 40–41

vehicle (metaphor), 3, 7, 55, 72, 144
Virgil, 82–83, 85–86, 91

visual metaphor, vii, 10, 14, 61, 103, 138, 203, 215–233, 238, 240, 242, 244–245, 248–249
  cartoons about climate change, 227–229
  cartoons about racism, 225–227
  in advertising, 18, 215, 233, 241
  law and justice, 220–225
vocabulary, 48, 59, 236

Waletsky, J., 28
Walters, K., 220

Waterloo (song), 17–18
Whitman, J., 80
Wilson, D., 6, 57–58, 72–73
Wright, Jeremiah, 171, 173, 178, 180, 182, 184–185
Wuthering Heights, 29

Zhong, C. B., 8, 67
Zhu, M., 63
Zimbardo, Phil, 133
Zwaan, R. A., 68–69, 236, 245, 248